Morrissey

Morrissey
Fandom, Representations and Identities

Edited by Eoin Devereux, Aileen Dillane and Martin J. Power

intellect Bristol, UK / Chicago, USA

First published in the UK in 2011 by
Intellect, The Mill, Parnall Road, Fishponds, Bristol, BS16 3JG, UK

First published in the USA in 2011 by
Intellect, The University of Chicago Press, 1427 E. 60th Street,
Chicago, IL 60637, USA

A catalogue record for this book is available from the
British Library.

Cover designer: Joe Gervin
Copy-editor: Rebecca Vaughan-Williams
Typesetting: Mac Style, Beverley, E. Yorkshire

Hardback ISBN 978-1-84150-417-9
Paperback ISBN 978-1-84150-596-1

Printed and bound by Gutenberg Press, Malta.

Contents

Acknowledgements

For all of their help and support the editors would like to thank:

Paul Boland; Boz Boorer; Len Brown; Ellie Byrne; The late Pat Bugler; Phil Collins; David Collopy; Sheena Doyle; Paula Dundon; Peter Finan; Joe Gervin; Girl in A Coma; Kerri Koch; Gavin Murphy; Anne McCarthy; Tina O'Toole; Issac Ramos; Jelena Stanovnik and These Charming Men. At the University of Limerick we would like to acknowledge the support received from the Faculty of Arts, Humanities and Social Sciences; the Department of Sociology; Irish World Academy of Music and Dance and the Research Office. Grateful thanks to the following for their permission to reproduce original images: Douglas Cape; Andrew Cope; Erin Hazard; Graham Humphreys and Linder Sterling.

Individual thanks from each of the editors to the following:

Eoin Devereux: Liz, Joe and Gavin for all their love and all the laughs; Michael Breen for sound advice; Leo Halpin for talking to strangers in airports; Sarah Moore for all the support and encouragement and the "Moz Posse" – Ger Fitzgerald; Mikey Ryan; Natalie Harford and Jane Bruce for all of the Morrissey gigs and aftershows all over the world.

Aileen Dillane: The Gilbert boys, Lochlann, Senan and Rossa, and especially Hayden, for his unwavering support, and the Dillane Clan, Maureen, Seamus, Deirdre, Noreen, and, in particular, Fionnuala, for her advice and inspirational example.

Martin J. Power: For Marian and Fiona. Thanks to my family and friends for making me who I am. Thanks to Dr Amanda Haynes for moulding me into an academic. Last, but certainly not least, I would like to dedicate this book to the late Jimmy Farrell, a great friend who introduced me to The Smiths on a rainy Sunday afternoon in 1985. You are "a light that never goes out".

And finally, thanks to Morrissey for the songs that saved our lives.

Preface

Back in the winter of 2008, when I received advance warning of the University of Limerick's second academic symposium on Morrissey – *The Songs That Saved Your Life (Again)* – I emailed the charming Mancunian for his reaction. Having been voted second in the BBC's Greatest Living Icons poll – behind Sir David Attenborough, ahead of Sir Paul McCartney – I could not help remarking that this was another extraordinary achievement; to be celebrated by an international bunch of boffins with brains bigger than Bolton was surely a tremendous honour for a Salford lad who had suffered education in reverse and entered the world of work (*that* four letter word!) with barely a couple of O-levels to cover his modesty.

Although initially my email met with radio silence, I would argue that Morrissey responded stylishly and humorously on the eve of the Symposium in April 2009 with the release of his 'I'm Throwing My Arms Around Paris' single. The supporting track – as throwaway-brilliant as many of The Smiths' B-sides had been – opened with the lines: "Because of my poor education, I don't expect your invitation".

The introduction to this enlightening collection of essays uses the phrase "deliberate construction" in relation to "a man consumed with his public persona and its mediation". For the average human on the Chorlton omnibus, sporting a soiled 'Meat Is Murder' T-shirt and a rain-soaked quiff, this means that Morrissey knows exactly what he is doing and, inspired by one of his teenage heroes Andy Warhol, closely controls how he presents himself and his art. There are no coincidences in the world of Morrissey. Nothing is accidental; everything is planned to perfection, from beautifully-crafted pop masterpieces and iconic photo opportunities to manufactured media controversies.

To me, Morrissey is a work of art. From the moment I first saw him onstage with The Smiths, back in the autumn of 1983, I felt there was something special, different, unusual, charismatic, awkward, abnormal, extraordinary, original (delete to taste) about the man. Getting to know him in my guise as an *NME* journalist and later as a TV producer and writer, I have never been disappointed by any of my encounters with the Moz. He has always been charming company, brilliantly witty, fantastically knowledgeable about popular culture and provocatively opinionated on subjects close to his heart. No one can ruffle feathers or rattle cages like him. True, there have been times when I have winced on hearing some of his more controversial views but, as my lovely long-lost Mum once observed, "you'll learn nothing from only listening to people who agree with you".

It is hugely significant that this well-researched work on Morrissey has been spawned in the great cradle of Irish learning. The man himself remains fiercely proud of his Celtic roots, and Ireland has been the homeland of many ghostly muses who have inspired and illuminated Morrissey's work over the past 30 years. When scholars talk reverently about classical art forms, they stress how crucial it is that artists mirror life, that they speak fundamental and universal truths, and remind us why we are here. Swift's *Gulliver's Travels* declared that the function of art was "to mend the world". Yeats passionately believed it was the role of the poet to "speak the truth for his generation" and defended "the right of every man to see the world in his own way". While well-beloved Wilde claimed that the secret of life is art and argued that true artists must always seek to extend the subject matter of art.

In my entirely subjective opinion, Morrissey has extended the subject matter of popular music more than any other artist over the last 30 years. With his "lovely singing voice", he has used the three-minute pop song to embrace society's outsiders and tackle taboo subjects with an old-fashioned, almost Victorian reforming zeal: everyday issues such as child murders, suicide, poverty, animal rights, violence, vegetarianism, racism, mental illness, football hooliganism, paedophilia and police corruption. The very subjects that 99.9 per cent of all recording "artists" *avoid* for fear they will smear their lovely careers are faced head-on in Moz songs. "And if a double-decker bus crashes into us …"

No doubt some critics will argue that an old cult like Morrissey does not deserve such intense academic interrogation or investigation. I would passionately disagree. Middle-aged white blokes with beards (and nothing better to do) continue to write countless books analysing the artistic output of Bob Dylan, putting every mumbled word under the microscope, celebrating the genius of a twentieth-century lyrical wizard. Obviously Dylan qualifies as one of the great modern pop artists but he has said little to me since 1983 and his magic has rarely been mirrored in live performance. In contrast, onstage Morrissey is transformed from solitary, shy and disillusioned poet into one of the most charismatic and emotional performers of our or any time. You have to see it to believe it.

If you are even vaguely interested in original thinking on the art of pop culture, then – as if studying a living sculpture – everything about Steven Patrick Morrissey remains deeply fascinating and thought-provoking; from obscure lyrical references and playful plagiarism to his public image and gestures, from provocative politically-incorrect pronouncements to his celebration of alternative sexual codes ("I'm not the man you think I am").

For example, in this volume Andrew Cope suggests that Morrissey's poses in publicity photos and on record sleeves are knowing references to religious artworks such as the devotional image of the Christ known as *The Man of Sorrow* and Michelangelo's *Dying Captive*. Meanwhile Lawrence Foley's chapter explores links between John Betjeman, British identity and Morrissey's "mystical bond" with Manchester, focusing partly on how the artist's happy memories of his youth in Queen's Square Salford were eradicated (by friendly bombs) in the slum clearances of the late 1960s.

As these diverse, insightful and critically-opinioned chapters all confirm, Morrissey's life – this deliberately constructed work of art – continues to raise more questions than answers. Some of the chapter titles may, initially, wilt your academic asparagus ("Tropes of Hyperbole and Sentimentality in Morrissey's Musical Expression"!), but I whole-heartedly recommend that you cast aside all prejudices and embrace this intellectual experience. *How do you know if you haven't tried?*

Forgive the cheap alliteration employed by this toothless, ageing, old *NME* hack, but I believe you will find this book enlightening, educational and entertaining. Personally, it brings back fond memories of a warm, friendly and stimulating weekend spent in Limerick in the spring of 2009, in the company of Dr Eoin Devereux and many intelligent, articulate and naturally sensitive Smiths/Moz fans. You see, despite my poor education, I accepted the invitation.

Morrissey, you should have been there. You might have learnt something.

Len Brown, May 2011

Introduction

But Don't Forget the Songs that Made You Cry and the Songs that Saved Your Life ...

Eoin Devereux, Aileen Dillane and Martin J. Power

As a multi-layered (and sometimes reluctant) icon, Morrissey has attracted the attention of scholars interested in questions concerning class, ethnic, gender and sexual identities. Morrissey's transnational appeal and the intense fandom, which he continues to attract, have also been of interest. Organised around the themes of fandom, representations and identities, this collection of essays – focused primarily on Morrissey's solo career – examines one of the most controversial,[1] complex and iconic figures within popular culture. Our intention is to add significantly to the emerging body of academic research which has begun to engage seriously with Morrissey as a solo-artiste and leader of The Smiths.[2]

The seeds for this book were planted at the second of two symposia held at the University of Limerick, Ireland in April 2009.[3] Some of the writers featured in this anthology have been intrigued by Morrissey from his early days with The Smiths to the present, having grown up with songs that accompanied formative experiences and created significant others. Some have come to Morrissey a little later but proclaim firm commitment to, and a deep-felt personal ownership of, his sounds, sentiments and semiotics. Undoubtedly, this thematic thread of the articulating (and hopefully articulate) "fan" speaks out from virtually every chapter. Given, then, that most of the authors here listened to Morrissey long before they began their academic/writing careers lends a particular bottom-up perspective that rings true in all of the chapters.

But does being a fan first result in compromised objectivity? Far from it, we would argue. What emerges is a passionate scholarship underpinned by a politics of admiration which enriches, not detracts from the arguments and analyses presented here, though we appreciate such things are not without their tensions (see for example Snowsell, Chapter 4). In fact, these very tensions and contradictions when discussing Morrissey and his elusive positioning on a variety of social, political, cultural and musical issues are at the heart of this collection of essays. But as Erin Hazard points out in Chapter 1 of this volume, there is huge potential for "the fan" to engage in a creative act when occupying that very role. This paradigm, so prevalent in both active audience studies and cultural studies, is, we hope, taken to a new critical level, harnessing genuine interest while at the same time taming hero-worshiping, and channeling "passions just like mine" into a series of essays that postulate, provoke, prise apart and play. This collection is not a fanzine nor is it music journalism or criticism. It is a scholarly book, but, taking our cue from its subject, it is also a creative act featuring wry humour alongside serious rhetoric, and a compilation of individual as well as collective ideas, lyrically as well as critically framed. This is not to say that to read this book you need to be a Morrissey fan. As with George Eliot's pier-glass, our aim is to provide a variety of perspectives on this artist, whom you may know intimately or whom you are just about to meet. So, like eating a good (vegetarian) cookie, you can start from anywhere in this volume, but we do recommend listening to Morrissey's music just before, during or subsequently. After all, that is really where it all begins and ends – with "the *songs* that saved your life" again (and again).

Sing your life: Themes and topics

This collection stretches across a range of disciplines and theoretical homes, from cultural studies to gender studies and queer theory, from sociology and media studies to musicology and musical analyses, and from visual culture to semiotics. A number of thematic threads predominate but are by no means exhaustive. The tension previously spoken of in relation to the critical position taken by the fan/author also plays out when considering Morrissey's championing of "Others" (marginalized, different) in some instances and his almost narcissistic focus on a carefully constructed self in others. In the case of the former, Morrissey is understood as a "raconteur of the marginalized" (Power, Chapter 5), particularly of the working-class but also of those who are cast as somehow different (Manco, Chapter 6). Morrissey's songs give voice to the voiceless or to those who are generally unheard, thereby using his music as a vehicle for challenging the socio/political *status quo*. Yet Morrissey's representations of, as opposed to *for*, the working-class and subaltern in particular are by no means straightforward. His borrowing from skinhead and punk cultures, as much as from British dandies (see the chapters by Baker, Foley and Hawkins), paints a picture of a Romantic nationalist fearful of the change brought about by mass immigration in the United Kingdom (often leading to racist charges against Morrissey). At best, such views, which may be reproduced by fans, are laced with a kind of ersatz nostalgia (see Jacobs and Jeffrey, Chapter 13), a longing for something that never truly was, complicating Morrissey's stance as a hero of the working-class given that the material existence of the underprivileged can be recast in a kind of noble savage rhetoric through his recreations.

In the case of the latter, where the focus is on Morrissey's image, the careful, deliberate construction of a deeply coded, textually rich self, where every gesture, sound, and image is almost painfully self-conscious, presents a man consumed with his public persona and its mediation. In such an era of mass media, the colours and textures of the messenger/harbinger prove as important as the message in the music. As carefully constructed codes splatter out from the body of the song into the careful composition that is "Morrissey", a rich textual reading is invited. Visual representations of the performing body feature prominently here, from decoding album covers (see Connor, Chapter 7) to reading the potential provenance of gestures in Morrissey's self-conscious poses (see Cope, Chapter 8), where the play with authenticity is at its sharpest. The lexicon from which Morrissey draws is rich in allusion and allegory. Eclectically mining the sounds and styles of cultural icons, musicians, poets, writers, Morrissey comes across as someone keen to pay tribute, to eulogize, and as a savvy bricoleur (see Brooks, Chapter 14 and Hazard, Chapter 1). The strategy sometimes involves ventriloquism and dialogism (see Martino, Chapter 12), invoking those with a literary sensibility, for example, that may speak for and through him, and him through them (see Hawkins, Chapter 17). The outcome is a play, a deferral, a subversion and an elusiveness that makes it impossible to know the "real" Morrissey (including the gendered Morrissey – see Woronzoff, Chapter 15), resulting in considerable ambiguity in his, literally, *(re)presentations* of *them* as *him* and *vice versa*.

Given this is a book about a singer, it is natural that there is a focus on specific songs too and the primary modus of their delivery, Morrissey's voice (see Sjöstedt, Chapter 16). A number of chapters are given over to detailed analysis where the emphasis is not just on music or the performer in context, nor on music as a mere vehicle for the lyrics or words, but rather as a structured sound world central to the communicative play (see Devereux and Dillane, Chapter 10). Formal considerations come under the microscope, involving both syntax and process (see Askerøi, Chapter 11; Hawkins, Chapter 17). It is not simply the case that Morrissey's words and music somehow reflect or record society. They also structurally question, contest and even generate it (Attali 1985) as, arguably, all good (pop) music should. Such arguments about the worth of pop are touched upon in numerous essays (see Brett, Chapter 9; Sjöstedt, Chapter 16), involving discussions on the aesthetics of Morrissey's works and the degree to which they are and should be canonized or cannibalized.

Finally, to complete the full circle, we return to the idea of the fan and the manner in which Morrissey is celebrated and celebrates others through his music and visual representations. Many of the essays play with quasi-religious undertones, from discussions of meta-pilgrimage (Hazard, Chapter 1) and martyrdom of St Steven/Wilde (Devereux and Dillane, Chapter 10) to the iconicity of the vicar in a tutu (Martino, Chapter 12) and the imagery of Joan of Arc getting down to Morrissey and The Smiths on a New York dance floor (Jacobson and Jeffrey, Chapter 13).

The resultant collection, then, offers a multitude of positionalities and a myriad of possible identifications with Morrissey, his music, his beliefs and his strategies of representation, in all of their often-unresolved, controversial and contradictory glory. Some essays offer close analysis of words and music, enriching the social context or even generating it recursively. Other essays ask, "what if?" in terms of demonstrating the new layers of meaning to be uncovered when certain paradigms act as prisms (or pier-glasses) once focused upon Morrissey and his creative output. Most of all, each essay acts as a particular starting point, not as a full stop, in the discussion of one of the most interesting, sometimes infuriating, but always engaging artists of our time.

Notes

1. Morrissey has maintained his reputation as a controversial artist, with his world-view largely being Left wing and indeed very radical. His republican views, his "hostility to everyone from Thatcher to Bush" and his comments on "immigration and the protection of British culture from outside influences" continue to court controversy (Brown 2009). However it is perhaps animal rights and vegetarianism that are the issues closest to Morrissey's heart, and which have resulted in some

of his most controversial utterances. He has publicly defended the actions of the Animal Rights Militia, stating that he believes such violence is acceptable because it is perpetrated against those who farm fur or conduct animal experiments, people who had therefore "brought it on themselves" (Allardyce 2006). In his most recent controversy he described the treatment of animals in China as "absolutely horrific", arguing in response that "you can't help but feel that the Chinese are a subspecies" (Topping 2010). While such views are controversial (and hugely problematic), "when it comes to animal rights and animal welfare, he's absolutely unshakable in his beliefs. In his view, if you treat an animal badly, you are less than human" (Armitage cited in Topping 2010).

2. See for example, Michael Bracewell (2009) *England is Mine: Poplife in Albion*. London: Faber and Faber; Sean Campbell and Colin Coulter (eds) (2010) *Why Pamper Life's Complexities? Essays on The Smiths*. Manchester: Manchester University Press; Eoin Devereux (2009) 'I'm not the man you think I am: authenticity, ambiguity and the cult of Morrissey', in E. Haverinen, U. Kovala and V. Rautavuoma (eds) *Cult, Community, Identity*. Finland: Research Center for Contemporary Culture of the University of Jyväskylä; Eoin Devereux (2006) 'Being Wild(e) about Morrissey: fandom and identity', in M. Corcoran and M. Peillon (eds) *Uncertain Ireland: A Sociological Chronicle 2003–4*. Dublin: IPA; Stan Hawkins (2002) *Settling the Pop Score*. Aldershot: Ashgate; Stan Hawkins (2009) *The British Pop Dandy: Masculinity, Popular Music and Culture*. Farnham: Ashgate; Gavin Hopps (2009) *Morrissey: The Pageant of His Bleeding Heart*. London and New York: Continuum; Nadine Hubbs (1996) 'Music of the "fourth gender": Morrissey and the sexual politics of melodic contour', in T. Foster, C. Stiegel and E. E. Berry (eds) *Bodies of Writing, Bodies in Performance*. New York: New York University Press; Pierpaolo Martino (2007) 'I am a living sign: a semiotic reading of Morrissey', *International Journal of Applied Semiotics*, 6: 1; Antti Nylén (2004) 'Morrissey and Me', available www.eurozine.com; Antti Nylén (2009) *On Consolation*. Helsinki: Antti Nylén; Simon Renyolds and Joy Press (1995) *The Sex Revolts: Gender, Rebellion and Rock 'n'Roll*. Cambridge, MA: Harvard University Press; Julian Stringer (1992) 'The Smiths: repressed but remarkably dressed', *Popular Music*, 11, pp. 15–26; Taina Viitamäki (1997) 'I'm not the man you think I am: Morrissey's fourth gender', *Musical Currents*, 3, pp. 29–40; Suzanne Weaver (2008) (ed.) *Phil Collins: The World Won't Listen*. Yale: Yale University Press; Nabeel Zuberi (2001) 'The last truly British people you will ever know: The Smiths, Morrissey and Britpop', *Sounds English: Transnational Popular Music*. Chicago: University of Illinois Press.

3. *The Songs That Saved Your Life (Again): A Symposium on Morrissey* featured 20 academic papers, a panel discussion, documentary screenings as well as a live performance by The Smiths/Morrissey tribute band These Charming Men. The symposium featured the European premiere of Kerri Koch's documentary on Morrissey's growing Latino fanbase called "Passions Just Like Mine" (2009) as well as the screening of the Indonesian version of video-artist Phil Collins' film *The World Won't Listen*.

References

Allardyce, J. (2006) 'Morrissey supports animal rights violence', *The Sunday Times*, 15th January, available: *http://www.timesonline.co.uk/tol/news/uk/article788698.ece*.

Attali, J. (1985) *Noise: The Political Economy of Music*, trans. by Brian Massumi. Minneapolis: University of Minnesota Press.

Brown, L. (2009) 'Morrissey turns 50', *The Guardian*, 21st May.

Topping, A. (2010) 'Morrissey reignites racism row by calling Chinese a "subspecies"', *The Guardian*, 3rd September, available: *http://www.guardian.co.uk/music/2010/sep/03/morrissey-china-subspecies-racism?intcmp=239*.

Chapter 1

'Suedehead': Paving the Pilgrimage Path to Morrissey's and Dean's Fairmount, Indiana

Erin Hazard

Introduction

In January of 1992, as a 16 year old on the heels of Morrissey, I made a pilgrimage to Fairmount, Indiana, home of James Dean and site of Morrissey's first "promotional film" (or video) for the single 'Suedehead'.[1] Filmed in Fairmount in February of 1988 and directed by the late Tim Broad, 'Suedehead', as Melissa Connor demonstrates elsewhere in this collection, solidified Morrissey's reputation as a solo artist distinct from The Smiths.

Drunk from witnessing Morrissey's triumphant *Kill Uncle* US tours, I managed to convince my parents to make the drive from our home in Milwaukee, Wisconsin, to Fairmount, Indiana, about eight hours each way. By this point, they recognized Morrissey as a surrogate member of the family whose voice could always be heard in my bedroom and whose image dominated the family television. In my imagination, Fairmount was as much Morrissey's as Dean's. Upon arriving, we visited the record store on Main Street where we found a homespun bulletin board with several amateur photographs of the 'Suedehead' shoot. It read: "Morrissey was here [...] the video [...] the equipment [...] crew [...] star" (Figure 1.1); I documented this documentation of Morrissey's visit with my Kodak disc camera and purchased two photographs taken during the filming of the video, one a rear view of Morrissey's hat and overcoat and another of a shivering Morrissey next to the Indian motorcycle used in the shoot. The presence of this display and the hawking of these paparazzi-esque snapshots attest to the numbers of travellers like me, who came to Fairmount seeking some cocktail of Morrissey and Dean, heavy on the Morrissey.

As a teenage pilgrim, I intuited that Morrissey must understand my obsession with seeking out all the books, films and figures to which he alluded. Morrissey, after all, shared a similar attitude towards his cabinet of heroes, in which Dean occupied a privileged position. In 1981, before forming The Smiths, Morrissey (then Steven Morrissey) had published a short book on Dean, *James Dean is Not Dead*. As Morrissey's star rose, he maintained communication with his idols, transparently weaving them into the worlds of Smithdom and eventually Morrisseydom. In 1984, Morrissey was photographed with his framed photograph of Dean for *Smash Hits* and explained his fascination with the actor: "His entire life seemed so magnificently perfect. What he did on film didn't stir me that much but as a person he was immensely valuable [...] Even though he was making enormous strides with his craft, he was still incredibly miserable and obviously doomed [...] That kind of mystical knowledge that there is something incredibly black around the corner. People who feel this are quite special and always end up in quite a mangled mess."[2] In 1986, Dean was featured as

Figure 1.1: Morrissey was here ... Reproduced by kind permission © Erin Hazard (2011).

the cover star for The Smiths' single 'Bigmouth Strikes Again'. Dean's presence continues to inform the iconography and mythology of Morrissey, as Dean and his *East of Eden* co-star Dick Davalos have appeared in recent pre-concert show reels. Morrissey's sustained and studied reverence for Dean, and his many other heroes, not only elicited a similar attitude towards Morrissey from me, but also convinced me that in order to understand Morrissey, I must also study those he had worshipped.

The double layers of associations at Fairmount – those of Dean's upbringing and Morrissey's subsequent 1988 pilgrimage to the site – thus inspired my 1992 pilgrimage. Now, nearly 20 years after the trip, I am interested in how 'Suedehead', the video, remade Dean's Fairmount into Dean's and Morrissey's Fairmount, allowing me to visit the town first for its associations with Morrissey, and then for those with Dean. 'Suedehead' casts Morrissey as a pilgrim to Dean's Fairmount. Receiving a parcel containing Antoine de Saint-Exupéry's *Le Petit Prince* from a golden-haired visitor to his house, Morrissey travels to Fairmount. There he visits a series of sites associated with Dean, sites which had entered the Dean canon when *Life* magazine photographer Dennis Stock photographed Dean in Fairmount in 1954. Morrissey's trip not only borrows its stations from Stock's photographs, but the trip is also visually presented using a series of images that directly borrow Stock's photographic compositions with Morrissey in the position of Dean. Thus, 'Suedehead' takes Stock's photographic exploration of Dean's 1954 homecoming and transforms it into Morrissey's pilgrimage to Dean's Fairmount. 'Suedehead's telling of Morrissey's pilgrimage, however, paves the way for a reception that would remake Dean's Fairmount into Dean's and Morrissey's Fairmount; it accomplishes this through the aesthetic strategy of allegory.

Allegory and the doubling of meaning

Allegory refers to a text, whether a piece of literature, a painting or even a video, that communicates a double meaning. Angus Fletcher writes that "In the simplest terms, allegory says one thing and means another" (1964: 2). Fletcher also points out that a singular reading of an allegory's most literal sense often makes reasonable sense, but that a probing of its secondary meaning provides for a more productive interpretation: "The whole point of allegory is that it does not *need* to be read exegetically; it often has a literal level that makes good enough sense all by itself. But somehow this literal surface suggests a peculiar doubleness of intention, and while it can, as it were, get along without interpretation, it becomes richer and more interesting if given interpretation" (1964: 7).

In traditional art history, a painting like Bronzino's (1546) *An Allegory with Venus and Cupid* is exemplary of allegory: Father Time in the upper right rips a curtain away, revealing Venus and her son Cupid mid-embrace. Folly in the right middle ground approves and prepares to bombard the incestuous couple with roses, while in the left middle ground Jealousy tears her hair out. These figures personify abstract concepts like time, folly and jealousy and in one visual form they convey two meanings: first, a scene in which mother and son (Venus and Cupid) embrace to the pleasure of some and horror of others and, at the same time, a commentary on the consequences of such contact. By the late nineteenth and early twentieth centuries, traditional allegory, with its dependence on an interaction between literary association and visual form, was pretty much reviled by purist painters and critics, who preferred the exploration of paintings as paintings to stodgy allegories in which tales about the present were told using images from the past. Walter Benjamin, in his *The Origin of German Tragic Drama* (1928), was notable for his analysis and defence of allegory.

Drawing heavily on Benjamin's analysis, the critic Craig Owens – writing in the journal *October* – declared allegory a constituent "impulse" of postmodernism. Owens broadly defines allegory as a structure in which "one text is *read through* another" (1980: 68). In postmodernist art practice, according to Owens, allegory is realized through the tactics of "appropriation, site-specificity, impermanence, accumulation, discursivity, and hybridization" (1980: 75). Response to this reading of allegory was varied; some objected that by the end of the twentieth century, everything and anything had become allegory. That debate is not within the scope of my discussion. Instead I am interested in thinking about how 'Suedehead', the video, works in Owen's sense of the term allegory, as it turns the accumulated text of Dean's Fairmount into Morrissey's Fairmount, using many of the same aesthetic tactics Owens identified as constituting allegory – for example, appropriation, accumulation and hybridization. For Owens, this doubling of text is always a process of usurpation in which the original text genuflects to its appropriator. 'Suedehead', in contrast, keeps Dean's Fairmount alive as it becomes Morrissey's Fairmount. This respect for the layers of texts is crucial: in its simultaneous preservation of Dean's Fairmount and transformation of that Fairmount into Morrissey's Fairmount, 'Suedehead' articulates the tremendous creative potential of being "a fan".[3]

'Suedehead': A postmodern allegory?

Before Morrissey ever visited the state of Indiana, Fairmount had achieved iconic status as Dean's hometown, not only through its biographical associations, but also through *Life* magazine's 1955 publication of Dennis Stock's photographs of Dean in Fairmount.[4] Dean's aunt and uncle had raised him on a farm on the outskirts of the town. In the winter of 1954, with *East of Eden* wrapped but not yet released, Dean made the trip home with Stock. Dean's visit had the potential – a potential that came to be tragically realized – to transform the stuff of his Midwestern upbringing into mythology. Stock captured Dean walking the small town's Main Street. He returned to the farm where his aunt and uncle raised him, playing his bongo drums among the farm animals and reading in the hayloft. Dean visited the high school where his acting career had started. The accumulated text of biographical and associative material constituting "Dean's Fairmount" as presented in Stock's 1954 photographs is the text that 'Suedehead', as Owens puts it, "doubles".

Tim Broad's video for 'Suedehead' begins with views of a London West-End square and the Royal Borough of Kensington and Chelsea signs. The camera pans to (what purports to be) Morrissey's upper storey window and then invites us into Morrissey's bathroom, which serves as a study and a temple to the worthies of Byron, Dean and Davalos. Using two of Owens' strategies of allegory, specifically accumulation and hybridization, the bath sequence places Morrissey in the simultaneous positions of hero and fan. In place of narrative, the accumulation, or layering of objects, sets the scene. In other words, we do not care why Morrissey's in the bath; instead, a proliferation of artefacts in his Elysium of a bathroom tells us that Morrissey worships and is worshipped. Morrissey, the fan, soaks beneath a large-scale photograph of his heroes Dean and Davalos. His typewriter, a letter from Dean and a volume of Byron's poetry (Byron was Dean's middle name) rest atop a makeshift desk over the tub while a copy of *The Fairmount News* memorial edition to Dean (a facsimile of which is available for purchase on a Fairmount Dean pilgrimage) rests on a nearby stool. The homemade bathmat reading 'There Is A Light That Never Goes Out' (apparently crafted by a fan) lies on the floor next to the bath (Bret 2004: 105), reminding the viewer that just as Morrissey genuflects to Dean, so do his followers to him. Spatially positioned between objects attesting to his love of Dean and others' love of him, Morrissey is presented as a mediator of heroes and fans. As in a traditional allegorical painting, the objects presented are not simply of visual interest but rather, as the accumulation of parenthetical information above indicates, they are clues demanding interpretation.

The London segment of 'Suedehead' alerts us to another strategy of allegory identified by Owens: hybridity. As a medium, video generically works through hybridization as it combines music, lyrics and images. More specifically, 'Suedehead' explicitly plays with what Owens describes as "the reciprocity [...] between the visual and the verbal: words are often treated as purely visual phenomena, while visual images are offered as script to be deciphered" (1980: 74). While the presentation of the various objects accumulated in Morrissey's bathroom is "offered as script to be deciphered", the introductory London footage also alerts us to the visual interest of words as it includes the Royal Borough of Kensington and Chelsea signage, the title "Byron" on the cover of the book above the bath, the Olympia label and the numerous keys on the typewriter, the letter in Dean's handwriting, *The Fairmount News* and the bathmat. If the seemingly decorative objects are actually texts communicating Morrissey's work as hero and fan, the textual elements transform into visual elements. The iconic script on the London signage, the antique type on the cover of the Byron volume, the mechanical appearance of the typewriter lettering and the idiosyncrasies of Dean's own script appeal to the eye. While the allegorical doubling of 'Suedehead' allows for a collapse between Morrissey's positions as hero and fan, it also works through a doubling of visual and textual interest as it presents images and objects as texts to be interpreted and words as visual motifs.

The transition between London and Fairmount is not motivated by narrative complexity but rather announced by the arrival of an object in the hands of a child: a golden-haired visitor in an antique pilot's hat, played by Morrissey's nephew Sam, delivers a book-shaped parcel to Morrissey's front stoop. Upon Morrissey's arrival in Fairmount's downtown, the parcel reveals itself to contain Dean's favourite book: *Le Petit Prince*. Inspired by Saint-Exupéry's experiences after his plane crashed in the Sahara, *Le Petit Prince* tells the story of a blond little prince who leaves his planet, Asteroid B-612, to visit inhabitants of other sites in the universe. A fox the prince encounters on his travels articulates the primary lesson of these sojourns: "it is only with the heart that one can see rightly. What is essential is invisible to the eye" (Saint-Exupéry 1943: 87).[5] Thus, once the viewer understands the parcel to contain *Le Petit Prince*, the child visitor proves a fitting transition from London to Fairmount. Beyond simply bearing Dean's favourite book, the child, with his blond tousled hair and aviator's hat, appears to be a hybrid of Saint-Exupéry and his favourite character. Furthermore, the child's hat and his status as Morrissey's nephew also allude to Stock's photographs of Dean in Fairmount, which include Dean's nephew Markie, who likewise wears an aviator's hat, in the Fairmount cemetery and playing soapbox derby in the driveway. Furthermore, the message of the book delivered by the child ("What is essential is invisible to the eye") assumes new import in the context of 'Suedehead', reminding viewers that the various clues strewn throughout its presentation are not simply there to be looked at but also to be interpreted.

Owen's allegorical strategies likewise guide the presentation of Morrissey's trip to Fairmount. Accumulation and hybridity continue to allow for the doubling of texts (Dean's Fairmount and Morrissey's Fairmount), as appropriation is also introduced. While hybridity has thus far been discussed as the reciprocity between the visual and textual interest of words and images, the hybridity of video as a medium that combines music, words and images informs the opening sequence of Morrissey in Fairmount's downtown. As Morrissey sings, "Why do you come here?" he walks on the Fairmount sidewalk with its hanging street lights and nineteenth-century main street architecture in the background. Through the hybridity of voice and image, surprising interpretations emerge. For example, when watching and listening to 'Suedehead', the video, the words that sounded like a mournful questioning of an estranged one on the record alone ("Why do you come here?") sound and look like an interrogation of the ritual of fan pilgrimage in the context of the video: Why do fans go to these places? What are they looking for? The play with words treated as images directs the video's presentation of the search for Dean's Fairmount. While Broad's camera plays with Fairmount's signage (e.g. the Walk/Don't Walk signals, the highway signs, the Indian Motorcycle label, the Gas City water tower, child Dean's name and hand/footprints in the barn), it also captures Morrissey's own camera transforming "Fairmount", "Dairy Queen", "Fairmount Water Works" and "High School" into photographs. Likewise, Morrissey's graffiti scrawl and chalkboard messages at the Fairmount high school ("Morrissey February 7th 1988", "Put on a Happy Face, No" and "You Can't Go Home Again") are as interesting as visual emblems of Morrissey as they are for their content and layers of associations with literature and Dean.

The primary strategy of allegory at play here, however, is appropriation. 'Suedehead' communicates Morrissey's trip to Fairmount through a series of images that directly recall Stock's photographs of Dean. The allegorical strategy of appropriation binds together the presentation of Morrissey in Fairmount's downtown, Dean's old school, the old Dean farmstead and the Fairmount graveyard. For Owens (1980: 69), appropriation is the dominant strategy of allegory:

> Allegorical imagery is appropriated imagery; the allegorist does not invent images but confiscates them […] The first link between allegory and contemporary art may now be made with the appropriation of images that occurs in the works of Troy Brauntuch, Sherrie Levine, Robert Longo, and others – artists who generate images through the reproduction of other images. The appropriated image may be a film still, a photograph, a drawing; it is often itself already a reproduction.

In the instance of 'Suedehead', the appropriated imagery is Stock's photographs of Dean's visit to Fairmount. Morrissey's visit to the town is communicated visually through a re-creation of Stock's photographic compositions with Morrissey in the position of Dean. The shot of

Morrissey walking down the Fairmount sidewalk with the corner bank building in the background reproduces Stock's earlier image of Dean travelling the same path, albeit with a cigarette in his mouth. At Dean's alma mater, Stock photographed the actor sitting slouched atop a desk with a distant gaze. At the now derelict high school devoid of classrooms fully stocked with desks, 'Suedehead' recreates the image with Morrissey in a classroom gazing out the window and then in a chair centre stage in Dean's high school auditorium. At the Dean farmstead, Stock shot Dean playing his beloved bongo drums in the farmyard amidst the cows. Likewise, 'Suedehead' captures Morrissey playing bongos with the cows at the Deans' farm. Some of the appropriated imagery in 'Suedehead' conflates elements from more than one of Stock's photographs. For example, the footage of Morrissey reading James Whitcomb Riley in the Deans' hayloft combines Stock's photographs of James Dean reading James Whitcomb Riley at his aunt and uncle's kitchen table with another photograph of a suit-clad Dean reading in the hayloft. The shot of Morrissey in the Fairmount graveyard in front of a tombstone reading "Cal Dean" recreates Stock's photograph of Dean at the same site and in the same pose; the tombstone of an ancestor named Cal in the Fairmount graveyard resonated for the actor who had just put to rest the role of Cal Trask in *East of Eden*.

After the presentation of Morrissey in front of the Cal Dean tombstone, the appropriation of Stock's photographs halts for the remainder of 'Suedehead'. Instead Morrissey sits at twilight in the snow at Dean's grave surrounded by wreaths and flowers. Obviously there is no precedent in Stock's photographs for such a scene, but the appropriated image rears its head one last time at the close of the video. Superimposed film footage of Dean looks down at Morrissey and his own grave and then looks away. The image of Morrissey at once at Dean's grave and the object of Dean's gaze brings to mind the book that initiated the pilgrimage. At the close of *Le Petit Prince*, the little prince tells the narrator, "It was wrong of you to come. You will suffer. I shall look as if I were dead; and that will not be true." He continues, "You understand [...] It is too far. I cannot carry this body with me. It is too heavy" (Saint-Exupéry 1943: 106). Building upon the book's message that "What is essential is invisible to the eye", the little prince assures the narrator that though he may *look* dead, "In one of the stars I shall be living. In one of them I shall be laughing" (Saint-Exupéry 1943: 106). Though the pilgrimage to Fairmount appears to present Dean as a dead actor reduced to sites, objects and monuments, the conclusion of 'Suedehead' presents Dean living in the stars, just like the hero of his favourite book, looking down on one of his fans who also happens to be a hero to many.

Accumulation, hybridity and appropriation – these are the mainstays of Owens' interpretation of postmodern allegory, and 'Suedehead' puts them to good use towards a doubling of meaning in which Dean's Fairmount becomes also Morrissey's Fairmount. For Owens', however, allegory – with its reliance on the double reading of a text – is also a process of usurpation. The allegorist, writes Owens, "does not restore an original meaning that may have been lost or obscured [...] Rather, he adds another meaning to the image. If the allegorist adds meaning, however, she does so only to replace: the allegorical meaning supplants an antecedent one; it is a supplement" (1980: 69). To reiterate, according to

Owens, "The appropriated image may be a film still, a photograph, a drawing; it is often itself already a reproduction. However, the manipulations to which these artists subject such images work to empty them of their resonance, their significance, their authoritative claim to meaning" (1980: 69). For Owens, allegory is seductive for its potential to wrest artworks and texts of their original meanings or intentions and to supplant them with the allegorist's "supplement". What happens here is less the doubling of a text than the substitution of one meaning for another. Beyond 'Suedehead', allegory and appropriation are recurrent in the lyrics and visual culture of The Smiths and Morrissey. With cover art consisting solely of reproduced film stills and photographs and lyrics built of lines taken "on loan", The Smiths seemed to be the quintessential postmodern pop group. Yet, to cast Morrissey in the position of Owens' postmodern artist vacuuming images and texts of their original meanings does not add up. In this respect, Morrissey's and 'Suedehead's use of allegory, though both revel in the strategies identified by Owens, in the end resembles more closely Fletcher's explanation of allegory as a text that can be read on only one level, but yields more if read doubly.

'Suedehead' presents Morrissey as a Dean fan visiting Fairmount, walking down Main Street, playing the bongos amidst the farmyard animals, and visiting James Dean's grave. Certainly the casual viewer could view the video as little more than that, though such a viewing would probably induce some confusion (why the bongos?). Once the beholder understands Morrissey not just as a Dean fan visiting Fairmount, but as a Dean fan visiting Fairmount at the same time that he is a hero performing his pilgrimage for fans, a fuller interpretation of 'Suedehead' emerges. Like Bronzino's *An Allegory with Venus and Cupid*, 'Suedehead' offers its viewers a moral: this is how to worship. Proceed carefully not just with your eyes but also your heart and mind. Pay attention to the trail of clues laid for you, decipher these objects and allusions, and you might learn how to transform the rites of fandom into your own creative activity. This message would be completely lost if one imputes 'Suedehead' with the allegorical usurpation of meaning described by Owens; that would be tantamount to saying the video transforms Fairmount, the home of Dean, into a site linked only to Morrissey's celebrity. Such a reading would be polemical and, what is more, totally off the mark. For such a transformation would position Morrissey as only a hero and negate his position as a fan. The instructional value of this particular allegory relies on exactly this doubling of Dean and Morrissey, hero and fan, for Morrissey's audience. 'Suedehead' perpetuates Dean's history in Fairmount while also imbuing the site with Morrissey's residue, rendering Fairmount now James Dean's Fairmount and Morrissey's Fairmount. 'Suedehead' laid the foundation for this transformation, a transformation that was fully realized by countless Morrissey fans' pilgrimages to Morrissey's (and then Dean's) Fairmount, Indiana.

The reception of 'Suedehead', or my Morrissey scrapbook

The two layers of 'Suedehead's allegory motivated my visit to Fairmount in 1992. Surely, Morrissey's filmed pilgrimage to the town made the trip an imperative, but the town's associations with Dean exerted a secondary pull. The photographs I shot in Fairmount demonstrate an application of the aesthetic strategies observed in 'Suedehead'. The photographs fall into two main categories: first, re-creations of shots from Broad's footage and those photographs that Morrissey is presented as taking and, secondly, photographs of my friend and I acting the part of Morrissey. My snapshots of the corner bank building and street lights imitate Broad's opening footage of Fairmount, while the Dairy Queen and water tower photos are re-creations of the photos Morrissey is presented as taking. Presumably, many of these subjects – like those of the Fairmount water tower, the hanging street lights and the Dairy Queen ice cream franchise – were chosen for inclusion in 'Suedehead' not simply on the basis of their Dean associations, but also because they must have appeared to Broad and Morrissey as curiosities, exotic images of Midwestern America. I lived in the shadow of a similar water tower and had played on a Little League baseball team sponsored by our local Dairy Queen, but I nevertheless faithfully photographed similar sites in Fairmount. Yet, the activity of taking these photographs suggests something beyond the making of facsimiles. As we shot these photographs, we were recreating the very premise of 'Suedehead'. For if much of the video shows Morrissey re-enacting Dean's 1954 encounter with Fairmount, as we shot our photos we were recreating those moments in Morrissey's 1988 pilgrimage not appropriated from Stock's photos but instead showing Morrissey, the tourist, snapping photographs. As Morrissey recreated Dean's homecoming to Fairmount, we recreated Morrissey's pilgrimage to Fairmount.

The second category of photos from the trip shows my friend and me taking turns photographing each other in Morrissey's posture. At the café on Main Street (refurbished since Morrissey's visit), we took turns contemplatively sipping tea and reading our newly purchased facsimile copies of *The Fairmount News* (Figure 1.2). We gained entry to the old high school and paced and photographed the schoolroom Morrissey had visited. We travelled out to the graveyard, where we found Dean's grave covered with lipstick impressions, and photographed each other stooping tenderly next to the gravesite. While our excursion was motivated by a desire to feel some closeness to our hero Morrissey, looking back at these photographs now demonstrates how we were also learning to explore the potential of acts of appropriation, as we were photographed as Morrissey had been, just as Morrissey had been filmed by Broad as Dean had been photographed by Stock. For us, and all those other kids buying snapshots of Morrissey at the downtown record store, the allegory of 'Suedehead' had transformed Dean's Fairmount, Indiana, into Dean's and Morrissey's Fairmount, Indiana.

Our holiday jaunt was just that: an excursion to Dean's *and* Morrissey's Fairmount, Indiana. Had we made the journey with only the end in mind, of appropriating Morrissey's appropriations, a reading of 'Suedehead' as exemplary of Owen's postmodern definition of allegory would be spot on; 'Suedehead' would have succeeded in usurping Dean's Fairmount and transforming it solely into Morrissey's. But Morrissey's appropriation of Stock's imagery did not efface its original in the manner predicted by Owens. Instead, we also came to Fairmount to learn about Dean. We had prepared with weekend Dean film festivals, staying up all night to watch all three films in chronological sequence. We were not sated by a

Figure 1.2: The Fairmount News. Reproduced by kind permission © Erin Hazard (2011).

reading of Morrissey's *James Dean is Not Dead*, but had added David Dalton's (1974) *The Mutant King* to the bibliography as well. In Fairmount, we attentively toured the James Dean museum and were touched by a drive past the old farm not because it was the site of Morrissey's legendary tractor test drive, but because it was where Dean himself had grown up. Similarly, Morrissey's lyrical loans never commandeered their originals in the fashion articulated by Owens, but instead sent me to the library for copies of Shelagh Delaney's *A Taste of Honey* (1959) and *Sweetly Sings the Donkey* (1964). Each instance of appropriation was a clue to follow; together they formed an archive to excavate and catalogue. For me, this kind of investigation eventually became a way to turn imitation and reverence into creativity.

The tropes of hero worship Morrissey modelled in 'Suedehead' could be applied not only to Fairmount, but also to the trail of Mancunian landmarks and sites rife in The Smiths' and Morrissey's lyrics and imagery. While these sites were certainly the terminus of many pilgrimage paths pre-'Suedehead', it is notable that the first official Manchester Smiths convention was held the summer after 'Suedehead's release on 28th and 29th July, 1988.

Watching Morrissey visit the sites associated with Dean potentially solidified the sites associated with Morrissey through his biography, words, videos and album art into a formal itinerary: The Salford Lads Club, his childhood homestead on Kings Road, the iron bridge and St. Mary's, Stretford. 'Suedehead' instructs its viewers on how to interact with these sites, encouraging them to prepare by reading the hero's favourite books, to document the journey through photographs that appropriate the imagery associated with the hero, and to leave graffiti marks on its stations using words borrowed from the hero.

Though I was only able to read of the first Smiths convention in the *New Musical Express*, a group of fanzine pen friends and I completed a pilgrimage to The Smiths' and Morrissey's Manchester several years later in which we applied all these lessons. While Broad photographed Morrissey as Dean in Fairmount, we stood as The Smiths for a Salford Lads Club photo op. As Morrissey had done in Dean's schoolroom and as countless others had done before us, we left graffiti messages (see Devereux 2010). I chose to appropriate Morrissey's words about appropriation: "I can't help quoting you 'cos everything that you said rings true." At "the old grey school" of St. Mary's in Stretford, I posed at a desk contemplatively for the camera, as Morrissey had done in the Fairmount theatre and as Dean had done on his 1954 visit to his alma mater.

The moral of the meta-pilgrimage to Morrissey's Fairmount

While I have problematized the categorization of 'Suedehead's allegory as quintessentially "postmodern", in Owens' sense of the term, above, I would also like to note that the particular type of fan pilgrimage communicated in 'Suedehead' is not unique. Morrissey was not the first hero to perform the part of pilgrim and, in so doing, transform the destination of his pilgrimage into a site associated with both his hero and himself. In 1815, the American writer Washington Irving visited Stratford-on-Avon, the birthplace of William Shakespeare and then published a literary retelling of his pilgrimage as "Stratford-on-Avon" in *The Sketch-Book of Geoffrey Crayon, Gent* (1819–20). Irving's account recounts his experiences at all of the requisite Shakespeare sights in Stratford including the house where Shakespeare was born, the church where his remains rest, and Charlecot, the estate where the young Shakespeare was traditionally believed to have poached a deer, a deed that sent him on his route to London. Interestingly, Irving's "Stratford-on-Avon" also created a new stop on the Stratford tourist's itinerary, this one not associated with Shakespeare but rather with Irving: the Red Horse Inn where Irving stayed during his visit to Stratford. While Irving's "Stratford-on-Avon" relays his frustrated attempts to secure an object or place authentically linked to Shakespeare, he spares his readers the same disappointment as he describes the chair he occupied and fireplace poker he used at The Red Horse Inn, cunningly laying a foundation for their eventual transformation into attractions linked to Irving.

Like Morrissey, Irving precariously positioned himself as the simultaneous hero and fan. Like Morrissey, he was able to communicate the experience of fandom and simultaneously elevate that communication into an artefact worthy of veneration. And, also similar to Morrissey, Irving was the recipient of an intense blend of reverence and identification from his readers. He spent the later years of his life at his Hudson River cottage Sunnyside near Tarrytown, New York, where visitors sought him out, begging a souvenir, a kind word or a dinner invitation. Sunnyside became America's first proper literary landmark during Irving's lifetime as its image was reproduced and its location was included in gazetteers to the Hudson River region. I bring up this likeness between Irving and Morrissey for two reasons. First, the similarity dispels the notion that the Morrissey phenomenon can be readily explicated by an appeal to the postmodern Zeitgeist with Morrissey as the quintessential usurper of culture. Moreover, it suggests that the figure who simultaneously articulates the positions of hero and fan inspires intense devotion from his readers or listeners, who see in him at the same time an ideal and a reflection of themselves.

Irving's Stratford pilgrimage and Morrissey's Fairmount pilgrimage are special types of journeys, allowing their protagonists to pay homage to their heroes while creating a trail for future meta-pilgrimages to Irving's Stratford or Morrissey's Fairmount. While the cynical receiver of 'Suedehead' might identify the video's lesson with an "Oh, typical, Morrissey hubris! 'Worship me as I have worshipped Dean,'" I prefer a gentler, more generous reading. Rather than simply aggrandizing Morrissey in this fashion, the allegory of 'Suedehead' actually allows for a poignant articulation of the potentially productive position of fandom. If Fairmount was once Dean's Fairmount, post-'Suedehead' it is Dean's and Morrissey's Fairmount. This doubling of text opens up a space of tremendous possibility. The attentive Morrissey fan realizes, thus, that if Dean's Fairmount is now Morrissey's and Dean's Fairmount, it might also some day be her own Fairmount too, or at least that – heeding Morrissey's example – out of fandom she might forge a way to make her own mark. The message veiled in the allegory of 'Suedehead' finds more direct expression in Morrissey's lyrical directive to "*Sing your life* / Walk right up to the microphone / And name / All the things you love / All the things that you loathe."

Confirmation of the potential productiveness of being a fan arrives in 'Suedehead's companion piece, Morrissey's second solo video for 'Everyday Is Like Sunday'. At the close of 'Suedehead', Dean looks down on Morrissey in the Fairmount graveyard, while at the end of 'Everyday Is Like Sunday', a Morrissey fan looks through a telescope to find Morrissey, face shielded, with an image of the fan screened on his t-shirt. In his wardrobe choice, Morrissey, the hero, imitates the costume of a fan, replacing his image with hers. Read together, these two conclusions emphasize the fluidity that Morrissey announces between the positions of hero and fan, a fluidity that acknowledges the potential of reverence to transform into a creative act worthy itself of recognition. Allegory allows this same point to come through in one text and thus poignantly articulates the collapse between hero and fan constituent of the lyrics, iconography and performance of Morrissey.

Notes

1. Broad had worked previously with The Smiths on the videos for 'Stop Me If You Think That You Heard This One Before' and 'Girlfriend In A Coma'. 'Suedehead' is available on two Morrissey video compilations: *Hulmerist* and *¡Oye Esteban!* Broad continued to direct videos for Morrissey until his death in February of 1993. Broad directed 'Everyday Is Like Sunday', 'The Last Of The Famous International Playboys', 'Interesting Drug', 'Ouija Board, Ouija Board', 'November Spawned A Monster', 'Sing Your Life', 'Pregnant For The Last Time', 'My Love Life', 'We Hate It When Our Friends Become Successful', and 'You're the One For Me Fatty'. I make no concrete claims for Broad's or Morrissey's intentions or authorship, preferring instead to conduct a close reading of the video itself.
2. 'The Morrissey collection', Morrissey interviewed by Ian Birch for *Smash Hits*, 21st June–4th July, 1984, reprinted: *http: //foreverill.com/interviews/1984/collection.htm*, accessed 14th April, 2010.
3. In the decades that followed the acknowledgement of criticism and reading as a creative act, many scholars turned their attention to fandom and its potential for the production of new media texts. On fan culture, see Henry Jenkins, *Textual Poachers: Television Fans and Participatory Culture* (1992) and Jenkins, *Fans, Bloggers, and Gamers: Exploring Participatory Culture* (2006). For a useful overview of the literature on the subject, see Jeroen de Kloet and Liesbeth Van Zoonen, 'Fan Culture – Performing Difference', in Eoin Devereux (ed.) *Media Studies: Key Issues and Debates* (2007).
4. Stock's photographs of Dean in Fairmount are republished in Dennis Stock, *James Dean Revisited* (1986).
5. Morrissey unwraps the package, revealing its contents to be *Le Petit Prince*, just after walking past Fox TV and Appliances in Fairmount. Given this juxtaposition, the signage on the Fox TV and Appliances store becomes yet another clue typical of an allegorical presentation; it alludes to the moral of the book Morrissey is about to unwrap.

References

Benjamin, W. (1998 [1928]) *The Origin of German Tragic Drama*. London and New York: Verso.

Birch, I. (1984) 'The Morrissey collection', *Smash Hits*, 21st June.

Bret, D. (2004) *Morrissey: Scandal and Passion*. London: Robson Books.

Dalton, D. (1974) *James Dean: The Mutant King, a Biography*. San Francisco: Straight Arrow Books.

Delaney, S. (1964) *Sweetly Sings the Donkey*. London: Metheun.

Delaney, S. (1959) *A Taste of Honey*. New York: Grove Books.

Devereux, E. (ed.) (2007) *Media Studies: Key Issues and Debates*. London: Sage.

Devereux, E. (2010) '"Heaven Knows We'll Soon Be Dust": Catholicism and devotion in The Smiths', in S. Campbell and C. Coulter (eds) *Why Pamper Life's Complexities? Essays on The Smiths*. Manchester: Manchester University Press.

Fletcher, A. (1964) *Allegory: The Theory of a Symbolic Mode*. Ithaca, NY: Cornell University Press.

Irving, W. (1978 [1819–20]) *The Sketch Book of Geoffrey Crayon, Gent*. Boston: Twayne.

Jenkins, H. (2006) *Fans, Bloggers, and Gamers; Exploring Participatory Culture*. New York: New York University Press.

Jenkins, H. (1992) *Textual Poachers: Television Fans and Participatory Culture*. London: Routledge.

Morrissey, S. (1981) *James Dean is Not Dead*. Manchester: Babylon Books.

Owens, C. (1980) 'The allegorical impulse: toward a theory of postmodernism', *October*, 12, pp. 67–86.

Saint-Exupéry, A. (1971 [1943]) *The Little Prince*. New York: Harcourt, Brace & World Inc.

Stock, D. (1986) *James Dean Revisited*. London: Plexus.

Chapter 2

"The Seaside Town that They Forgot to Bomb": Morrissey and Betjeman on Urban Regeneration and British Identity

Lawrence Foley

Morrissey and Betjeman: Establishing the link

Morrissey has never been shy about his literary influences; indeed, such is Morrissey's fixation with the life and works of Oscar Wilde that Len Brown's (2008) latest offering on the singer contains over 30 references to the Victorian aesthete. However, in contrast to the omnipresence of Wilde, the position of Sir John Betjeman in Morrissey's literary coterie has received decidedly peripheral attention in recent works on the singer. Prior to the publication of Hopps' (2009) study of the singer's work, Betjeman's influence on Morrissey had been consistently understated and underestimated in the proto-academic studies offered up by music journalists and Morrissey aficionados. Though there are limitations to Hopps' work, which I will point out later, it is undeniable that he succeeded through its publication in bringing Morrissey into the realm of "serious" academic consideration. Moreover, it is fair to say that Hopps has also brought the relationship between Morrissey and Betjeman into sharper focus, even if the cultural concerns that both men articulate are perhaps more closely related than he has suggested. But the failure to establish a meaningful link between the two, prior to Hopps' work, is somewhat surprising, particularly given Morrissey's overt engagement with the former Poet Laureate throughout his career. Indeed 'Everyday Is Like Sunday' seems rooted in the apocalypticism of Betjeman's 'Slough', borrowing its call for bombs to wreak destruction upon an inert and dismal land. Morrissey has claimed that this similarity was an unconscious one, but his use of another Betjeman poem, "A Child Ill" is anything but accidental. Utilized by Morrissey as a walk-on piece during his 2002 tour, a recording of the same poem was also chosen as the final track of *NME*'s *Songs To Save Your Life* CD, compiled by the singer. If Morrissey has a "Wilde man" in his head, as he somewhat gratuitously claimed in 'I'm Not Sorry', then he just as surely has Betjeman on the brain.

Morrissey seemed to confirm the link with Betjeman in 2006, when interviewed for the BBC *Culture Show's* 'Living Icons' poll. Asked about his own heroes, he responded: "Living: Nobody. Dead: Thousands. Sir John Betjeman, I think he would be my personal vote" (BBC, *The Culture Show*, 9th December, 2006). Such a statement is clearly significant, even if – as ever – there is an element of irony in Morrissey's answer. After all, naming a deceased living icon is just a way to underline his denunciatory indictment of what he perceived to be the stagnant repose of British culture. Furthermore, the comment also succeeded in undermining the claims for the title by his rivals Sirs Paul McCartney and David Attenborough. In typical Morrissey style, when asked about the merits of the latter, he responded, "he has a nice voice". But if the rules of the poll were unimportant, then it is surely surprising that he plumped for Betjeman as his choice, particularly in light of his well-documented and self-confessed obsession with Wilde. Certainly there is an obvious appeal for Morrissey: the irony and melancholia associated with Betjeman's poetry are defining characteristics of Morrissey's lyrical style, but this alone cannot account for his selection.

More interesting in plotting the correlation between Morrissey and Betjeman is to consider alternative aspects to Betjeman's multifaceted contribution to British culture, which was not limited to his poetic achievements. In addition to holding the post of Poet Laureate for 12 years and being arguably the most widely read, accessible and popular British poet of the twentieth century, he was a prominent architectural critic. Betjeman's architectural understanding and the rapport he held with the British public led to him enjoying a long and successful career in radio and television, making programmes related to Britain's architectural vernacular and community life on an increasingly regular basis. Indeed, it was during Morrissey's formative childhood years that Betjeman's television and radio career was at its peak. This fact, coupled with the assumption that Morrissey would at some point (either contemporaneously, or later) have become aware of these aspects to Betjeman's career, are crucial in any attempt to locate the genesis of Morrissey's engagement with him. Simon Goddard makes an important, if somewhat obvious, observation when noting that Morrissey's overt interest in the poet should "coincide with his move to Betjeman's native north London in the early 90s" (Goddard 2009: 31). It seems improbable that Morrissey could have remained ignorant of the wider reaches of Betjeman's career; in selecting him as a British icon, Morrissey was speaking as positively about Betjeman's defence of British buildings as he was about his poetry.

This chapter examines the link between Morrissey and Betjeman, focusing on the similarities between the concerns and attitudes expressed by both men on the issue of architectural regeneration, particularly in the urban space. It is my contention that the locus of these similarities is sited in a shared interest in the relationship between individuals and places. Furthermore, I will argue that both expressed significant concerns at the levelling down of society and the undermining effect that large-scale urban regeneration had on individual identity and community cohesion, which in turn was perceived as having destabilizing implications for national identity. I suggest that these are the factors which stimulate and provide the foundations for the ostensible link between Morrissey and Betjeman, and will examine the various ways in which they attempt to articulate these problems. The chapter will conclude by considering the ideological implications of these beliefs, placing the issue of architectural regeneration – and objections to it – within the context of increasing levels of immigration in post-war Britain.

Betjeman and post-war planning

In his paper considering the term *urban regeneration* as a metaphor, Rob Furbey discusses the history of the term and its ideological implications (1999: 419–445). Furbey makes the significant claim that it is only since the 1980s that the term has come into wide usage as a means of describing urban policy, replacing the post-war "reconstruction", and the "redevelopment" or "renewal" of the 1960s and 1970s (Furbey 1999: 419). Though the *Oxford English Dictionary* traces the term back as far as 1850, Furbey is correct in his assertion that the term became fully established in urban policy lexicon in the context of Margaret Thatcher's "radical right-wing agenda" during the 1980s (Furbey 1999: 421). The connotations of the term lent themselves well to the kind of "rebirth" that Britain was supposedly undergoing during Thatcher's government, but it is arguable that essentially, it was no more than a simple re-labelling of the processes and policies of urban planning during the preceding decades. However, *urban regeneration* differed from that earlier terminology because it seemed an attempt to promote a sense of social inclusion in the urban sphere, simultaneously gesturing towards the questions of immigration and integration. By associating the word *regeneration* with urban policy, ministers were able to imply the arrival of new urban spaces and new identities, new places and new people. Whilst "renewal" would have meant an improvement on what existed, "regeneration" implied a starting anew, and a significant move away from the past.

If we accept "urban regeneration" as a term of the past two decades, then an attempt to apply the term to Betjeman might seem anachronistic given his death in 1984. Indeed, to many people Betjeman is perhaps more recognizable as the voice of complaints about urban sprawl than a champion of traditional urban architecture. This reputation is in no small part attributable to the difficulties he felt with modernist architecture during his tenure as editor of *The Architectural Review* in the early 1930s. However, this chapter makes no effort to reposition Betjeman in the "urban" camp of any abstract architectural quarrel with the "rural". Rather, it is an attempt to illustrate that the destruction wrought across British cityscapes during the Second World War had a major impact on Betjeman's architectural concerns, forcing him into a re-evaluation of the value of urban architecture. Morrissey fits more comfortably into a discussion of urban regeneration, not least since his own childhood was affected by large-scale urban planning initiatives, and whose creative impulse and artistic career was borne out of the very era of Thatcherism that instituted "urban regeneration" as a mainstay in the lexicon of urban policy.

In 1930 Betjeman was appointed as assistant editor of *The Architectural Review*, a role which forced him to rein in his previously overt distaste for modernist architecture. The magazine's readership was comprised mostly of professional architects, whose new messiah was Le Corbusier and whose architectural tendencies were best described as minimalist and modern. The interests of such a readership were far removed from the concerns of rural England, and since Betjeman had become a staunch defender of those concerns, he became increasingly frustrated at his inability to pursue this agenda. Bevis Hillier has described his task at the time as "trying to reconcile what he likes with what he is required to like" (2007: 103). After leaving the magazine in 1935, Betjeman spent the rest of the decade "protecting and publicizing English vernacular architecture" and "lobbying town-planning policy affecting the impact of modern developments on the countryside" (Hiscock 2000: 195–196). When war broke out, Betjeman had been considered unfit for military duty, but the impact of the war on his remit as an architectural conservationist was profound. The destruction caused in British cities led the national architectural policy to be switched from "town-planning" to "reconstruction": a term which had serious and damaging implications for the future of Britain's cityscapes.

The individual and the place

It is perhaps Betjeman's love of Britain's architectural vernacular and his work as an architectural conservationist that represents the source of his attraction for Morrissey. Like Betjeman, Morrissey's work is saturated with references to particular places and buildings, and his lyrics are often infused with a certain nostalgia attached to these locations. In 1985 he responded to a question asking him if he was in love:

> The things that stir me are schools and buildings and I'm quite immersed in the past and in the history of this country and how things have evolved.
>
> (cited in Woods 2007: 13)

In the same interview he admits to having wanted to become a librarian, attributing the impulse behind this desire to the "romance" of old libraries. He describes the lot of the librarian as seeming "like the perfect life: solitude; absolute silence; tall, dark libraries", and apparently, the only thing that prevented him from following through with this early ambition was the modernization of those buildings, which turned them into "these little pre-fabs and they had no romance whatsoever" (cited in Woods 2007: 12).

Morrissey's attachment to places has been noted by Hopps (2009: 116–119), who argues that his lyrics "evince a peculiar sensitivity to the distinctive resonance of [...] particular places". From this point of interpretation Hopps is offered the opportunity to position Morrissey within the same poetic genealogy as Betjeman and Philip Larkin, which he does, noting the collective tendency to concern themselves with the poetry of "everyday" or "commonplace". This assessment is insightful and not without merit, not least in his posing the question: "who else could – and would want to – interest us in all-night chemists?" But it is at this point – and with this example – that Hopps could go further, and his failure to do so would seem to miss something vital in the attempt to align Morrissey with Betjeman and Larkin, and the former in particular. For Morrissey's celebration of the kitsch, his desire to "force high art to make room for the 'lowly'", is often set against the backdrop of urbanity. One could not imagine an all-night chemist in a quaint English village, nor could we envisage the iron bridge of 'Still Ill' providing the focal point for any environment other than a cityscape. Hopps's final example of Morrissey's elevation of the lowly, "Drinking tea with the taste of the Thames", provides emphasis to the point being made here, and the point which Hopps ultimately fails to make: that Morrissey's attachment to the city, and his celebration (or at times, denunciation) of its apparently banal features, is a significant feature of his lyrical discourse.

Indeed, one of the crucial elements in the connection between Morrissey and Betjeman and their affection for architecture is their shared belief in the profound connection between people and places. Hillier (2007: 289) argues that Betjeman's attitude towards architecture was similar to Freud's ideas about the human psyche, namely that childhood experiences have a profound effect. In 1971 Betjeman addressed this issue directly, writing: "what makes you like architecture are the things seen and reacted to as a child" (cited in Hillier 2007: 289). Like Morrissey, his first attraction to buildings was on aesthetic grounds, but Betjeman also possessed an awareness of the wider sociological implications of architecture, and the personal attachment of individuals to places. His poetry is permeated with a clear affection for, and appreciation of, buildings and places. But tellingly, he also makes frequent observations on the relationship between people and the places they inhabit. Refuting the description of him as a "pure poet of place" in 1947, Betjeman maintained "I write primarily with *people* in mind and relate the people to the background" (cited in Hillier 2007: 287–288).

Morrissey's Manchester

The consequences of urban planning were personally relevant to Morrissey, having had a profound and turbulent effect on his childhood. He has spoken movingly about the experience of his childhood home being demolished, most memorably in a television interview for the BBC's *Oxford Road Show* during which he discusses his childhood and specifically the house on Queen's Square near Old Trafford in which he spent his early childhood. Having moved there in 1965, his parents remained on the street until it was redeveloped as part of a regeneration project during the late 1960s, leaving the entire surrounding area completely transformed. Morrissey compared the demolition of these buildings to "having one's childhood wiped away":

> Well there's nothing at Queen's Square now as you can see. Everything has just vanished, it's just like the whole thing has been completely erased from the face of the earth. I feel great anger; I feel massive sadness. It's like a complete loss of childhood, because although I've always lived in Manchester, I've always lived relatively close to here, to this part of Manchester. Now, when I pass through here or even being here today, it's just so foreign to me.
>
> (BBC, *Oxford Road Show*, 22nd March, 1985)

This anger and sadness is perhaps expressed most clearly in 'Back To The Old House,' the 1984 B-side to 'What Difference Does It Make?' Whilst Johnny Rogan has suggested that the song is Morrissey "indulging" in a "bleak sense of loss for something that was evidently unrealized" (Rogan 2006: 44), this reading of the song is somewhat underwhelming and

– surprisingly for Rogan – understated. Certainly the song hints at some unrequited or unrecognized love, but this is not the overarching message that the song conveys, which lies in the deeper ambivalence towards the titular subject of the song.

The song opens up by insisting that he would "rather not go" back to the house and the explanation offered is that there are "too many bad memories" attached to the place. The two middle verses then seem to undermine this claim; instead of reciting a negative, formative childhood experience, Morrissey describes the sight of somebody – presumably significant – cycling by as being the "saddest thing I've ever seen". The disparity between the listener's interpretation of this image and the profound sadness attached to it by the speaker is important. By attributing all his sadness to this one – seemingly frivolous – recollection, Morrissey is using the memory to signify a deeper sadness; it becomes symbolic of his nostalgia for an irrecoverable past. Indeed, after expressing regret at never having told this individual how much he "really liked them", he ends his address by asking if they have moved away. The lyrics then refocus on the house, the speaker having undergone a complete reversal in attitude, now stating that he "would love to go". The song ends with the repetition of the line "I never will", implying a regret at being unable to go in contrast to the determination not to return in the song's opening. If we can take the liberty of deducing that the house in question is the one on Queen's Square, then his realization that he "never will" go back is possibly because it no longer exists. By insisting that the memories attached to this place are negative in the song's opening, the automatic reading of the middle two verses is to assume that this specific memory is picked out for illustration and support of that claim. However, an alternative and altogether more helpful reading is that the memory serves to convince him of his desire to go 'Back To The Old House' and as such represents a source of nostalgia. The regret in having not told the addressee of the song how much he really liked them is actually a wish for the chance to do so now, or to return to the past.

In 'Late Night Maudlin Street' Morrissey once again articulates sadness at moving home. What is important in the understanding of Morrissey's connection with this place is once more the ambivalent attitude that he appears to hold in relation to the fictitious 'Maudlin Street', which would seem to represent one of his two childhood homes on either Queen's Square or Kings Road. The line "don't leave your torch behind, a power-cut ahead; 1972, you know", places it in the context of the miners' strikes over pay in that year and the likelihood is that the subject of the song is the latter residence. When discussing Kings Road, Morrissey is largely negative, describing it as "quite bland, quite uneventful", adding "there's not a really great deal to say about Kings Road" (*Oxford Road Show*, 22nd March, 1985). However, he does credit it with affording him creative inspiration, suggesting that the sterility of the street and the ennui it prompted inspired him to write. "The only way that I could find any mental relaxation", he says, "was to simply go out and walk, and to walk around these streets, which can seem quite depressing to most people" (*Oxford Road Show*, 22nd March, 1985). But for Morrissey this was "fuel", the anger and frustration that the relocation to this soulless street caused, leading him to go home and "write furiously" (*Oxford Road Show*, 22nd March, 1985).

Like 'Back To The Old House', this song expresses an ambivalent attitude to the childhood home. Whilst there is an undoubted attachment to the place, there is always an undermining element to that affection. His insistence on taking the keys to the house away and his having to remind himself that it's "only bricks and mortar", are undercut by lines such as "I never stole a happy hour around here". However, the overwhelming ambience of the song is nostalgic and not jubilatory at bidding farewell to the "half-life" that the street represents for him. This ambivalent attitude is reflected in Morrissey's attitude to Manchester – and indeed England – generally. In the *Oxford Road Show* interview quoted above, he also analyses his link to Manchester, saying:

> Now for the very first time I'm in a situation where I could leave the North and live in a place of my choice quite comfortably. But do I want to? I don't think I do. It's very difficult to say how things will be in the future, because we tend to change our minds about places. But right now I don't feel that I want to, I feel quite cemented and I feel quite attached to all the things that I know. Why? Who knows? This mystical bond.
>
> (*Oxford Road Show*, 22nd March, 1985)

Despite describing his connection with Manchester as being like a "mystical bond", he left not long afterwards to live in north London. However – as is the norm with Morrissey – he soon became dissatisfied with life in the capital city also, and indeed he went on to live in Dublin, Los Angeles and most recently, Rome. It is clear to see that Morrissey's gradual withdrawal from England occurred in tandem with the increasingly negative press reaction towards him. Moreover, his own disdain for the state of the music industry and culture generally fed into this separation to such an extent that England and Morrissey seemed to find one another equally repellent. The source of Morrissey's nomadic tendency seems to be the perceived erosion of all those things that made him feel "cemented" in Manchester and England. Another difficulty would have been that his working-class background and Irish immigrant heritage sat uncomfortably with his newfound fame and fortune. This much was alluded to in his 1992 single from *Your Arsenal*, 'We Hate It When Our Friends Become Successful', where the listener is assured "if they're Northern that makes it even worse". The irony of course is that the success enjoyed by The Smiths was largely due to their working-class image, or as Andrew Warnes (2008: 137) has suggested, the "deft mythologisation of a postindustrial, post-socialist, white proletarian identity".

Betjeman: From urban sprawl to urban conservation

As Morrissey's relationship to British cities weakened over time, Betjeman's strengthened with its passage, if only in the wake of catastrophe. If Betjeman's primary pre-war concern was urban sprawl, then the destruction wrought in cities across Britain between 1939 and 1945 convinced him that the redevelopment of British cities was of paramount importance.

In line with his fundamental conviction about the importance of the relationship between people and places, Betjeman had severe concerns about the sociological impact of such large-scale redevelopment and modernization, and these concerns soon took precedence over his pre-existing quarrel with town planners over urban sprawl. By the end of the war, one-third of Britain's housing stock had been damaged. After defeating Winston Churchill in the 1945 general election, Clement Attlee's government (1945–51) sought to remedy this situation, overseeing the building of over one million public houses. Moreover, the introduction of the 1947 Town and Country Planning Act put planning under the control of local authorities. Though the act gave local authorities power to control outdoor advertising and protect woodland – and in effect saw the creation of the modern listed building system – centralized planning was not without its problems (Tewdwr-Jones 2005: 392). This centralization meant that architects were being employed predominantly by public authorities. As Betjeman puts it, they no longer had to "design single houses, but whole groups of houses", the result being that "the scope for individual design" grew smaller.

The subscription of town-planners to the Corbusian ideal meant being concerned with housing as many people as possible in the smallest area possible. The result was the erection of tall blocks of flats known as "tower blocks", which sprung up, according to Betjeman, "particularly in areas bombed by the Germans or built by the Georgians". He possessed grave concerns over the detrimental effect these buildings had on society and communities, feeling that they were erected "with no thought at all of the psychological effect on families with children who were forced to live in them" (Betjeman 1972: 97–101). Betjeman's attitude towards tower blocks is best illustrated by his 1969 programme for the BBC, *An Englishman's Home*, where he thrives in his polemical element, decrying the state of East London's Docklands after the devastation of war:

> The Germans bombed the little streets, which had been home for thousands. After that – partly to keep the rates up, partly to get as many as possible into a minimum space – out of the devastation, slabs arose. Sometimes they called them towers, and these replaced the liveliness of streets.
>
> (BBC, *Birds Eye View: An Englishman's Home*, 1969)

With more than a hint of irony, Betjeman insists "Oh, the planners did their best", denouncing the towers as badly thought out, ugly, cumbersome and damaging to the family unit. The issue becomes one which undermines the fundamental compassion in society as he asks, "where can be the heart that sends a family to the twentieth floor of such a slab as this?", before providing the answer to his own question with the unequivocal, "it can't be right". Granted, Morrissey's own childhood homes did not leave him and his family "caged halfway up the sky", nor was he moved to a tower block after the demolition of Queen's Square, but the kind of faceless housing that Betjeman objects to was not strictly limited to high-rise buildings. The final moments of the film depict aerial shots of vast building sites, with newly built developments rising out of destruction and dereliction: so-called New Towns. Betjeman's voiceover sounds like an offering from the pulpit:

> New Towns, new housing estates,
> New homes, new streets, new neighbours,
> New standards of living,
> New financial commitments,
> New jobs, new schools, new shops,
> New loneliness, new restlessness,
> New pressure, new tension.
> And people,
> People who have to cope with all this newness.
> People who cannot afford old irrelevancies.
> People who have to find a God who fits in.
>
> (BBC, *Birds Eye View: An Englishman's Home*, 1969)

Betjeman brought the issue of planning to the forefront of public debate intentionally; he wanted to stimulate a national debate on the issue (Tewdwr-Jones 2005: 407). But his criticism of the high-rise flats was offensive to some, who viewed his sentiments as in some way anti–working-class, arguing that the buildings provided good quality housing that was long overdue (Tewdwr-Jones 2005: 406). However, Betjeman's deep-rooted cynicism struck a chord with the public imagination throughout the 1960s and beyond. This may have been in part due to the fact that during this period town planning was at its most potent and pervasive. Through his use of the medium of television as a polemical instrument, Betjeman made the issue accessible to millions of Britons. Moreover, Betjeman correctly identified the issue of community as being vital in widespread doubts over modern urban planning policy. People were being uprooted from their homes, withdrawn from established communities, and placed in new and alien surroundings: towers, flats and maisonettes where one did not know one's neighbours and the social problems created by the new housing outweighed any spatial advantages.[1] The reality of life in the new developments was a stark contrast to the dream and promise of regeneration; as Terence Davies (2008) puts it when describing his own experience of regeneration in Liverpool: "we had hoped for paradise, we got the anus mundi".

Regeneration, immigration and the urban palimpsest

The tension that Betjeman detects was partly communicated as a reaction against the planners, or whoever was deemed to have "put them there", but there is arguably a racially charged undertone to such discourse also. In addition to the rebuilding works forced by war, increased pressure was placed on the housing infrastructure in British cities by a sharp rise in post-war immigration. The 1948 British Nationality Act granted citizens of the Commonwealth and of the United Kingdom and its colonies the right to enter, settle and work in Britain. The consequences of such legislation led to the relocation by people of West Indian, African and Asian origin growing sharply in the 1950s and beyond. Occurring as it did in parallel with the rapid redevelopment of areas and the consequent dissolution of large communities, immigration became a question which was characterized by a perceived territorial threat. In 1968, just a year prior to the airing of *An Englishman's Home*, Enoch Powell had infamously declared that English people were finding "their homes and neighbourhoods changed beyond all recognition", referring to "the transformation of whole areas [...] into alien territory" (cited in Smith 1989: 120). We might then consider the undoubted significance in the programme's title, *An Englishman's Home*, since such a title inherently poses the question of what it means to be English. Furthermore, it also poses a more politically charged question about what an Englishman may call his home, and indeed, whether or not England remains his home.

Betjeman was notoriously suspicious of foreignness, writing to Patrick Balfour in 1930 that "it is useless to pretend that I enjoy myself abroad" (cited in Hillier 2007: 117). Again in 1932, he writes "the South of France has always been in my mind something worse than Maidenhead", before declaring to Alan-Pryce Jones in 1939 that "abroad is so nasty" (Betjeman 2007: 119–120). Given Maidenhead's ignominious mention in Betjeman's attack on Slough, such a comment is disparaging indeed. The 1971 poem, "The Costa Blanca" tells the story of British expats in Spain, who find after several years of living abroad that they long to return to England, bitter at the "Dago" who "caught the wife and me all right!" (Betjeman 1984: 381) This suspicion translated into his architectural interests and as early as 1932, he had acknowledged the threat to national architectural vernaculars, saying that in future, architecture "would not consist of the varying indigenous styles of a county or a country, but of one style for a continent" (*The Times*, 22nd July, 1932). Though Betjeman was never outspokenly critical of mass immigration into Britain, his antipathy towards foreignness and his championing of "Englishness" meant that his architectural thoughts intrinsically possessed nationalistic undertones.

Betjeman's concern at the undermining of British identity was articulated through his architectural conservation work and antipathy towards modernist architecture, both of which were tinged with the kind of nostalgic nationalism that has come to be associated with Morrissey. The reactionary stance Betjeman adopted towards modernity – and specifically the modernization of buildings – resonates through Morrissey, who admitted in a 1987 interview, "I don't like anything new – I'm not really modern to any degree at all. Take houses – I like old, dark properties, Victorian or Georgian preferably" (cited in Simpson 2003: 168). As with Queen's Square and the libraries, the destruction of such properties is anathema to Morrissey's elegiac view of Britain. As Mark Simpson (2003: 164) has argued, "England is the past he [Morrissey] never had". Unable to realize a forgotten culture, Morrissey attaches himself to the residue of bygone eras, namely their buildings, which become palimpsestuous for him.

Morrissey's Manchester, like Betjeman's Britain, is at once almost unrecognizable in its current condition and yet enduring in its "original" form within the imagination. In this respect it resembles De Quincey's palimpsest of the mind, whose writing "repeatedly *performs* [the] resurrection" of his dead sister Elizabeth and "continually enacts the impossibility of his forgetting of her" (Dillon 2005: 246). The explicit admiration by both Betjeman and Morrissey for buildings from the past can thus be viewed as an express desire to achieve the same with their romanticized notions of England. Morrissey and Betjeman simply shift the emphasis of resurrection from individual human being to architectural vestiges of the past, simultaneously preserving their own idealized constructions of culture and national identity. The enduring existence of some of these buildings acts as a constant reminder of the past, whilst they sit concurrently in stark contrast to modern buildings, highlighting the "newness" of the present as much as – if not more than – they underscore the "oldness" of the past. As Tim Edensor (2008: 313) states:

The speed of social and spatial change throughout the twentieth century means that the contemporary era is the site of numerous hauntings, for the erasure of the past in the quest for the ever-new is usually only partial. Modern imperatives to swiftly bury the past produce cities that are haunted by that which has been consigned to irrelevance. Accordingly, the contemporary city is a palimpsest composed of different temporal elements, featuring signs, objects and vaguer traces that rebuke the tendencies to move on and forget.

Morrissey: Nostalgic nationalist or cultural commentator?

The destruction of Queen's Square was symptomatic of the changing architectural, cultural and social landscape of the era, and in the late 1960s, Manchester was particularly affected. In 1967 Nikolaus Pevsner wrote that "Manchester is engaged in one of the largest slum-clearance enterprises of all-time." Considering the impact of redevelopment, and what was to replace the demolished terraced housing Pevsner could be confused with Betjeman, asking: "do we really want these towers of flats everywhere?" His conclusion that those very flats would be the slums "of fifty years hence" was prophetic (cited in Stamp 2007: 139); indeed in many areas, they already were the slums. Just as Manchester followed the contemporary inclinations of British cities in terms of its urban planning, so too did it experience vastly increased levels of immigration during the 1950s and 1960s, predominantly from the Caribbean and South Asia (Kaplan and Lei 2006: 193).

Having grown up during the 1960s, Morrissey experienced first-hand the rapid cultural change that mass-immigration prompted, and his artistic responses to the subject have predictably triggered accusations of racism. On the whole, these allegations have been based on the provocative titles of a few songs: 'Bengali In Platforms', 'Asian Rut' and 'National Front Disco' to name a few. The ironic, teasing tone of 'Bengali In Platforms' in particular has been interpreted as revealing condescension and intolerance. But the most objectionable lines from the song, "shelve your western plans" and "life is hard enough when you belong here", seem to be addressing the problems of integration, even if it connotes that Bengalis do not belong in Britain. It certainly cannot be suggested that Morrissey resorts to stereotypes in his choice of attire for the subject of his song, whilst his insistence that "he only wants to embrace your culture" does not follow the presupposition that immigrant communities accepted cultural segregation. Instead, the plea to "shelve your western plans" and the repeated insistence that "life is hard enough when you belong here" seems to be more a damning verdict on England than a territorial warning. Dissatisfied as Morrissey was with Britain, the lyrics seem to express incredulity at any desire to belong "here", leaving any warning that can be seen to exist as one motivated by a humorous and self-deprecating compulsion to impart his own negative experience of his country.

'The National Front Disco' is perhaps the one song where Morrissey would seem to express, if not endorsement, then sympathy with far-right supporters. The song laments the loss of a young man to the National Front, spurred on by his dreams of an "England for the English". However, the fact that this line seems to be spoken by the protagonist rather than Morrissey himself tends to be overlooked by those who seek to take umbrage with its content. There is no overt identification with the racist National Front and instead the song seems to follow in Morrissey's long-standing tendency to be fascinated by outsiders. Whilst he is keen to position himself on the margins of society, the characters in his songs frequently occupy a similar territory. The release of The Smiths' single 'Panic' in 1986 had been met with similar claims of racism, mostly by the musical weekly press. The key to understanding what Morrissey is trying to say in this song would seem to be to read it as a song about cultural integration and the experience of living through vast social and cultural upheaval. One of the most notorious lines of that song, "the music that they constantly play, says nothing to me about my life" undoubtedly poses questions about who *they* are, but more importantly seems to address the disparity between the insider and the outsider in cultural terms. As it turns out that particular line and the equally controversial call to "hang the DJ" fit more comfortably against the context of the rise of the dance music genre in the 1980s. Nevertheless it remains a paragon of Morrissey's obsession with rapid change in the urban space, with its comprehensive listing of British cities and subsequent observation of the panic engendered on their streets by the pace of that change.

Conclusion

In light of the connections drawn above, and in addition to the overt and plentiful references to literature in his lyrics and interviews, there can be little doubt about the importance of literary figures and works to the ideas expressed in Morrissey's lyrics. But past studies that have attempted to consider the impact of literature on the singer have underestimated the influence of Betjeman on those ideas, treating him either as a peripheral figure (Brown 2008) or failing to grasp fully the nature of his influence (Hopps 2009). Such an oversight is unfortunate and in truth, inexplicable. What is clear, however, is that Betjeman's iconic status as perceived by Morrissey relies on more than the former's literary output and stature. Rather, Morrissey's interest in Betjeman owes much to the vigour with which Betjeman upheld what he imagined it meant to be English, or indeed British. Central to Betjeman's attempt to achieve this were his architectural conservation endeavours, his championing of the British architectural vernacular, and his opposition to the post-war utilitarian housing, which he saw springing up across British cityscapes. The most fundamental correlation between Betjeman and Morrissey then is that as the former expressed concern at the rapid change of Britain's architectural vernacular, the latter lived through the change. Significantly, this architectural revolution occurred in tandem with a monumental overhaul of Britain's racial demographic, linking the two issues in the hearts and minds of many Britons, and particularly those in urban areas. Growing up in Manchester, Morrissey felt the tensions created by these issues, and whilst he addresses the resultant tensions in his lyrics, he does not purport to suggest solutions to them. What Morrissey does in songs like 'Asian Rut', 'National Front Disco' and 'Bengali In Platforms' is address the issues engendered by rapid social change in an observational way, providing an authentic, personal and at times uncomfortable representation of the experience of vast cultural change as he lived it, and as he imagined others lived it.

The effect of such expeditious and fundamental change on Morrissey was to create a sense of alienation, a feeling of "not-belonging" in his homeland. The solution he finds to the feeling of unfamiliarity fostered by this cultural milieu is to attach himself to the buildings of the past, imbuing them with a form of idealized "Britishness" and turning them into bastions of a lost national identity. To describe Morrissey as placeless, or nation-less would not be an overstatement. Indeed, in some respects, Morrissey has always been this way: the very essence of both his artistry and his popular appeal is in no small part attributable to this outsider status. However, just how much of this outsider status is self-invented, and how much created by the social turbulence of his youth, remains debatable. Whilst it evidently cannot be argued that urban regeneration was stimulated by immigration, or vice versa, the very fact that the two reached their zenith simultaneously made them inextricably linked in the cultural overhaul experienced by Morrissey. Indeed, in 2007 he addressed the subject of immigration directly, allegedly telling *NME* that "the higher the influx into England the more the British identity disappears". He reportedly went on to say that "England is just a memory now", and whilst agreeing that immigration enriches British identity, he maintains that accepting the change that immigration engenders means having to "say goodbye to the Britain you once knew" (See Duff 2007). Morrissey is not just referring to "Britain" in an idealized and abstract cultural sense; he also recognizes and laments the change that immigration engenders in the visual, namely architectural, landscape of Britain.

The Britain that Morrissey laments the loss of, the Britain he sees encapsulated in the aged and symbolic architectural monuments of its history, is one to which he has never belonged. Betjeman did, perhaps, but Morrissey's Britain is a past he has never known. Morrissey's conception of Britain is one that is rubbed out, though not fully, and then written over by immigration, urban regeneration and the ensuing alliance between multiculturalism and modernity. Thus the Britain that Morrissey idealizes is a cultural and architectural palimpsest; he detects traces of it in the architecture of the urban environment, but it remains ephemeral and intangible. Of course, Britain's cultural and architectural transformations were well underway before Morrissey witnessed it. In fact in as much as cultural and architectural change are concerned, the 1960s and 1970s are more aptly thought of as the aftershock than the social earthquake, which had been stirred into activity in the immediate aftermath of the Second World War. As Morrissey felt internally the cultural shift in Britain, he witnessed the acceleration rather than the onset of architectural change in its towns and cities. The issues of immigration and urban regeneration are thus interlinked, if not directly, then at least in the perceptions of those who experienced their crescendo. The Betjeman-inspired song 'Everyday Is Like Sunday' contains no inflammatory remarks about racial issues, nor does it romanticize architecture in the way that Morrissey has done elsewhere in interviews. But for Morrissey, the combined effect of immigration and urban regeneration is the disintegration of British identity and the creation of a vast cultural wasteland. The "seaside town" imagined in 'Everyday Is Like Sunday' represents an articulation of that wasteland, where "everything is silent and grey" and where uniformity reigns supreme.

Note

1. See Rod Hackney, *The Good, the Bad and the Ugly*, London, Frederick Muller, 1990, pp. 39–47.

References

Betjeman, J. (2007) *Tennis Whites and Teacakes: An Anthology of Betjeman's Prose and Verse*. London: John Murray.
Betjeman, J. (1984) *John Betjeman's Collected Poems*. London: John Murray.
Betjeman, J. (1972) *A Pictorial History of English Architecture*. London: John Murray.
Betjeman, J. (1932) *The Times*, 22nd July.
Birds Eye View: An Englishman's Home (1969) BBC 2, 5th April.
Brown, L. (2008) *Meetings with Morrissey*. Malta: Omnibus Press.
Davies, T. (2008) *Of Time and the City*. Liverpool: Hurricane Films.
Dillon, S. (2005) 'Reinscribing De Quincey's palimpsest: the significance of the palimpsest in contemporary literary and cultural studies', *Textual Practice*, 19: 3, pp. 243–263.
Duff, O. (2007) 'Morrissey Blames Immigration for "disappearance" of British Identity', available: *http://www.independent.co.uk/news/uk/home-news/morrissey-blames-immigration-for-disappearance-of-british-identity-760825.html*.
Edensor, T. (2008) 'Mundane hauntings: commuting through the phantasmagoric working-class spaces of Manchester, England', *Cultural Geographies*, 15, pp. 313–333.
Furbey, R. (1999) 'Urban regeneration: reflections on a metaphor', *Critical Social Policy*, 19, pp. 419–445.
Goddard, S. (2009) *Mozipedia: The Encyclopedia of Morrissey and The Smiths*. Bodmin: Ebury.

Hackney, R. (1990) *The Good, the Bad and the Ugly*. London: Frederick Muller.

Hillier, B. (2007) *John Betjeman: The Biography*. London: John Murray.

Hiscock, K. (2000) 'Modernity and "English Tradition": Betjeman at The Architectural Review', *Journal of Design History*, 13: 3, pp. 193–212.

Hopps, G. (2009) *Morrissey: The Pageant of His Bleeding Heart*. London: Continuum.

Kaplan, D. and Li, W. (2006) *Landscapes of the Ethnic Economy*. Lanham: Rowman & Littlefield.

Oxford Road Show (1985) BBC 2, 22nd March.

Rogan, J. (2006) *Morrissey: The Albums*. London: Calidore.

Simpson, M. (2003) *Saint Morrissey*. London: SAF Publishing.

Smith, S. (1989) *The Politics of 'Race' and Residence*. Cambridge: Polity.

Stamp, G. (2007) *Britain's Lost Cities*. London: Aurum Press Ltd.

Tewdwr-Jones, M. (2005) '"Oh, the planners did their best": the planning films of John Betjeman', *Planning Perspectives*, 20: 4, pp. 389–411.

The Culture Show (2006) BBC 2, 9th December.

Warnes, A. (2008) 'Black, white and blue: the racial antagonism of The Smiths' record sleeves', *Popular Music*, 27: 1, pp. 135–149.

Woods, P. (2007) *Morrissey in Conversation: The Essential Interviews*. London: Plexus.

Chapter 3

In the Spirit of '69? Morrissey and the Skinhead Cult

John H. Baker

Introduction

In early 1992 it was announced that Madness, inactive since 1986, were to re-form for a one-off concert, headlining a festival called "Madstock" at Finsbury Park in North London on Saturday, 8th August. The other acts would include Ian Dury and The Blockheads, Flowered Up and The Farm. Tickets for the gig sold so rapidly that a second date on Sunday, 9th August was added. Shortly before the event, The Farm were removed from the bill for both dates, despite the fact that many of their fans had already bought tickets to the gig. They were replaced by Gallon Drunk, a London band whose work had been critically acclaimed but never popular, and, by contrast, one of the best-known British performers of recent musical history: Morrissey.

Morrissey's brief performance at Madstock – he was on stage for little more than half an hour – has come to assume an importance in relation to his career that no one could have imagined at the time. Despite the fact that his set was videoed and recorded, as well as witnessed by thousands of people, it has come to assume a grotesquely distorted character as a major piece of evidence in the case against Morrissey, for those who wish to depict him as a flag-waving British nationalist with a nasty racist streak. A great deal of the subsequent discussion of Finsbury Park simply replicates the entirely hostile account of the event given, notoriously, in the edition of the *NME* dated 22nd August, 1992 (Fadele et al. 1992). It is the contention of this chapter that this account of Finsbury Park is, to say the least, distorted – by the predictable vagaries of memory and the common tendency to believe the most sensational account of an event as much as by deliberate spinning – and that a much more accurate analysis of Finsbury Park and its significance in terms of Morrissey's career can be reached through an examination of the singer's curious fascination with one of the most notorious youth subcultures in recent British history – the skinhead cult.

Why Morrissey played Madstock

Morrissey had been a solo artist since 1987 and retained both a large and fanatical fanbase and considerable critical support. His third studio album, *Your Arsenal*, would be released the same week as Madstock. Morrissey's decision to accept a rare non-headlining slot may appear odd, but he had often spoken of his admiration for Madness. His 1991 album *Kill Uncle* had been produced by Madness's producers and featured Madness's bassist, Bedders, and vocalist, Suggs. Suggs had also provided backing vocals on Morrissey's 1989 single 'Piccadilly Palare', and a still from Madness's video for their single 'Cardiac Arrest' appears briefly in the video for Morrissey's early 1992 single 'We Hate It When Our Friends Become Successful'. Ominously, in the light of subsequent events, Morrissey told the French press that he had been particularly attracted by what he saw as the "Britishness" of the event: "Madness are old friends of mine. I wouldn't have done it otherwise. Gallon Drunk will be there, and maybe The Kinks. Paul Weller should be there. The entire 'British Family'! It will be an expressly British weekend – no rave, no rap, no Americans! Just Vespas, Union Jacks, and afternoon teas" (Bret 1994: 155).

It seems likely that Morrissey made the inclusion of Gallon Drunk on the bill a condition of his appearance. He was a fan of the band and would employ them as his support act on his subsequent American tour in the autumn of 1992.

Morrissey had not performed in Britain since October 1991, and had cancelled a performance at 1992's Glastonbury festival. Unsurprisingly, a large number of his fans purchased tickets for Madstock – the vast majority for the newly announced second date, which meant that Morrissey would perform the chief support slot on the first date in front of a crowd consisting almost entirely of fans of the other acts. Only a very small percentage of the crowd would be there specifically to see him.

Morrissey agreed to perform at Madstock because he admired the headliners, but it seems likely that Madness's fanbase also played an important part in this decision. Madness's roots lie in the ska revival of the late 1970s. At the turn of the decade, British bands like The Specials, The Selecter and The Beat took a contemporary spin on ska, the Jamaican precursor to reggae, into the British charts. Many of these bands were multiracial, hence the "2 Tone" name given both to the genre and its best-known record label, but all of them played music with Jamaican roots. Although all the members of Madness are white, their first singles were essentially ska – indeed, their debut single, 'The Prince', is a tribute to ska legend Prince Buster.

Skinheads made up a large percentage of Madness's early fanbase, as well as that of many other "2 Tone" bands. Both Suggs and Chas Smash were skinheads in the late 1970s. Madness's skinhead fans were among their most devoted, and many of them travelled from all over the United Kingdom to Finsbury Park in August 1992 to bid an emotional farewell to their heroes. Little did they know that the band would sporadically re-form as years went on, and eventually record new music.

By 1992, Morrissey had developed an interest in the skinhead cult. This interest has occasioned considerable controversy throughout Morrissey's career. The late afternoon of 8th August, 1992 is the most significant moment in the history of Morrissey's skinhead fascination, since it remains the only moment at which the singer has come face-to-face with a large number of real skinheads – obviously, no-one was counting shaven scalps on the day, but there were at least several thousand in the Madstock crowd.

The Skinhead cult

One of the main problems with most of the accounts of Finsbury Park and Morrissey's relationship with the skinhead cult is a lamentable ignorance of the cult itself on the part of many critics, who frequently assume that a shaven head and racist thuggery are automatically linked. Yes, some skinheads were (and are) racist, but to link the cult unambiguously to racism is misleading. It is certainly problematic when it comes to investigating Morrissey's complex relationship to the cult. What, then is the "skinhead cult"? What sort of people was Morrissey confronting at Finsbury Park?

The original skinheads

The cult can be helpfully viewed as having had two main phases.[1] The first phase lasted from the mid-to-late 1960s to the early 1970s, while the "skinhead revival" has extended from the late 1970s to the present. The original British skinheads emerged from the Mod subculture of the mid-1960s, which was based around fashion – Mods were consumerists who always wanted to be at the cutting-edge – and music, mainly American soul and Jamaican ska and rocksteady. Many working-class youths, however, could not afford the ostentatious display beloved of the so-called Peacock Mods. By around 1965 a tough subspecies of Mod had developed in reaction: the "Hard Mod", or "Gang Mod". Stanley Cohen neatly encapsulates the subdivisions that had, by this time, developed within the Mod movement: he distinguishes between "the Hard Mods (wearing heavy boots, jeans with braces, short hair, the precursors of the Skinheads, usually prowling in large groups with the appearance of being jumpy, unsure of themselves, on the paranoiac edge, heavily involved in any disturbance) and the smooth Mods (usually older and better off, sharply dressed, moving in small groups and usually looking for a bird)" (Cohen 2002: 158). Hard Mods, also nicknamed "Peanuts", wore their hair much shorter than other Mods, and sported an image of clean, working-class toughness. Their tight jeans, shirts, braces, and Doc Marten boots were smart but affordable, and reminiscent of the clothes worn by the working-class men of the time. For sociologist John Clarke, this working-class imagery is crucial to an understanding of the class-based anxieties that contributed to the formation of the style: "the Skinhead style represents an attempt to re-create through the 'mob' the traditional working-class community, as a substitution for the real decline of the latter [...] the underlying social dynamic of the style, in this light, is the relative worsening of the situation of the lower working-class, through the second half of the sixties" (Clarke 2006: 80). This straightforwardly proletarian and masculine image, together with their short hair, separated them both from wealthier Mods and long-haired hippies – in Dick Hebdige's words, it was a "systematic exaggeration of those elements within the mod style which were self-evidently proletarian, and a complementary suppression of any imagined bourgeois influences" (Hebdige 2009: 55). Clarke, too, emphasizes the exaggerated nature of this "proletarian" display, presumably unconscious on the skinheads' part, referring to "an image of what [working-class] community was" as the basis of skinhead style (Clarke 2006: 81). It is important to emphasize that these "Hard Mods" wore their hair short – a number one crop – but did not entirely shave their heads. The completely shaven head, or "bonehead", which is often associated with neo-Nazism (particularly in America), was not part of the original skinhead scene.

By 1969 the "Hard Mods" had come to be known as "skinheads" – a memorable nickname that stuck, perhaps because the word *sounds* hard (it is almost impossible to sound the 'h' without sounding a bit of a fool). They were especially associated with London's East End – "the archetypal working-class community", in John Clarke's words – but also with other working-class inner-city neighbourhoods (Clarke 2006: 82). They retained their Mod predecessors' passion for music, particularly ska. This is a particularly baffling feature of the original cult to those who associate skinheads with racism – the music the original skins danced to was almost exclusively produced by black musicians. This is partially down to the cult's origin within the Mod subculture, but there is a more profound explanation that undermines the simplistic stereotype of the racist skinhead. Many Jamaicans worked in the docks of the East End – alongside many white working-class youths. The "outsider" status of the young working-class – what Clarke calls "a sense of being excluded and under attack from a variety of points" – paralleled that of young Jamaicans in late 1960s Britain, and it is unsurprising that friendships developed that transcended racial boundaries (Clarke 2006: 81). White youths visited clubs in areas of London like Notting Hill and Brixton, dancing to the latest ska sounds from Jamaica, and the Jamaican influence on the emergent skinhead style is undeniable. The Jamaican "Rude Boy" – a sharply dressed habitué of the Kingston dancehalls, often associated with gang violence and the brutal pastime of "dance crashing" rival sound systems – particularly contributed to the original skinheads' visual style: "the clean-cut, neatly pressed delinquent look" (Hebdige 2009: 56). It would make a dramatic reappearance at the end of the 1970s with the sharp suits and pork-pie hats worn by The Specials. In Hebdige's words, "a somewhat mythically conceived image of the traditional working-class community with its classic focal concerns, its acute sense of territory, its tough exteriors, its dour 'machismo' [...] was overlaid with elements taken directly from the West Indian community (and more particularly from the rude boy subculture of the black delinquent young)" (Hebdige 2009: 55–56). The skinheads "borrowed individual items of dress (the crombie, the crop), argot and style directly from equivalent West Indian groups" (Hebdige 2009: 56).

Jamaican singers like Desmond Dekker and Prince Buster became skinhead heroes: something which baffles those who automatically associate skinheads with racist violence, but makes much more sense to those familiar with what Hebdige calls "the dialectical interplay of black and white 'languages' played out through their clothes, speech and behaviour" (Hebdige 2009: 57). Skinheads can take a good deal of credit for getting ska classics like Dekker's 'Israelites' into the charts at a time when Jamaican music was granted little airplay. However, the skinheads' other obsession – football – would form a rather less savoury part of their reputation. By 1968–69 fights between rival football supporters had become commonplace, with skinheads widely perceived as enthusiastic participants in the violence. In Clarke's words, "football, and especially the violence articulated around it, also provided one area for the expression of the Skinheads' concern with a particular, collective, masculine self-conception, involving an identification of masculinity with physical toughness, and an unwillingness to back down in the face of 'trouble'" (Clarke 2006: 82). These hooligan skins came to be known, as the 1970s went on, as "bootboys" – not all skins joined in the macho mayhem, but enough did to give the cult a deeply intimidating reputation.

The original skinheads had little interest in politics. The movement was intensely masculine (although there were female skinheads) and working-class, and offered its members both a feeling of belonging and a powerful, intimidating image. Hebdige stresses the importance of black West Indian culture as a powerful model for disenfranchised white working-class youth in the late 1960s: "[H]ere was a culture armed against contaminating influences, protected against the more frontal assaults of the dominant ideology, denied access to the 'good life' by the colour of its skin" (Hebdige 2009: 57). A resentment of authority, particularly the police, was part of the skinhead movement from the start, but this resentment was accompanied by a loathing for hippies, students and the middle-class. Hippies – or, more generally, men with long hair – were seen as effeminate and in need of a good kicking, while open homosexuality was definitely a no-no in this macho culture. As Clarke puts it, "Queer-Bashing" may be read as a reaction against the erosion of traditionally available stereotypes of masculinity, especially by the hippies. The skinhead operational definition of "queer" seems to have extended to all those males who by their standards looked "odd" (Clarke 2006: 83). Many skinheads added Asian immigrants to Britain to their hate list, particularly after Enoch Powell's notorious "rivers of blood" speech in April 1968. However illogical it may seem, many skinheads chose to bolster their sense of identity by targeting Asian immigrants in a gruesome phenomenon which became known as "Paki-bashing", in Hebdige's words "a displacement manoeuvre whereby the fear and anxiety produced by limited identification with one black group was transformed into aggression and directed against another black community […] Every time the boot went in, a contradiction was concealed, glossed over, made to 'disappear'" (Hebdige 2009: 58). The macho skinhead culture undeniably glorified "masculine" aggression; some skinheads, unsurprisingly, indulged in what Clarke calls "the ritual and aggressive defence of the social and cultural homogeneity of the community against its most obviously scapegoated outsiders [i.e., Asian immigrants and men perceived as somehow 'unmanly']" (Clarke 2006: 83). Nevertheless, it would be inaccurate to see this disposition towards racist violence on the part of some skinheads as representative of any organized neo-Nazism on the part of the original skinheads as a whole.

These, then, were the original skinheads: proudly working-class, aggressively masculine, and deeply divided when it came to race. The appeal of the cult should be obvious – it offered its members strength in numbers (the sight of thousands of massed skinheads on the terraces of football stadiums in England in 1969 was terrifying – which was essentially the point), a superficially straightforward image of clean, working-class toughness and the excitement of violence. By the turn of the decade the skinheads had largely displaced Mods and Rockers as the hate-figures of "straight" society – "folk devils", in Stanley Cohen's phrase. Cohen's seminal study of the "Mods and Rockers" hysteria of the mid 1960s, *Folk Devils and Moral Panics*, discusses skinheads only tangentially, but the fearful figure of the racist skinhead, anxious for aggro, takes its place in the gallery of deviant post-war figures discussed by Cohen in the preface to the book's third edition, which also includes violent schoolchildren, drug users, paedophiles, single mothers and asylum seekers (Cohen 2002: viii–xxi). The movement did not last, however, for all its notoriety.

Second wave

By 1971 many of the original skins had grown up somewhat and the movement's association with violence had lost its appeal. A number one crop could result in too much hassle, so many skins grew their hair into a longer, but still short and neat, style that became known as a "suedehead". Eventually this name was applied to a subgroup of former skinheads, who dressed more like their Mod predecessors, often in suits, ditching the boots for brogues and ska for the slower, more romantic sound of rocksteady. The suedeheads were a more relaxed lot than the skinheads, and violence was not really their thing; those who wished to continue the macho mayhem concentrated on football violence, and many of the bootboys – later "casuals" – who wreaked mayhem on the terraces throughout the 1970s were former skins. The appeal of Jamaican music had begun to wear off, as well: "as reggae became increasingly preoccupied with its own blackness, it began to appeal less and less to the skinheads who were gradually edged out at a time when the cycle of obsolescence had, as far as this particular subculture was concerned, almost run its course" (Hebdige 2009: 59). By 1972 the skinhead cult seemed to have had its day, and lingered in the collective memory, as the decade went on, mainly for its violent and racist associations. This entirely negative "folk devil" depiction of the cult was notoriously bolstered by the Canadian writer James Moffat – never a skinhead himself – who, writing as Richard Allen, produced a series of notorious novels from 1970 onward, including *Skinhead* and *Suedehead*, depicting skinhead life as an unending round of sex, booze, casual racism and violence (Allen 1992). These pulp novels provided many an illicit thrill to early 1970s teenagers – including Morrissey, as he told Len Brown in 1988 – but their grim depiction of the cult is one-sided, to say the least (Brown 1988).

Remarkably, however, this was not the end of the cult. The punk movement of the late 1970s stimulated a re-emergence of the skinhead "look", at least as far as hairstyle was concerned, among many youths who took the cropped punk look – a contemptuous rejection of the lustrous manes sported by "old farts" like Pink Floyd and Led Zeppelin – to its logical extreme by shaving their heads. This "second wave" of skinhead had relatively little in common with the original cult, but it retained the working-class identity and love of music. This time round, many skins listened exclusively to British music, particularly the "street punk" of bands like Sham 69, The Angelic Upstarts and The Cockney Rejects, rather than soul and reggae. Morrissey developed a taste for some of these bands in the 1990s:

some of their songs featured on the "intro tapes" played before his concerts, chosen by the singer himself, and he befriended Mensi, the skinhead frontman of The Angelic Upstarts. These bands' music was, like punk, fast-paced and aggressive, but the themes of the songs were more exclusively working-class. Come the early 1980s, many of these bands would be lumped into a musical movement called "Oi!" – a title suggested by the journalist Gary Bushell. Although none of the major Oi! bands were openly racist, and several, like The Angelic Upstarts, were explicitly anti-racist, the movement became indelibly associated with racism after a notorious riot in 1981 at the Hambrough Tavern in Southall during which Asian youths firebombed a pub hosting a gig by three Oi! bands in the belief that it was a neo-Nazi gathering. The tabloid media subsequently blamed racist skinheads – some of whom *were* definitely at the gig – for the violence, and the Oi! movement never really recovered (Marshall 1994: 107–29). Much of the automatic association of skinheads with neo-Nazism dates from this period.

It cannot be denied that some second-wave skinheads were neo-Nazis. Particularly notorious in this regard was the "Rock Against Communism" movement that emerged in the late 1970s, a subgenre that had a good deal in common with Oi!, but whose lyrics were openly and unrepentantly nationalistic, racist and anti-Semitic (Marshall 1994: 131–151). The most notorious band in this grim movement was Skrewdriver, whose thuggish leader, Ian Stuart Donaldson, remains a hero to many racists despite his death in 1993.[2] Fortunately for his admirers, Morrissey has never demonstrated the slightest interest in this movement.

Not all of the second-generation skinheads listened to Oi!; many of them became devotees of the "2 Tone" bands that emerged around 1979. Many of these bands, like The Specials and The Selecter, were multiracial; most of them also espoused an explicitly left wing and anti-racist political stance.[3] These bands swiftly accrued a large skinhead following, which ultimately explains the presence of so many skinheads at Madstock. Madness, unlike many other "2 Tone" bands, have never been explicitly "political", and they have had, and continue to have, some racist fans; nevertheless, this racist following was, and remains, a minority. To automatically equate Madness's skinhead fans with racism would be both highly inaccurate and deeply unjust. Morrissey did not walk out to face a seething ocean of sieg-heiling Nazi skins at Madstock. The skinhead phenomenon is, therefore, a complex one, and the simple equation of a shaven head with Nazism is simplistic. When Morrissey performed at Madstock, he was not participating in a White Power rally. None of the bands playing at Madstock were racist. Nevertheless, his decision to play the gig is indicative of more than his liking for Madness's music. It is the most striking moment in the history of his engagement with the skinhead cult, to which we must now turn.

Morrissey and the Skinhead cult

Morrissey was born in Manchester in May 1959, into a working-class Irish family. His sense of class identity should be stressed: as he sings in his 2004 single 'On The Streets I Ran', a "working-class face" stares back at him from the mirror. Although he was brought up in a loving atmosphere and never knew the sort of grinding poverty familiar to, say, John Lydon, he was not born into privilege. He has often spoken and sung about the dark, grimy working-class Manchester he grew up in. The Smiths' songs like 'Rusholme Ruffians' and 'Jeane' deal eloquently with working-class life, while 'The Headmaster Ritual' memorably depicts the horrors of Morrissey's comprehensive education at St Mary's Secondary School in Stretford. He left school with three O levels, including one in English literature, but at a time when the prospect of higher education was out of reach to all but a few working-class students (Goddard 2009: 376). His notorious reluctance to seek employment and decision to retreat into his bedroom and live on the dole – as he says in 'You've Got Everything Now', "I've never had a job / Because I never wanted one" – can be seen as a rejection of the limited opportunities available to an intelligent working-class youth in the late 1970s. Though not a "political" songwriter in the mould of Billy Bragg and Joe Strummer, Morrissey's lyrics often express resentment at the numerous ways in which the working-classes are patronized and discriminated against in modern British society (see Power's chapter in this volume).

Nevertheless, Morrissey's class identity did not lead him to identify explicitly with any of the youth movements of the 1970s, the skinhead cult included, unless we can see him as part of the Glam movement associated with Marc Bolan and David Bowie. He was only ten years old in 1969, and seems by his own account to have been a somewhat sensitive and isolated teenager, unsuited to the rougher lifestyle of the skinheads or bootboys. Indeed, the teenage Morrissey sounds like a likely target for skinhead ire. He wore his hair long (and, by his own admission in the song 'I Know Very Well How I Got My Name', once dyed it gold), adored T. Rex, Roxy Music and David Bowie, and was seen as somewhat effeminate by several contemporaries. This image may be deceptive – he was an outstanding athlete at school, which protected him to a degree from bullying – but connections between the youthful Morrissey and the skinhead cult are hard to find. Indeed, in a recent interview, when asked about David Bowie, he sounds fairly contemptuous of the skinheads of his youth: "[H]e was so important to me because his vocal melodies were so strong and his appearance was so confrontational. Manchester, then, was full of bootboys and skinheads and macho-macho thugs, but I saw Bowie's appearance as the ultimate bravery. To me, it took guts to be David Bowie, not to be a shit-kicking skinhead in a pack" (Nolan 2009). Nevertheless, one aspect of the cult seems to have appealed to the young Morrissey – the music. Morrissey remembers some of the ska tunes beloved of the early skins with fondness – the sleeve notes to his collection of favourite tunes, *Under the Influence*, mention Jimmy Cliff's 'Vietnam', Dave and Ansell Collins's 'Double Barrel', Bob and Marcia's 'Young, Gifted and Black' and 'Swan Lake' by The Cats. The latter track – a reggae version of the Tchaikovsky composition – is included in the album.

All the same, Morrissey's engagement with the skinhead cult is essentially associated with his solo career, and particularly with an increasing interest in traditionally intensely masculine occupations like boxing and violent criminality that became particularly prominent in his work during the 1990s. The Smiths split up in 1987, and Morrissey's debut single as a solo artist, 'Suedehead', was released in February 1988. Neither the song itself nor its promotional video concern the skinhead cult, but its title has caused some discussion. In an interview published in the *NME* in February 1988, Morrissey admitted that he had read Richard Allen's novel of the same title "when it came out" and that he "was interested in the whole Richard Allen cult", but, essentially, he just liked the word itself (Brown 1988). Nevertheless, his use of the title is the first indication of his interest in the cult.

By 1991 Morrissey was ready, for the first time, to make explicit use of skinhead imagery in the rarely seen video for his 1991 single, 'Our Frank', which preceded his second studio album, *Kill Uncle*. The video shows Morrissey singing the song alone, interspersed with shots of a group of mostly male skinheads wandering around London and misbehaving in a variety of fairly innocuous ways – one of them climbs on top of a bus shelter at one point, and at another some of the skinheads seem to be clambering on some sort of memorial. The skinheads never commit any acts of violence, although at one point a close-up shot of a slightly nervous looking uniformed railway official of Asian appearance is briefly used, and at one point one of them seems to be pursuing a member of the public and attempting to engage him in conversation. The member of the public moves on swiftly.

The skinheads in the video are depicted in a contemporary setting (i.e. early 1990s) and seem to be in their late teens or early twenties. These are not skinheads of the first generation. This is obvious when one looks at the completely shaven heads sported by most of the group, which would not have impressed most original skins. In fact, the completely shaven look, the "bonehead", has become particularly associated with neo-Nazi skinheads since the late 1970s. The dark jackets and jeans worn by most of the group also give them a certain sinister uniformity.

The overall impact of the video is hard to assess. The juxtaposition of Morrissey (who appears very briefly in the skinheads' "world" at the start of the video, using a telephone in a railway station, but thereafter is seen alone, illuminated in darkness, singing directly to the camera) and the skinheads is particularly striking. The singer, wearing a red shirt and a plaster above his left eye, performs in his characteristically flamboyant fashion while the skinheads' behaviour is stereotypically masculine and rowdy. At one point they race through an underpass directly towards the viewer, an intimidating sight. The lyrics to the song do not directly mention skinheads but seem to betray an impatience with the life of the mind and a desire to embrace the simpler pleasures of the flesh: the protagonist is sick and tired of "frank and open / Deep conversations," since they "get him nowhere"; instead, he calls for "a cigarette" and "a drink" in the hope that these bodily indulgences will stop him "from thinking all the time". Here Morrissey, long regarded as one of pop's few intellectuals, expresses weariness with a life of thought and a desire for action – or at least oblivion. If this analysis is correct, the video makes more sense: the skinheads symbolize a healthy (if slightly intimidating) lack of sophistication – and communal spirit – that the singer can only envy. The plaster worn by the singer in the video may be seen as an attempt to link himself with the harder, more rough-and-tumble world of masculinity; Morrissey would return to this sort of graphic display in more florid form in later years, even wearing fake cuts and bruises and posing rather unconvincingly with a knuckleduster. He also often spoke of the "gang mentality" that gave The Smiths such inner strength; here, the solo Morrissey seems to lament the loss of this security and envy it in others. The song 'The Ordinary Boys', which features on *Viva Hate*, carries a similar message; the singer simultaneously envies and despises the "ordinary boys" of the title, "happy knowing nothing / Happy being no one but themselves". The Smiths song 'I Want The One I Can't Have' is not dissimilar. As Morrissey told Tony Parsons in 1993, while discussing "macho, working-class youth":

> [A]bove all, I envy their sense of freedom. They don't need to use their imagination all that much, they act upon impulse – and that's very enviable. Theirs is a naturalness which I think is a great art form, which I can't even aspire to. I don't feel natural even when I am fast asleep. The only impulse I have ever served is making records and doing sleeves. That was the opening for it all. Before that, it was all twisted.
>
> (Parsons 1993)

This perhaps rather patronizing view of the working-class youth as a sort of "noble savage" recurs sporadically throughout Morrissey's later career in songs like 'Teenage Dad on His Estate', 'The Boy Racer' and 'Dagenham Dave', and is an important part of his interest in the skinhead cult.

The history of this "skinhead" video is a curious one. It has never been released on any of Morrissey's video compilations. It is easy to track down online, but has only ever been legally issued on a video compilation in Japan – a country without any particular associations between skinheads and racism.[4] The video's "disappearance" may be associated with the "racism" controversy that erupted after Madstock, which, if so, demonstrates the sensitivity with which the use of skinhead imagery – rightly or wrongly – is viewed. It is certainly ironic that a song prominently featuring a raga violin, played by Nawazish Ali Khan, is – indirectly – associated with racism.

Skins: Alive and kicking

Shortly after the release of *Kill Uncle*, Morrissey discussed his interest in the skinhead cult in some detail during an interview with Stuart Maconie in the *NME*. The way he chose to dress for this interview seems to have been carefully considered. Maconie met him in a hotel bar in Berlin, and he was "an unmistakable figure, even though there are certain unusual accoutrements: the beer, the magenta nail varnish, the T-shirt, with its garish illustration of legs ending in half-mast jeans and fearsome six-hole 'Docs', and bearing the legend 'Skins: Alive and Kicking'" (Maconie 1991). Surrounded by an entourage of press officer, personal assistants and band, "sipping large glasses of Pils", Morrissey, in Maconie's view, could almost have been "one of the lads" (Maconie 1991).

The T-shirt's illustration is significant: its allusion to the skinhead cult is explicit and threatening, and the way it focuses on the boots draws emphasis to the cult's association with violence. Indeed, many an old-school skin would view it as somewhat crude and perpetuating the old stereotypes. Nevertheless, Morrissey's decision to wear nail varnish at the same time as this aggressively masculine image undermines it completely. The Morrissey who wears nail varnish, like the isolated Morrissey of the 'Our Frank' video, may admire the skinhead's world – or, at least, the simple world of the skinhead stereotype – but he is ultimately separate from it. His garb is simultaneously expressing admiration for the cult and an ironic distance from it. The straightforwardly masculine and aggressive image on the T-shirt is cut across by the "queerness" of the magenta nail varnish, with its deliberate connotations of sexual ambiguity; a man who simultaneously wears both is choosing to send out deliberately contradictory signals.

Later in the interview Morrissey draws attention to the T-shirt when responding to a question about his attitudes towards race: "I'm incapable of racism, even though I'm wearing this T-shirt and even though I'm delighted that an increasing number of my audience are skinheads in nail varnish. And I'm not trying to be funny, that really is the perfect audience for me" (Maconie 1991). Morrissey is plainly aware of the automatic association Maconie may make between skinheads and racism, and seems deliberately to stray into dangerous waters. Maconie asks Morrissey to elaborate, and the singer explains that "as you're perfectly aware, the audience for all those groups from that little island of Manchester all dress in completely American style which befuddles me. So the sight of streams of skinheads in nail varnish [...] it somehow represents the Britain I love" (Maconie 1991). Maconie asks the singer to explain further, and Morrissey, by now sounding rather snappy, replies "well, correct me if I'm wrong, but I thought the skinhead was an entirely British invention" (Maconie 1991). The conversation then moves on to Morrissey's nostalgic pining for a "mythical Britain" (Maconie 1991). Morrissey seems to have been arguing that skinheads were somehow uniquely "British", and therefore that their "look" appeals to him rather more than the "American" look worn by many contemporary music fans (the baseball boots worn by Robert Smith of The Cure strike him as particularly obnoxious).

As we have already seen, Morrissey's admiration for the skinhead cult as an "entirely British invention" is, to say the least, inaccurate. Morrissey does not in any way acknowledge the Jamaican influence on the cult discussed by Hebdige, here or elsewhere, choosing instead to focus on what he sees as their emblematic status as representatives of the British working-class. If Morrissey's skinhead obsession can in any way be seen as racist, perhaps this is where his "racism" lies – in his apparent refusal to admit that his beloved "British" skins found their cultural origins in Kingston, Jamaica, as much as in the East End of London.

Madstock

1992, however, was the year in which Morrissey's interest in skinheads contributed to the most controversial episode of his career. By the time of Madstock Morrissey had assembled a new band that he would go on to work with for many years. The band were drawn from the contemporary rockabilly scene, and their quiffs, turned-up jeans and (in the case of bassist Gary Day) extensive tattooing gave them a tough and intensely masculine "look", which contrasted strikingly with the more ambiguous appearance and manner of their employer. Morrissey's decision to employ these musicians stemmed in part from his love for rockabilly, but also seems to have been part of a desire on his part to adopt, if only to undermine, a more traditionally masculine aesthetic. This desire has continued, more or less, to the present day, as anyone familiar only with the Morrissey of the early 1980s would immediately notice on seeing his more "manly" contemporary incarnation, a thick-set gentleman of middle years whose tendency to wear smart suits and chunky gold jewellery gives him the aura of an East End gangster of the 1960s. Morrissey would come to refer to his new band as "the lads" and accounts of his relationship with them testify to a newly boisterous Morrissey that one could not have imagined while he was in The Smiths.

The very sound of his new album, *Your Arsenal*, contributed to this sense that Morrissey was asserting his masculinity and distancing himself from his former "sensitive" image. The album's producer, Mick Ronson, gave the songs a tough, glam-influenced sound, and overall the album was Morrissey's "rockiest" work yet. Some of the songs' lyrics contributed to this impression of confrontation. 'Glamorous Glue' laments the deleterious effects of American-led globalization on British society: "we look to Los Angeles for the language we use / London is dead." The uniquely Cockney idiolect is being eroded by the imported mass popular culture of America. We are reminded of Morrissey's disgust at Robert Smith's baseball boots. 'We'll Let You Know' is sung from the perspective of a football hooligan, and ends with the ominous declaration that "we are the last truly British people you will ever know". Most controversially, in 'The National Front Disco' a young man's friends and mother mourn the loss of their son to the National Front: the song contains the line (in quotation marks) "England for the English", and attempts to explain the appeal of neo-Nazism to the youth: "you want the day to come sooner / When you settle the score". While the song is, lyrically, in no way a racist anthem, its title alone troubled contemporary critics and it would be brought forward as one of the pieces of "evidence" for Morrissey's supposed racism after Madstock.

What really happened at Madstock?

What transpired during Morrissey's set at Finsbury Park has often been misinterpreted. Morrissey's critics would have you believe that he was bottled off stage by hordes of neo-Nazi skinheads who had interpreted his attempts to ingratiate himself with them (the backdrop, the flag, the "dodgy" songs) as mockery. This version depicts Morrissey as at best naive and more likely openly racist, and skinheads as the usual bootboy caricatures. Morrissey's defenders see him as a misunderstood ironist whose adroit subversion of skinhead imagery was designed to infuriate them and expose them as the thugs they are. Skinheads, unsurprisingly, emerge as moronic yobs in both versions. So what really happened at Madstock?[5]

Signs of the trouble to come were noticeable during Gallon Drunk's set earlier in the afternoon: several objects had been thrown at the band, and they had been the target of some abuse. Morrissey's slot was awkwardly timed: the huge crowd had just enjoyed Ian Dury's set and were growing impatient for the arrival of Madness. Morrissey had chosen an extremely striking image of two skinhead girls – a cropped version of a picture taken by Derek Ridgers in Brighton in 1980 – to be used as the backdrop for his performance, and had decided that it would be appropriate to face thousands of drunken Madness fans wearing a gold lamé shirt – that Liberace would probably have rejected as excessively camp – open to the waist to reveal a lean bare torso.[6] Contemporary footage shows him walking onstage to the esoterically dramatic sound of Klaus Nomi's 'Wayward Sisters' and receiving a generally positive reception.[7] Crucially, he holds a Union flag, which he drops onto the stage before heading over to the microphone and greeting the crowd with a shriek. What transpired over the next 40 minutes or so – or, at least, subsequent accounts of it – has haunted Morrissey ever since, and has been repeatedly used to link him to the skinhead cult in the most negative of ways.

Fortunately, Morrissey's set was videoed by someone in the crowd and can be viewed online.[8] There is also at least one bootleg audio recording extant. The footage shows that the area closest to the stage was occupied, unsurprisingly, by Morrissey fans, who supported their hero throughout his set by clapping and cheering. Nevertheless, Morrissey fans were a tiny minority at this gig. Morrissey was in the unusual position (for him) of performing to an audience who were largely indifferent to him. This explains why his set was not received with undiluted adulation, and also explains the irritation the footage clearly shows him feeling as the set goes on. Three years later he would, for the only time in his career as a solo artist, agree to tour as a support act – to David Bowie – and the tour ended in disaster when Morrissey abruptly quit, apparently angry at having to perform to largely indifferent crowds of Bowie fans.

The set begins well. Morrissey is cheered on his entrance and upon the conclusion of his first song. However, the mood begins to sour during the second song, 'Glamorous Glue', during which the singer, notoriously, picks up the Union flag he had carried on earlier and proceeds to wave it about.[9] He at no point "wraps himself" in it, as was later alleged – indeed, in my opinion he treats it with scant respect, whipping the stage with it, flailing about with it, and finally tossing it into the crowd before the end of the song. To see this performance as some sort of racist display seems perverse. The National Front had, since the late 1970s, attempted to appropriate the flag as a racist symbol, but Morrissey does not treat the flag with reverence. If there is a nationalist agenda here, it is anti-American rather than racist – the song itself laments the bland effects of globalization on British culture, and Morrissey's declaration that "London is dead" does not seem to go down well with many of the crowd; Madness are a London band. If anything, it is this statement that seems to have particularly riled some Madness fans. It should also be emphasized that the "skinhead backdrop" depicts two skinhead *girls* – unusual figures, in that they have close-cropped hair unlike the longer style usually worn by female skinheads. The girls in the picture are somewhat androgynous, and Morrissey's choice of this image profoundly undermines the intensely masculine skinhead stereotype and reflects the blurring of gender stereotypes Morrissey has undertaken throughout his career. Morrissey had similarly "queered" skinhead imagery through his choice of T-shirt and make-up when meeting Stuart Maconie the previous year. Had Morrissey chosen a more conventional image of male skinheads, the "message" of the backdrop would be rather different.

From this moment on, Morrissey becomes the target of abuse from some of the crowd, which grows steadily throughout his set. The footage shows various missiles (usually plastic water bottles, it would seem) being thrown at the stage, though most of them fall short – they are not, after all, being thrown by Morrissey's fans, but by people further back. It is not a "hail" of missiles, and Morrissey is not "bottled off", as would later be reported. Most of the people in shot seem to be on Morrissey's side. Interestingly, the footage does not clearly show a single "skinhead" in front of the stage – pretty much everyone has fairly long hair. Morrissey is also the target of verbal abuse – "wanker" is a popular insult, and a small number of people can be seen making the "wanker" gesture or giving him two fingers as the set goes on. There is some chanting, apparently by Madness fans impatient for the band's arrival. Johnnie Craig, a Morrissey fan, claims in a 2009 online article on Madstock that he was mocked on his entrance to Finsbury Park by "a lager-swilling huddle of bovver-booted neo-Nazis" for wearing a polka-dot shirt, and that "bald giants" with "swastika'd necks" "refused to budge" from their positions at the front of the stage on Morrissey's entrance and greeted him with "a hate-filled crescendo", while "hate-filled missiles (oranges and plastic bottles) rained onstage" (Craig 2009). The terrifying "bald giants", it must be said, are conspicuous only by their absence from the contemporary footage, and Craig's depiction of events seems, to say the least, "coloured" by subsequent accounts and the "folk devil" stereotype of skinheads as racist imbeciles.

Chris, a skinhead since 1979 and a big Madness fan, provides another perspective.[10] He describes a very different atmosphere, with Finsbury Park full of a largely good-natured crowd of Madness fans, including many families as well as quite a few skinheads. It was a very hot day and many of the crowd had been drinking heavily by the time Morrissey was preparing for his entrance. Chris was quite close to the front and found himself next to some working-class men in their forties singing football chants. These men were, according to Chris, not skinheads but "your average guy you see down the pub". Chris says he rather liked The Smiths himself and was looking forward to seeing Morrissey perform, but he was surprised at his presence on the bill since many skinheads viewed Morrissey and his fans as "weirdoes and poofters" – which makes one think that some of the crowd may have objected to Morrissey's performance on the grounds of his perceived sexuality as much as anything else.

Chris says that the crowd became quite rowdy during Morrissey's set and that keeping his footing was difficult at times (a not uncommon experience at big gigs). He did not notice the backdrop until after the gig, when he viewed some photographs taken by a friend, and says that as far as he could tell Morrissey's antics with the flag did not bother the crowd. The main problem, he claims, was caused by the "blokes" mentioned earlier, whose booze-fuelled impatience for the arrival of Madness led them to shout abuse at Morrissey throughout his set, including charming remarks like "I'd rather be a Paki than a Smiths fan." Despite this, Chris maintains that "there were no Nazi skinheads sieg-heiling at that gig", which conflicts with much of the subsequent media reportage. His account of the affair is of considerable interest because, as far as I know, no one has ever bothered to ask a real, living skinhead what he made of Morrissey's performance. The footage shows Morrissey consulting with his band about half way through the set and gesturing at the set-list: he is evidently deciding to cut the set short. After nine songs Morrissey abruptly walks off stage, swiftly followed by his band. His performance was followed by Madness's live return, which was ecstatically received by the crowd. Morrissey proceeded to disappoint his fans by cancelling his appearance at the second date, blaming his early exit on "the abysmal behaviour of a small group of loathsome yobbos" – perhaps the drunken racists mentioned by Chris (Bret 2004: 185).

The aftermath

The following week the *NME* accused him of flirting dangerously with right-wing imagery and Morrissey's refusal to discuss the matter or defend himself, except in the most general terms, ignited a controversy about his alleged "racism" that has rumbled on to this day. In his only detailed discussion of the event, during an interview published in December 1992, he stated that "I know there were a lot of people there from the National Front, but I don't think they were particularly interested in me. And even though there were reports of me being booed and pelted off-stage – which of course never happened at all – I don't believe that it was the National Front who did that. I think it was a small selection of rather dull north Londoners. Now the press claim that every skinhead in London wants my blood, which is twaddle. Nobody mentioned that Madness themselves also received missiles" (Chalmers 1992). He later defended his use of skinhead imagery to the French journalist Emmanuel Tellier in 1993: "not all skinheads are racists. Skinheads and the National Front are two different things. Skinheads are emblematic of the British working-classes. I have no ties whatsoever with racism. I like boxing! Does that make me violent?" (Bret 2004: 190).

Nevertheless, Morrissey has been very cautious in his use of skinhead imagery (in the United Kingdom, at least) since Madstock. He continued to use the "skinhead girls" backdrop on his tour of North America in Autumn 1992, and the image also appeared on T-shirts, the tour programme and the tour passes. However, the image was dropped when he returned to the United Kingdom in December 1992, probably due to the racism accusations.[11] The Union flag was never used on stage again at all (Morrissey must have been wryly amused by its very visible reclamation by Britpop artists like Blur and Oasis in the mid 1990s). His interest in tough, "manly" pursuits continued to be manifested in his mid-1990s passion for boxing and songs like 'Dagenham Dave', 'Boxers' and 'Roy's Keen', as well as his continued interest in crime, best displayed in his hit 2004 single 'First Of The Gang To Die'. He has continued, on occasion, to play songs by The Angelic Upstarts and The Cockney Rejects before his shows, and wrote the preface to the autobiography of Jeff Turner, singer in the latter band, as well as invited them to perform at the Meltdown Festival he curated in 2004 (Turner 2010: vii–viii). A weird moment came in 1997, when he decided, briefly, to adopt a much shorter, almost skinhead, hairstyle – this writer recalls his shock at seeing Morrissey walk onstage at the start of his performance at Battersea power station in December 1997 without his famous quiff. Evidence for this can be seen in the rather strange promotional video for his contemporaneous single 'Alma Matters', which depicts Morrissey writhing suggestively in a grim-looking basement. His performance is interspersed with brief, blurred shots of a group of male and female skinheads fighting outside, and at one point Morrissey hurls the contents of a bowl of cornflakes into the face of a tough-looking female skinhead who is haranguing him. The significance of the video is hard to assess, and remains unavailable on DVD, perhaps because of its (admittedly mild) violence and skinhead imagery.[12] As the promotional video for the opening single from one his least successful albums, it was little seen at the time.

Conclusion

What, then, was Morrissey trying to achieve with his performance at Madstock, assuming that he was not attempting either to set himself up as a fascist leader, or to deliberately insult Madness's skinhead fans? A clue is given in an interview he gave to the Swedish magazine *Slitz* in 1992, in which he explains his interest in the cult in the following manner:

> Most youth cultures come from the U.S.A. Except skinheads, which as I understand, is an exclusively British invention. That the rest of the world around us looks upon skinheads as people who tattoo swastikas in their foreheads and throw fruit at innocent football supporters is a shame. Of course I'm aware of the fact that there exist such 'skinheads'. But the original idea of skinheads was just about clothes and music. And in England it still is to a pretty great extent. Style and everything it involves for me have their roots in the British working-class. That's where all culture I appreciate passes on and in some degree is updated. The British working-class and its youth cultures are never vulgar or excessive. Whereas the middle class never has created a bit.
>
> (Lokko 1992)

He would defend his interest in skinheads in a similarly class-based fashion to Emmanuel Tellier in 1993, as we have seen, valuing what Hebdige calls their "undiluted 'classfulness', a romantic conception of the traditional whole way of (working-class) life revived twice weekly on television programmes like *Coronation Street*" (Hebdige 2009: 86–87). Morrissey's passion for *Coronation Street*, particularly the 1960s incarnation of his youth, is well known (Goddard 2009: 80–81).

In Morrissey's eyes, then, the skinhead cult is to be admired as an essentially British working-class youth cult, entirely free of the American influence he decries in 'Glamorous Glue'. As we have seen, this focus on the skinheads' essential "Britishness" is somewhat problematic, in that it elides the enormous Jamaican contribution to the cult. Morrissey also fails to acknowledge the way in which many of the original skinheads enjoyed the specifically American musical genre of Soul, like their Mod predecessors. Even so, to see his fantasy vision of Madstock as "an essentially British weekend" as somehow racist is missing the point, unless a declaration of nostalgia for a lost "Britishness" in the face of what Morrissey sees as the negative influence of American culture can be seen as racist. I would argue that Morrissey's decision to use the flag to underline this message during 'Glamorous Glue' was premeditated, not spontaneous – indeed, he had behaved in a similar manner during his performances at two European festivals in July 1992, which elicited no controversy whatsoever. The "skinhead girls" backdrop can also be seen as part of Morrissey's tribute to the cult, with a deliberately gendered twist that undermines the cult's aggressive "masculinity"; had he been able to get hold of a photo of one of his mythological "skinheads in nail varnish", he would almost certainly have used that. As he admitted to Maconie in their 1991 interview, Morrissey nostalgically admired the skinheads for what he saw, somewhat inaccurately, as their unapologetically working-class "Britishness" – in Hebdige's words, for the way they "theorised and fetishised their class position, in order to effect a 'magical' return to an imagined past" (Hebdige 2009: 120). They were, in his personal iconography, "emblematic of the British working-classes" (Bret 2004: 190). He also envied them for the toughness, outsider status and gang mentality so clearly displayed in the videos for 'Our Frank' and 'Alma Matters'. His decision to play at Madstock was his attempt to pay public tribute to the cult. I would argue that it failed disastrously, due to a toxic combination of deliberate media misinterpretation and his own rather arrogant belief that a crowd almost entirely indifferent to him – and impatient for the arrival of their heroes – could be bothered to decode his complex message.

Notes

1. The most detailed sources for information on the cult are George Marshall's *Spirit of '69: A Skinhead Bible*, 2nd edn, London, S. T. Publishing, 1994 and Nick Knight's *Skinhead*, London, Omnibus, 1992. Dick Hebdige's *Subculture: The Meaning of Style*, Padstow, Routledge, 2009, although it is not exclusively focused on the cult, contains some of the most penetrating analysis of it to date, even though it is now over three decades old.
2. A useful source on this squalid outfit (from an avowedly anti-Nazi perspective) is Nick Lowles and Steve Silver's *White Noise: Inside the International Nazi Skinhead Scene*, London, Searchlight Magazine Ltd, 1998. Those with strong stomachs will find a somewhat different take on the band at *www.bloodandhonourworldwide.co.uk*, but visiting this thoroughly revolting site is not recommended.
3. For more information on 2 Tone, see Dave Thompson's *Wheels Out of Gear: 2 Tone, The Specials and a World in Flame*, London, Helter Skelter, 2004.

4. The video can be viewed at *http: //vids.myspace.com/index.cfm?fuseaction=vids.individual&VideoID=1271445*.
5. It should be noted that the author of this chapter was not at the gig himself.
6. The photograph of the two girls was taken in Brighton in 1980 by Derek Ridgers. His (somewhat unhappy) account of how the image came to be used by Morrissey can be found at *http: //www.derekridgers.com/homepage/Blog/Entries/2010/5/21_Skinhead_girls,_Bank_Holiday,_Brighton_1980.html*.
7. See *http: //www.youtube.com/watch?v=CnoJkMY1x7c*.
8. The whole gig can be viewed at *http: //www.youtube.com/watch?v=CnoJkMY1x7c&feature=PlayList&p=2F72CFA64677BEA6&playnext_from=PL&index=0&playnext=1*.
9. Morrissey's performance of 'Glamorous Glue' can be viewed at *http: //www.youtube.com/watch?v=M6DnMA5IiB8*.
10. Interview with Chris (private communication).
11. See *http: //www.passionsjustlikemine.com/gigs/moz-gi9212ukeur.htm*.
12. The video can be viewed at *http: //www.youtube.com/watch?v=C_pfMoUVNPw*.

References

Allen, R. (1992) *The Complete Richard Allen Volume One: Skinhead, Suedehead, Skinhead Escapes.* London: S. T. Publishing.
Bret, D. (2004) *Morrissey: Scandal and Passion.* London: Robson.
Bret, D. (1994) *Morrissey: Landscapes of the Mind.* London: Robson.
Brown, L. (1988) 'Born to be Wilde', *NME*, 13th February.
Chalmers, R. (1992) 'Morrissey flowers again', *Observer*, December.
Clarke, J. (2006) 'The Skinheads and the magical recovery of community' in S. Hall and T. Jefferson (eds) *Resistance Through Rituals: Youth Subculture in Post-War Britain.* Oxford: Routledge, pp. 80–83.
Cohen, S. (2002) *Folk Devils and Moral Panics.* Oxford: Routledge.
Craig, J. (2009) 'My Favourite Worst Nightmare – Morrissey and Madstock', available: *http: //www.state.ie/2009/10/features/my-favourite-worst-nightmare-morrissey-madstock/*.
Fadele, D., Collins, A., Kelly, D. and Martin, G. (1992) 'Caucasian rut', *NME*, 22nd August.
Goddard, S. (2009) *Mozipedia: The Encyclopaedia of Morrissey and The Smiths.* Bodmin: Ebury Press.
Hebdige, D. (2009) *Subculture: The Meaning of Style.* Padstow: Routledge.
Knight, N. (1982) *Skinhead.* London: Omnibus.
Lokko, A. (1992) 'Fan-mail', *Slitz* (Sweden), September.
Lowles, N. and Silver, S. (1998) *White Noise: Inside the International Nazi Skinhead Scene.* London, Searchlight Magazine Ltd.
Maconie, S. (1991) 'Morrissey comes out! (for a drink)', *NME*, 18th May.
Marshall, G. (1994) *Spirit of '69: A Skinhead Bible*, 2nd edn. London: S. T. Publishing.
Nolan, P. (2009) 'I've something to get off my chest', *Hot Press* (Ireland), 1st April.
Parsons, T. (1993) 'What now, Mozzer?', *Vox*, April.
Thompson, D. (2004) *Wheels out of Gear: 2 Tone, The Specials, and a World in Flame.* London: Helter Skelter Publishing.
Turner, J. (2010) *Cockney Reject.* London: John Blake.

Chapter 4

Fanatics, Apostles and NMEs

Colin Snowsell

Introduction

This chapter examines the difficulty many fans of Morrissey find themselves in when the subject of their admiration engages in the mediated public sphere by uttering statements and adopting positions which seem to conflict ethically and philosophically with the more liberal and progressive views commonly attributed to The Smiths, and to the world of independent ("indie") music more generally. This chapter suggests that fandom occurs along a continuum, where Morrissey's preferred term for dedicated admirers ("apostles") may be situated between "fans" at one end and "fanatics" at the other.[1] Using the controversial 2007 *New Musical Express* (*NME*) cover interview with Morrissey as an example, this chapter argues that, although fanaticism may represent the most extreme position on the continuum, the irrational support demanded of, and offered by fanatics, harms both the reputation of Morrissey and his community of supporters. It suggests that a revalorization of fandom, one that entails the interrogation of the present over-prioritization of fidelity at all costs, is essential to reinvigorating the fan community with recognition that critique of specific public positions undertaken by the artist, may be an act of sincere, mature and reasoned fandom, not its negation.

Fidelity

> [B]ush was the movement and the cause.
>
> (Kristol cited in Bumiller 2006)

Reynolds (1990: 15) suggests that loyalty, "fidelity" in his formulation, in pop music is the primary and only necessary quality to resist commodification. "The one thing that makes rock more than an industry, the one thing that transcends the commodity relation is fidelity, the idea of a relationship. There are voices you turn to as a friend, and you don't just turn your back on your friends if they do go off the rails. You hang around." This, of course, is nonsense.

The one thing that makes rock *precisely* an industry is the way fans are cultivated, the same way consumers and markets are cultivated. In order to do this, singers and bands are packaged in distinct ways so that they may be differentiated from the competition. Adorno refers to this as pseudo-individualization (2002: 445). Naomi Klein calls it branding. Klein's (2000) indictment of branding as the most pernicious tool of late industrial capitalism is based on its substitution of symbolic meaning for quality or physical need as imperative reasons for purchase. She reminds us that the goal of any successful company is to create a brand that can "escape almost all that is earthbound and to become pure idea, like a spirit ascending" (Klein 2000: 25). Moving from corporate to human branding is not much of a stretch, as Klein repeatedly asserts. The passage above continues: "This is a goal that is available not only to companies, but also to people. We have human brands as well as company brands and they, too, are cutting ties with what might be broadly described as 'doing things'" (Klein 2000: 25).

When people covet, or imagine themselves incomplete without the Nike swoosh, irrespective of the horrible manufacturing conditions – and their attendant human toll – this marks, as Klein demonstrates, the emergence of a new strain of capitalism, albeit one not without precedent. Klein concludes her essay in what in retrospect reads as an unduly optimistic note on the power of enlightened consumers to reject the omnipotent demands of lifestyle branding, and insist that the companies behind the brand engage in ethical business practices.

> If brands are indeed intimately entangled with our culture and identity, then, when they do wrong, their crimes are not easily dismissed as another corporation trying to make a buck. Instead, many of the people who inhabit these branded worlds feel complicit in their wrongs, both guilty and connected. And this connection is a volatile one, akin to the relationship of fan and celebrity; emotionally intense but shallow enough to turn on a dime.
>
> (Klein 2000: 28)

But Klein underestimates the depth of fandom to be found further along the continuum. The fan–celebrity relationship may tend to be as fickle as she imagines; in this formulation, the connection hinges solely on fame which, when exhausted, ends the sole cause of fandom. Indeed, Klein's mistaken optimism stems from the comparison of brand loyalty between fan and celebrity, when the relationship seems much more like the one we see between fans and Morrissey or, as Kristol notes (cited in Bumiller 2006) the relationship between Republicans and George W. Bush. In short, Morrissey *fanatics* define goodness as whatever Morrissey does; there is no higher proof. Morrissey is no mere celebrity. To such fanatics (as opposed to fans), he is everything. So desirable is such a relationship that the advertising industry came into existence to try to create it. As such, loyal fanatics are anything but the antithesis of the commodity relationship, as Reynolds (1990) would have it; they are rather the manifestation of a highly successful and eminently desirable one. Surely Morrissey, as much as any contemporary popular music artist, understands the intensity of the fan–performer relationship? At the age of 22, shortly before forming The Smiths, Morrissey published a book on James Dean. At the age of 18, he was president of the UK branch of the New York Dolls fan club, and wrote obsessively (and largely unsuccessfully) to the independent British music weeklies, sometimes in defence of his musical heroes.[2]

Transformation and utopianism

To scholars of critical cultural studies, the primary interest in Morrissey (and The Smiths) has always revolved around his perceived delivery of cultural studies' transformative and emancipatory goals.[3] Even the *NME*, in an article suggesting Morrissey might be racist, acknowledges that "Morrissey has held, and continues to hold, sway over the minds of a generation who take tips from his every utterance, try to model themselves on his sense of fashion and live their lives at least partly according to codes he's laid down with a flourish (just try imagining the number of people who converted to vegetarianism upon hearing The Smiths' 'Meat Is Murder')" (Kelly, Martin and Maconie 1992). Being a fan of Morrissey has never been an idle declaration of a passing fancy with no particular meaning attached to it. Being a fan has always been a declaration of dissatisfaction with an unjust world, a recognition that amidst the darkness of despair, there is one voice who understands the solitude and who is prepared to light the way out. And that this relationship between fan and pop singer exists has always seemed to justify what has been the great hope for pop culture, that through supposedly disposable, irrelevant, pop cultural commodities, a challenge to the world that produces such loneliness may be found. "Fandom is, at least potentially, the site of the optimism, invigoration and passion which are necessary conditions for any struggle to change the conditions of one's life" (Grossberg 1992: 65).[4] Or, as Frith (1996a: 123) asks, could it be that we look to music and we look to the popular, because in combination it could be this that "gives us a real experience of what the ideal could be"?

Morrissey certainly thinks so. Changing people's lives through music has always been his stated goal:

> It's a matter of life and death to me. Music affects everybody and I really think it does change the world! Everybody has their favourite song and people's lives do change because of songs.
>
> For the most part products are disposable, but just for that extra one song that changes your direction in life, the importance of popular music cannot be stressed enough. Music is the most important thing in the world.
>
> (cited in Worral 1983)

Morrissey's (1983) belief in the power of popular music might now seem quaint, but there can be no doubt that Morrissey, as solo artist and as member of The Smiths, intended his music to be read as a political rejection of the social world in which his band was formed, and as hope to those individuals afflicted by that world. As Morrissey said: "[I] don't want The Smiths in any way to be attached to any kind of trend. But, yes, we do have our political views and I think it really is quite obvious the way we feel about most things if you just study the lyrics and the music anyway" (West 1985: 17).

Previously, I have argued (Snowsell 2002: 87–88) that Morrissey's critical transformative interventions may be divided into three broad categories: his rejection of liberated sexuality and his preference for expanded options of sexual identity;[5] his dissatisfaction with the limited identity options offered to working and middle-class youth; and his celebration of the (British) past as a form of retro Blochian utopia, that is, "a critique of what is present" (Bloch 1998: 12). It was understood that there was an explicit progressive, critical project underlying Morrissey's pop cultural project; fandom was based on this understanding.

As Frith reminds us, pop music is useful not so much for what it tells us about the performer, but what it tells us about the audience and the community that is created between the constituencies: "The question we should be asking is not what does popular music reveal about the people who play and use it but how does it create them as a people, as a web of identities?" (Frith 1996: 121). When the textual meaning, implicit and explicit, offered through the singer or performer changes, it's not just s/he who has changed; all of the audience who accepts uncritically the shift will necessarily have changed as well.

The 2007 *NME* scandal is a scandal only when seen in this light. It is not that Morrissey said or did anything that a host of conservative (or centrist or liberal, or even leftist) politicians had not already said or done. It is the fact that, given the context I have outlined above, Morrissey's 2007 statements represent not a continuation of the progressive utopianism of The Smiths. Rather, I would argue that they represent a rejection of these ideals.

The old enemy

In the 27th November, 2007 issue of *NME*, Morrissey appeared on the cover under the headline: "Big Mouth Strikes Again [...] Oh dear, not again" and accompanied by the following quote attributed to him from the interview: "The gates of England are flooded. The country's been thrown away" (Jonze and *NME* 2007). The appearance rekindled a previous (as John H. Baker notes elsewhere in this collection) and still lingering controversy, also caused by a Morrissey cover story published in the *NME*, in 1992. As evidence of emergent racism, *NME* offers a close reading of selected lyrics, combines this with an equally close reading of a single performance, at Finsbury Park, throws in a collection of supposedly damning quotes, and recommends more care in the future: "Therefore when [Morrissey] sends out signals on subjects as sensitive as those discussed above there seems little room for playfulness, never mind ambiguity" (Kelly, Martin and Maconie 1992). Both the original and the subsequent discussions of Morrissey as racist have been exhaustively covered. To be clear, accusations of racism overreach.[6] What I do wish to argue is that, at best, Morrissey's position in regard to immigration and other fraught political questions – such as Palestine – has been ambivalent, and that he has demonstrated a tenacious lack of awareness as to how many of his statements, taken in isolation, or together, must inevitably be interpreted in some camps amidst the broad Morrissey fan community.

Whether an artist or mass-mediated celebrity has any responsibility to consider the effect his or her behaviour may have on fans who seek to emulate (often misguidedly, or inaccurately) is an issue of ethics and is not the concern of this chapter. However, that there is a direct correlation between celebrity action/utterance and the emulative behaviour of dedicated admirers is beyond contention. Dedicated admirers of influential mass-mediated celebrities do attempt to adopt the actions, physical attributes and behaviour, and attempt to mimic the overall worldview of the admired, in an attempt to establish the conviction of their devotion (Chia and Poo 2009: 23–26; Boon and Lomore 2001: 432–436; McCutcheon et al. 2002). Morrissey's seemingly stubborn refusal to recognize how these passages of wilful ambiguity might be interpreted by some of his fans (the fanatics, for instance) is surprising given his own intense experiences of fandom, and given his penchant for celebrating the intense admiration he provokes in his followers.[7]

This is not your country?

As Simpson (2007) observes, if you did not know the author behind each of the following quotes it would be difficult to discern the source. To wit:

> [W]ith the issue of immigration, it's very difficult because although I don't have anything against people from other countries, the higher the influx into England the more the British identity disappears. If you travel to Germany, it's still absolutely Germany. If you travel to Sweden, it still has a Swedish identity. But travel to England and you have no idea where you are [...] If you walk through Knightsbridge you'll hear every accent apart from an English accent.
>
> (in Simpson 2007)

> While, to the immigrant, entry to this country was admission to privileges and opportunities [...] the impact upon the existing population was very different. For reasons which they could not comprehend, and in pursuance of a decision by default, on which they were never consulted, they found themselves made strangers in their own country.
>
> (in Simpson 2007)

The latter quote is from Enoch Powell's (1968) "Rivers of Blood" speech. The former is from the 2007 *NME* Morrissey interview/cover story (Jonze and *NME* 2007). Powell was dismissed from the shadow cabinet, of which he as a Conservative party Member of Parliament was a member, for the speech, and there was widespread revulsion, particularly amongst the educated, at the imagery Powell's speech invoked (Dorey 1995: 98). Nonetheless, the speech was popular at the time, and, as Simpson (2007) observes, however controversial Powell's speech may have been amongst certain segments of society in 1968, its sentiment – opposing or limiting immigration – has become widely routinized (not uncritically accepted) as a subject for debate in the United Kingdom. Moreover, the idea that the national interest would be best served by limiting immigration has become commonly a platform of many centrist, rightwing (conservative) and supposedly left wing parties (for example New Labour) throughout the western world. As Simpson (2007) argues, "[I]f Morrissey can be pilloried for expressing similar views to [Leader of the British Conservative party] David Cameron, is it any wonder he prefers to live abroad"?

Simpson's quote, the last line of his article, begins to mark the divide between Morrissey fanatics, on one hand, and the community around indie music in general, on the other. Through his London solicitors – Russells – Morrissey threatened to sue the *NME*, and editor Conor McNicholas, personally, for defamation (*True To You: A Morrissey Zine* 2007).[8] The letter does not specifically request that publication be halted, but dated as it is a day before the *NME*'s scheduled publication, the implication that the text, and headline, and emphasis of the immigration theme in the offending issue will be considered malicious and defamatory upon publication seems clear. The letter reads, in part: "Our client is understandably extremely concerned that the Article will be defamatory to him, in particular carrying expressly or by imputation the false assertion that our client is a racist or holds racist views" (*True To You: A Morrissey Zine* 2007).

This is interesting for it is Morrissey, through his lawyers, who raises the question of racism. If we accept, as I do, that Morrissey is not racist, the quotes given by Morrissey in this interview remain provocative, and are worthy of discussion. "The gates of England are flooded. The country's been thrown away", is a newsworthy quote, irrespective of the person uttering it. I would argue that any editor and any writer who reports on, and critically evaluates, indie bands and their recordings would, on the grounds of journalistic integrity, find it obligatory to feature as incongruous such a statement. This was McNicholas's position also when he wrote to then-Morrissey manager Merck Mercuriadis in advance of the article's publication to advise him that Morrissey's comments had forced *NME* to shift the focus of the interview. McNicholas writes, "While Morrissey is obviously entirely entitled to his point of view we're not beholden to re-print them without comment. And given that his views are not those that we'd normally expect to come from someone in the very liberal world of rock'n'roll, we're not able to either support them or print them without comment" (*True To You: A Morrissey Zine* 2007).

Restrictionist immigration policies may have become de rigueur for contemporary conservative and centrist (and even leftist) politicians; in the world of indie, emerging as it does from an alternative and post-punk environment, such a sentiment remains, as I have argued above, antithetical to the entire project. A conservative position on immigration is not anti-Thatcher; it is *essential* Thatcherism. "The election of Mrs. Thatcher as leader of the Conservative Party in 1975 marked the beginning of the present strongly Restrictionist period in Conservative immigration policy. Mrs. Thatcher was sympathetic to [Enoch] Powell's views" (Cornelius et al. 1994: 286).

In addition to the threatened legal action, Morrissey, through Mercuriadis, sought to make an issue out of the *NME*'s interviewer, Tim Jonze's request to have his name removed from the article (which is why the attribution is joint between Jonze and *NME*; Jonze is credited with the interview, *NME* with the story). The allegation from Mercuriadis was that Jonze himself was bothered by the allegations in the piece. This interpretation was rejected unequivocally by Jonze in a *Guardian* blog post in which he claims the opposite; he asked his name to be removed because he did not think the article took a strong enough position *against* Morrissey's comments on immigration (Jonze 2007). Jonze writes, "If Morrissey holds these opinions he should either be sticking to his guns and standing by them or – more honourably – educating himself on race issues, realising why his comments were both offensive and inflammatory, and apologising for them as quickly as is humanly possible" (Jonze 2007).

Morrissey did no such thing; what he did do was issue a blog post (also through *The Guardian*) of his own in which he apologized for nothing, except for speaking to the *NME*, and then made a predictable "some of my favourite artists/singers are/were/(might someday become) black/brown" defence before a series of digressive lamentations about the state of music journalism (Morrissey 2007). Then, months later, he resorted again to his solicitors.

The Word, a British monthly music magazine, published a review of Morrissey's 2008 *Greatest Hits* album (Decca), in which the reviewer criticized Morrissey along the same lines I have outlined, only using much more aggressive language. The review concludes:

> Never mind that as the child of an immigration parent he really should know better than to attack immigration […] For his waving of the flag […] for his ingrained habit of paying lip service to anti-racism while talking like an old Tory immigration spokesman, and for his abandonment of everything that made The Smiths a band for outsiders, Morrissey should be ashamed of himself. Sadly, he never will be.
>
> (Quantick 2008: 93)

Morrissey sued *The Word* magazine on the grounds that the above paragraph could be construed to suggest he was a racist, or held racist opinions, or was "a hypocrite" (*True To You: A Morrissey Zine* 2008). Morrissey won the case since, the court argued, the complaint against the *NME* was still being pursued and, as such, *The Word* might have been repeating material which could still be ruled libellous. *The Word* apologized. Morrissey responded, "The NME have calculatedly tried to damage my integrity and to label me as a racist in order to boost their diminishing circulation" (*True To You: A Morrissey Zine* 2008).

I would argue that Morrissey's victory could be seen as the predictable victory of the tyrant with a superior economic advantage. Billy Bragg, long-time admirer of Morrissey as "the most articulate pop star of the past 25 years", makes the same point:

> From a man whose whole career has been based on the articulation of sensitivity and victimhood, this is more than just heavy-handedness. Any court case will only result in his questionable assertions on immigration being aired anew – something you'd imagine he'd want to avoid. He may hope, in going to law, to shut the *NME* up, wait until the fuss dies down and quietly withdraw the writ. But that has been the tactic down the ages of those wealthy folk who are self-centred enough to believe that they are above criticism.
>
> (Bragg 2007)

Bragg proved prescient, although not in the exact consequence he predicted.

Close upon the heels of the 2007 *NME* controversy Morrissey started a new furore when he announced his decision to play at the Heatwave Festival in Tel Aviv, Israel on 29th July, 2008. This despite the artistic boycott currently in place and supported by such traditional allies of post punk as Bono and British filmmaker Ken Loach, not to mention Desmond Tutu. How did the Palestinian Campaign for the Academic and Cultural Boycott of Israel respond to his decision? The organization used Morrissey's own words, taken from Morrissey's *Guardian* blog in response to the *NME* interview, to point out the hypocrisy they see in Morrissey's decision to play in Israel:

> "I abhor racism and oppression or cruelty of any kind and will not let this pass without being absolutely clear and emphatic with regard to what my position is. Racism is beyond common sense and I believe it has no place in our society." It is "absolutely clear" that your performance in Israel would betray a regrettable double standard, if not a categorical negation of those noble ideals.
>
> (Palestinian Campaign for the Academic and Cultural Boycott of Israel 2008)

This then outlines the detente between Morrissey, on one hand, and the music press, formerly allied pop stars such as Billy Bragg, and aggrieved advocacy groups on the other. However, what interests me here is the way some fans of "brand" Morrissey have responded to these events. And it is here then that the question of fandom and the methodology necessary to understand the behaviour of singular fans as collective phenomena becomes troubled.

Voyeuristic observation

Frith admits in the second chapter of *Performing Rites* that he has no way around the impasse of studying the reasons for appreciation of music or a musical artist generally, and specifically when it comes to "self-declared fans", on the grounds that their terms of judgement are "likely to be a bit peculiar". By this, Frith seems to mean that fans tend to like things produced by the subject of their fandom simply because the subject of their fandom has produced them. He considers this "extreme and obsessive" but argues that this is the nature of appreciating an artist's contributions (Frith 1996b: 48). Academics who write about fans have long struggled with the difficulty in evaluating fans who value things *excessively*. This is often the result of a desire not to criticize audiences involved in "active readings", and/or because of the perceived difficulties inherent in the fan/scholar duality.[9] However, if fanatics are defined by their irrational inability to stop emulating their admired, then the critique of individual instances of supposedly aberrant fanatic behaviour is really a critique of the admired, when the admired has engaged in behaviour or expressed opinions that seem unworthy of emulation.

I conclude by examining the tensions created in the collision between Morrissey's pernicious ambiguity around politically fraught questions and the unquestioning acceptance by those fanatics, that Morrissey's actions are invariably good. Frith gets himself out of the methodological impasse inherent in questions of fandom by resorting to what he calls "Mass-Observation", a combination of voyeuristic observation and the use of such tools as people's diaries (Frith, 1996b: 52–53). My discussion of Morrissey fandom stems from two things: my own situation as a fan, which I discuss below; and my participation on Morrissey fan communities, as both fan and voyeuristic observer.

Boon and Lomore's study of 213 Western Canadian undergraduates who experienced "strong feelings of attraction" for a mass-mediated celebrity (including one Morrissey admirer) revealed compelling evidence that celebrity fans had conclusively altered their lives in "nontrivial" ways, including the assumption of voluntary major identity transformations (Boon and Lomore 2001: 446). Despite this, when asked, most participants denied that their preferred celebrity had altered their lives in "powerful and enduring ways" (Boon and Lomore 2001: 445). Awareness among fans that intense fan–celebrity relationships are often viewed negatively (sometimes as a form of mental illness) causes savvy fans to deny or downplay the importance of such a relationship when asked to comment on it directly (particularly by a scholar, one might presume); this significant methodological problem leads Boon and Lomore to caution subsequent researchers to consider collecting data about fans from other sources, a caution that correlates with Frith's "Voyeuristic Observation" (Boon and Lomore 2001: 457–459). The study also suggests that the greater the investment in the celebrity (for instance through regular participation in fan forums, a secondary activity that follows the heavy consumption of a mass-mediated text), the greater the likelihood that fans have intentionally cultivated strong feelings of attachment towards their idol, the necessary precursor to a willingness to alter the self in order to preserve this imaginary, mediated relationship.

Admirers and apostles

> Oh, whatever he has done, I have done.
> (Morrissey/Marr, 'Suffer Little Children', 1983)

In Bracewell's introduction to Linder Sterling's *Morrissey Shot*, Howie Klein is seen to marvel at the sort of fan Morrissey had called into being: "It's like he's a guru or something" (Bracewell 1992: 1). Klein, perhaps, had been watching video footage of George Harrison in India when he chose this particular word or perhaps he was, like all of us who attended shows of this era, lost for words, since the spectacle before us, and in which we participated, seemed to lack historical precedent from the world of post-Beatles popular music. The imagery of Sterling's book, a photo essay of Morrissey's 1990 and 1991 tours, captures artistically the unique combination of mayhem and devotion summoned by Morrissey from his audiences of this era, but equally compelling evidence exists in the astonishing footage of Morrissey performing on *The Tonight Show Starring Johnny Carson* (1991), and later *The Tonight Show*

With Jay Leno (1992), where even the audio indicates an intensity, a rabidness of fervour simply present amongst no (or few) other live-to-tape North American TV audience post-The Beatles (Carson and de Cordova 1991; Leno 1992).

I suffered the crush of the pit at Morrissey's 1992 Vancouver show (the first time I had seen him perform) at the PNE forum – just four days before the Leno appearance – and spent the next 15 years describing it, without hyperbole, as not just the best concert of my life, but the defining moment of my life. I do not blame Klein, in other words, for reaching for "guru". To everyone who experienced it, the magnitude of what we experienced seemed created as a direct challenge to the power of language to represent adequately experiences that seemed to go deeper than our daily language could ever hope to express. And so we pilfered through forgotten language like the bright-eyed curious at a rummage sale, marvelling at the artefacts whose world had long since vanished: thus mania, thus guru.

But guru is not the right word. Morrissey is not, surely, an influential teacher or even a revered mentor as the *Canadian Oxford Dictionary* (2004: 627) has it. Probably Klein (cited in Bracewell 1992: 1) did not intend to suggest he was. In the common Western usage, a guru, then, is a leader in his/her field or, according to the *American Heritage Dictionary of the English Language* (2000/09) "an acknowledged and influential advocate, as of a movement or idea". We could see, perhaps, Morrissey as having been, or continuing to be, a guru for (as samples of a list that could be much longer) vegetarianism, celibacy, the importance of pop music as transformative, the enduring critical legacy of Marc Bolan and, as we have seen, for The New York Dolls, and James Dean. Yet the mania for Morrissey that Klein (cited in Bracewell 1992: 1) attempts to describe stems from none of these things in particular and would exist in the absence of any single one of them, or all of them. Which is why guru does not fit. If Morrissey advocates for any idea, that idea is called Morrissey. And such circularity, particularly in the context of a word with spiritual and religious origin, seems to preclude that particular usage. Some of Morrissey's followers, I will attempt to argue, do so not because of what he has attained or what he represents, but because he is he. The "idea" is that there is no greater idea beyond the individual as embodiment of the idea, and that as such there cannot be any greater philosophical value than loyalty at all cost. What word to use to describe such a relationship?

Reynolds, in the 1988 *Melody Maker* interview, offers "fanaticism". It is a term (at least in its shortened form "fan" as indicated in the Pye quote) considered previously and rejected by Morrissey (Reynolds 1990: 15). Morrissey's rejection of fan seems to stem from the commonness for which the abbreviated form of the noun is used to express a casual and fleeting appreciation, even with an adjectival modifier, for any sort of whim or fancy: big fan of cheese; big fan of Britney. The word "fan" does seem to have become exhausted, through abbreviation, of its originary meaning. Yet "fanatic" whether or not Morrissey agrees is the correct word to describe the group of fans who excessively model their attitudes and behaviour according to Morrissey's example.

If we place the casual fan (as discussed above) at one end of the continuum, we might place apostles in the centre, and fanatics on the other end. The concept of fandom occurring along a continuum appears also in the work of Chia and Poo (2009), in their study of adolescent

Singaporean fans of mass-mediated celebrities. Drawing upon Burke's (1969) identification theory, and the 2002 Celebrity Attitude Scale (CAS), developed by McCutcheon et al. (2002), Chia and Poo suggest that the intensity of fan identification with celebrities may be separated into three categories. Fans seeking either a way to belong socially or an escape from reality have *entertainment social-values* met through celebrity identification. More intensely, some fans develop *intense personal feelings* towards the admired celebrity. At this stage "fervent admiration often translates into aspirations to look, behave, or even think like the celebrities" (Chia and Poo 2009: 25). Finally, some fans develop *borderline pathological* tendencies where they may find it difficult to imagine life without the relationship they have developed with the mass-mediated figure (Chia and Poo 2009: 23–26).

Morrissey seems to use "apostle" when "fanatic" is the sort of fan he means to describe (Pye 1984).[10] It is an interesting semantic distinction from Morrissey in that it is an indication of preference for one term used to signify religious or spiritual devotion of intensity over another term used to signify religious or spiritual devotion of intensity. Moreover, it is a preference for a Christian term over a Pagan one; the Latin root of fan is fanaticus, a person who, as an adherent of a fanum, the Latin word for temple, is prone to frenzy, caused by an overabundance of zeal caused by, or as expression of devotion to, whichever god is getting his or her dues at that particular fanum (Merriam-Webster 1991: 169; Jenkins 2006: 17). As an indicator of a greater level of commitment implied by the casual use of "fan", the word apostle is an improvement. In every other respect, it is not.[11]

In common usage, an apostle continues to carry the dominant religious meaning, that is – messenger of Christ. Difficult to detach from the modifying quantifier "12", the designation "apostle" represents a promotion from the broader ranks of disciples, a word defined as learners or students. To become an apostle, then, meant you had learned all you needed to know about Christ and his teachings, and were capable of representing these knowledgeably, maybe not as comprehensively as Christ, but as an expert on the subject.

Not one of the 12, but more famous than any of them or any of the subsequent apostles, Paul in Athens, throwing down with the Epicureans and the Stoics, provides us with the clearest behavioural expectation of an apostle, versus a fanatic.[12] Paul in Athens was able to engage in rational discourse about why he thought the Athenians' gods were false, and why his God represented a better *rational* choice. That is *apostledom*. *Fanatics* in Athens would have defended their God the way football hooligans stereotypically defend their team's honour: with fists and threats of fists, and a complete inability to ever imagine switching teams. Morrissey may have apostles as well, but what he seems, particularly as a solo artist, to have cultivated more of is fanatics.

The sycophantic slags all say

Morrissey ends the song 'The Harsh Truth Of The Camera Eye' with a stanza in quotations. The song, a plaintive plea from a photographer's subject, contains a sentiment that, no doubt, most humans share:

Oh, I don't want
to be judged anymore
I don't want to be judged
I would sooner be Loved
I would sooner be
just blindly Loved.

(Morrissey/Nevin, 'The Harsh Truth
Of The Camera Eye', 1991)

Taken in context with Morrissey's own invocation of his fans as apostles (in the sense he intended it: as uncritical followers), there is a clear preference for, and concomitant creation of, a type of fan – the fanatic – willing to accept and defend any position adapted by Morrissey, even when the position runs contrary to the goals and values of the movement from which Morrissey, as lead singer of The Smiths, emerged and even when these beliefs and positions contradict beliefs and positions adapted previously by Morrissey himself. Dislike of reprimand and reproof might, one could speculate, be universal. However, there are few historic examples of the decision by a leader to surround himself or herself with acolytes unwilling to offer critique or engage in philosophic debate being regarded as illustratively wise.

When we return to the two imbricated public positions adapted by Morrissey – the renewed controversy over Morrissey's positions on British immigration, as it played out in lawsuits against the *NME* and *The Word Magazine* in late 2007, and Morrissey's decision to play Israel in 2008, despite an international artistic boycott of that state – we see that many fans have responded to Morrissey not as rational actors, or as apostles, but, rather, as fanatics. The move from fan to fanatic is often marked through the display of this irrational over-identification (Chia and Poo 2009: 25).[13]

I have been attempting to argue that the position of fanatic is unsound, grounded as it is in irrationality that manifests itself as support for a movement, a cause or a person, even when the values originally symbolized have shifted. Boon and Lomore (2001: 433) found that admirers of mass-mediated celebrities often measured their own self-worth according to how closely their behaviour and attitudes remained modelled on their admired celebrities. The research "strongly suggests that this perceived affinity between admirer and idol promotes important attitudinal and behavioral changes on the part of the admirer that may, in turn, increase the admirer's perceptions that the idol has affected his or her identity and feelings of self-worth" (Boon and Lomore 2001: 434). Once a fan (anywhere along the continuum) begins to change his or her attitudes and behaviour to emulate the admired, it becomes difficult to resist perceived subsequent necessary change. If we may speculate that "fanaticism" correlates roughly with Chia and Poo's (2009: 25) third, and most extreme, degree of fandom, the borderline pathological, we see that selective behavioural and attitudinal change (contrary to Morrissey's own opinion, or any rational criticism of the behaviour of the admired) becomes difficult, if not impossible, because such fans "are perceived to have lost control of their thoughts and to be irrational".

It should be obvious that all fans, irrespective of their position along the continuum, by definition, tend in the main to support Morrissey on most matters uncontroversial and appreciate his music, irrespective of what non-fans think. It is when Morrissey finds himself representing positions antithetical to previous positions (as a Smith) and more broadly definitive indie positions (as McNicholas states above) that observation (voyeuristic, a la Frith) bears fruit. The understood definition of "fanatic" implies a desire to achieve universal consistency with the admired's attitudes and behaviour. When the positions of Morrissey are controversial, the support of the "true" fan(atic) remains. Fans and apostles retain control over their admiration. They are able to appreciate Morrissey for a host of different reasons while refusing to emulate him blindly. They do not hesitate to criticize him when his behaviour or utterances seem to warrant it. The fanatic cannot, literally, make such a distinction. I have chosen to focus on the perceived anti-immigration remarks from the 2007 *NME* interview and the Israel boycott because, in both instances, Morrissey's behaviour and attitudes were, as I have documented, roundly criticized in virtually all sources reporting on them; it was only on Morrissey-solo.com where a concerted, and extremely vitriolic, defence from the fanatics I have been discussing could be found. The threads at Morrissey-solo.com documenting the Israel boycott story are illustrative, typical and, I would argue, entirely consistent with the discourse of such fanatics elsewhere on the site in response to any news item perceived as hostile to, or critical of, Morrissey.[14]

This is the first exchange (all posts are unedited) (discussion forum at Morrissey-solo. com, initiated by Tseng 2008).[15]

> Honestly [...] who cares.
>
> Anonymous

To which another anonymous responds: "i bet you're a us citizen, aren't you??? oh god, please help us from the ignorance and insensitivity of some people [...] How times have changed and how moz fanbase has changed over the last years."

Later on yet another anonymous responds: "This is so ridiculous. I think everyone forgets that this is about the music. Stop making it about everything else."

The debate proceeds along similar lines. The occasional critique of Morrissey, based in an observation that Morrissey's decision seems like a contradiction of his previous positions, and, in any case, is in terribly poor form for someone to whom progressive, political beliefs are often ascribed, is met by a series of attacks, either formed by vitriol or indifference or some combination of both. For instance, yet another anonymous writes, "What a bunch of crap. Sorry to say this, but muslims [*sic*] are not usually known for their love of culture, and I don't mean moderate muslims [*sic*], I mean all the assholes who scream FATWA everytime someone dares to question their blind faith. I'm sick of this crap. "

And later, from a poster who uses the name "Mozkateer" "Go MORRISSEY, Go!!!!!!!!!!! What Israel's people celibrate [*sic*] is the 60th anniversary of their return from exile [*sic*]. Palestine is not, nor has ever been a state – merely a large gang of squatters which once resided on property they did not own. – The Mozkateer" (Tseng 2008).

Conclusions

Ce qu'il y a de certain c'est que moi, je ne suis pas Marxiste.
(Karl Marx, cited in Kemple 1995: 1)

Unwelcome actions or utterances by misguided, ill-informed and rash followers under the banner/guise of fidelity to a person or for a cause would hardly be without precedent. Yet if the nature of the fanatic is to emulate as much as possible the admired, there must be evidence of a misunderstanding before we can dismiss the behaviour of fanatics as unrelated to the behaviour of the admired. Fanatics serve as a sort of mirror. They are unable to prevent themselves from doing exactly as they imagine their admired would do, or has done already. In the emulative behaviour of Morrissey's extreme fanatics, we find, then, indicators of what those most obsessed by him believe him to signify culturally. Until Morrissey has endeavoured to explain at which point his fanatics have misunderstood him, he cannot, unlike Marx, distance himself from the critical corruptions of these followers. Silencing critics and dissenters with a heavy hand, not deigning to respond to reasonable critiques from within the community – as this chapter has argued, this behaviour now, regrettably, seems to represent Morrissey with great accuracy. Many fanatics may mistake this intolerance as the highest proof of their devotion. It is not. Any point on the continuum that attempts to reduce or remove the reciprocal exchange of reasonable views and interpretations (between fellow fans of the community, and also the admired public figure directly) must be regarded as the beginning of a degradation.

As we have seen, some of Morrissey's public positions have been reasonably interpreted by a range of public figures (scholars, fellow musicians, music journalists), many of whom, including myself, self identify (or did so formerly) as fervent Morrissey admirers, as antithetical to the established position of Morrissey of The Smiths, and to the broader world of "indie" popular music. At the very least, Morrissey should encourage the discussion his comments have provoked. Using his solicitors to silence debate threatens to silence also the sort of fan/apostle who still wants to appreciate Morrissey's artistic contributions, but who, out of a more reasoned version of admiration, wants to ponder publicly the contradictions. No one is asking Morrissey to be consistent on the grounds that Oscar Wilde, another to whom Morrissey gave his fandom, was correct when he wrote, "Consistency is the last refuge of the unimaginative" (Wilde 1996: 40). But Wilde never said anything about valorizing the bully, which is the category to which Morrissey and these fanatics seem to run, too often. Between "fanatics", who support every controversial statement blindly and "apostles", who support him because no one has ever expressed or embodied the hope for a better world more brilliantly, there really ought not to be a choice. Perhaps Morrissey could reflect upon what many of the fanatics, brought into being through his own discourse, do and say, and what they understand him to mean. Yes, this represents change. Is it the change Morrissey intended when he said music could change the world?

Epilogue

> You are sleeping. You do not want to believe.
>
> (Morrissey/Marr, 'Rubber Ring' 1987)

While the manuscript for this book was under review, Morrissey remarked to Simon Armitage, who was interviewing him for *The Guardian*, that "You can't help but feel that the Chinese are a subspecies" (Armitage 2010: n.p.). More inflammatory, offensive and crude than any of Morrissey's previous utterances, many commentators speculated that, for once, the singer had painted himself into a corner from which no legion of fans could possibly extricate him. "What are the apologists going to say this time? It looks like in his old age Morrissey has forgotten to include the ambiguity, like he has done in the past. Maybe he just doesn't care anymore", music journalist Simon Price told *The Guardian* (Topping 2010: n.p.).

It was lost on no one, critics and fanatics alike, that Morrissey's comment was in condemnation of China's alleged appalling animal rights record. Morrissey's self-defense rested entirely on the re-emphasis of this worthy point. "If anyone has seen the horrific and unwatchable footage of the Chinese cat and dog trade – animals skinned alive – then they could not possibly argue in favour of China as a caring nation. There are no animal protection laws in China and this results in the worst animal abuse and cruelty on the planet. It is indefensible" (Contactmusic 2010: n.p.). That the cause of animal rights has in Morrissey a keen and tireless advocate is without question. But the logical leap from outrage on behalf of defenceless animals to the labelling of more than a billion people – millions of whom, one presumes, have never harmed an animal, and are as appalled at animal cruelty as is Morrissey – as categorically inferior is, while breathless in its audacity, a rational impossibility; it requires, at minimum, wilful ignorance of the seemingly self-evident rudimentary logical fallacy at the heart of his outburst.

For Martin Smith, British organizer of Love Music Hate Racism, an organization that has previously accepted $44,000 in donation from Morrissey, the "Chinese subspecies" incident was a bridge too far.

> But this time … you know, everyone's entitled to be wrong or change their mind once. I think the problem we've got with Morrissey is that he's done it several times.
>
> I don't believe it's a mistake. I think it's conscious, and I think he's gone too far. In our organization, some of the bands have already met and talked about it, and we don't want to be associated with him. We feel it's not helpful to anybody […] "Subhuman" is crude racism, to put it mildly. If someone like Adolf Hitler said that, you'd talk about biological racism, which everyone knows is genocidal. So I feel he's really crossed the Rubicon on it really.
>
> (Billet 2010: n.p.)

Despite the egregiousness of Morrissey's comment, condemnation was not as swift or as pervasive as it has been for the 2007 *NME* remarks. As Price and Smith both observe, there is no equivocation in the remark – no possible rational defense for it exists, and no apology could ever fully reverse the blight. The relative lack of outrage serves, then, as a useful benchmark of Morrissey's reputation; the 2007 controversy shocked the dwindling portion of the public that still concerns itself with Morrissey. We wanted to be wrong about what we knew was not right. The publication of Armitage's interview removed whatever vestigial plausible deniability remained. It seemed to confirm what many of his dearest fans tacitly understood. Morrissey flirting with racism was no longer particularly newsworthy in 2010; it is de rigeur when discussing him now, as much a part of his legacy as gladioli and a quiff.

At Morrissey-solo.com, of course, the subspecies comment, although vigorously discussed, hardly seemed to make a dent in Morrissey's reputation (Tito 2010: 1–8). Predictably, a rash of Morrissey fanatics emerged as heretofore closeted anti-Chinese racists. The dissenting voices of reasoning admirers, so prevalent during the 2007 controversy, were reduced and muted, as though a generation of admirers had simply thrown up its hands and walked away, finally willing to relinquish Morrissey to the fanatics he has cultivated. A user posting under the name "Cornflakes" summarizes the tone of the discussion: "It's a good job Morrissey has racist fans who are able to explain why it's not racist to be racist, otherwise where would he be" (Tito 2010: 2)?

Fair question, Cornflakes.

Notes

1. I am indebted to the editors of this book for suggesting the exploration of fandom occurring along a continuum.
2. From *Melody Maker* in 1975 (6th September). "Aerosmith are one of those American dance-a-rama scenic bands with enough punch to see the Stones on pensions and enough make-up to last them through the winter. Their music is that of a confused struggle, with vocalist Steven Tyler sounding as though he is using the microphone to brush his teeth. They are as original as a bar of soap and have as much to offer Seventies rock as Ena Sharples. Aerosmith are just another street-corner rock 'n' roll band, using notorious Zeppelin riffs in an effort to steal our love and devotion. But when one ruminates over the fact that 'Toys In The Attic' is the band's THIRD album ! Thanks, but no thanks, Aerosmith. I'll stick with the New York Dolls for my rock 'n' thrills. – Steve Morrissey, Kings Road, Stretford, Manchester."
3. Perhaps Jonathan Sterne states most clearly the foundational and motivational ethos of cultural studies: "If you don't believe in social transformation then we have little to discuss – and frankly I have no idea why you'd want to do cultural studies. But if you believe that societies have radically changed over the past few centuries or eons, perhaps you believe they can change again. If this be the case, then it is worthwhile to think about what kind of world we should want to live in" (Sterne 2005: 99).
4. The impulse to divide fans of mass-mediated texts into "good" fans and "bad" fans along moral and political lines remains, although problematic, central to critical cultural studies. Fan communities

that retain or develop politically resistant, Marxist discourses remain valorized; fan communities that display apolitical tendencies or worse tend to be pathologized. Studies of fandom that try to avoid this binary by resisting judgement are themselves critiqued for evading the core critical principle of cultural studies, as expressed by Sterne above. See especially the conversation between Matt Hills and Henry Jenkins (Jenkins 2006: 9–12), Hills (2002) and Staiger (2000: 43–60).

5. The most provocative examination of Morrissey's sexuality may be found in Hubbs (1996).

6. On the particular question of racism, see especially Zuberi (2002); see also Mark Simpson (2003/05), particularly pp. 160–170; for a round-up of mass-mediated discussions of the 2007 controversy, see the forums at Morrissey-solo (Kewpie 2007).

7. The intensity of Morrissey's devotion to James Dean, for instance, is captured here: "I had a very small bedroom and I remember going through periods when I was 18 or 19 where I literally would not leave it for three to four weeks. I would be in there day after day, the sun would be blazingly hot and I'd have the curtains drawn. I'd be sitting there in near darkness alone with the typewriter and surrounded by masses of paper. The walls were totally bespattered with James Dean, almost to the point of claustrophobia" (Van Poznack 1984: n.p.).

8. McNicholas resigned as editor of *NME* in 2009 (Luft 2009).

9. See Fiske (1987: 62–83) for a discussion of active audiences and their polysemic readings of mediated texts. See Hills (2002: 1–24) and Jenkins (2006: 13–15) on the fan/scholar/intellectual role.

10. The Pye interview contains, as far as I have been able to ascertain, the earliest use of the term "apostles" by Morrissey: "I get terribly embarrassed when I meet Smiths apostles – I hate the word fan. They seem to expect so much of me. Many of them see me as some kind of religious character who can solve all their problems with a wave of a syllable" (Pye 1984).

11. Morrissey invites the religious comparison through his insistence on the term "apostles" but, in any case, discussions of fervent fandom tend typically to compare the degree of fan fervour to religious or spiritual devotion. On whether it is pathologizing to compare fans of mass-mediated texts to religious devotees, see Jenkins (2006: 16–23). On the usefulness (and problems of) of religious comparisons to fans of some mass-mediated, cultic figures, see Frow (1998: 197–210); and Duffett (2003: 513–522).

12. For more on Paul in Athens, see Piettre (2005).

13. Chia and Poo base their methodology here in part on the work of McCutcheon et al. (2002: 25), in particular their "absorption-addiction" model.

14. The first discussion forum responding to Quantick's 2008 review in *The Word* is itself illustrative of the way Morrissey fanatics defend their admired. There is some very reasoned discussion of the article; many fans/apostles suggest Quantick was right to criticize Morrissey's stance on immigration, observe that he is a credible and funny journalist who has previously reviewed Morrissey favourably, and suggest Morrissey's *NME* interview is indefensible. Interspersed with these however are an array of offensive comments.

15. Founded by David Tseng in 1997, the Morrissey-solo fan website operates as the central repository for discussions of everything regarding Morrissey. Through his "official" site, true-to-you.net (founded as another fan site, but now used by Morrissey to issue statements), Morrissey has referred to Morrissey-solo as "MorrisseySoLow", apparently in an attempt to distance himself from the content posted there. Morrissey's use of this term provoked, perhaps, one of the more serious fan outcries against him, many regular visitors to Morrissey-solo pointing out that much of Morrissey's contemporary success is attributable to Tseng, who, in no small measure, grew Morrissey's fanbase for him, particularly as the site's popularity coincided with Morrissey's commercial nadir, between 1997 and 2003, when the singer had no record deal (Sistasheila 2009).

References

Adorno, T. (2002) *Essays on Music*. Berkeley and Los Angeles: California, University of California Press.

Armitage, S. (2010) 'Morrissey interview: big mouth strikes again', *The Guardian*, 3rd September, available: *http: //www.guardian.co.uk/music/2010/sep/03/morrissey-simon-armitage-interview*.

Barber, L. (2002) 'The man with the thorn in his side', *The Observer*, 15th September, available: *http: //www.observer.co.uk/magazine/story/0,11913,792189,00.html*.

Billet, A. (2010) 'A clarion call for the movement', *Socialist Worker.org*, 17th September, available: *http: //socialistworker.org/2010/09/17/clarion-call-for-the-movement*.

Bloch, E. (1988) *The Utopian Function of Art and Literature: Selected Essays*. Cambridge, MA and London: The MIT Press.

Boon, S. D. and Lomore, C. D. (2001) 'Admirer–celebrity relationships among young adults: explaining perceptions of celebrity influence on identity', *Human Communication Research*, 27: 3, July, pp. 432–465.

Bracewell, M. (1992) 'Introduction', in L. Sterling *Morrissey Shot*. New York: Hyperion.

Bragg, B. (2007) 'Bigmouth was better', *The Guardian*, 12th December, available: *http: //www.guardian. co.uk/commentisfree/2007/dec/12/comment.music*.

Bumiller, E. (2006) 'An outspoken conservative loses his place at the table', *New York Times*, 13th February, available: *http: //www.nytimes.com/2006/02/13/politics/13letter.html?_r=1&adxnnl=1&adxnnlx= 1204844849-B5Bx4JCMyUM04ViG6FjWLQ*.

Burke, K. (1969) *A Rhetoric of Motives*. Berkeley: University of California Press.

Carson, J. (Writer) and de Cordova, F. (Director) (1991) 'The Tonight Show Starring Johnny Carson' (Television series episode), in F. de Cordova (Executive Producer) *The Tonight Show Starring Johnny Carson*. New York: National Broadcasting Company, 14th June.

Chia, S. C. and Poo, Y. L. (2009) 'Media, celebrities, and fans: an examination of adolescents' media usage and involvement with entertainment celebrities', *Journalism and Mass Communication Quarterly*, 86: 1, Spring, pp. 23–44.

Contactmusic.com (2010) 'Morrissey – Morrissey Won't Retract "Subspecies" Remark', 6th September, available: *http: //www.contactmusic.com/news.nsf/story/morrissey-wont-retract-subspecies-remark_1163838*.

Cornelius, W. A., Martin, P. L. and Hollifield, J. F. (1994) *Controlling Immigration: A Global Perspective*. Stanford: Stanford University Press.

Dorey, P. (1995) *British Politics Since 1945 (Making Contemporary Britain)*. Oxford and Malden, MA: Blackwell.

Duffett, M. (2003) 'False faith or false comparison? a critique of the religious interpretation of Elvis fan culture', *Popular Music and Society*, 26: 4, pp. 513–522.

'Fanatic', in Merriam-Webster Inc, *The Merriam-Webster New Book of Word Histories*. United States: Merriam-Webster, p. 169.

Fiske, J. (1987) *Television Culture*. London: Routledge.

Frith, S. (1996a) 'Music and identity', in S. Hall and P. du Gay (eds) *Questions of Cultural Identity*. London: Sage, pp. 108–127.

Frith, S. (1996b) *Performing Rites: On The Value of Popular Music*. Cambridge, MA: Harvard University Press.

Frow, J. (1998) 'Is Elvis a God? cult, culture, questions of method', *International Journal of Cultural Studies*, 1: 2, pp. 197–210.

Gallagher, T., Campbell, M. and Gillies, M. (1995) *The Smiths; All Men Have Secrets*. London: Virgin.

Grossberg, L. (1992) 'Is there a fan in the house?: The affective sensibility of fandom', in L. A. Lewis (ed.) *The Adoring Audience: Fan Culture and Popular Media*. London and New York: Routledge, pp. 50–68.

'Guru', in K. Barber (ed.) (1998) Canadian Oxford Dictionary. Don Mills, ON: Oxford University Press, p. 627.

'Guru', in *American Heritage Dictionary of the English Language, Fourth Edition* (2000/09), available: *http: //www.thefreedictionary.com/guru*.

Hills, M. (2002) *Fan Cultures*. London: Routledge.

Hubbs, N. (1996) 'Music of the "fourth gender": Morrissey and the sexual politics of melodic contour', in T. Foster, C. Siegel and E. Berry (eds) *Bodies of Writing, Bodies in Performance*. New York: New York University Press, pp. 266–296.

Jenkins, H. (2006) *Fans, Bloggers, and Gamers: Exploring Participatory Culture*. New York and London: New York University Press.

Jonze, T. and *NME* (2007) 'Bigmouth strikes again', *NME*, 27th November.

Jonze, T. (2007) 'Morrissey, *NME* and me', *The Guardian*, 30th November, available: *http: //www. guardian.co.uk/commentisfree/2007/nov/30/timjonze*.

Kelly, D., Martin G. and S. Maconie (1992) 'This alarming man', *New Musical Express*, 22nd August, available: *http: //motorcycleaupairboy.com/interviews/1992/caucasian.htm*.

Kemple, T. M. (1995) *Reading Marx Writing: Melodrama, The Market, and The 'Grundrisse'*. Stanford: Stanford University Press.

Kewpie (2007) 'The Official *NME* Story Coverage Thread' (Msg 1), 29th November, message posted to: *http: //forums.morrissey-solo.com/showthread.php?t=80869&highlight=conor*.

Klein, N. (2000) 'The tyranny of the brands', *New Statesman*, 24th January, pp. 25–28.

Leno, J. (Host) (1992) 'The Tonight Show with Jay Leno' (Television series episode), in H. Kushnick (Executive Producer) *The Tonight Show with Jay Leno*.New York: National Broadcasting Company, 9th October.

Luft, O. (2009) '*Top Gear* appoints *NME*'s Conor McNicholas as editor', *The Guardian*, 24th June, available: http: //www.guardian.co.uk/media/2009/jun/24/top-gear-nme-conor-mcnicholas.

Maurice E. (2008) 'new Word Magazine; perhaps most vicious attack ever on Moz (in Greatest Hits review)', 13th February, messages posted to *http: //forums.morrissey-solo.com/showthread.php?t=8 3955&highlight=quantick*.

McCutcheon, L. E., Lange, R. and Houran, J. (2002) 'Conceptualization and measurement of celebrity worship', *British Journal of Psychology*, 93: 1, pp. 67–87.

Morrissey, S. (1983) *James Dean is Not Dead*. London: Babylon.

Morrissey, S. and Marr, J. 'Suffer Little Children', *The Smiths*. London: Rough Trade.

Morrissey, S and Marr, J. (1986) 'Frankly, Mr. Shankly', *The Queen is Dead*. New York: Sire Records.

Morrissey, S. and Nevin, M. E. (1991) 'The Harsh Truth Of The Camera Eye', *Kill Uncle*. Maidenhead, UK: HMV.

Morrissey, S. and Whyte, A. (1992) 'The National Front Disco', *Your Arsenal*. Maidenhead, UK: HMV.

Morrissey (2007) 'I abhor racism and apologise – for speaking to the *NME*', *The Guardian*, 4th December, available: *http: //www.guardian.co.uk/music/musicblog/2007/dec04/morrisseyresponds*.

Palestinian Campaign for the Academic and Cultural Boycott of Israel (2008) 'Morrissey: celebrating Apartheid in Tel Aviv? An open letter from PACBI', *The Palestinian Campaign for the Academic and Cultural Boycott of Israel*, 15th April, available: *http: //www.pacbi.org/etemplate.php?id=715*.

Piettre, R. (2005) 'Paul and the Athens Epicureans: between polytheisms, atheisms and monotheisms', *Diogenes*, 52: 1, pp. 47–60.

Powell, E. (1968) 'Rivers of Blood', speech presented at Conservative Association Meeting, Birmingham, UK, 20th April, available: *http: //www.telegraph.co.uk/comment/3643823/Enoch-Powells-Rivers-of-Blood-Speech.html*.

Pye, I. (1984) 'A hard day's misery', *Melody Maker*, 3rd November, available: *http: //foreverill.com/interviews/1984/misery.htm*.

Quantick, D. (2008) 'The King is Dead', *The Word*, March, pp. 92–93, available: *http: //forums.morrissey-solo.com/showpost.php?p=783644&postcount=50*.

Reynolds, S. (1990) *Blissed Out*. London: Serpent's Tail.

Simpson, D. (2007) 'Morrissey vs *NME*: Mozgate Part II', *The Guardian*, 27th November, available: *http: //www.guardian.co.uk/music/musicblog/2007/nov/28/mozgate*.

Simpson, M. (2003/05) *Saint Morrissey*. New York: Touchstone.

Sistasheila (2009) 'Statement from Morrissey – true-to-you.net', 14th July, available: *http: //www.morrissey-solo.com/article.pl?sid=09/07/14/151241*. ·

Snowsell C. (2002) '"My Only Mistake is I'm Hoping": Monty, Morrissey and mediatized utopia', Master's Thesis, Graduate Program in Communication Studies, Calgary: University of Calgary.

Staiger, J. (2000) *Perverse Spectators: The Practices of Film Reception*. New York and London: New York University Press.

Sterling, L. (1992) *Morrissey Shot*. New York: Hyperion.

Sterne, J. (2005) 'The burden of culture', in M. Bérubé (ed.) *The Aesthetics of Cultural Studies*. Malden, MA and Oxford: Blackwell Publishing, pp. 80–102.

Tito (2010) 'with Morrissey fans supporting Morrissey's racist remarks' (Msg 31), 6th September, message posted to: *http: //forums.morrissey-solo.com/showthread.php?t=110828&highlight=subspecies&page=2*.

True To You (2007) 'Morrissey vs. the *NME*', *True To You a Morrissey zine*, 27th November, available: *http: //true-to-you.net/morrissey_news_071127_01*.

True To You (2008) 'Morrissey court victory', *True To You a Morrissey zine*, 3rd April, available: *http: //true-to-you.net/morrissey_news_080403_01*.

Tseng, D. (2008) 'Palestinians call on Morrissey to boycott Israel', 16th April, messages posted to: *http: //www.morrissey-solo.com/article.pl?sid=08/04/16/1534234*.

Van Poznack, E. (1984) 'Morrissey: The Face interview', *The Face*, July, available: *http: //foreverill.com/interviews/1984/mozface.htm*.

West, M. (ed.) (1985) *The Smiths in Quotes*. Todmorden, Lancs: Babylon.

Wilde, O. and Beckson, K. (eds) (1996) *I Can Resist Everything Except Temptation: And Other Quotations from Oscar Wilde*. New York: Columbia University Press.

Worral, F. (1983) 'The cradle snatchers', *Melody Maker*, 3rd September, available: http: //www.foreverill.com/interviews/1983/cradle.htm.

Zuberi, N. (2002) '"The Last Truly British People You Will Ever Know": Skinheads, Pakis, and Morrissey', in H. Jenkins, T. McPherson and J. Shattuc (eds) *Hop on Pop*. Durham and London: Duke University Press, pp. 539–556.

Chapter 5

The "Teenage Dad" and "Slum Mums" are Just "Certain People I Know": Counter Hegemonic Representations of the Working/ Underclass in the Works of Morrissey

Martin J. Power

Introduction

The "understandable preoccupation" with Morrissey's sexuality has seen "other forms of social identity" which inform his body of work, particularly social class, being neglected to a certain extent (Coulter 2010: 160). In this chapter I examine Morrissey's representation of the working/underclass in an era where neo-liberalism and the ideology of personal responsibility have obtained a global hegemonic or dominant position. My particular interest in Morrissey's creative work lies in wider sociological debates around the continuing relevance and representations of social class. This chapter will document how Morrissey has continuously dealt with the "hidden injuries of class" that characterize contemporary society (Coulter 2005: 6). Ultimately, the chapter will demonstrate that Morrissey's work presents a counter narrative/alternative lens with which to critically examine the hegemonic neo-liberal view of the working/underclass.

The fragmentation of class structure, neo-liberalism and the emergence of class disgust

The "death of class" debate (Pakulski and Waters 1996) occurred in conjunction with the emergence of a political rhetoric of inclusion, meritocracy and social mobility, with terms like social exclusion and underclass replacing discussions centred on the working-class (Skeggs 2005: 47 cited in Tyler 2008: 20). This change occurred at a time when there was grave concern about the escalating polarization caused as a result of the "crisis of Keynesian economics", and the ensuing "neoliberal reordering of public policy" (Hayward and Yar 2006: 10). The emergence of the "New Right" ideology of personal responsibility (Dixon and Hyde 2003: 25) in the political doctrines of Thatcher and Regan was a major factor in the acceptance of neo-liberalism in public discourse. In the UK, Thatcher advocated individualism as the basis of what she styled the "Healthy Society", where the vast majority of citizens are encouraged (and where necessary compelled) to accept responsibility for the provision of their own welfare, and to live with minimal reliance on the state (Thatcher 1977: 81 cited in George and Wilding 1985: 23). One way in which this "New Right"/neo-liberal ideology became part of popular discourse was through the use of the media, where neo-liberal policies favouring the "restructuring" of the welfare state were aided by a "moral panic" (Golding and Middleton 1982; Clarke and Newman 1997).

As part of this process neo-liberal individualistic ideologies inject myths into public discourse, which are constructed as "fact". These myths stigmatize feckless members of the working-class as "undeserving" of the assistance they receive (Lens 2002: 144), consequently absolving the state, and the system of stratification resulting from global capitalism, of any responsibility (Edelman 1998: 134). The discourse of the dominant ideology of individual responsibility (Lens 2002: 137–138) is successfully communicated through key words like "welfare", "dependency" and "personal responsibility". These words act as a cognitive prompt, framing the issues of social exclusion and poverty as individual problems, and function as a linguistic reference facilitating the general public in strengthening previously held beliefs about the causes of social exclusion and those who experience it (Edelman 1998, cited in Lens 2002: 144). The construction of dependency and empowerment myths renders participation in the workforce as a "normal" empowering process (Adair 2001b: 461), stigmatizing those who do not conform as deviant "others" (Devereux 2003: 127) who choose a life of welfare dependency, and are a resultant drain on wider society (Adair 2001a: 161–62). I would argue that future generations may come to see our era as characterized by "newspeak [...] half-truths and lies" which were "used to justify policies [...] which are in opposition to established norms of morality [...] grounded in the dominant democratic ideology" (Hersh 2004: 3).

While discourse about the underclass originally resulted from the pathologizing of sections of the working-class in relation to "socially productive labour", the contemporary underclass figure of the "chav" is also pathologized in relation to patterns of consumption (Hayward and Yar 2006: 10–11). In the context of fluctuating definitions of class, the denigration of the chav should be seen as an indicator of middle-class aspirations to redefine class confines (Tyler 2008: 18). In this context middle-class representations of the chav serve to negatively stereotype them as reprehensible, shameful and disgusting (Law 2006: 28), in the process producing approval for middle-class values, and maintaining the "symbolic order" (Skeggs 2005: 970). Chavs have been constructed through reference to "crime, disease, drugs, and over-breeding", are said to lack social skills or any form of work ethic, and live mainly on local authority housing estates (Law 2006: 28). In essence they have been constructed as the antithesis of a respectable, peaceful and hard-working society, and chav culture is seen as the root of all of society's ills rather than as "a symptom of extreme social polarisation and inequality" (Law 2006: 28–29).

Media representations of the working-class

The mass media could confront hegemonic beliefs about poverty and those who experience it (Carroll and Ratner 1999 cited in Bullock et al. 2001: 243), but most often the media controls the type of information that reaches the general public, shaping and/or limiting our social knowledge and the way in which we construct our social world (McCullagh 2002: 22; see Croteau and Hoynes 2000: 214–222 for a discussion on working-class invisibility). Audiences have agency in decoding media messages (Hall 1999; Smith and Bell 2007: 82) but it is important to note that audiences are limited in their capacity to assess the accuracy of the media they consume without direct personal experience or detailed information on any issue (Bullock et al. 2001: 229–230).

The media thus operates as a powerful institution for the dissemination of ideologies and discourses (Devereux 2003: 103), which have been used to cultivate and shape national consciousness (Adair 2001b: 454) and construct the underclass as the "undeserving poor" (Golding and Middleton 1982; Lens 2002: 144; Bullock et al. 2001: 229–230; Hayward and Yar 2006: 11–12). Media portrayals of poverty are important as they impact on public opinion. If public attitudes are informed by inaccurate, ideological and stigmatizing representations of the poor, then policies preferred by the public (and political elites) are unlikely to seek to tackle the structural causes of inequality (Clawson and Trice 2000: 61). In essence, this works to ensure that the working/underclass are positioned in a top-down society created for them, and they are expected to involve themselves in that society under those prearranged social constructs (Woronzoff 2009).

Counter-hegemonic ideologies

Although (media) discourses of "undeserving poor" are hegemonic, it is important to recognize that counter-hegemonic ideologies have also emerged, though these are far fewer in number and do not penetrate into popular discourse to a similar extent. In essence a lack of access to the mechanisms of "symbolic production" has ensured there have been limited occurrences[1] of sustained critiques of "middle-class pretensions" (Skeggs 2005: 975–976). In a society where the hegemonic discourse is produced by the upper- and middle-classes, the capacity to articulate a contradictory narrative to the marginalized is aided by the "reach" of popular music (Botta 2006: 123).

Speaking early in his career Morrissey argued that "The Smiths create their world and not many people do that" (*The South Bank Show* 1987). Morrissey's work has the ability to realize people and places in a believable manner, creating innovative modalities to visualize them. He manages to do this through a process of layering "textscapes", "soundscapes" and "landscapes" into his work (Botta 2006: 123). Morrissey's "textscapes" consist of the lyrics and song titles which refer to people and places, while his "soundscape" is conveyed through the use of local dialect, accent or sounds. Lastly, the "landscape" is portrayed through visual elements such as his covers, posters, photographs, videos and stage backdrops etc., which may reflect a particular place, individual or way of life, often a valorized/iconic form of (white) working-class identity (Botta 2006: 123).

Characters in Morrissey's lyrics are often people that are trapped in a humanity that is imposed upon them (Woronzoff 2009). Yet, his work offers the opportunity for a negotiated reading of such texts. Morrissey's friend Linder states that as a result of the ambiguity present in his work "you are never quite sure who he is singing to or who he is singing about [...] so therefore whoever you are when you listen to the songs you can interpret them to fit your life" (*The South Bank Show* 1987). Additionally, the writer Zoe Williams believes that his music allows "you [to] make the connection on your own and having made the connection on your own gives you a sense of belonging, it makes you think there is a common understanding between you and Morrissey" (*Salford Lad* 2007). Thus a negotiated reading of his "scapes" has the ability to turn Morrissey's music into an influential instrument for re-imagining people and places and assemble alternative images of the working/underclass, which ultimately work their way around the planet (Botta 2006: 123).

A proletarian hero?

Morrissey's repertoire has consistently championed working-class values. In 1986 The Smiths played in Newcastle as part of the Red Wedge[2] tour and also played in the "From Manchester With Love" benefit gig to raise money for the 49 Liverpool councillors who were taken to court by the Conservative Government (Rogan 1992: 243). He has argued "it was important to confront people [...] sometimes when you are from a working-class background you have to be overtly demonstrative in order to be heard and in order to get anywhere" (*The South Bank Show* 1987). But there are contradictions/paradoxes in Morrissey's stance on class. For example, fandom typically involves levels of conspicuous consumption, and there is a strong argument that Morrissey deliberately exploits the commercial aspect of his representations of social class.[3] Yet in spite of this legitimate argument, and even though he is now obviously a wealthy individual, Morrissey is fiercely anti-establishment, has continued in his role as a raconteur of the marginalized, and, in the process, remains a "proletarian hero to many of his fans" (Edwards 2006).

In essence Morrissey represents "the outsider, and the outsider is always political"[4] (*Girls and Boys: Sex and British Pop* 2008). This identity of a "political outsider" in part comes from his formative experiences. He was the younger child of an Irish immigrant family in Manchester, yet he was also the self-educated son of an assistant librarian, spending several of those formative years in a moderately well-to-do suburb. These autobiographical strains permeate his work in various ways (Coulter 2010: 165) and one explanation for his conflicting mix of upper-class articulation and working-class absorption, Northern values and "Little Englander" identity is his inability to fit in anywhere (Kallioniemi 1999: 308).

Speaking of his childhood he commented "I can simply remember being in very dark streets, penniless" (cited in Pye 1984). His formative experiences served as a vital source of inspiration for him, which he acknowledged in an early interview. "It was absolutely crucial to me, absolutely crucial, to go through those things and grasp the realities of life, which so very few people seem to manage" (cited in Pye 1984). Morrissey's experience of secondary school would also serve to instil a sense of class consciousness in him. He recalled

It was a very deprived school [...] total disinterest thrust on the pupils, the absolute belief that when you left you would just go down and down and down [...] There was no question of getting GCSEs [...] never mind a degree in science or something! It was just, "All you boys are hopeless cases so get used to it"

(cited in Pye 1984)

It is little wonder then that Morrissey remembers his youth as being characterized by feelings of isolation and marginalization (Woronzoff 2009). Accordingly, I would argue that Morrissey's upbringing ultimately instilled in him a desire to question the social and political order through his artistic endeavour.

Early in his career Morrissey said "I want people to enjoy the music and also to think about what's being said" (cited in Worrall 1983). Yet he has always been acutely aware that barriers exist which restrict his ability to do just that, as not only is society "dedicated to the class system [...] it's rife throughout the music industry" (cited in Pye 1984). To be a "successful" artist means blindly conforming to hegemonic discourses and ideologies and certainly not questioning the validity of the status quo (Edwards 2006). In addressing this necessity to conform, Morrissey said "it's easy to get in line all the time and to please everyone, to please the media [...] But I can't do that" (*The Culture Show* 2006). Accordingly, he spits venom at contemporary pop stars and the music industry in general in 'The World Is Full Of Crashing Bores'. He reminds us that

> It's just more lock jawed pop stars,
> Thicker than pig shit, nothing to convey,
> They're so scared to show intelligence,
> It might smear their lovely career,
> This world, I am afraid, is designed for crashing bores,
> I am not one.

Such views are unlikely to gain Morrissey many admirers in the Establishment. But Morrissey's lyrics strive to create an alternative cultural text, which documents working-class life; in doing so he re-contextualizes class and challenges the hegemonic neo-liberal political ideology. He might not make much difference in practical terms but "if people can discover literature though pop music then why not politics? Sometimes a seed needs only to be sown" (Pye 1984).

Re-imagining people and places

The UK Conservative Party (in reality New Right and staunchly neo-liberal) government of the 1980s attacked organized Labour, stressed personal responsibility, and depoliticized the working-class,[5] in the process presenting them as merely "a phenomenon of culture" (Zuberi 2001: 21). Thus "commercial popular-cultural memory" has a vital role to play in how working-class identity is "contested and negotiated" (Zuberi 2001: 21).

Thematically, Morrissey's catalogue demonstrates veneration for a simpler way of life (Arellano 2002). Much of this representation is his nostalgic remembering of an imagined working-class world. He stimulates a communal recollection of the proletarian, white, English working-class past, often in contradictory ways (Zuberi 2001: 20), conveying to us a world of the unemployed and the work-shy, usually from the perspective of an outsider trying to fit in. He articulates feelings of alienation and anomie, yet his ability/desire to acknowledge and discuss those lived realities (which are largely absent in mainstream popular culture) offer one explanation for his global appeal (Devereux 2009: 105–115). Morrissey's appeal to his Latino fans, for example, may lie in the fact that he provides a public voice which acknowledges "the injustices of a social order that confines them to the margin" and allows them the possibility of escape from "the limited identity options entrenched in peripheral, working – and middle-class culture" (Snowsell cited in Arellano 2002). In essence, these Latino fans from a "community who were seen as an underclass in the United States" seem to have found "a kindred spirit in this Northern proletarian hero" (*Salford Lad* 2007).

As the rest of this chapter will demonstrate, Morrissey continues to produce songs that critique a highly unequal and highly ideological political doctrine, which has achieved an un-questioned global hegemonic position. These acts of rebellion (no matter how small), which re-imagine people and places, serve to challenge the dominant neo-liberal discourse of the "pathological" working/underclass. In essence they should be seen as "the expression of a [...] political sensibility [...] that is appalled at living in a society that venerates the few while seeking to humiliate the many" (Coulter 2010: 168).

The de-industrialization of the North of England

When you're Northern, you're Northern for ever. You're instilled with a certain feel for life that you can't get rid of.

(Morrissey on *Later with Jools Holland* 2004)

Morrissey's representation of the working/underclass can initially be understood in the context of the de-industrialization of the North of England (Kallioniemi 1999: 312), particularly during Thatcher's period in power. Thatcher's programme incorporated a free-market economy, privatization of state-owned industries, lower direct taxation and retracting the welfare state (Bhattacharyya 2002: 63). The destruction of the traditional working-class industries in the North of England was a consequence of her government's economic policies, policies which were concerned with preserving the "relative advantage of one section of capital, explicitly political, and intended to destroy the capacity of the organised trade union movement in its citadels of power" (Byrne 1999: 65). Thatcher's policies "threatened to amputate the welfare state from the body politic" and encouraged a growing reliance on Victorian values and service provision. Her radical market-driven policies saw unemployment rates hit 3 million in 1981 (Rogan 1992: 132–133). In reality the situation in the North of England could be said to have resulted from "a prejudice against a region dominated by working-class problems" (Singer 2007: 407–409) and the decline of heavy industry which saw the North increasingly associated with bleakness, coldness, decay, social problems, working-class exploitation and a lack of hope[6] (Schmid 2007: 349; Tonnies 2007: 305).

Manchester was an urban wasteland by the late 1970s, characterized by derelict factories, boarded up warehouses and deserted office blocks.[7] But Morrissey was intent on renovating the dreary Mancunian landscape through his art (Pordzik 2007: 330–331) and took on the mantle of representing the downtrodden working-class in Thatcher's Britain (O'Donovan 2007). Morrissey's writing "epitomises the overlaying of individual messages with a broad variety of divergent bits of texts and meaning bearing patterns adapted from different realms of creative thought" (Pordzik 2007: 327; see also Brett's chapter in this volume). He successfully "photographs" the decline of the North, turning the landscape into "a poetic mirror for existential desolation and class resentments" (Zuberi 2001: 35–36). In this sense Morrissey's work constructs "representational spaces which overlay the actual physical space", and in the process transmits a strong social condemnation of Thatcherite Britain (Tonnies 2007: 307–314; see Brooker 2010 for an interesting discussion of The Smiths/Morrissey and Thatcherism).

The music of The Smiths made reference to "iron bridges", "disused railway lines" and "cemetery gates" (Botta 2006: 124) and the band were photographed posing in front of factories, smokestacks, cobbled streets and red-brick terraced houses, which have been a part of how people see Manchester going back to the descriptions of Engels[8] and Dickens (Shields 1991 and Moretti 1998 cited in Botta 2006: 123–124). An iconic image saw The Smiths photographed outside Salford Lads Club on Coronation Street[9] for the inside gatefold of *The Queen is Dead*, while the video for 'Stop Me If You Think That You've Heard This One Before' saw Morrissey and a number of his "fans" cycling through the streets of Manchester and Salford. Morrissey looks longingly at boarded up terraced houses, and shop fronts with traditional North of England surnames, in the process attempting to take ownership of the now desolate working-class landscape (Zuberi 2001: 48). In essence, The Smiths gave expression to the vacant and crumbling "temples of capitalism", vividly illustrating that when the capitalist economy goes through a period of "adjustment", unemployment rises and whole neighbourhoods are left in need of physical and social regeneration (Botta 2006: 124).

In 1987 the "Iron Lady" argued that "there is no such thing as society. There are individual men and women, and there are families. And people must look to themselves first. It's our duty to look after ourselves […] People have got the entitlements too much in mind" (Thatcher 1987). The dissemination and subsequent general acceptance of such discourse was central to the "successes" of Thatcher's neo-liberal agenda. In a perverted version of Thatcher's views on society, a good number of the pictures in British photographer Paul Graham's book *Beyond Caring* suggest that a feeling for the needs of others was a luxury that people could no longer afford in Thatcherite Britain (Tonnies 2007: 309–310). Morrissey however, refused to accept such discourse and was particularly outspoken regarding the agenda of the Thatcher administration. His abhorrence of the woman and what she represented were obvious. In an interview in 1984 he stated that the "only thing that could possibly save British politics would be Margaret Thatcher's assassin" and the "sorrow of the Brighton bombing [...] is that she (Thatcher) escaped unscathed" (cited in Pye 1984). Morrissey also used his musical canon to bombard his nemesis and four years after he lamented the inability of the IRA to assassinate her, Morrissey called on the "kind people" of the UK to do the job instead. 'Margaret On The Guillotine', the final track on his debut solo album *Viva Hate* was an obvious protests against Thatcherism. Morrissey sang of the "the kind people" having a wonderful dream of Margaret on the guillotine, and he implored his listeners not to "shelter this dream" but rather to "make the dream real". In doing so he signalled his intent to ensure that his solo career would continue to express his disgruntlement with the neo-liberal state and its resulting inequalities, in the same manner that the music of The Smiths had.

The community of the working-class

Thatcher guaranteed working-class voters' upward mobility if they deserted the trade union movement and the Labour Party, which she argued were full of obsolete principles (Zuberi 2001: 40–41). Many observers at that time spoke of "the working-class disappearing through a process of embourgoisement", yet in reality the implementation of Thatcher's policies created enormous unemployment and a new "underclass" (Zuberi 2001: 40–41). In spite of this, her "guarantee" resulted in even the disaffected voting for the Conservatives, and Thatcher's party were returned to power time and time again[10.]

Morrissey's catalogue is littered with references to the community of the working-class, and he refers to various working-class locations throughout England. He has an uncanny ability to write songs which reflect his understanding of white, Northern English, working-class life, an understanding which presents an evocative view of working-class communities (Devereux 2009: 115; Zuberi 2003: 540) and a disappearing Manchester (Pordzik 2007: 335). In the 1960s, Manchester and Salford implemented a slum clearance project, which sought to move residents to more modern housing estates, in the process destroying an entire way of life which was cherished by the likes of Morrissey and the artist L. S. Lowry (Schmid 2007: 357). Morrissey vocalized the impact of the destruction of this way of life when he stated "most of the houses I grew up in were demolished and most of the schools I attended [...] strong working-class communities were completely eradicated [...] it was almost like a political movement to completely squash the body of people" (*The South Bank Show* 1987). "The place where I grew up no longer exists apart from here in the local history library, photographic evidence [...] in a way it was like having ones childhood wiped away [...] I feel great anger, I feel great sadness. It's like a complete loss of childhood" (*Oxford Road Show* 1985).

It is hardly surprising then that Morrissey's lyrics fêted that disappearing Northern working-class identity, portraying a world characterized by kindliness, community and humility, which he believed had finally been obliterated by the policies of successive Thatcher governments (see Coulter 2010: 161). In doing so, his reminiscence and criticisms of modernity emphasize "authenticity" and particularly working-class simplicity (Cloonan 1997: 58–65 cited in Baxter-Moore 2006: 148). Morrissey's lyrics vibrantly deal with the manifold "hidden injuries of class", disaffection, indignities and humiliations that are indisputable characteristics of neo-liberal capitalist society. The Smiths produced a "cultural politics", which illustrated that there are multiple social realities and class is entirely central to them all (Coulter 2005: 5–6). This process continued in Morrissey's solo career.[11]

His "outsider" understanding of working-class tensions is honestly addressed in 'On The Streets I Ran' where Morrissey delves into the subliminal attitudes of the people on those streets. In 'Ordinary Boys' Morrissey sees working-class people as being "happy knowing nothing. Happy being no-one but themselves". In spite of them having such monotonous, thankless lives, he believes they are content with their existence because they know nothing better. This is in direct contrast to the feelings of indecision and anxiety that the narrator (Morrissey) feels, so he appears genuinely envious of them. Even his decision to record The Jam song 'That's Entertainment' is significant, as it describes the dire conditions of working/underclass life. Morrissey often does not appear to foresee a future which is anything other than the inevitable product of contemporary forces, which makes the present so hard to bear for certain groups. In such a situation, the past becomes even more appealing (Baxter–Moore 2006: 156) and may further explain the nostalgic longing for his valorized community of the Northern English, white working-class.

Celebrating working-class hardness, idleness, criminality and social indifference

In Morrissey's solo career, many of his tracks celebrate working-class hardness, idleness, criminality and social indifference (Botta 2006: 124). His descriptions imply "a gay viewpoint" on some occasions and "a straight viewpoint" on others, but "every instance is fraught with ambiguity" (Hubbs 1996: 269; see also Stringer 1992; Simpson 2004). Morrissey's sexuality is vague and open to elucidation (Brown 1991) and his fascination with hard working-class males in particular can be read as homoerotic attraction. Indeed, reading this fascination with working-class hardness from a Queer Theory perspective might well see these characters as "rough trade" (Sheppard 2003).

Hubbs (1996: 285) argues that Morrissey "chooses to explore queer themes, in the most knowledgeable 'inside' of queer-insider language", and while the message is delivered in an ambiguous manner it "is abundantly meaningful to other insiders: for queer listeners, Morrissey's work is about queer erotics and experience". However, Hubbs (1996: 285) acknowledges that she knows many "straight fans" who have no idea that Morrissey's work has anything to do with "queerness". Such a viewpoint is easily accounted for given mainstream society's "ignorance of queer codes", and the impact of "the economy of compulsory heterosexuality". I am in agreement with Hubbs (1996: 288) assertion that those who ignore "the relevant codes and secret languages" are missing "a crucial part of the picture", but to simply restrictively classify Morrissey's work as a form of "gay rock" is to miss the point entirely. As such Morrissey's fascination with working-class hardness should also be seen as identification with the marginalized other (Zuberi 2001: 51). Coulter (2010: 166) suggests that Morrissey's "gaze" on hard working-class males could also be "the result of another form of envy or desire", one that suspects that these characters are "in some way authentically working-class in a way that he can never possibly be". It is that understanding that informs the next section of this chapter.

There are multiple ways of being a working-class male; there is however a dominant hegemonic form of masculinity, which defines (a stereotypical version of) what it is to be a man (Coulter 2010: 166). In post-war Britain, manufacturing jobs presented opportunities for (predominantly white) working-class males, yet this form of employment also accumulated a particular type of masculine "body capital" (Nayak 2006: 813–814). With industrial decline, working-class youths had to negotiate a now uncertain transition to manhood via government training schemes or the dole[12] (Bates 1984 cited in Nayak 2006: 814), in the process underpinning the class society (Beck 1998: 35 cited in Nayak 2006: 814), which in turn detrimentally impacted on their masculine identity (Nayak 2006: 816). Yet "real and symbolic acts of violence" offered young working-class males the prospect of maintaining their "tough" masculine identity (McDowell 2002 cited in Nayak 2006: 821). These young males began to adapt to the social inequalities they faced by performing an unrepentant "posture of survival" that was hard and streetwise, in order to demonstrate a survivalist response to the neo-liberal "reforms" that left many of their communities completely abandoned (MacDonald, 1999 cited in Nayak 2006: 826–827). The importance of place, locality and regional identities cannot be underestimated, and in spite of major physical and economic regeneration, the traditional working-class culture/identity of these young males steadfastly refuses to be erased (Nayak 2006: 828). In such a context Morrissey's work makes extremely interesting reading.

'Reader Meets Author'[13] sees Morrissey castigate middle-class fascination with the working-class (Zuberi 2001: 60). The parachute journalist in this track writes their stories from afar (safety) without ever understanding what it means to live in such locations. Morrissey sees his work as providing a more authentic view of working-class life, though from the perspective of an outsider who never really fitted into that way of life. Songs such as 'Dial A Cliché', 'He Cried' and 'Certain People I Know' illustrate Morrissey's fascination with working-class hardness. Additionally, his 'Rusholme Ruffians', 'Sweet And Tender Hooligan(s)', 'Suedehead'(s) and skinheads can all be seen as part of his "reclamation of the working-class" (Zuberi 2001: 52; see Bakers' chapter in this volume).

'We'll Let You Know' deals with English football hooligans, presenting them as tragic figures (Zuberi 2001). Morrissey sings "We're all smiles then, honest, I swear, it's the turnstiles that make us hostile." He speaks of those involved descending "on anyone unable to defend themselves" and finishes by describing these individuals as the "last truly British people you will ever know". Zuberi argues that this song therefore "evokes a hard line British nationalism"

(Zuberi 2001: 57). Yet there are alternative views about the origins and meaning of football hooliganism, and consequently alternative ways of reading this particular song. I would argue that Morrissey illustrates hooliganism as a "practice rooted in a particular segment of class struggle" (Smith cited in Zuberi 2001: 59). Ian Taylor (1971 cited in Frosdick and Marsh 2005: 89) for example argues that the embourgoisement of football was part of the disintegration of the time-honoured working-class weekend. Football hooliganism could therefore be understood as a response to the social alienation and lack of social support experienced by working-class youths, the disintegration of the traditional working-class, and an effort to reinstate the traditional working-class weekend with its masculine, tribal characteristics (Frosdick and Marsh 2005: 89; Piotrowski, 2006).

Morrissey has worn a West Ham United Football Club T-shirt on stage on a number of occasions,[14] and West Ham hooligans (the Inter City Firm – hereafter ICF), were one of the biggest and most feared hooligan groups in the UK. The members of that group claimed to only fight with other hooligan firms, and the values fêted by the ICF echo the dominant values of East-End working-class culture, specifically a strong "in-group solidarity" and an intense suspicion of representatives of the Establishment (Spaj 2006). This solidarity was illustrated by one ICF member who stated "we pride ourselves in sticking together no matter what happens. We look after one another". Furthermore, although the majority of hooligans were white males, a number of the ICF's core members were black (Cass Pennant for example) or from other minority ethnic groups (Spaaij 2006). Finally, it is noteworthy that contrary to the image of explicit racism linked with hooligan firms throughout the 1970s and 1980s, only a minute fraction of ICF members were ever connected to Far-Right organizations such as the National Front, BNP or Combat 18; in fact there are instances where ICF members fought on behalf of the Socialist Workers Party against supporters of the National Front (Dunning et al. 1988: 182). As such, rather than presenting a hard line, right wing British nationalism, the "last truly British people you will ever know" could be interpreted as referring to the decline of working-class culture and the reaction of some groups trying to halt that process.

Morrissey's work also addresses the issue of idleness/fecklessness among the working/underclass. 'Nobody Loves Us' gives voice to how society at large views such individuals. Yet Morrissey venerates such idleness. 'Still Ill' and 'You've Got Everything Now' are absolutely derisive in their anti-work stance (Rogan 1992: 190) and 'Heaven Knows I'm Miserable Now' contends that getting a job is no guarantee of contentment (Zuberi 2001: 33). In reply to the disparaging resentment of mainstream society, Morrissey offers a defence of the poverty-stricken, methadone-using, 'Teenage Dad On His Estate'. He implies that the dominant view of the underclass is in reality an ill-informed opinion obtained through the media ("You defer to the views of the television news, Let someone do your thinking for you, and you still buy a daily newspaper and you find everything there – but the news"), which fuels the jealous derision ("you can't help feeling used and you hate the teenage dad on his estate because he's poor But he's happier than you") of discontented and alienated members of the middle-classes. This theme of jealousy is also evident in Morrissey's discussion of the 'Boy

Racer' where he states "He's just too good-natured and he's got too much money and he's got too many girlfriends, I'm jealous, that's all."

Furthermore, Morrissey deals with criminality in an alternative way. Crime as a shortcut to celebrity is the focus of 'The Last Of The Famous International Playboys', a song that is an analysis of twisted morals (Garrett 2006). Morrissey intones

> Dear hero imprisoned [...]
> And now in my cell (well, I followed you) [...]
> Reggie Kray – do you know my name? [...]
> Ronnie Kray – do you know my face?

It could be argued that Morrissey is not only associating himself with the Kray twins, he is also re-contextualizing them, presenting them as more than just gangsters and murderers. Clark et al. (1975: 100) for example recognize the Kray twins as constituent elements of an exceedingly differentiated criminal subculture that existed in the East End of London, which was in fact part of the "normal" existence and culture of the East End working-classes (see also Cope's chapter in this volume). Alternatively, the song can be read as Morrissey criticizing the media's glamorization of individuals such as the Krays, Ronnie Biggs etc., a glamorization which in turn encourages people to emulate them ("in our lifetime those who kill, the news world hands them stardom, and these are the ways on which I was raised [...] I never wanted to kill, I am not naturally evil, Such things I do just to make myself more attractive to you"), but which ultimately results in ruined lives.

Morrissey further exhibits his gallery of "loveable" rogues in the 'First Of The Gang To Die' where he discusses Latino gangs in LA. He again presents the subject matter in an alternative manner, where the main character, Hector (despite being someone who "stole from the rich and the poor and the not-very-rich and the very poor") is given iconic status ("he stole all hearts away") as he was the "first of the gang with a gun in his hand, and the first to do time, the first of the gang to die". Yet Morrissey tries to show the futilities of that way of life when describing Hector as "such a silly boy".

'Ganglord' continues this theme but from the perspective that the actions and attitudes of the police drive the narrator into the arms of the 'Ganglord'. Morrissey sings of how the police are "haunting me, taunting me, wanting me to break their laws [...] And I'm turning to you to save me [...] They say 'to protect and to serve' but what they really want to say is 'Get back to the ghetto!'" Morrissey appears to be promoting the idea that the police see the narrator (and his kind) as working/underclass ghetto-dwellers, and by extension he appears to be stating that if you come from such a background, the police will never respect or protect you. "To protect and to serve" is the motto of the Los Angeles Police Department (LAPD), yet here "To Protect and Serve" is conveyed as "To Harass and Dominate", where defending the peace is dependant on the narrator becoming subservient to the police officers' instructions and compliant "to the boot of his enforcement" (SARTRE 2003). While the song appears to be directed at the LAPD's treatment of Latino immigrants, it is ambiguous enough to apply to any location, for example it could just as easily be read and understood by those who have experienced the actions and attitudes of the police in Gare du Nord train station in Paris in the aftermath of the riots that took place in its poor, mainly immigrant, suburbs in 2005.

Morrissey's glamorous, exalted and alternative representation of those engaged in criminality serves to set such criminal subculture elements of the working/underclass apart from the dominant understanding of crime, in the process building a counter-hegemonic discourse and image of those who engage in such behaviour.

Attacking neo-liberal discourse

Morris (1994: 80) identifies two general theoretical or ideological positions with respect to the socially excluded (who have been constructed by governments and dominant discourse as an "underclass"). The cultural position sees the source of social exclusion as lying in the attitudes and behaviour of the underclass itself, while the structural position sees it lying in the structured inequality of the labour market and the state, which disadvantages particular groups in society. For those who accept the cultural version of this discourse, the way to bring about social inclusion is by "fixing" the individual failings with which the excluded are afflicted. Proponents of the "stronger" form of the discourse stress the role of those elites who are allowing this exclusion to take place, and seek solutions, which address the structural aspect of exclusion (Veit-Wilson 1998: 45). It is apparent that most discourse and public policy on the subject tends to be of the cultural variety and the excluded are therefore perceived as having personal deficits (Byrne 1999: 128). In current political debate the Moral Underclass Discourse (a variant of the weak definition of social exclusion) stresses "moral" and "cultural" sources of poverty and exclusion, and is thus primarily obsessed with the "moral hazard" of welfare dependency (Levitas 2000: 360). This discourse reaffirms long existent themes about dangerous classes (see Skeggs 1997), stressing the moral and cultural weaknesses of certain groups such as lone parents and the long-term unemployed (Levitas 2000: 360). The Moral Underclass Discourse is concerned with blaming the excluded for the situation they find themselves in and conveniently ignores the structural causes of exclusion which predominate in the current neo-liberal era. "One hears about 'the marginalized' and the 'socially excluded', but there is little discussion on who is excluding or marginalizing them" (Allen 2000: 37).

Morrissey tackles that very subject in 'Interesting Drug', which examines social exploitation, moral deceit and an unaccommodating state (Garrett 2006), in the process adopting a structural position (Morris 1994) on social exclusion and reaffirming his concern for society's outcasts and dispossessed. He sings about being on "a government scheme designed to kill your dream". In doing so he draws attention to the immorality of the neo-liberal state, which denies certain people an equal chance in life. In the songs' video there are additional references, with the pupils, for example, clearly writing "There are some bad people on the Right" on the wall, and the lead actress carries a placard which states "Unfairly Dismissed". In such circumstances Morrissey intones "Once poor, always poor, you wonder why we're only half-ashamed [...] Look around [...]can you blame us?"

This song may have been an attack on the social and economic policies of Thatcher's Britain, yet the subject matter remains as relevant now as it was then, and Morrissey could just as easily be singing about the situation in contemporary Ireland or elsewhere. The mass availability of cheap credit combined with certain sections of the media continually promoting the mantra that people must buy immediately or run the risk of never being able to buy a home stimulated a property bubble, and young people were encouraged to avail of 30- and 40-year mortgages in order to buy houses (Allen 2009: 107–122). As a result, many of those managing to purchase houses in a massively inflated market are now crippled with colossal debt repayments and negative equity (Allen 2009: 180–185). Therefore, I am certain that the line "young married couple in debt ever felt had?" will resonate with many people.

The US administration's multibillion dollar bail out of its financial institutions has debunked the neo-liberal myth that capitalists are independent risk-taking wealth creators, which was the main justification for inequality. In fact, those who previously supported such risk taking became fervent supporters of "corporate welfare" almost overnight (Allen 2009: 63–64). Accordingly, the response to the current global economic crisis has concentrated on restoring "order" to public finances, with government mantra being that excessive resources are exhausted by the poor through social welfare for example (Allen 2009: 5–7). Simultaneously we have seen money required for the provision of vital public services being diverted to "recapitalize" the near-bankrupt banking system. In such circumstances people are entitled to wonder why financial institutions are deemed to be more important than ordinary people. Once more Morrissey appears to have captured the answer that many people might offer to this question when he sings "they're saving their own skins by ruining people's lives".

It is interesting that in the UK, New Labour was far more enthusiastic about the neo-liberal agenda (particularly the privatization of core public services) than even Thatcher dared to be (Byrne 2005: 56).[15] In this regard Morrissey signalled his continuing hostility to neo-liberal policies with the lines "I've been dreaming of a time when the English are sick to death of Labour and Tories" in 'Irish Blood, English Heart'. In 'All You Need Is Me' he sings "I was a small fat child in a welfare house, there was only one thing I ever dreamed about and fate has just handed it to me, whoopee." He is effectively describing happenstance, where fate rather than any state policy or intervention is responsible for an improvement in the narrators' circumstances. In the process Morrissey directly challenges the meritocratic ideology/discourse which has camouflaged the perpetuation of privilege in neo-liberal states.

While public discourse attributes agency to those who participate in the labour force, it ignores the integral role of the structural, social and political forces in determining their employment status (Lens 2002: 140). Welfare recipients have become scorned (Adair 2001b: 455), with discourses reflecting their construction as a liability to the "decency" of the "deserving" working members of our society (Adair 2005: 823). Morrissey personally experienced such disdain. Having quit from a Civil Service job after two weeks, he returned to the welfare office to be told by a DHSS officer that "People like you make me sick" (Rogan 1992: 85). In view of that, it is no surprise that Morrissey questions the role and influence that civil servants have on people's lives in contemporary neo-liberal societies. In 'Mama Lay Softly On The River Bed' he poignantly asks "Mama, who drove you to it? Was it the pigs in grey suits persecuting you? Uncivil servants unconcerned at how they frighten you?" While Morrissey's lyrics are often deliberately ambiguous, making it difficult to identify the actual source of his scorn in 'How Can Anybody Possibly Know How I Feel', I also read this track as a comment on the abuse of authority by those in positions of power within the apparatus of the state.

Challenging class disgust

The use of the chav as a marker of class disgust is most evident through the construction of the chavette or "pramface",[16] complete with hoopy earrings, tracksuit, ponytail ("Croydon facelift") and multitude of mixed-race kids. She has been constructed as the archetypal sexually extreme lone mother who is an "immoral, filthy, ignorant, vulgar, tasteless, working-class whore" (Tyler 2008: 26). Wilson and Huntington (2005: 59) argue that a new set of feminine norms has emerged (where the idyllic life-course of middle-class women now conforms to the neo-liberal needs of the economy, via higher education and increased female participation in the labour market), resulting in the denigration of the chavette (Tyler 2008: 30). When middle-class women delayed having children so as to participate in the labour market, it increasingly caused non-working (young) mothers (especially those on welfare) to be viewed as problematic. Essentially the chavette was stigmatized as a result of "normality" being defined by "white middle-class cultural practices and family forms" (Griffin 1993: 38 cited in Wilson and Huntington 2005: 67).

The class disgust discourse on the chavette or "slum mum" also conveniently allows governments to deflect attention away from cuts in welfare provision once they have framed the issue as an individualistic social problem (Skeggs 2005: 968). Accordingly, concerns for teenage mothers are almost always articulated through the discourse of welfare dependency, the ideological basis of which is camouflaged (Wilson and Huntington 2005: 62). Instead of framing such women's poverty in terms of structural deficiencies (such as inadequate childcare, low levels of educational attainment, declining wages, less sustainable employment etc.), these women are most often depicted in a manner that "makes" them responsible for their own misfortune. This is highly significant as a "political shift from redistribution to recognition politics" has occurred, and those who are not "respectable" now cannot "morally" seek assistance from the state (Skeggs 2005: 977).

In this context the 'Slum Mums', which laments a coloured lone mother's existence, powerfully critiques the impact of some of the myths which are continually advanced by neo-liberal governments through the Moral Underclass Discourse. The song begins with the sound of wailing children, before Morrissey adopts the role of the welfare officer to narrate this particular story. He sings from a patronizing/superior position to the 'Slum Mum', questioning her audacity in trying to receive assistance from the state, "you turn to us for succour because you think we're just suckers". His apparent glee while doing so is so vibrant – "We may be welfare, but we don't care and we're paid to despise your council house eyes" – that it demonstrates the contempt and inhumanity that many people have for this group of the "undeserving" underclass. In this context, signifiers such as accent, dress and address etc. serve as markers which are decoded by welfare officers as signs that the individual is not to be trusted (see Power 2009). Morrissey sings "You can change your name and you can bleach your skin, camouflage your accent so that even you don't recognise it, but you won't escape from the slum mums because you are one, because you live and breathe like one." The stereotypical view of the undeserving slum mums continues with reference to the "six filthy children from six absent fathers". The effect that this discourse has on the ability of such individuals to gain their rightful entitlements from both the state and its representatives (i.e. the welfare officer) is portrayed in detail – "The office of the Social Service is strategically placed in a dowdy, rowdy part of town to discourage you from signing. We make you feel as if you're whining when you claim what's legally yours."

The final verse of the song is the most disturbing. "Take you and your rat pack brood to the long grass of the meadow, administer seven doses lethal and illegal which may render you elsewhere." Morrissey's (in his role as the welfare officer) encouragement of the "slum mum's" infanticide appears to suggest that she is better off killing her children so as to save them from the indignities of a life spent as a member of the underclass. In assuming the role of the taunter, as well as her potential liberator, Morrissey forces the audience to deal with our own prejudices (Rogan 1992: 300). Accordingly a negotiated reading of these codes (Hall 1999) may evoke a more compassionate/understanding view of the "slum mums" of this world.

Conclusions

In conclusion, Morrissey's body of work makes an important contribution to wider sociological debates around the continuing relevance and representations of social class. The neo-liberal individualistic ideology of personal responsibility has framed the issues of social exclusion and poverty as individual problems (Lens 2002: 137–144), facilitating an "abdication from acknowledging class relations" (Skeggs 2005: 54), causing the identification of class discrimination and the specificity of class cultures/identities/struggle to be suppressed (Tyler 2008: 20).

Yet, Morrissey recognizes that class is a central element of our social identity and his work demonstrates a shift from an objective to a subjective analysis of class, vividly illustrating the validity of Skeggs' (1997) claim that the academic abandoning of class as a theoretical concept does not mean it no longer exists. Morrissey challenges postmodern arguments that individualization weakens class identities by reconfiguring class analysis, and centrally locating "issues of cultural identity" (Bottero 2004: 988), in the process demonstrating that individualization has merely altered how class operates. Despite the fact that communal class identities are fragile, our subjective identities continue to involve "relational comparisons" with those from other classes, signifying "the reforming of class cultures around individualized axes" (Savage, 2000: xii cited in Bottero 2004: 989). In such a context, by continuously using his work as a powerful tool for re-imagining people and places, Morrissey has built a counter-hegemonic discourse and image of the working/underclass (Botta 2006: 123). As such it would appear that Morrissey's *Years of Refusal* have been very well spent.

Notes

1. *The Royle Family* (BBC) and *Shameless* (Channel 4) for example.
2. Red Wedge was a collective of British musicians who attempted to connect music fans with the Left wing policies of the UK Labour Party prior to the general election of 1987, with the intention to remove Thatcher's Conservative Party from government. There are some suggestions that Morrissey was ambivalent about Red Wedge, and that it was really Johnny Marr that pushed for the involvement of The Smiths in Red Wedge (see Devereux 2010: 77).
3. See Devereux (2010: 74) for a similar discussion in relation to Morrissey's commercial exploitation of religion.
4. This assessment comes from Alice Nutter of the anarchist pop group Chumbawumba (*The South Bank Show* 1987), a woman who was so radically political that she advocated theft, and urged fans of their music who could not afford to buy their CDs to steal them from large music chain stores in 1998 (Harris 1999: 96).
5. Morrissey made reference to this "strategy" on his 2004 tour when using a version of the 'Imperfect List' by Big Hard Excellent Fish as an intro tape. This intro makes reference to "the Tory invention of the non-working-class […] fucking bastard Thatcher. […] racist […] hunger[…] greed […] overdraft like a mountain […] poll tax, commie bashers […] the breakdown of the NHS […] homelessness […] and the all-American way".
6. The North of England remains an area that is characterized by higher unemployment and lower wages, and by a higher crime and a lower economic activity rate (Singer 2007: 407).
7. This is brilliantly captured in Grant Gee's 2008 documentary film, *Joy Division: Their Own Story in Their Own Words*.
8. Engel's *The Condition of the Working Class in England* casts a gloomy light on a city made up of dwellings hardly fit for human habitation (Schmid 2007: 347).
9. Coronation Street has come to symbolize the archetypal Northern working-class street in popular consciousness (Zuberi 2001: 36).
10. 'Glamorous Glue' refers to this trend. "We won't vote Conservative because we never have. Everyone lies, everyone lies."
11. There are discernible differences in Morrissey's representations of class over time. I would argue that in The Smiths he tends to focus on an objective analysis of class while as a solo artiste he concentrates more on how class location is bound up with social identity.

12. For many working-class males there was only a depressing choice between "shit jobs and govvy schemes" (Coffield et al. 1986: 86 cited in Nayak 2006: 814).
13. This track is reported to be about the journalist Julie Burchill.
14. Some have speculated that Morrissey's 1994 interview with Julie Burchill was his inspiration in writing this song. See Goddard 2009, 344.
15. David Cameron's coalition government seem eager to continue this process.
16. See Lizzie Hopley's (2005) play of the same name which portrays this construction of the chavette and denigration of the working-class as a form of social racism.

References

Adair, V. (2005) 'US working-class/poverty-class divides', *Sociology*, 39: 5, pp. 817–834.

Adair, V. (2001a) 'Poverty and the (broken) promise of higher education', *Harvard Educational Review*, 71: 2, pp. 217–239.

Adair, V. (2001b) 'Branded with infamy: inscriptions of poverty and class in the United States', *Signs: Journal of Women in Culture and Society*, 27: 2, pp. 451–471.

Allen, K. (2009) *Ireland's Economic Crash: A Radical Agenda for Change*. Dublin: The Liffey Press.

Allen, K. (2000) *The Celtic Tiger: The Myth of Social Partnership in Ireland*. Manchester: Manchester University Press.

Arellano, G. (2002) 'Their charming man: dispatches from the Latino Morrissey love-in', *Orange County Weekly*, 8: , September.

Baxter–Moore, N. (2006) '"This Is Where I Belong": identity, social class, and the nostalgic Englishness of Ray Davies and the Kinks', *Popular Music and Society*, 29: 2, pp. 145–165.

Bhattacharyya, G. (2002) *Sexuality and Society: An Introduction*. New York: Routledge.

Botta, G. (2006) 'Pop music, cultural sensibilities and places: Manchester 1976–1997', in proceedings of the ESF-LiU Conference *Cities and Media: Cultural Perspectives on Urban Identities in a Mediatized World*, pp. 121–125, Vadstena.

Bottero, W. (2004) 'Class identities and the identity of class', *Sociology*, 38: 5, pp. 985–1003.

Brooker, J. (2010) 'Has the world changed or have I changed?: The Smiths and the challenge of Thatcherism', in S. Campbell and C. Coulter (eds) *Why Pamper Life's Complexities? Essays on The Smiths*. Manchester: Manchester University Press, pp. 22–42.

Brown, L. (1991) 'I'll Astonish You', *Details*, March, available: http: //www.rocksbackpages.com/ article.html?ArticleID=6746.

Bullock, H., Fraser Wyche, K. and Williams, W. (2001) 'Media images of the poor', *Journal of Social Issues*, 57: 2, pp. 229–246.

Byrne, D. (2005) *Social Exclusion*, 2nd edition. Maidenhead: Open University Press.

Byrne, D. (1999) *Social Exclusion*. Buckingham: Open University Press.

Clark, J., Hall, S., Jefferson, T. and Roberts, B. (1975) 'Subcultures, Cultures, and Class', in K. Gelder (ed.) *The Subculture Reader*. New York: Routledge, pp. 100–111.

Clarke, J. and Newman, J. (1997) *The Managerial State. Power, Politics and Ideology in the Remaking of Social Welfare*. Thousand Oaks: Sage Publications.

Clawson, R. and Trice, R. (2000) 'Poverty as we know it: media portrayals of the poor', *Public Opinion Quarterly*, 64, pp. 53–64.

Coulter, C. (2010) '"A Double Bed and a Stalwart Lover for Sure': The Smiths, the death of pop and the not so hidden injuries of class', in S. Campbell and C. Coulter (eds) *Why Pamper Life's Complexities? Essays on The Smiths*. Manchester: Manchester University Press, pp. 156–178.

Coulter, C. (2005) "'A Double Bed and a Stalwart Lover For Sure': The Smiths, the alchemy of class and the end of pop', paper from *Why Pamper Life's Complexities? A Symposium on The Smiths*, pp. 1–8, Manchester, available: *http: //www.nic.fi/~east/CHORUS/DOKUMENTIT/colins.pdf*.

Croteau, D. and Hoynes, W. (2000) *Media Society: Industries, Images, and Audiences*, 2nd edition. Thousand Oaks: Pine Forge.

Devereux, E. (2009) 'I'm not the man you think I am: authenticity, ambiguity and the cult of Morrissey', in E. Haverinen, U. Kovala and V. Rautavuoma (eds) *Cult, Community, Identity*. Finland: Research Center for Contemporary Culture of the University of Jyväskylä, pp. 103–118.

Devereux, E. (2003) *Understanding the Media*. London: Sage Publications.

Devereux, E. (2010) 'Heaven knows we'll soon be dust: Catholicism and devotion in The Smiths', in C. Coulter and S. Campbell (eds) *Why Pamper Life's Complexities? Essays on The Smiths*. Manchester: Manchester University Press, pp. 65–80.

Dixon, J. and Hyde, M. (2003) 'Public pension privatisation neo-classical economics, decision risks and welfare ideology', *International Journal of Social Economics*, 30: 5, pp. 633–650.

Dunning, E., Murphy, P. and Williams, J. (1988) *The Roots of Football Hooliganism: An Historical and Sociological Study*. London: Routledge & Keegan Paul.

Edelman, M. (1998) 'Language, myths and rhetoric', *Society*, 35: 2, pp. 131–139.

Edwards, B. (2006) 'The Politics of Morrissey', available: *http: //liberation.typepad.com/ liberation/2006/08/the_politics_of.html*.

Frosdick, S. and Marsh, P. (2005) *Football Hooliganism*. Cullumpton: Willan Publishing.

Garrett, D. (2006) 'Elegant Rock (Or, Impressing Posterity): The Best of Morrissey and Ringleader of the Tormentors', available: *http: //www.compulsivereader.com/html/index.php?name=News&file=ar ticle&sid=1353*.

George, V. and Wilding, P. (1985) *Ideology and Social Welfare*. London: Routledge.

Girls and Boys: Sex and British Pop Episode 3: Tainted Love (2008) BBC 4, 23rd Jan.

Goddard, S. (2009) *Mozipedia*, Bodmin: Ebury Press.

Golding, P. and Middleton, S. (1982) *Images of Welfare: Press and Public Attitudes to Poverty*. Oxford: Martin Robertson.

Hall, S. (1999) 'Encoding, decoding', in S. During (ed.) *The Cultural Studies Reader*, 2nd edn. New York: Routledge, pp. 507–517.

Harris, R. (1999) *A Cognitive Psychology of Mass Communication*. Mahwah: Lawrence Eribaum.

Hayward, K. and Yar, M. (2006) 'The "chav" phenomenon: Consumption, media and the construction of a new underclass', *Crime Media Culture*, 2: 1, pp. 9–28.

Hersh, J. (2004) 'Old speak/newspeak of (neo)liberalism on development', *The Interdisciplinary Journal of International Studies*, 2: 1, pp. 3–19.

Hubbs, N. 'Music of the "Fourth Gender": Morrissey and the sexual politics ofmelodic contour', in T. Foster, C. Stiegele and E. Berry (eds) *Bodies of Writing, Bodies in Performance*. New York: New York University Press, pp. 266–296.

Kallioniemi, K. (1999) 'Rock discourse, mass mediations, and cultural identity: the imaginary England of pop-poet Stephen Patrick Morrissey', in S. Inkinen (ed.) *Mediapolis, Aspects of Texts, Hypertexts, and Multimedial Communication*. Berlin: De Gruyter, pp. 291–320.

Later With Jools Holland (2004) BBC 2, 21st May.

Law, A. (2006) 'Hatred and respect: the class shame of Ned "Humour"', *Variant*, 25, pp. 28–30.

Lens, V. (2002) 'Public voices and public policy: changing the societal discourse on welfare', *Journal of Sociology and Social Welfare*, 29: 1, pp. 137–154.

Levitas, R. (2000) 'What is social exclusion?', in D. Gordon and P. Townsend (eds) *Breadline Europe*. Bristol: The Policy Press, pp. 357–364.

McCullagh, C. (2002) *Media Power: A Sociological Introduction*. New York: Palgrave Macmillan.

Morris, L. (1994) *Dangerous Classes: The Underclass and Social Citizenship*. London: Routledge.

Nayak, A. (2006) 'Displaced masculinities: chavs, youth and class in the post-industrial city', *Sociology*, 40: 5, pp. 813–831.

O'Donovan, D. (2007) 'Carry on Morrissey: the persistence of white Britishness', in S. Petrilli (ed.) *White Matters /Il bianco in questione*. Rome: Meltimi, pp. 236–246

Oxford Road Show (1985) BBC 2, 22nd March.

Pakulski, J. and Waters, M. (1996) *The Death of Class*. London: Sage.

Pordzik, R. (2007) 'Of popular spaces: Northern heterotopias, Morrissey and the Manchester Britpop scene', in C. Ehlan, *Thinking Northern: Textures of Identity in the North of England*. New York: Rodopi, pp. 325–346.

Piotrowski, P. (2006) 'Coping with football-related hooliganism: healing symptoms versus causes prevention', *Journal of Applied Social Psychology*, 36: 3, pp. 629–643.

Power, M. J. (2009) '"Outwitting the gatekeepers of the purse": The impact of micro-level interactions in determining access to the Back To Education Allowance Welfare to Education Programme', *International Review of Modern Sociology*, 35: 1, pp. 25–42.

Pye, I. (1984) 'A Hard Day's Misery', *Melody Maker*, 3 November.

Rogan, J. (1992) *Morrissey & Marr: The Severed Alliance*. London: Omnibus Press.

Salford Lad (2007) BBC Radio 2, 21st and 28th April.

SARTRE (2003) 'To Protect and Serve', available: *http: //batr.org/gulag/071603.html*.

Schmid, S. (2007) 'Between L. S. Lowry and Coronation Street: Salford cultural identities', in C. Ehlan, *Thinking Northern: Textures of Identity in the North of England*. New York: Rodopi, pp. 347–362.

Sheppard, S. (2003) *Kinkorama: Dispatches From the Front Lines of Perversion*. New York: Alyson Books.

Simpson, M. (2004) *Saint Morrissey*. London: SAF.

Singer, C. (2007) 'Northern England in facts & figures', in C. Ehlan, *Thinking Northern: Textures of Identity in the North of England*. New York: Rodopi, pp. 407–433.

Skeggs, B. (2005) 'The making of class and gender through visual moral subject formation', *Sociology*, 39: 5, pp. 965–982.

Skeggs, B. (1997) *Formations of Class and Gender: Becoming Respectable*. London: Sage.

Smith, P. and Bell, A. (2007) 'Unravelling the web of discourse analysis', in E. Devereux (ed.) *Media Studies: Key Issues & Debates*. London: Sage, pp. 78–100.

Spaaij, R. (2006) *Understanding Football Hooliganism: A Comparison of Six Western European Football Clubs*. Amsterdam: Amsterdam University Press.

Stringer, J. (1992) 'The Smiths: repressed (but remarkably dressed)', *Popular Music*, 11(1), pp. 15–26.

Thatcher, M. (1987) 'There is no such thing as society', *Women's Own* magazine, 31st October, available: http: //www.conservativevault.com/wiki/There_is_no_such_thing_as_society.

The Culture Show (2006) BBC 2, 9th December.

The South Bank Show (1987) ITV, 18th October.

Tonnies, M. (2007) 'Constructing an emblematic Northern space under Thatcherism: The New Brighton photographs of Martin Parr and Tom Wood', in C. Ehlan, *Thinking Northern: Textures of Identity in the North of England*. New York: Rodopi, pp. 305–324.

Tyler, I. '"Chav Mum Chav Scum" Class disgust in contemporary Britain', *Feminist Media Studies*, 8: 1, pp. 17–34.

Veit-Wilson, J. (1998) *Setting Adequacy Standards*. Bristol: Policy Press.

Wilson, H. and Huntington, A. (2005) 'Deviant (m)others: the construction of teenage motherhood in contemporary discourse', *Journal of Social Policy*, 35: 10, pp. 59–76.

Woronzoff, E. (2009) '*Because the Music That They Constantly Play, It Says Nothing to Me About My Life': An Analysis of Youth's Appropriation of Morrissey's Sexuality, Gender, and Identity*, monograph, Simmons College of Arts and Sciences Graduate Studies.

Worrall, F. (1983) 'The cradle snatchers', *Melody Maker*, 3rd September.

Zuberi, N.(2003) 'The last truly British people you will ever know: skinheads, Pakis and Morrissey', in H. Jenkins, T. McPherson and J. Shattuc (eds) *Hop on Pop: The Politics and Pleasures of Popular Culture*. Durham: Duke University Press, pp. 539–555.

Zuberi, N. (2001) *Sounds English: Transnational Popular Music*. Urbana: University of Illinois Press.

Chapter 6

In Our Different Ways We are the Same: Morrissey and Representations of Disability

Daniel Manco

Introduction

Years prior to forsaking his first and middle names and ascending to international stardom – first as vocalist and lyricist for the seminal 1980s rock group The Smiths and, in the 20-plus years since that ensemble's disbandment, as an accomplished solo artist – Steven Patrick Morrissey mounted the public stage under the pseudonym "Sheridan Whiteside". Not as a would-be pop idol, however: it was, rather, as a music journalist penning concert reviews in the unofficial capacity of Mancunian correspondent for the British music weekly *Record Mirror* (Bret 1995: 16; Chalmers 1992) that Morrissey had adopted the penname, sourced from the 1943 film *The Man Who Came to Dinner*.[1] Sheridan Whiteside is that film's central character, a cosmopolitan critic and radio personality equally notable for his arch wit and domineering personality. While on a national lecture tour that deposits him in the parochial town of Mesalia, Ohio, Whiteside slips on an icy step and, having apparently broken his hip, finds himself relegated to a wheelchair. Constrained to straitened convalescence in the home of a local conservative businessman, sharp-tongued Whiteside proceeds to wreak manipulative havoc in the personal and professional lives of his attendant staff and host community. Ultimately given a clean bill of health and granted permission to continue his tour, Whiteside elects instead to feign continued infirmity, remaining wheelchair-bound that he might continue his social machinations uninterrupted.

Morrissey's selection of the name "Sheridan Whiteside" as an early pseudonym was no doubt overdetermined. The man who would later rail in song against humdrum towns that drag you down ('William, It Was Really Nothing') surely empathized with Whiteside's profound aversion to his temporary provincial lodgings. Moreover, Whiteside's caustic repartee bears striking similarity to that of Morrissey's beloved idol Oscar Wilde, and prefigures the vicious wit that Morrissey himself would come to evince with seeming ease. What I wish to emphasize here, however, is the way in which Morrissey's use of the Whiteside *nom de plume* introduces at a very early stage in his career – one might even say, in its prehistory – a discourse of disability that has steeped the man's *oeuvre* from inception to present. Whiteside is, after all, manifestly a character persistently ensconced in a wheelchair. As such, his representation delineates a portrait of disability such as has been subjected to scrutiny by scholars working under the rubric of disability studies, an interdisciplinary field of relatively recent provenance but growing prominence; its scholars "examine the social meanings and interpretations of disability, with emphasis on how cultural constructions and representations of disability and disabled persons shape public and institutional responses to these conditions and people" (Ghaziani 2005: 276). That Morrissey the pop music artist would return time and again to the trope of disability – not only in song, most famously his April 1990 single 'November Spawned A Monster', but also in such flourishes as his renowned sporting of a hearing aid and National Health Service (NHS) spectacles (Bret 2004: 49, 52, 80) – was thus portended by his provisional adoption, as an aspiring music journalist, of the "Whiteside" moniker. This chapter offers some commentary on the character of and possible motivation impelling Morrissey's perennial and, as I shall argue, equivocal recourse in his work to images of disability.

Understanding disability

A central project of the field of disability studies is to dispute any apprehension of disability as a static phenomenon or natural category of human experience. Its scholars have sought, on the contrary, to historicize disability, tracing from the available evidence its ever-shifting configuration over the centuries and across cultures. Davis (1995) demonstrates that such contemporary and taken-for-granted terms as "average", "normal" and "abnormal" are relatively recent inventions in Western discourse, emerging discernibly in their current semantic guises only in the mid-nineteenth century. It was at this historical juncture that the rise of the new branch of knowledge known as statistics provided apparently scientific justification of bourgeois hegemony via its championing of moderation and middle-class ideology. Through its measurement of the distribution of human features (e.g. weight and height) and subsequent identification of the physically average man, statistics worked simultaneously to produce a morally average man, virtuous in his temperate immunity to the debilitating extremes of human experience. Under statistics' "normal distributions", extremities, or deviations from the virtuous norm, became devalued. For the non-normative disabled body, this development was calamitous; "in a society where the concept of the norm is operative", Davis writes, "people with disabilities will be thought of as deviants" (1995: 29). Nor were disabled persons alone in their disparagement: the nonstandard population joining them in ignominy was an indiscriminate composite of all those with allegedly undesirable traits: criminals, the dissolute, the poor, the sexually licentious – all those with not only physical but mental "defects" as well (Davis 1995: 35, 37).

Garland-Thomson (1997: 8) has usefully coined the term "normate" in order to name "the veiled subject position of cultural self, the figure outlined by the array of deviant others whose marked bodies shore up the normate's boundaries". This normate is a social figure which accords definitive humanity, a mantle that when assumed endows its bearer with the authority to wield power. Of course, given the admixture of devalued traits (including those pertaining to class, ethnicity, gender and sexuality) whose exclusion shores up the boundaries of "normativity", the normate body emerges as an exceedingly narrowly defined rubric under which only a very small minority of people fall. Turning her attention to the normate's obverse, Garland-Thomson refers to the corporeal difference subsumed under the label "disability" in all its manifestations as "extraordinary bodies" (1997: 5). This designation simultaneously registers the non-normativity of the disabled body and preserves it from denigration via the positive connotations that the term "extraordinary" bears in certain usages.[2]

Although numerous models of disability have circulated in discourse about the rejected body (Shakespeare 2006: 9), it is the social model that pre-eminently orients the field of disability studies. An appreciation of this model's significance hinges on an understanding of the precedent model of disability to which it is principally opposed: the medical model. Under this latter conception, disability is regarded as a problem that resides in the individual. Corporeal difference or impairment is understood to be inherently disabling; disability is viewed as a biological matter, with its relationship to the social environment bracketed out of view. Because biological, disability is thus considered properly the province of medical intervention (Siebers 2008: 25). The anomalous bodies of disabled persons are subjected to the medical gaze in a highly unequal relation of power, rendering disabled persons the dreaded, pitiable, tragic and utterly dependent "helped" at the mercy of valiant "helpers" (Johnstone 2001: 16–18). Within this inequitable power relation, the disabled patient is seen as defective, with medicine's goal being to fix or cure the anomalous body – that is, to normalize the abnormal.

The social model of disability

Championed by many disability studies scholars in explicit opposition to such a view is the social model of disability. This social model – sometimes called the "minority model" (Mason et al. 2004: 58) to denote how persons with disabilities, like other minority groups, have historically been denied rights, access and protection – eschews essentialist, reductionist and biologically determinist conceptions in favor of positing disability as a social construction. The social model deflects attention away from the individual body and its perceived physical or mental deficits in order to illuminate the context of a social environment that excludes or fails to accommodate the person with disabilities: "[r]ather than disability being inescapable, it becomes a product of social arrangements, and can thus be reduced, or possibly even eliminated" (Shakespeare 2006: 29). At the heart of the social model of disability is the distinction between impairment and disability. This distinction was summarized in a 1974 publication by the British organization Union of Physically Impaired Against Segregation (UPIAS) titled *Fundamental Principles of Disability*, which asserted the following (cited in Barton 2004: 286):

> In our view, it is society which disables physically impaired people. Disability is something imposed on top of our impairment by the way we are unnecessarily isolated and excluded from full participation in society. Disabled people are therefore an oppressed group in society. Thus we define impairment as lacking all or part of a limb, or having a defective

limb, organism or mechanism of the body; and disability as the disadvantage or restriction of activity caused by a contemporary social organisation which takes little or no account of people who have physical impairments and thus excludes them from participation in the mainstream of social activities.

Because on this view disability is located not in the body but in a disabling environment, disability studies scholars have asserted that in a world in which none were ignorant of sign, deafness would not be construed as a disability (Wendell 1996: 29), while locomoting in a wheelchair is a disadvantage only in a world of staircases (Young 2002: xii).

The reference here to wheelchairs hearkens back not only to my opening discussion of Sheridan Whiteside, that impaired fictional character whose name Morrissey appropriated in his early forays into music journalism, but in the present context inevitably calls to mind Morrissey's solo single 'November Spawned A Monster'. This song takes as its subject matter a young, physically impaired girl, her own attitudes towards her disability, and the attitudes theretoward of the putative able-bodied persons around her. Certainly, references to and representations of disabled persons had surfaced in Morrissey's *opus* beginning with his earliest work with The Smiths,[3] but the release of 'November' inaugurated a two-year period in which Morrissey's interest in corporeal difference, signaled by the cameo representations of disability that had marked his work up to that point (as well as by his erstwhile brandishing of the hearing aid prop and NHS spectacles), would become a central preoccupation of his art. As such, 'November Spawned A Monster' – like those songs dealing with other varieties of corporeal non-normativity that followed in its wake – affords a richer opportunity to examine attitudes towards disability posed by Morrissey's work.

Moreover, 'November Spawned A Monster' rates among the highest-profile entries in the Morrissey canon, having been included on compilations including *Bona Drag* (1990), *Suedehead: The Best of Morrissey* (1997) and *The Best of Morrissey* (2001). The song has also been a recurrent fixture in Morrissey's live performances, as reflected by its inclusion on the 1991 VHS release *Live In Dallas* as well as on the live albums *Beethoven was Deaf* (1993) and *Live at Earls Court* (2005). Moreover, a promotional music video produced for the song's release was not only broadcast contemporaneously but has since been issued on the video collections *Hulmerist* (1991) and *¡Oye Esteban!* (2000) and achieved an even wider dissemination when it was included in the 1994 'Blackout!' episode of the animated MTV show *Beavis and Butt-head*. Not surprisingly, those title characters voice their thoroughgoing antipathy towards the clip: "Get up off the ground and stop whining, you wuss", Butt-head admonishes Morrissey's televised image, to which Beavis, having registered his own revulsion with a spit-take, appends, "Get up, stand up straight, quit acting like a wuss, quit whining, go out and get a job and some good clothes" – sentiments such as are frequently directed against such disabled persons as the one portrayed in the song's lyrics (Barnes 1993: 14–15). Public reaction to the controversial song was, however, more conflicted. While some objected that the song tastelessly lampooned disabled persons in a way that both reflected and reproduced the prejudices of ableist ideology, others defended

Morrissey with the insistence that the song mounted rather a compassionate portrayal of the fraught character of disabled identity (Bret 1995: 102–103; Brown 2008: 166; Rogan 2006: 151–152). An analysis of the track's words and music, as well as of the accompanying music video, suggests that the song's ambivalence offers bases to recommend both points of view.

While numerous methodologies have been brought to bear in analyses of images of disability across various media (Mitchell and Snyder 2000: 15–40), it is the negative-image school that seems to have most coloured the perspectives of those critics who have found grounds for censure in such disability-themed lyrics of Morrissey's as 'November Spawned A Monster'. Scholars working within the negative-image school comb the representational archives in order to identify and interrogate those pernicious stereotypes that have served historically to devalue people with disabilities by limning demeaning, reductive portraits that fail to do justice to the reality of human complexity. This scholarly perspective is predicated upon the notion that demeaning images of disability circulated in literature, film, television, print and other media are inherently disabling because they (re)produce dehumanizing public attitudes towards disabled people which in turn find expression in the architectural, institutional, legal and other barriers erected to foreclose the disabled from full participation in society (Gartner and Joe 1987: 1–3). Viewed against the ground of disability studies scholars' catalogues of disability stereotypes (Barnes 1993; Longmore 1987; Kriegel 1987), Morrissey's portrayal of disability experience in 'November' receives a modicum of exoneration. In particular, his modest desire at the song lyrics' conclusion that his disabled protagonist be permitted someday to select her own garmenture ("Oh, one fine day, let it be soon / She won't be rich or beautiful / But she'll be walking your streets in the clothes / That she went out and chose for herself") adroitly subverts the stereotype of The Disabled Person as Super Cripple (Barnes 1993: 12). Under this representational convention, disabled persons, figured as protagonists of "narratives of overcoming" (Sandahl 2004: 584; Lerner and Straus 2006: 2) are assigned superhuman, quasi-magical compensatory abilities that allow them to transcend their impairments. Within the resultant "rhetoric of triumph" (Couser 2002: 111), disabled individuals may undergo what Longmore (1987: 71) terms "dramas of adjustment" wherein "God or nature or life compensates handicapped people for their loss, and the compensation is spiritual, moral, mental and emotional." A widely circulated iteration of this stereotype is the biography of Beethoven, who – as the title of Morrissey's 1993 live album reminds – was deaf, yet is remembered as having surmounted that obstacle to compose some of the most revered works of Western art music (Cizmic 2006: 24). The dangers that inhere in the "super cripple" stereotype are multiple (Barnes 1993: 12–13): first, the "super cripple" figure promotes exaggerated and inaccurate beliefs about the abilities of disabled people which might result in their being denied needed services; furthermore, an inordinate emphasis on disabled achievement implies that acceptance into the broader community demands overcompensation on the part of disabled persons; and finally, the inordinate emphasis on disabled achievement implicitly devalues the experiences of "ordinary" people (able-bodied and disabled alike) as inconsequential.

Inasmuch as Morrissey merely wishes that his disabled protagonist be able to choose her own clothing, he aspires for her a minimal degree of non-heroic agency. Hereby the disabled girl, even if she has had no say in her corporeal figuration, can at least elect to ornament (and conceal) it is as she prefers, thereby attaining a measure of influence over the ableist gaze. Moreover, that Morrissey foresees neither pulchritude nor wealth for her not only testifies to the perdurability of socially constructed norms of beauty predicated on the fiction of the normate body; it is also presciently consonant with a January 2008 British charity report which found that low employment levels, education discrimination, and insufficient benefits among the UK's disabled population resulted in their being twice as likely as the non-disabled population to suffer economic hardship (Smith 2008). To be sure, Morrissey's reference in these lines to "walking" does puzzle. Because Morrissey is vague on the precise details of the disabled girl's embodiment – exploitatively inviting the listener thereby to imagine her in the most unsettling of terms – it is impossible to say whether the act of "walking" (which I assume Morrissey intends to be understood literally, as a perambulatory technique of the normate body) is something that, through physical therapy, surgical intervention, prosthesis or physical aid, she could be plausibly expected to approximate, or whether in wishing her this fate, Morrissey is steering her towards "super cripple" aspirations. It can be prudently asserted, in any case, that Morrissey's portrayal of disability in 'November' predominantly avoids explicit and hackneyed evocation of the "super cripple" stereotype.

Morrissey can also be seen in 'November' to countermine the stereotype of the Disabled Person as Sinister and Evil (Barnes 1993: 11). A staple of literary characterization, this formula poses disabled persons as menacing figures whose corporeal deformation indexes "disfigurement of personality and deformity of soul" (Longmore 1987: 68). Barnes notes that the linkage of disability to sin, the sinister, monstrous, criminal and violent – in short, to evil – is a persistent feature of disability characterization that poses "a major obstacle to disabled people's successful integration into the community" (1993: 11). The evil attributed to the disabled figure that Kriegel names "the Demonic Cripple" is purported to result from "a pervasive sense of absence [that] forces each of them to plot and scheme and burn with the need for revenge [...] trying to bend the world's will to his own" (1987: 34–35). Echoing Kriegel, Longmore (1987: 67) cogently observes that

[g]iving disabilities to villainous characters reflects and reinforces, albeit in exaggerated fashion, three common prejudices against handicapped people: disability is a punishment for evil; disabled people are embittered by their "fate"; disabled people resent the nondisabled and would, if they could, destroy them.

To be sure, 'November' would seem at first blush to invoke the stereotype of the 'Demonic Cripple' through the portentously bestial sonics that issue from its heavily distorted guitar, punctuating the song at its introduction, fadeout and horrific intermediate "birthing" interlude. Moreover, the stereotype is evoked through Morrissey's inflammatory (and deliberately provocative, in view of the prominence bestowed by its placement as the final word of the song's title, where it is encouraged to linger in the memory) use of the word "monster" to denominate his disabled protagonist. However, rather than serve as an endorsement of this derogatory signification, the boldness with which the aspersion is uttered suggests that Morrissey engages here in what Mitchell and Snyder (2000: 35–36) call "transgressive resignification":

> As opposed to substituting more palatable terms, the ironic embrace of derogatory terminology has provided the leverage that belongs to openly transgressive displays [...] The embrace of denigrating terminology forces the dominant culture to face its own violence head-on because the authority of devaluation has been claimed openly and ironically [...] The effect shames the dominant culture into a recognition of its own dehumanizing precepts [...] that detracts from the original power of the condescending terms.

Rogan opines that Morrissey's use of the word "monster" constitutes an "outrage [that] outweighs whatever noble intentions he may claim" (2006: 152). I argue on the contrary that in putting forward so loaded a term, Morrissey issues an implicit invitation to interrogate language – always a critical issue when considering the interests of disabled persons (Wendell 1996: 77–81) – and, in turn, to confront our own views on, and prejudices towards, disability. To be sure, the song's inflammatory musical and lyrical rhetoric is ironized and, ultimately, derailed by such countervailing factors as the disabled girl's unblemished juvenescence and by her earnest, borderline naïve and decidedly undemonic appeal to Christ for aid ("Jesus made me, so Jesus save me / From pity, sympathy / And people discussing me").

But if Morrissey can be credited with repudiating certain disability stereotypes, he can equally be charged with re-inscribing others. His repeated description of his disabled protagonist as a "poor twisted child, so ugly" and as a "hostage to [...] the wheels underneath her" participates, for instance, in the stereotype of the Disabled Person as Pitiable and Pathetic (Barnes 1993: 7–10), according to which disability is synonymous with illness and suffering. This equation justifies portrayals of disabled persons as wretched, passive and dependent, their tragic neediness enabling the fundamental benevolence and sensitivity of their non-disabled benefactors to emerge into view – Morrissey's bathetic invitation of "oh hug me, oh hug me" being apposite to such a point. Such depictions of disability – patronizingly sentimental rather than genuinely compassionate in a way that might usefully alter public perceptions – are complicit with the medical model of disability in their location of the "problem" of disability in the individual body and in their (inaccurate) depiction of life with impairment as a tragic and life-shattering experience, one which necessarily eventuates in social isolation. This manner of presentation shrouds disability in the kind of fearsomeness that ableist culture feels it must indeed, to borrow Morrissey's phrase, put out of its mind.

Perhaps even greater consequence can be discerned in the deployment in 'November' of the stereotype of the Disabled Person as Sexually Abnormal (Barnes 1993: 16), wherein persons with disabilities are limned as incapable of sexual activity – the dire corollary to this perceived impotency being that their lives are deemed unworthy of living. Barnes assails the accuracy of the stereotype, observing that while certain "normal" sexual activities can be hindered by impairment, the range of alternate sexual behaviors available may nevertheless remain rather large, and thus the equation of disability with impotence speaks more to the able-bodied world's lack of knowledge about sex than to its knowledge of disability. I will have more to say about this stereotype below, but for the moment it suffices to say that the depiction of the disabled protagonist of 'November' – her whom none would dare to kiss, even under cover of darkness; this "symbol of where mad, mad lovers / Must pause and draw the line" – appears to be in full complicity with the cliché. Morrissey may be stirred by the girl's sexual abjection, but he does not explicitly challenge it.

This manner of deconstruction could continue apace for several paragraphs more, but the point would remain that if in 'November Spawned A Monster' Morrissey discredits select injurious disability stereotypes, he advertises certain others. Of course, to accept the validity of this contention is not to conclude that Morrissey necessarily endorses whatever troubling sentiments he articulates. Such a logical leap fails to appreciate the subtlety of Morrissey's artistry. But then, Zuberi, in a consideration of representations of race and nationalism in Morrissey's work, underscores how problematic Morrissey's manner of artistry can be (2001: 64).

> As a studious fan I want to concede to Morrissey the escape clause of irony – that he doesn't really mean it, and he's just provoking the Brits to think [...] Listening to the songs repeatedly suggests that Morrissey is a ventriloquist, posing different voices against each other. You're never very sure which voice belongs to him [...] As much as an ironic mode has the potential to critique certain versions of history, irony can serve to evade realities and new possibilities as it takes apart the same decaying body of [...] cultural concerns again and again with its blunt scalpel.

Zuberi's misgivings vis-à-vis Morrissey's discourse of race and nationalism apply equally well to Morrissey's representations of the disabled other. Following his lead, I argue that in 'November Spawned A Monster', Morrissey plays the role of cultural ventriloquist whose aim is to force his audience into a confrontation with the violence of its own ableist prejudices. In order to avoid the appearance of brute didacticism, however, Morrissey engages in a circumspect strategy of multivocal ambiguity which could easily be mistaken for at least partial collusion with ableist ideology.

Still, the vigilant eye can discern junctures at which Morrissey tips his hand as *agent provocateur*. Several shots in the music video filmed to promote the 'November' single, for instance, depict Morrissey kicking or pawing at the earthen floor of California's Death Valley (Bret 2004: 135), sending up clouds of dust and stone. One tracking shot propels the camera gliding towards Morrissey's oncoming figure, and just as it draws nigh, he flings a handful of dirt and rocks hurtling towards its lens. Such pugnacious gestures achieve germane resonance when decoded with reference to Douglas's influential study *Purity and Danger: An Analysis of Concepts of Pollution and Taboo*. Although not a treatise on disability specifically, Garland-Thomson finds Douglas's work of considerable interest to disability studies (1997: 33–34).

> Douglas speculates about the relativity of dirt in ways that can be applied to the cultural meaning of disability. Dirt, she observes, is "matter out of place [...] the by-product of a systematic ordering and classification of matter, in so far as ordering involves rejecting inappropriate elements" [...] Dirt is an anomaly, a discordant element rejected from the schema that individuals and societies use in order to construct a stable, recognizable, and predictable world [...] Douglas's interpretation of dirt as anomaly, as the extra-ordinary, can be extended to the body we call "disabled" as well as to other forms of social marginalization. Like dirt, all disability is in some sense "matter out of place" in terms of the interpretive frameworks and physical expectations our culture shares. Visible physical disability lies outside the normative ordering system and can only be included and comprehended under Douglas's classifications of "aberrant" or "anomalous", categories that accommodate what does not fit into the space of the ordinary [...] Because cultures do not tolerate such affronts to their communal narratives of order, what emerges from a given cultural context as irremediable anomaly translates not as neutral difference, but as pollution, taboo, contagion.

Within Douglas's conceptual framework, political significance can thus be discerned in the very act of Morrissey's release of a single (and accompanying music video) that takes as its novel subject matter the experience of disability: 'November Spawned A Monster' emerges in this view as an artistic and commercial effort that deposited a sizable clod of cultural dirt onto the terrain of the popular musicscape. Within the music video itself, this transgressive act is visualized in the shots of Morrissey kicking up dirt and flinging it at the camera – by implication, at the viewer. It is helpful to note here that, as Garland-Thomson observes (1997: 35), one coping mechanism identified by Douglas as a means whereby cultures respond to the existence of the anomalous – of cultural dirt – is outright avoidance of it, achieved through enclosure, exclusion, regulation and segregation. In writing, recording and performing 'November Spawned A Monster', Morrissey works to undermine the strategies of avoidance and segregation that help preserve the devaluation of disfavored cultural categories.

Further covert meaning can be discerned in the hearing aid that Morrissey sports in the 'November' video, an updated model of the prosthesis-cum-accoutrement that it had been his wont to wear in the early days of The Smiths. His reprise of the accessory here reminds the cognizant viewer that Morrissey had, by his own account, originally worn the contrivance as a demonstration of solidarity and support after receiving a fan letter from a deaf girl (Rogan 1993: 185–186). One can reasonably infer that the return of the prop in the 'November' video, whatever problematic ambiguities of tone are otherwise presented, registers Morrissey's assertion of a comparable solidarity with that song's disabled protagonist. It is a gesture, moreover, which tacitly cultivates a nascent sense of community predicated upon disabled identity, presupposing as it does a certain parity between two disparate forms of disabled embodiment – impaired hearing and congenital deformity.

Indeed, in subsequent years, Morrissey would grow that community incrementally as a widening variety of anomalous bodies would come to populate his songscape: the aphonia of 'Mute Witness' (1991), the chronic maternity of 'Pregnant For The Last Time' (1991), the corpulence of 'You're The One For Me, Fatty' (1992) and the short-heightedness of 'It's Hard To Walk Tall When You're Small' (2004). I lack the space to discuss these other songs at any length, but I will venture two general observations. First, each of these songs follows the lead of 'November' in affording Morrissey the occasion to evince provocatively equivocal attitudes towards figures of corporeal non-normativity, alternately embracing and disavowing the rejected body. Second, the sheer variety of disabled embodiment and attendant cultural meanings that these songs successively present intrinsically advocate for an ever-expansive conception of disability and disabled identity.

Nowhere, however, in Morrissey's *oeuvre* is the boundary separating the normate from the rejected body more aggressively troubled than in the track 'At Amber', issued as the B-Side to Morrissey's October 1990 single 'Piccadilly Palare'. Released just six months after 'November Spawned A Monster', 'At Amber' comprises a kind of postscript to that antecedent text. Its lyrics situate a despondent Morrissey in a hotel foyer from which he telephones an "invalid friend"[4] in order to bewail his unsatisfactory accommodations and disparage the inebriation and sexual profligacy of the other patrons. After being chided by his disabled auditor for ingratitude – after all, he is at least fortunate enough to have functioning limbs – Morrissey rejoins with a remarkable declaration: "oh, my invalid friend", he sings, "in our different ways we are the same". Because these words conclude Morrissey's lyric, nothing follows to specify what meaning underlies this tension proffered between identity and difference vis-à-vis Morrissey's relationship to disability. Nor do the precedent lines offer a sufficient basis from which to evolve a clear understanding. Explication must be sought elsewhere, and the lead I wish to pursue necessitates a return to the stereotype of the Disabled Person as Sexually Abnormal.

Disability is equated in the cultural imaginary with physical lack; so too is the female body, which psychoanalysis figures as a castrated male, discursively linking two categories such that the phrase "disabled female sexuality" becomes tautology (Siebers 2008: 173; Garland-Thomson 1997: 19). Disabled male sexuality, on the other hand, resonates with themes of emasculation and effeminacy. Indeed, as Longmore (1987: 73) observes, "[m]ore than one male character with a disability refers to himself as 'only half a man'". This, of course, is not impertinent to an artist whose quasi-autobiographical (Rogan 2006: 81) 1987 composition 'Half A Person' finds its young male protagonist checking into the YWCA. To be sure, Morrissey's gender nonconformity and indeterminate sexual identity constitute well-trod, if still unsettled, ground; therefore, I will not rehearse their associated speculations here.[5] I will, however, draw attention to the way in which Morrissey's rhetoric of gender and sexual identity resounds with his rhetoric of disability. Take, for example, Morrissey's pronouncement in a 1986 interview that "I always thought my genitals were the result of some crude practical joke" (Pye 1986). (Morrissey added an indirect gloss to this assertion when in a 1991 interview he asserted that "I've always felt closer to transsexuality than anything else" (Brown 1991).) This constituted an only slightly more provocatively terse expression of a sentiment that had been thematized in The Smiths' 1984 track 'Pretty Girls Make Graves'. Here Morrissey describes a seaside stroll with a carnally ravenous female whose sexual aggression vis-à-vis Morrissey's own demure corporeal insecurities ("she's too rough and I'm too delicate") rewrites conventional gender roles. Certain lyrical passages circumspectly intimate (through the innuendo of "rise" in particular) that Morrissey as narrator is marked by sexual impairment, dysfunction or insufficiency:

> I'm not the man you think I am
> And Sorrow's native son
> He will not rise for anyone
> […]
> I could have been wild and I could have been free
> But Nature played this trick on me.

Morrissey's characterization here of Nature as trickster prefigures his subsequent remark (cited above) regarding his sexual organs being cosmic subterfuge. Both pronouncements in turn prefigure the ascription of blame to a greater power made by the disabled protagonist of 'November Spawned A Monster' for the "frame of useless limbs" by which she has been burdened: "Jesus made me, so Jesus save me." And all these utterances in turn foretoken Morrissey's thematization of frustrated sexual desire on his 2004 single 'I Have Forgiven Jesus':

> I was a good kid
> I wouldn't do you no harm
> […]
> But Jesus hurt me
> When he deserted me, but
> I have forgiven Jesus
> […]
> Why did you give me so much desire
> When there is nowhere I can go
> To offload this desire?
> […]
> Why did you stick me in
> Self-deprecating bones and skin?

The above-cited passages demonstrate that the lyrics of 'Jesus' echo those of 'November' in bringing together themes of blameless youth, dysfunctional corporeality, social and sexual abjection, and divine culpability.

One might well ponder the associative chains[6] that link Morrissey's rhetoric of gender and sexual identity to his rhetoric of disability and conclude that Morrissey exploits disability by invoking it as a proxy through which to articulate his own gender and sexual concerns, obscuring disability's real self by arrogating it as a "master trope of human disqualification" (Mitchell and Snyder 2000: 3). As philosopher Anita Silvers has written (2002: 232–233), "[a] signature thesis of disability studies is that art inherently appropriates and exploits the figure of disability [...] using disability symbolically to signify something other than itself, and thus with diverting attention from disability in order to hide it [...]impairment is veiled by being treated as broadly symbolic of disempowerment [...]of all those, whether or not impaired, whom the dominant society excludes and oppresses". This "history of metaphorical opportunism" eventuates in what has been termed "the representational double bind of disability. While disabled populations are firmly entrenched on the outer margins of social power and cultural value, the disabled body also serves as the raw material out of which other socially disempowered communities make themselves visible .[...] In fact, once the bodily surface is exposed as the phantasmatic façade that disguises the workings of patriarchal, racist, heterosexist, and upper class norms, the monstrous body itself is quickly forgotten" (Mitchell and Snyder 1997: 6–17).

Such criticisms seem at first consideration to be wholly appropriate to a discussion of disability representation in Morrissey's *oeuvre*. That his disability-themed songs traffic in certain clichés and stereotypes can be understood, as I suggested earlier, as a kind of cultural ventriloquism whereby Morrissey brings to attention a variety of attitudes regarding disability, proffering them for contemplation; in this view, Morrissey is exculpated from any endorsement of ableist prejudice against disabled persons, emerging instead as a provocateur who has what he perceives to be the interests of disabled persons in mind even as he alternately ridicules and expresses sympathy for them in song. This is perhaps the most generous view that can be taken of Morrissey's discourse of disability. A more persuasive argument might be built upon the suggestion that Morrissey's recourse to tropes of disability is less about disabled persons themselves and more about their utility as proxy symbols of other forms of social marginalization of greater interest to Morrissey – non-normative sexual and gender identity in particular. This latter reading of Morrissey's discourse of disability sees it as deeply implicated in the "metaphorical opportunism" decried by disability studies scholars.

Such concerns might well be mitigated by recalling the observation that the normate is a figure defined through the exclusion of devalued traits that fall along multiple axes of identity – not just able-bodiedness, but class, gender, ethnicity and sexuality as well; as such, disability cannot be fully disentangled from these latter identity categories. The recognition that disability has always been inflected by issues of gender, sexuality, ethnicity (Garland-Thomson 1997: 9) and so on reframes Morrissey's symbolic use of disability and deployment of mutually inflecting rhetorics of gender/sexuality and disability as less egregious exploitation than empathetic manoeuvre. Indeed, Morrissey's use of disability imagery implicitly subsumes multiple marginalized identities of interest to the artist (including national, religious and class identity; after all, Morrissey grew up a working-class second generation Irish Catholic in class-conscious Protestant England (Rogan 1993: 30–36)). This strategy is suggested by Morrissey's biographer David Bret's (2004: 135) comment regarding 'November Spawned A Monster': "The song (though otherwise unconnected with its title) does fit into the category known by the French as 'Les enfants de novembre' – collectively, the oppressed peoples of the world, whether this be by way of creed, colour, sexuality, war, or in this instance disability".

Still, even if regarded as fair use rather than semiotic colonialism, Morrissey's recourse to tropes of disability is subject to the criticism that opening too broad an umbrella in order to assert a commonality among different kinds of social marginalization erases the political value that accrues from cultivating a distinct sense of disabled identity, as Susan Wendell has observed (1996: 74–75).

> Emphasizing differences from the dominant group [...] often creates a strong sense of solidarity among those who share them and makes it easier to resist the devaluation of those differences by the dominant group. In addition, some people with disabilities do not particularly want to be assimilated into non-disabled social life or non-disabled political groups, either because they fear that unless social values are changed quite radically, they will always be at a disadvantage in integrated settings, or because they value qualities of their separate lives and organizations.

> [...] In separate groups of people with disabilities, powerful "givens" of the larger culture that put them at a disadvantage, such as the non-disabled paradigm of humanity, the idealization of the body, and the demand for control of the body, can be challenged openly and even made irrelevant.

Wendell (1996: 70) complicates this perspective, however, with her assertion that "[i]t is [...] important not to assume that people with disabilities identify with all others who have disabilities or share a single perspective on disability (or anything else)"; that is, the obfuscation of differences among the proliferating varieties of disability diverts attention away from the specific experiences of and remedies available to any individual disabled person. However, a certain political value undoubtedly inheres in an expansive conception of disability that troubles its traditional narrow colloquial definitions, exposing its articulations to other forms of marginalized identity: as Wendell notes (1996: 74), "[e]mphasizing similarities between people with and people without disabilities seems to hold the promise of reducing the 'Otherness' of those who are disabled by enabling the non-disabled to identify with them, recognize their humanity and their rights, paving the way to increasing their assimilation into all aspects of social life".

Indeed, it is worth noting in the context of the present discussion that despite the emphasis in so much of Morrissey's work on the isolation of the individual, there exists a countervailing discourse of community and solidarity that emerges at junctures. Pertinently, the phraseology through which such community is limned is tinged with the language of corporeal impairment and disability. For instance, on the track 'Nobody Loves Us', the B-Side of his 1995 single 'Dagenham Dave', Morrissey posits himself as a member of a community of unloved "born-again atheists" and "practicing troublemakers". His description of this coterie as "useless" deploys the same adjective used to describe the impaired corporeality ("frame of useless limbs") of the disabled protagonist of 'November Spawned A Monster'. He also describes this unloved fraternity as "bog-eyed and cross-eyed" (stigmatized physical differences both) and asserts that "we are just stood here / Waiting for the next great wound" – again conjuring up the motif of bodily impairment. Then too, the concluding track of Morrissey's 1991 album *Kill Uncle*, 'There's A Place In Hell For Me And My Friends', similarly thematizes the marginalization of Morrissey and his confrères, whose extreme social abjection is registered by the song's title. To the mainstream culture which has so ostracized them, Morrissey addresses the following lines:

> All that we hope is when we go
> Our skin and our blood and our bones
> Don't get in your way, making you ill
> The way they did when we lived.

These lines lay emphasis on the revulsion caused by the corporeality of Morrissey and his stigmatized companions, evoking the threat discerned by ableist culture in the rejected body. Moreover, Morrissey's lyrics, with its image of unpleasantly obtruding carnage, align well with Mary Douglas's analysis of the cultural figuration of socially marginalized identities (including disability) as dirt, matter out of place, pollution and contagion.

To be clear, I am not suggesting that the communities being imagined in these songs are expressly fraternities of the disabled. Such a focus would be far too narrow for an artist whose 2006 single 'The Youngest Was The Most Loved' – a song about a shy, overprotected child who grows into a murderous adult – tendered the blanket proclamation, "There is no such thing in life as normal." I argue instead that Morrissey is using the trope of disability in order to stake out a sodality whose indeterminate boundaries are flexible enough to accommodate multiple socially marginalized identities, whether predicated on gender, sexual, racial, ethnic, national, class or physical and mental differences. Yet inasmuch as disabled identity is an acknowledged constituent of this commodious disfavored populace, Morrissey's art works to diminish the ableist prejudice that gazes at the disabled body and sees only otherness. Like the unforeseen broken hip of Sheridan Whiteside, it is therefore allied to one of the central projects of disability studies: to re-imagine disability as, in the words of Snyder, Brueggemann and Garland-Thomson (2002: 2), "a bodily condition and a social category [that] either now or later will touch us all. The fact that many of us will become disabled if we live long enough is perhaps the fundamental aspect of human embodiment".

Notes

1. The film would, in turn, be cited by Morrissey in the early days of his celebrity as occupying a place among his ten favourite films (Morrissey 1983).
2. With different emphasis, Wendell – like Garland-Thomson, a feminist disability studies scholar – uses the terms "rejected" and "negative body" to name the cultural violence enacted on those aspects of non-normative corporeality "that are feared, ignored, despised, and/or rejected in a society and its culture" (1996: 85). The resulting prejudice that would reduce a body to its stigmatized disability has been labelled "ableism" by activists and academics within disability studies (Siebers 2008: 81).
3. A few examples suffice to make the point. The titular siren of The Smiths' 1983 B-side 'Wonderful Woman', for instance, callously importunes both "I'm starved of mirth / Let's go and trip a dwarf" and "just to pass time / Let us go and rob the blind", while in the 1986 Smiths release 'Frankly Mr. Shankly', Morrissey declares "sometimes I'd feel more fulfilled / Making Christmas cards with the mentally ill". Nor are images of disability absent from Morrissey's later work; his 2004 solo single release 'First of the Gang to Die', by way of example, makes passing reference to the sun's rise "behind the Home for the Blind".
4. 'Invalid' constitutes an inexact designation which, according to the *Oxford English Dictionary Online* (2007), could range from temporary illness to permanent physical incapacitation; Colin Barnes notes that the term also contains the pejorative sense of not being valid, of lacking authority and efficacy (1993: 21) – rendering its appearance here provocative in a manner redolent of the use of the term "monster" in 'November Spawned A Monster'.
5. For a particularly cogent analysis of ways in which Morrissey's music and lyrics work to construct ambiguous gendered and sexual subjectivities, see Hubbs (1996).
6. It bears noting that similar associative chains recur in Morrissey's most recent work as well. In 'Because Of My Poor Education', the B-Side of his February 2009 single 'I'm Throwing My Arms Around Paris', Morrissey reprises the same linkages among corporeal difference, lovelessness, stigmatization and social abjection that had been thematized years previously in 'November Spawned A Monster'; here, however, the perspective is first-person, and the corporeal non-normativity is metaphorical: "Because of this strange indentation", Morrissey sings, "I live my life without affection / Kind-hearted view me and say / Thank God that's not me".

References

Barnes, C. (1993) *Disability Imagery and the Media: An Exploration of the Principles for Media Representations of Disabled People*. Halifax: The British Council of Organisations of Disabled People/Ryburn Publishing, available: *http: //www.leeds.ac.uk/disability-studies/archiveuk/Barnes/ disabling%20imagery.pdf._*

Barton, L. (2004) 'The disability movement: some observations', in J. Swain, S. French, C. Barnes and C. Thomas (eds) *Disabling Barriers – Enabling Environments*. Thousand Oaks, CA: Sage Publications, pp. 285–90.

Beavis and Butt-head (1994) Blackout, MTV, 11th April.

Bret, D. (2004) *Morrissey: Scandal and Passion*. London: Robson Books.

Bret, D. (1995) *Morrissey: Landscapes of the Mind*. New York: Carroll & Graf.

Brown, L. (2008) *Meetings with Morrissey*. New York: Omnibus Press.

Brown, L. (1991) 'I'll astonish you', *Details*, March, available: http: //www.compsoc.man.ac.uk/~moz/ quotes/details1.htm.

Chalmers, R. (1992) 'No sex please, I'm Morrissey', *The Observer*, 6th December, available: http: // motorcycleaupairboy.com/interviews/1992/observer.htm.

Cizmic, M. (2006) 'Of bodies and narratives: musical representations of pain and illness in HBO's Wit', in N. Lerner and J. N. Straus (eds) *Sounding Off: Theorizing Disability in Music.* New York: Routledge, pp. 23–40.

Couser, G. T. (2002) 'Signifying bodies: life writing and disability studies', in S. L. Snyder, B. J. Brueggemann and R. Garland-Thomson (eds) *Disability Studies: Enabling the Humanities.* New York: Modern Language Association of America, pp. 109–17.

Davis, L. J. (1995) *Enforcing Normalcy: Disability, Deafness, and the Body.* New York: Verso.

Garland-Thomson, R. (2006) 'Integrating disability, transforming feminist theory', in L. Davis (ed.) *The Disability Studies Reader.* New York: Routledge, pp. 257–73.

Garland-Thomson, R. (1997) *Extraordinary Bodies: Figuring Physical Disability in American Culture and Literature.* New York: Columbia University Press.

Gartner, A. and Joe, T. (1987) 'Introduction', in A. Gartner and T. Joe (eds) *Images of the Disabled, Disabling Images.* New York: Praeger Publishers, pp. 1–6.

Ghaziani, A. (2005) 'Anticipatory actualized identities: a cultural analysis of the transition from AIDS disability to work', *The Sociological Quarterly*, 45, pp. 273–301.

Hubbs, N. (1996) 'Music of the "Fourth Gender": Morrissey and the sexual politics of melodic contour', *Genders*, 23, pp. 266–96.

Johnstone, D. (2001) *An Introduction to Disability Studies.* London: David Fulton Publishers.

Keighley, William (dir.) (1942) *The Man Who Came To Dinner*, Film, US: Warner Bros.

Kriegel, L. (1987) 'The cripple in literature', in A. Gartner and T. Joe (eds) *Images of the Disabled, Disabling Images.* New York: Praeger Publishers, pp. 31–46.

Lerner, N. and Straus, J. N. (2006) 'Introduction: theorizing disability in music', in N. Lerner and J. Straus (eds) *Sounding Off: Theorizing Disability in Music.* New York: Routledge, pp. 1–10.

Longmore, P. K. (1987) 'Screening stereotypes: images of disabled people in television and motion pictures', in A. Gartner and T. Joe (eds) *Images of the Disabled, Disabling Images.* New York: Praeger Publishers, pp. 65–78.

Mason, A; Pratt H.D.; Patel, D.R.; Greydanus, D.E.; Yahya, K.Z. (2004) 'Prejudice toward people with disabilities', in J. L. Chin (ed.) *The Psychology of Prejudice and Discrimination: Disability, Religion, Physique and Other Traits.* Westport, CT: Greenwood Publishing Group, pp. 51–94.

Mitchell, D. T. and Snyder, S. L. (2000) *Narrative Prosthesis: Disability and the Dependencies of Discourse.* Ann Arbor: University of Michigan Press.

Mitchell, D. T. and Snyder, S. L. (1997) 'Introduction: disability studies and the double bind of representation', in D. T. Mitchell and S. L. Snyder (eds) *The Body and Physical Difference: Discourses of Disability.* Ann Arbor: University of Michigan Press, pp. 1–31.

Morrissey (2009) 'Because Of My Poor Education', *I'm Throwing My Arms Around Paris.* Polydor/ Decca.

Morrissey (2006) 'The Youngest Was The Most Loved', *The Youngest was the Most Loved.* Attack/ Sanctuary.

Morrissey (2005) *Live at Earls Court.* Attack.

Morrissey (2004) 'First Of The Gang To Die', *First of the Gang To Die.* Attack/Sanctuary.

Morrissey (2004) 'I Have Forgiven Jesus', *I Have Forgiven Jesus.* Attack/Sanctuary.

Morrissey (2004) 'It's Hard To Walk Tall When You're Small', *Irish Blood, English Heart.* Attack/ Sanctuary.

Morrissey (2001) *The Best of Morrissey.* Rhino/Reprise.

Morrissey (2000) *Suedehead: The Best of Morrissey.* EMI.

Morrissey (2000) 'November Spawned A Monster', Music Video, Dir. Tim Broad, *¡Oye Esteban!*, DVD. Warner/Reprise.

Morrissey (1995) 'Nobody Loves Us', *Dagenham Dave*. RCA Victor.

Morrissey (1993) *Beethoven Was Deaf*. HMV.

Morrissey (1992) *Live in Dallas*, VHS. Warner Bros.

Morrissey (1992) 'You're The One For Me, Fatty', *You're the One for Me, Fatty*. HMV.

Morrissey (1991) *Hulmerist*, VHS. Warner Bros.

Morrissey (1991) 'Mute Witness', *Kill Uncle*. HMV.

Morrissey (1991) 'Pregnant For The Last Time', *Pregnant for the Last Time*. HMV.

Morrissey (1991) 'There's A Place In Hell For Me And My Friends', *Kill Uncle*. HMV.

Morrissey (1990) 'At Amber', *Piccadilly Palare*. HMV.

Morrissey (1990) *Bona Drag*. HMV.

Morrissey (1990) 'November Spawned A Monster', *November Spawned a Monster*. HMV.

Morrissey (1983) 'Portrait of the artist as a consumer', *New Musical Express*, 17th September, available: *http: //www.morrissey-solo.com/content/interview/nme0983.html*.

Oxford English Dictionary Online, Version 3.1.1, 2007, Jerome Library, Bowling Green State University, Bowling Green, OH, available: http: //dictionary.oed.com.

Pye, I. (1986) 'Some mothers do 'ave 'em', *New Musical Express*, 7th June, available: http: //foreverill. com/interviews/1986/mothers.htm.

Rogan, J. (2006) *Morrissey: The Albums*. London: Calidore.

Rogan, J. (1993) *Morrissey & Marr: The Severed Alliance*. New York: Omnibus Press.

Sandahl, C. (2004) 'Black man, blind man: disability identity politics and performance', *Theatre Journal*, 56, pp. 579–602.

Shakespeare, T. (2006) *Disability Rights and Wrongs*. New York: Routledge.

Siebers, T. (2008) *Disability Theory*. Ann Arbor: University of Michigan Press.

Silvers, A. (2002) 'The crooked timber of humanity: disability, ideology and the aesthetic', in M. Corker and T. Shakespeare (eds) *Disability/Postmodernity: Embodying Disability Theory*. New York: Continuum, pp. 228–244.

Smith, L. (2008) 'Call for action to cut poverty among disabled people', *The Guardian*, 8th January, available: *http: //www.guardian.co.uk/politics/2008/jan/08/economy.uk*.

Smiths, The (1987) 'Half A Person', *Shoplifters of the World Unite*. Rough Trade.

Smiths, The (1986) 'Frankly Mr. Shankly', *The Queen is Dead*. Rough Trade.

Smiths, The (1984) 'Pretty Girls Make Graves', *The Smiths*. Rough Trade.

Smiths, The (1984) 'William, It Was Really Nothing', *William, It was Really Nothing*. Rough Trade.

Smiths, The (1983) 'Wonderful Woman', *This Charming Man*. Rough Trade.

Snyder, S. L., Brueggemann, B. J. and Garland-Thomson, R. (2002) 'Introduction: integrating disability into teaching and scholarship', in S. L. Snyder, B. J. Brueggemann and R. Garland-Thomson (eds) *Disability Studies: Enabling the Humanities*. New York: Modern Language Association of America, pp. 1–12.

Wendell, S. (1996) *The Rejected Body: Feminist Philosophical Reflections on Disability*. New York: Routledge.

Young, I. M. (2002) 'Foreword', in M. Corker and T. Shakespeare (eds) *Disability/Postmodernity: Embodying Disability Theory*. New York: Continuum, pp. xii–xiv.

Zuberi, N. (2001) *Sounds English: Transnational Popular Music*. Chicago: University of Illinois Press.

Chapter 7

"My So Friendly Lens": Morrissey as Mediated through His Public Image

Melissa Connor

Introduction

In this chapter I will consider the ways in which Morrissey has made use of visual imagery for album artwork and how this communicates within the spheres of visual art, portraiture and popular music, and specifically with his audience. With his first band, The Smiths, the album artwork was idiosyncratic. It was a distinct style of design recognizable by the "cover star" portrait, typography and absence of band members. As a solo artist it became necessary for Morrissey to forego a successful design style in favour of something else. What that "something else" is will be described as I look at Morrissey's solo album artwork from the single 'Suedehead', released in 1988, to the current "digital age", and how the construction of Morrissey as an icon has relied on carefully coded visual representations. The Internet has opened up new avenues for discussion about the visual component of Morrissey's work; it has also enabled fans to view album artwork before listening to any of the songs. For some fans it also becomes a place for sharing their own designs for alternate album artwork. The one consistent element of the album covers during the 21 years since 'Suedehead' has been Morrissey's insistence that his own face feature on each.

Artwork and the Smiths

The artwork for an album cover is a constructed visual image, loaded with signs which can be read as text by music fans. As described by Simon Frith and Howard Horne in their book *Art Into Pop* (1987), the album cover became aligned with visual art. Style became important. Style, as described by Dick Hebdige in his book *Subculture: The Meaning of Style* (1979) is an intentional communicator comprising choices such as clothing, pose and hairstyle. The choices Morrissey makes in his visual representations are deliberate and intentional communication with his audience. The album artwork can be considered an essential part of the "myth of Morrissey". Writers (including Julian Stringer and Gavin Hopps) and music journalists have remarked upon Morrissey's contradictions and unwillingness to conform. Stringer describes Morrissey as "a shy man who is also an outrageous narcissist" (Stringer 1992: 16). Due to this refusal to be pinned down, the album covers and concert backdrops become an important part of decoding Morrissey. Through his album covers the fan is able to gain awareness of the "Morrissey style" of dress, pose and gesture. There is also the pleasure of discovering the various "stars" and locations that Morrissey appropriates, whether on stage backdrops or in the films used before a concert. Watching the black and white images of Elvis Presley, The Shocking Blue, Lou Reed, Shelagh Delaney or Nico can seem like an exciting treasure hunt into discovering Morrissey's marginalized "heroes".

Because the album covers of The Smiths were so identifiable, Morrissey needed to abandon the visual style that he had been so involved in producing. The book *Peepholism* (1994) by Jo Slee provides a fascinating document of the "hands on" approach to album cover design by Morrissey. From the release of their first single in 1983, the album cover artwork of The Smiths carried a distinctive style, featuring popular culture reference points mined from Morrissey's nostalgic interest in music, film and literature. Choice of artwork served several purposes – as a means to resolve the problem of having a "band" image on the cover, as a branding device and as a means for Morrissey to display his cultural taste. The "cover stars" formed part of the overall Smiths package and helped to develop the public image of Morrissey as steeped in these popular culture references and perhaps as "the ultimate fan" as suggested by Andrew O'Hagan (2004).

Within the visual arts, the cover artwork of The Smiths shares similarities with the celebrity portrait silkscreens by American artist Andy Warhol. This similarity has also been noted by writers Michael Bracewell and Matthew Bannister to the extent that Bannister called Morrissey "the British Warhol", drawing comparisons between the "carefully fashioned public image" that they both share (Bannister 2006: 150). Bracewell compares Morrissey's position as a cultural brand transcending the limits of pop music to Warhol's ability to do the same in the art world (Bracewell 2002: 114–120). What both Bracewell and Bannister are referring to is Morrissey and Warhol's public image rather than any direct comparison between art forms. However, there are similarities in the way in which Warhol and Morrissey use the celebrity "cover star" image. In Warhol's silkscreens celebrities and the notion of celebrity itself are presented as unreal, particularly in the use of vibrant, unnatural colour rather than flesh tones, which render the celebrities similar; they become Warhol's stars. Like Warhol, Morrissey used publicly available images of celebrities, but, once placed on a Smiths album cover, they became appropriated as part of the "Morrissey" narrative rather than their own.

To me you are a work of art

Due to this strong identity of The Smiths album covers, it would have been difficult for Morrissey to continue to use this visual language of the "cover star", which necessitated an evolution of the "cover star" style. Morrissey chose himself and, in doing so, became the icon, deserving of cover star status. Morrissey's face became the mask-like image and, like the previously used "cover star", became a sign open to interpretation and symbolic readings. Antti Nylén refers to the Morrisey album covers as having an aura and the typography of Morrissey's name being "like a halo" (Nylen 2004). Gavin Hopps, in his book *The Pageant of*

His Bleeding Heart describes Morrissey's work as an "ongoing dramatisation of the self" with the song as the primary source of this dramatization (Hopps 2009: 41). However, I would also include the album artwork, merchandise and visual imagery such as stage backdrops and the films played before each concert as being part of the Morrissey dramatization. What Hopps does remind us of is the deliberate manner in which Morrissey presents his construction. No image enters the public arena by accident; each is considered and becomes part of the myth. Each album release becomes an "event", with fans and music media alike, trying to decode the images.

Photographic portraiture

Morrissey's album cover artwork falls into the artistic category of photographic portraiture. Portraiture is both a private and public act in that it is a private collaboration between artist and sitter, which is intended for public display. Historically, portraiture was used to render likenesses of religious icons and biblical parables; during the Renaissance, portraiture became a way for the wealthy and powerful to show off their status. Throughout its history portraiture has tried to capture the essence of a person and to evoke internal as well as external characteristics. The private nature of portraiture results in a collaborative relationship between artist and sitter with both wanting a portrait, which according to Nancy "touches, or else it is only an identification", and this results in images which show intimacy (Nancy 2005: 4). Nancy's definition of the intimate image conveys the sitter's indescribable essence, and there remains the possibility for a disjuncture between what the artist has created and the sitter's expectation.

Photographic portraiture differs from other forms, such as the painted portrait, in that it captures what is really there. Photography has the ability to show what Susan Sontag described as "immortality" and to capture events that have occurred "for all time" (Sontag 2002). John Gage discusses the photographic portrait as possessing qualities of "likeness" but reminds that this is subject to the influence of photographic devices of lighting, the focusing of the lens and how a photograph is framed or cropped (Gage 1997: 121–123). Useful to an understanding of the photograph is the work of Roland Barthes, particularly *Camera Lucida* (1981). Barthes' aim in the book was to gain an understanding of the power of the image and how the camera turns "subject into object" (Barthes 1981: 13). The idea of "studium" and "punctum" can be applied to the photographic images of Morrissey as a reminder that there is the "studium", which Barthes calls the "liking or not liking" of a photograph and operates as an initial response to the image (Barthes 1981: 27). And it is the "punctum" which provides the individual interest in a photograph, the element which means something to the individual viewer. This effect marks the photograph as a unique experience to each gaze, with each person finding that "something" in the image which individualizes their attention.

Just blindly loved

Since the release of 'Interesting Drug' (1989), the predominant visual feature of the cover artwork has been Morrissey's face. This repetitive use of his photographic portrait on albums needs to be considered as a part of the contextual landscape of the Morrissey persona; the photographs can be read as text. Just as the "cover star" on The Smiths' album was paired with Morrissey's lyrics, so are the images on the solo releases. In the images there are layers of textual coding – the choice of photographer, the location where the image was taken, Morrissey's body pose, gestures (see chapter 8 in this volume for a detailed discussion on this point), clothing and props etc. This textual coding is found in many of the photographs taken of Morrissey in landscapes, for example the cover photograph used for 'Certain People I Know'. This portrait is imbued with additional meaning through its connotative use of the location of the Hoxton Markets, a place which has links to the Kray twins. Two years into his solo career the use of Morrissey's self-portraiture became established. In the cover art for these releases there is no choice but to look at his face.

The release of *Bona Drag* in 1990 and, in particular, the single 'November Spawned A Monster' saw Morrissey exposing his body in a fashion which contradicted his former identity as the shy, slim singer of The Smiths. As he had done for The Smiths, it was common (and still is) for Morrissey to remove his shirt to expose his torso, an act which could be read as offering himself to his audience. This act presents something of a contradiction as the erotic/sexual photographs oppose statements of celibacy and asexualness as often attributed to Morrissey since he first became a public figure. It also contradicts notions of what a male "pop" star is supposed to do. In the film clip for 'November Spawned A Monster', Morrissey is seen in a semi-transparent black shirt, writhing around on rocks, clearly at ease with his body. This film clip playfully confuses notions of the private (sexual) self as it is performed in a public space. As Pierre Bourdieu states, the body can be a form of physical capital. Morrissey contrasts the visual spectacle of his fit, able body with the lyrics of his song.

At this stage in his solo career, for the audience there is little option but to look; Morrissey demands his audience's voyeuristic gaze. Stan Hawkins describes Morrissey as being "framed by the gaze" in his book on the male dandy in British pop music (Hawkins 2009: 72). The history of the "gaze" in visual art theory tends to focus on the female as the subject of the male gaze, reinforcing a stereotypical view of the active male and passive female as evident in art history's bias towards the male artist and the relegation of the woman to the role of a painted object. Hawkins interrogates the gaze asking "who it is directed to and why?" (2009: 72). Morrissey directs his audience to the vulnerability of his body, but there is also a sense of pleasure in his own body, an awareness of the attention that his display can bring. This contradiction between unease and narcissism has always been a feature of Morrissey's lyrics and persona.

It is of interest to note that the majority of the photographs between 1990 and 1991 were taken by Morrissey's long time friend and artist Linder Sterling, and reinforce the performative nature of photography. The act of being photographed is a performative one where the subject takes on a role or an identity. As Anne Marsh writes "the relationship with the camera is narcissistic […] the subject is always trying to act out an image of the ideal self" (Marsh 2003). Roland Barthes describes being in front of the camera as making another body, "I transform myself in advance into an image" (Barthes 1981: 10). Morrissey turns himself into an image through the specific gestural pose and composition within the photograph. This narcissistic and performative nature of photography seems to be at odds with the public utterances of Morrissey and creates a contradiction. Perhaps Morrissey is "acting out" his ideal image, shaping the way in which he would like to be seen. In the lyrics to 'The Public Image', he states that he is "ninety-eight per cent image" and that he has tried to "pass himself off as a human being" but the truth "exposed" him. In describing himself as nearly all "image", Morrissey speaks with the language of the commodity. His body is a product, in this case used to sell records, echoing the Warhol notion of turning the self into cultural entity.

Lad Moz

It is through some of the single release artwork from *Vauxhall and I* in 1994 and the accompanying promotional imagery that a new visual representation emerges – the beginning of what has become colloquially known through the music press as "Lad Moz", where Morrissey aligned with visual imagery of a "hardness or toughness" that could be identified through the visual clues of tattoos, scars and bruises. In two examples from this time – an inside picture from 'Hold On To Your Friends' and the promotional copy of 'The More You Ignore Me, The Closer I Get' – Morrissey is photographed in an intimate and seemingly unposed fashion, a break with the normal conventions of portrait photography. Through these spontaneous looking images Morrissey allows his audience an insight into an "authentic self". In the 'Hold On To Your Friends' inside portrait his gaze does not meet the viewer. He is standing in front of a bathroom mirror, unshaven, with the word "Honey" around his nipple. Morrissey's eyes are looking into the mirror at his reflected image rather than meeting those of the viewer. It appears that Morrissey is engaged in styling his hair and perhaps unconcerned that he is being photographed. To the right of the image are the lyrics to the song. The cover portrait features a dressed Morrissey in a pose similar to that in the inside photograph, although more conventionally staged. His eyes still avert the gaze and his hand remains on his hair. In the promotional image for 'The More You Ignore Me, The Closer I Get', Morrissey is captured with one arm around the photographer, Jake Walters, and the other clenched as a fist, perhaps towards the viewer or himself, as if issuing a challenge. It is an awkward image. The jewellery and background tone of the cover suggest that it was taken at the same time and location as the 'Hold Onto Your Friends' portrait. The images have an air of spontaneity and differ from the usual posed manner of previous album covers.

The "tough lad" imagery was taken further with the release of *Southpaw Grammar* in 1995. Unusually for his solo career the album artwork does not feature a photograph of Morrissey but rather of an image of a boxer that Morrissey selected from a boxing magazine called *The Ring*. The enclosed booklet accompanying the vinyl release contained photographic portraits of Morrissey, with cuts and bruises, taken by English photographer Rankin. Other promotional images from the time also showed Morrissey with fake cuts and scars. He was also photographed with boxers and in interviews discussed his recent attendance at boxing bouts. These outward signs taken at face value seem to suggest Morrissey's interest in boxing. However in an interview with Stuart Maconie for *Q* magazine in 1995, Morrissey is asked about boxing and if he would be interested in "getting in the ring"; Morrissey replies "No. I've got better things to do […] like planting bulbs". In answering this way Morrissey demonstrates that the image may not be a literal representation, it may in fact mean "nothing". When presented with an assumption based to some extent on publicity images. Morrissey denied any interest in participating in boxing and stated his preference for an activity less strenuous. Gavin Hopps refers to this as coyness, a strategy Morrissey uses to reveal "something" only for it to be refuted (2009: 132).

These "cuts" featured in the promotional material from the time could be viewed as Morrissey wanting to visually show the "cuts" he was feeling in his own self at the time, as an example of making the interior show on the exterior. In taking on an identifiably masculine image, although a damaged one, Morrissey is once again communicating a contradiction from his previous public image of the "shy and frail" man. But is it authentic? The cuts and bruises look fake (or we as the audience know they are fake). Perhaps this is where the rift in his audience occurred – the authenticity of the image was questioned. Discussions of authenticity within popular culture are difficult. Allan Moore describes authenticity as being natural and without artifice. This definition is clearly at odds with Hawkins' reading of Morrissey as a "pop dandy". Moore also describes authenticity as not contained within specific acts or gestures but located within the individual. It is the perception and interpretation of Morrissey's audience which determines authenticity (Moore 2001: 209–233). If Morrissey had previously been known for his authenticity and realism, then his audience would have felt confused by what could now be seen as a "character". Or perhaps the "cuts" are no less authentic than the hearing aid? In an interview with *Uncut* magazine, Jo Slee says of the images "He said something in an interview which stuck in my mind about his fascination with skinheads. He said that what he envied about these people – in a boyish, laddish way – was that they were natural and un-self-conscious, which I thought was very revealing" (Simpson 1998). Perhaps by being photographed with cuts Morrissey was trying on the identity of being "un-selfconscious" and breaking from his former public image.

The cover for his next album *Maladjusted* returned to an image of Morrissey, squatting against a background of silver. Or as Morrissey described it "the sleeve looked dreadful. I look like a mushroom or a leprechaun" (Spitz 2004). The stark, unhappy looking image for *Maladjusted* could be read as pairing with the music within and perhaps reinforce the "miserable Moz" tag. It seems Morrissey has realized the errors made in the album artwork selections for both *Southpaw Grammar* and *Maladjusted* as the notes written by Morrissey for the 2009 re-release of these two albums describe how the *Southpaw Grammar* image of the boxer may have lead to confusion amongst the record buying public. It appears that Morrissey, having established a visual style, now understands the importance of having his image on the album artwork.

Return to the past

After the seven "lost" years, the release of *You are the Quarry* in 2004 and *Ringleader of the Tormentors* in 2006 saw Morrissey align himself with an image that paid homage to the 1970s. A feature of the cover artwork for both these albums was the props used – the gun and the violin. Dressing up also seemed to be common to the publicity images from this time, with Morrissey dressing variously in gangster style, in a tuxedo, as a Seventies Eurovision performer and as a priest. As with the "Lad" images from the 1990s, these cover artworks could be read as Morrissey acting out an identity for the camera.

In the current "web 2.0" era it has become easier to not only download artwork images before the physical copy is in the shops, but it has also become easier to discuss the artwork within a fan community. The album *Greatest Hits* in 2008 featured two new singles 'All You Need Is Me' and 'That's How People Grow Up' and saw a return to the skin-baring images of the early 1990s. 'That's How People Grow Up' uses a previously unseen photograph from the *Vauxhall and I* era, however the greatest shock was found on the inside sleeve of the album. Contrasting with the serene, eyes-closed portrait on the front, this inside photograph credited as "Morrissey's arse photographed by Jake Walters" sparked intense speculation and debate amongst fans and mentions in mainstream music media. *The Guardian*, in an article titled 'Morrissey wears his arse on his sleeve', described the photograph as being "rich with readings" and then outlined potential readings of the image. The fan and media discussion of this image focused around the authenticity of the photograph and also raised questions as to why Morrissey would use this image. Was it a matter of making controversy for the sake of it, or was there some other reason behind it. In decoding this, Morrissey's long-time use of ambiguity, irony and camp references must be taken into account. From his early career with The Smiths, ambiguity and the use of camp imagery and references has been part of Morrissey's presentation of self. Ambiguity is not derived from the image, but from the meaning or narrative. Morrissey is able to present images which can be interpreted in more than one way. The issue is not so much "that it happened" but "why it is being shown". Stan Hawkins writes "[Morrissey] plays on notions of mystification by taunting the fan" (Hawkins 2009: 70). This follows Morrissey's strategy of seeming to reveal something while actually giving nothing away.

The issue of homoeroticism has long been stated as an almost indisputable part of the artwork of both The Smiths and Morrissey album covers. Simon Reynolds has described the albums *Your Arsenal*, *Vauxhall and I*, *Southpaw Grammar* and *Maladjusted* as testimony to "a growing homoerotic obsession with criminals, skinheads and boxers" (Reynolds 2011). Journalist Robert Chalmers described an "abundance of homoerotic imagery in his lyrics and album artwork" (Chalmers 1992). Both descriptions use loaded words to present the homoerotic as the only reading of Morrissey's lyrics and imagery. Morrissey has continually discussed his wish to "produce music which transcends boundaries [...] People are just sexual, the prefix is immaterial" (Hopps 2009: 156). Nadine Hubbs makes note of Morrissey's "refusal of both heterosexual and homosexual classifications" (Hubbs 1996: 270). While the homoerotic reading of the artwork is a *possible* reading, it is not the only reading and serves to continue the categorizing of sexuality in place of the ambiguity and breaking of gender norms which Morrissey has made central to his work.

The album artwork for *Years of Refusal* (2009) has Morrissey looking very assured. His full body stance towards the camera is confident and the direct gaze meets the camera, contrasting with the baby whose eyes are looking out of the frame. As babies are a metonymic sign indicating the future, it could be read as the baby representing "moving forward" or looking towards the future. The tattoos of a cocoon on Morrissey's arm and butterfly on the babies' forehead are suggestive of metamorphosis and need to be considered as a visual clue. If paired with the song lyrics and album title it could be suggestive of a rebirth. After the "whose baby is it?" riddle – or perhaps a literal reference to the "MozFather" label of *You are the Quarry* – what does the baby signify? Following the props of the gun and the violin, the baby could be viewed as revealing Morrissey's mindset. Music journalist Armond White wrote "that baby is a weapon" and when teamed with the word "refusal" could be viewed as a refusal to follow the norms of fatherhood and family (White 2009). *Years of Refusal* presents another example of Morrissey taking care with his album artwork and the layering of meaning.

The single release of 'I'm Throwing My Arms Around Paris' in 2009 sees an image of Morrissey on the front cover, however it was the inside image that sparked another "controversy". There we have Morrissey surrounded by the four male members of his band, naked but for seven inch vinyl records. In considering the proposition of this chapter – that Morrissey has used the album cover portrait as identity – then this recent photograph is an indicator of his current self. Looking at the image what I believe it is indicating is that having stripped away everything else, there is only music left, implying that this is what matters most and perhaps what has always been "there" for him. It also echoes the story that has been told about Morrissey asking acquaintances about the first record they bought. This is reflected in the second image where the four members of the band are seen holding 12-inch records towards the camera, perhaps as a clue to their first record-buying memory.

Conclusions

Morrissey has successfully used the album cover over the course of his music career to help accentuate and define his personal narrative as cultural identity. From the mining of his own nostalgia-laden past when part of The Smiths to the use of his self through the solo years, Morrissey has used the artwork as another means to display his sense of irony and ambiguity. The photographed portrait became the dominant cover artwork, with only three of his solo releases not featuring his own image. Narcissistic impulses along with an awareness of marketing strategies must be considered when trying to establish reasons for this continued use of his image. However as discussed through the chapter it is important to remember the degree to which an image of a public figure is a constructed image. Also, the ability for images to be open to multiple readings and interpretations needs to be considered when discussing the album artwork. Just as Morrissey's lyrics are a primary source of understanding, so the album cover allows for entry into Morrissey's "inner" self, but only as much as he wants us to see.

Bibliography

Bannister, M. (2006) *White Boys, White Noise: Masculinities and 1980's Indie Guitar Rock.* Aldershot: Ashgate.

Barthes, R. (1981) *Camera Lucida: Reflections on Photography*, 12th edn. New York: Hill and Wang.

Bracewell, M. (2002) *The Nineties: When Surface was Depth.* London: Flamingo.

Chalmers, R. (1992) "No sex please, I'm Morrissey", *The Observer.* 6th December.

Frith, S. and Horne, H. (1987) *Art Into Pop.* London: Methuen.

Hawkins, S. (2009) *The British Pop Dandy.* Farnham: Ashgate.

Hebdige, D. (1979) *Subculture: The Meaning of Style.* London: Methuen.

Hopps, G. (2009) *Morrissey: The Pageant of His Bleeding Heart.* US: Continuum.

Hubbs, N. (1996) 'Music of the "Fourth Gender": Morrissey and the sexual politics of melodic contour', in T. Foster, C. Stiegel and E. E Berry (eds) *Bodies of Writing, Bodies in Performance.* New York: New York University Press, pp. 226–296.

Moore, A. (2001) 'Authenticity as authentication', *Popular Music*, 21: 2, pp. 209–233.

Nancy, J-L. (2005) *The Ground of the Image.* New York: Fordham University Press.

Nylén, A. (2004) 'Me and Morrissey: notes on the essence and effects of a voice', *Eurozine*, available: *www.eurozine.com/articles/2004-08-24-nylen-en-html.*

O'Hagan, A. (2004) 'Cartwheels over broken glass', *The London Review of Books.* 26: 5, pp. 19–21.

Reynolds, S. (2011) 'The Smiths', *Encyclopædia Britannica* Online, available: http: //www.britannica.com/EBchecked/topic/549957/the-Smiths

Simpson, D. (1998) 'Manchester's answer to the H-bomb', *Uncut Magazine*, available: *www.morrissey-solo.com/articles/uncut0898b.htm.*

Slee, J. (1994) *Peepholism: Into the Art of Morrissey.* London: Sidgewick & Jackson Ltd.

Smith, R. (2002) 'Morrissey wears his arse on his sleeve', *The Guardian*, available: *http: //www.guardian.co.uk/music/musicblog/2008/feb/15/morrisseywearshisarseonhihttp.*

Sontag, S. (2002) *On Photography*, 3rd edn. London: Penguin.

Stringer, J. (1992) 'The Smiths: repressed (but remarkably dressed)', *Popular Music*, 11: 1. pp. 15–26.

Spitz, M. (2004) 'These things take time', *Spin Magazine*, available: *http: //m.spin.com/articles/these-things-take-time.*

White, A. (2009) 'Pop you can believe in', *New York Press*, available: *http: //www.nypress.com/article-19563-pop-you-can-believe-in.html.*

Chapter 8

"Because I've only got Two Hands": Western Art Undercurrents in the Poses and Gestures of Morrissey

Andrew Cope

"Does the body rule the mind?"

When The Smiths performed 'Vicar in a Tutu' on BBC Television's *The Old Grey Whistle Test* back in May 1986, the band's "voice", Morrissey, accompanied the song's final refrain of "I am a living sign" with a pointed skyward gaze. The sustained pose would become a recurring, and frequently caricatured, feature of the singer's flirtations with the camera (Figure 8.1). But today the image might be most usefully recalled to present an unusual, but highly significant, aesthetic presence to students of culture (and theatre studies in particular) as the moment captures a performer comfortably astride of two key and enduring perceptual realities, both appreciated as being well subscribed, especially in people's perception of the body, but each equally understood to be antagonistic towards the other. As such, Morrissey's simultaneous yet strangely harmonious appeal to the two world-views is as challenging as it is helpfully illustrative, and so fully deserving of scholarly attention.

The Old Grey Whistle Test's studio format located Morrissey in popular music's secular logics where the emphasis is on style rather than substance. But Morrissey's mesmerizing conclusion to 'Vicar in a Tutu', with its suddenly zealous Christian allusions, seemed to stray into sincerity and conspire with the singer's historically charged pose to fully invoke the religion's quite different relationship with embodied messages. In the former, postmodern rationale, the sign's status is no more than that of a communicative code, which brings about its meaning through a consensus that refers an audience elsewhere; we might agree then, that such a sign de-centres its messenger. However, in the competing religious view, an earthly accord counts for very little as it is an ultimate authority, that of a creator, which guarantees both the sign's meaning and the signifier's authenticity. To be "a living sign" in this logic then is to become the sensuous

Figure 8:1: Morrissey's much-caricatured skyward gaze. Reproduced by kind permission © Andrew Cope (2011).

expression of an absolute reality, and as such an unproblematic exchange of a sign with some kind of inner spirit or essence is assumed to be possible (Davey 1999).

The televised performance of 'Vicar in a Tutu' was then an example of Morrissey inviting his audience to follow a trail that leads away from him. Yet the diversion here was acute, as the referral process itself took its onlookers to the idea of access, not only to a message but also to a "doer" behind that message. The persona subsequently produced was both a beguiling paradox and perhaps something of an archetype which could help account for the wider Morrissey phenomenon, it being paradigmatic of the singer's almost ghostly (as opposed to contrived) public presence, at least insomuch as it managed to outflank, without ever actually denying, the "air of fictionality" which is generally associated with behaviour knowingly twice done (see Pywell 1994: esp. 85).

Morrissey is unlikely to concede the existence of (let alone explain) any stage technique. Indeed, in both conversation and promotion he neatly avoids any decentring, and potentially diminishing, idea of "restored behaviour" (Schechner 2002) by privileging notions of "appearing live" or "in person" rather than performing. But some glimpse into Morrissey's perception of his own persona might come from a brief interview for *The Observer* newspaper that occurred during his mid 1990s 'Boxers' tour (Bracewell 1995). Tellingly shifting between first and second person, Morrissey discusses his public profile with the author (and fan) Michael Bracewell, declaring that "The sound is too Ortonesque and the voice too absolutely real. I know my music will last." This seems insightful, not only because ideas of reality and theatre are pushed together (the postmodern concept of "performativity" also does this) but because art is un-problematically identified with the concrete. Wherein concepts of equivocality – notions often deployed by critics to explain the unfamiliarity of the Morrissey phenomenon – whilst not unfounded, seem scarcely sufficient to contain the significant complications (or, to concede something to the religious angle, the profound simplicity) of what is implied: that art, for Morrissey, is the prophetic call of some fundamental reality.

This chapter, then, will address the intriguing physical content and enduring success of Morrissey's "public" appearances; embodied scenarios that always seem to resist any level of postmodern disenchantment through an appeal to the very same aesthetic tactics that are often associated with the attitude's scepticism. The anticipated illumination will come from pursuing just some of the parallels that are perceived to exist between Morrissey's "doing" of the celebrated aspects of his own identity (particularly his performance of gender(s), rebellion and martyrdom) and the stylistic and formal tactics of Western fine art iconography, a longstanding aesthetic project and one which is similarly understood to defy any reductive status of artifice, particularly in the eyes of faithful beholders who tend to see through the affected component of an embodied representation in their deference to its centred and emotionally moving effects.

"I look at you and know"

Whilst the Western art tradition of iconography has its origins in the Ancient world's production of reality, it might be most usefully understood, at least for this academic exercise, as a "conceit" of the later Middle Ages – one which apparently foreshadowed Morrissey through its influential attempts to reconstitute the enchanted and centred exchanges of early Antiquity (with its *real* statues which were often chained down to prevent them from walking), via acknowledged strategies of representation that managed to maintain some expressive totality, despite the conflicts of its mimetic agenda. And much like the Morrissey phenomenon, such iconography, in presupposing man as God's image, esteemed and privileged the human figure (and its capacities), alongside narrative, in its production of apparently "authentic" meanings (Baudrillard 1983; Gill 1989).

"Obviously I'm interested in sex" said Morrissey in an interview in 1983 (in conversation with Dave McCullough, for the music paper *Sounds*). And whilst the singer has rarely been so upfront about his fleshy appetites since, his body has nevertheless been deployed to encourage an audience to privilege a sensual syntax from that which is, in actuality, semiotically open. In one characteristic and quietly seductive image from 1991, later used in a widely disseminated promotional image (Figure 8.2), the artist was captured (by

Figure 8:2: Morrissey poses for photographer Linder Sterling in London's East End c. 1991. Reproduced by kind permission © Linder Sterling (1991).

photographer Linder Sterling) posing with an outstretched hand on London's Vallance Road, one-time home of Ronnie and Reggie Kray, those archetypal British figures of a roguish and violent authority (as Power discusses elsewhere in this volume).

The origin of this pose might be traced back to the religious art of later Archaic and early Classical Greece, where a sculpted figure's outstretched arm would typically be extended towards the viewing position in order to present additional iconography to the faithful (see the replicas of *Athena Parthenos* for instance). And if today we read the posture as a portentous, and perhaps somewhat effeminate gesture, it might be due, at least in part, to the propagation of the pose through the derivative, cultish statues of Antinous, which were dispersed throughout the Roman Empire, during the second century AD (Lambert 1997).

By the time the Romans came to copy Greek art, a consistency in Hellene originals, and perhaps a familiarity with the lacuna left behind by iconoclasts, had arguably allowed the outstretched hand to become a representational strategy in itself. So when Emperor Hadrian attempted to elevate the status of his dead lover Antinous, to that of a god, the sedimentary effects of the reaching hand in figurative sculpture were perhaps an evocation enough of the divine pantheon to make any justifying attribute essentially superfluous, an argument that withstands even if a number of the Antinous type would originally have held some attribute to assist with identification. Given this, we might agree that in the case of the propagated Antinous figures, pose had become part of an aesthetic tactic – one that had the useful potential to obscure the interface between the rational world and an illusionary inner world. And in the event, it was arguably the comportment of these statues that helped to transform a much-discussed sexual relationship (with its famously controversial end) between an emperor and a boy into something infallible, rather than contentious and potentially shameful. An aegis that would, in time, come to transfigure the Antique representations of Antinous into an embodied "ideal for the gay 'uranist' movement of the nineteenth century which, boasted Oscar Wilde among its ranks" (Cawthorne 2005: 144).

Morrissey, then, seems to appeal to the enchanted meaning of the Antinous form, as an expression of an esteemed sexuality, and deploys it alongside no less centripetal ideas of Classical quality. In Linder Sterling's poetic outcome, this helped the singer to sustain the romantic reading of the Kray story privileged in his 1989 single 'Last of the Famous International Playboys'. Moreover, the subsequent double hermeneutic, created through posing in the marginalized situation of Vallance Road, ultimately challenges any gendered stereotypes which might be associated with the mannered body, to usher in an unusual and muscular vision of sensuality – a constitution which was arguably similar to the quirky persona which Morrissey had (in his earlier guise as a writer) attributed to the actor James Dean, who was apparently blessed with the enviable ability to "make good tea, grow geraniums and keep his house spotless without losing any of his obvious masculinity" (Morrissey 1983: 4). A presentation that attracts then, as it confounds an expectation, and so a pose that would perfectly anticipate the controversial re-inscriptions demanded by Morrissey's subsequent long player, 1992's *Your Arsenal*, the sleeve art of which would continue to perpetuate the singer's confident displays of sensuality, on this occasion through an unbuttoned shirt which reveals his (credited) appendix scar, an attribute that is itself pictured alongside the control of yet another proud appendage – the artist's microphone.

Whilst the effects of pose in figurative art have caught people up in its centring meta-fictions for centuries, it is possible to detect the emergence of a familiar and contemporary critical dissent in some later Renaissance examples. Michelangelo da Caravaggio, for instance, apparently recognized that the faith in a centred essence behind a gesture afforded art's representations of the body an amount of subversive potential. And much as Morrissey, particularly in his explorations of contemporary urban environments, uses pose to enfeeble the boundaries between lived lives and attractive ideals, so Caravaggio's paintings often used the viewer's investment in embodied meaning to straddle similar thematic realms.

Although the attributes and elements of the pose in Caravaggio's painting of *The Young Bacchus* (c.1596) point to an enchanted authenticity (Figure 8.3), the decaying fruit and the dirty fingernails of the young model are subversive insomuch as they locate any subsequent

Figure 8:3: After Caravaggio's *The Young Bacchus*. Reproduced by kind permission © Andrew Cope (2011).

veneration in the substance of a prosaic existence (Bolton 2004: 98). Moreover, the wine glass presented by the figure alludes to the Ganymede myth, which in-itself might be read as Classically austere but when it is combined with the subject's blushing cheeks and the suggestive tug at the belt of his garment, it seems to tempt the viewer and invite his or her flirtation, as much as any fettered academic admiration.

There is further slippage, literally, in the boy's attire and gaze, which recalls the revealing drapery and languid look associated with the Ancient statues of the 'Venus Genetrix' type (see, for example, *The Aphrodite of Frejus* in the Louvre's collection). And it is these same embodiments of physical desire that are re-stated in the plummeting necklines and heavy eyelids which Morrissey typically employs both to elevate, and to tease a sensual delight from, locations which have historically been allocated an unexceptional status. A pose which is perhaps best exemplified through Jurgen Teller's striking image of Morrissey in Battersea, which adorns the reverse side of *Bona Drag*'s album artwork, where a lamppost appears to be the recipient of a sensual tenderness which scarce few other pop stars would deem warranted by the circumstance.

Ostensibly then, Caravaggio and Morrissey could each be described as straightforward purveyors of traditional iconography, and yet in referring their audiences back to the disenchanted realm of lived life, they democratize the tradition by making once divine and aristocratic ideals universally available. Whilst such appropriation stops well short of iconoclasm (signs being preserved rather than destroyed), there is nevertheless some challenge to the sign's Antique integrity.

"It has been before, so it shall be again"

Morrissey has often chosen to identify himself with the theme of defiance. On the first European date of 2004's "comeback" "You are the Quarry" tour, the singer opened the Manchester Arena concert with a few (paraphrased) lines from Paul Anka's lyrical celebration of single mindedness 'My Way', restating a sentiment that Morrissey had visited through his own verse in "Quarry's" key ballad 'I'm Not Sorry'. But even in the days of The Smiths, when the singer professed to be enamoured by the gang-like mentality of being in a pop group (implicit in his choice of name for the band), Morrissey's public body would often be used to privilege the idea of disruption over any notions of unity, with group shots frequently featuring the singer posing significantly differently from the other members of the outfit. And sometimes Morrissey would seem minded to place some distance between himself and his cohorts, on occasion to an extent that seemed to guarantee that the other band members would drift out of the picture's focus (see Rogan 1994: 117 and 156).

In art history, the advocacy of such individualism is perhaps most closely associated with the Romantic movement of the late eighteenth and early nineteenth centuries. And it was Casper David Friedrich's image of *The Wanderer above the Mists* (1818) which came to embody best the idea of the introspective lone figure wresting with his thoughts, an image which would itself be inescapably recalled by Morrissey (Figure 8.4) as he posed for Anton Corbijin, photographing for *The Face* magazine, in 1990 (see Slee 1994: 95).

The conflicts between objective and subjective thinking, which defined the Romantic fine art movement, had been ably anticipated in Renaissance iconography, most notably perhaps in Raphael's fresco of *The School of Athens* (c.1510). The painting depicts a library full of scholars separated by their respective disciplines. And in the middle of the mural is the divisive image of Plato with his student, and proto-scientist, Aristotle (Figure 8.5). Whilst the latter holds his hand parallel with the earth in an appeal for moderation, Plato, who was preoccupied with thoughts of an otherworldly but fundamental reality, points skywards with a gesture that had been employed so much in previous iconography, to direct attention to God's heavenly dominion (Clark 1969), that it had arguably become symbolic of Christianity itself. And it is this persuasive appeal to an infallible truth that has been a recurring feature of Morrissey's stage act since the earliest days of The Smiths. The formal origins of the pose might be traced back to Roman antiquity where sculptors would privilege the subject's ability to command by friezing an outstretched arm gesture,

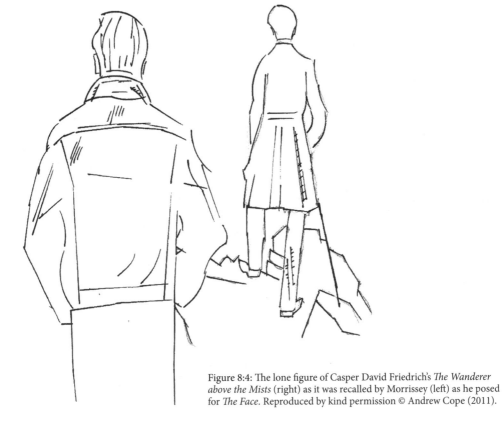

Figure 8:4: The lone figure of Casper David Friedrich's *The Wanderer above the Mists* (right) as it was recalled by Morrissey (left) as he posed for *The Face*. Reproduced by kind permission © Andrew Cope (2011).

Figure 8:5: The contrasting figures of Plato (left) and Aristotle, which take a central position in Raphael's *School of Athens* fresco. Reproduced by kind permission © Andrew Cope (2011).

known as the *adlocutio*, which would typically precede a statesman's address to the army (Pollitt 1993: 246).

In Ancient art the pointing gesture is perhaps most closely associated with the first century BC Augustus statue of the Prima Porta. Augustus (Octavius) was the first Roman Emperor proper, and such sculptures were central to the persuasive art project that was intended to affirm his disputed right to rule. In the nineteenth century, artist Jacques-Louis David, a neo-classicist who quite openly tended to borrow poses for his subjects from other works of art, would famously use the same outstretched arm, pointing skywards, in his 1801 depiction of the new hero of revolutionaries – First Consul Bonaparte, the gesture's appeal to the idea of fidelity arguably helping to give Napoleon's image the public importance of a political manifesto (Clark 1973: 26). But the Antique precedent also allowed David to anticipate Napoleon's imperial ambitions. We might agree then that in the realm of art, knowing might be said to be indistinct from copying; yet knowledge might also facilitate an amount of play which can, at least in effect, give artworks some level of agency (Schwartz 2000: 246).

The emotional impact of the sanguine outstretched arm was not wasted on those artists who sought to influence opinion in the twentieth century. Representations of Lenin for instance would typically show the leader of the proletariat recalling the poses of an art past. But significantly, in early images of the revolutionary leader, his arm is rarely raised skywards. Instead, his hand tended to hover level with the earth, echoing Aristotle's moderating gesture and perhaps Karl Marx's earthbound philosophy. However the passing of time can dull a population's appetite for change and to maintain impetus, rhetoric needs to become increasingly motivated, explaining why, in later imagery, Lenin's arm would become more elevated and his frame increasingly inclined, suggesting a growing momentum towards some metaphorical future (Gombrich 2002; Hobsbawm 2002: esp. illustration 5).

It is perhaps no accident then that Morrissey leans into a pointing outstretched arm on the sleeve of his 2005 DVD *Who put the M in Manchester?* Following a seven-year recording hiatus, the video captures a performer who was understandably eager to convince the world of the continuing relevance of the future envisioned in a playlist which included more established material, such as 'Shoplifters Of The World Unite', alongside new and no less inflammatory songs like 'Irish Blood, English Heart' which urges its listeners to "denounce […] [Britain's] royal line". Yet, whilst it is the faith in stable signs that has granted Morrissey some subversive success, the seditious tactic has meant that he inevitably upholds much of a sign's supporting apparatus in the moment of its critique (after Walter Benjamin cited in Huxley 1998: 277).

In one illuminating defence of his controversial use of imperial imagery at 1992's Finsbury Park appearance (for more on "Madstock" see the contributions elsewhere in this volume by Baker), Morrissey wrestled with the paradoxes innate in his performance by explaining that he "didn't invent the Union Jack, you do realise that don't you? I didn't knock it up on a spinning wheel in the front room. I can't account for other people's reactions […] I think it happened [the subsequent furore] because it was time to get old Mozzer" (Morrissey in conversation with Stuart Maconie 1995). In explaining the decentred character of the deployed emblem negatively ("I didn't invent […] I can't account"), Morrissey's assessment never alights on anything, and so could scarcely have been more in tune with the (potentially exonerating) fall of presence generally attributed to postmodern performances. Yet it is also as if Morrissey strangely meets himself when he is coming back from his own aesthetic diversions as he appears resigned, and perhaps even fated, to the objectifying consequence of being conditioned by the processes of iconography (after Butler 1999).

The artist himself then, would perhaps concede that his deployment of symbols, whilst not without humour and ultimately centrifugal, nevertheless thoroughly catches him up, and so ostensibly implicates him, in webs that are not of his making; a tragedy that perhaps underpins the (much misunderstood) aspect of Morrissey that is at once in awe of and enamoured by unsophisticated street crime and thuggish loutishness – behaviour he once described as "a great art form, which I can't even aspire to" (Morrissey cited in Parsons 1993).

"Learn to love me, assemble the ways"

Although the hegemonic aspects of Morrissey's decentring gestures may have left him exposed to an unmatched level of disapproving scrutiny, their centripetal effects have come to his rescue by defusing the damaging potential of his detractors' maligning critiques. In the fallouts which have succeeded his controversies, Morrissey has typically staged victim-as-martyr scenarios that are themselves reliant on the rhetorical agency of Christian art's representations – emotive iconography that inevitably shores-up the objective status of the righteous victim.

Barely a year after the release of The Smiths' first album, *NME* journalist Danny Kelly detected that the singer's "fountain of pronouncements [...] [had] started to grate" (Kelly 1985). In the subsequent interview, Morrissey apparently pitied his detractors, saying "They've lost faith". And the artist would recall the Christian model once more on the music weekly's cover which featured a clearly pleased Morrissey recreating the glowing and smiling Jesus of Matthias Grunewald's *Resurrection* image from around 1515.

The divinity of Jesus in Grunewald's sixteenth century painting is intended to resist doubt, as viewers witness the emergence of the Christ figure from the tomb. Likewise Morrissey, when confronted with suspicion, chose to restage the most enchanted moment of the Passion's narrative, which was designed to restore faith in the hearts of those with failing conviction. Whilst the *NME* image was primarily a parody, it nevertheless helped to both signpost and consolidate Morrissey's previous dalliances with the Christian art precedence. Stigmata, such as National Health Service spectacles, hearing aids and of course flowers, had already come to define the singer's public appearances; such "outings" apparently becoming opportunities for Morrissey to both venerate identities which were generally considered wretched, and to usefully mask the absence of any centred Morrissey persona in the process – flamboyantly fulfilling an aesthetic purpose which could be said to be indistinct from the two primary objectives of Christian iconography, at least as postmodern theory understands it (after Baudrillard 1983). Such practices of magical sympathy remain commonplace even in contemporary fine art. However, lest anyone forget, Morrissey is occasionally disposed to re-state the religious origins of such metamorphoses through his lyrics, most notably perhaps in 'Bigmouth Strikes Again', when he transports his hearing aid to fifteenth-century France in order to affiliate (or "melt") the object with the fiery scene of Saint Joan of Arc's public torching.

The allusion to sainthood, and particularly the relic which becomes radiant in the presence of belief, was furthered when Morrissey launched his solo career. Whilst the artwork of The Smiths' recording catalogue typically "starred" those actors from stage and screen who had captured the young Morrissey's imagination, subsequent releases would, by and large, frame only his chiselled features (as Connor demonstrates elsewhere in this volume). And much as a relic's fragmentation helped to maximize the dispersal of a saint's essence in the Christian tradition, so the reproduction of a record's picture sleeve would come to facilitate the widest distribution of Morrissey's signified proximity.

The extraordinary added-value provided by the photographed pose to Morrissey's own phenomenon might be registered in the fans' relationship with the gates of Salford Lad's Club which framed The Smiths on the inside of *The Queen is Dead*'s gatefold sleeve. Today, organizers facilitate a level of adoration through guided coach tours that take "pilgrims" to the red-bricked locale. And fans in high places seek to claim something of the institution's "enchanted" power by either attempting to recreate Morrissey's original composition for some subsequent dissemination; or by protecting its esoteric potential through attempting to regulate the amount of access that an adversary might have to the venue (see Woolf 2008), evidence, perhaps, of Morrissey's unrivalled and almost Midas-like ability to tease the precious from the prosaic (see also the chapter by Erin Hazard in this volume).

Morrissey signposted some readiness to accept the singular role of a quasi-religious icon through the artwork of his debut solo release, 1988's 'Suedehead', where the artist brandished an assertive elbow to demonstrate his willingness to collect veneration. It was a gesture that had frequently been employed in Dutch depictions of military leaders in the sixteenth and seventeenth centuries (see, for example, *The Laughing Cavalier* [c.1624] by Frans Hals), where the encroaching elbow would represent an army's struggle to extend and unify territory by claiming additional picture space (Spicer 1991: 97). In 'Suedehead's artwork an angle similarly nudges beyond the limits of the picture, suggesting that there is now no longer room for anyone else. And with this job done, Morrissey was free to directly emulate images of the divine on the cover of his subsequent long player.

In *Viva Hate*'s portrait photograph, Morrissey's features are bathed in light, recalling the luminous face that, in Renaissance iconography, often identified the Christ figure: A supposed sacred "glow" that the painter Albrecht Durer had previously borrowed to give a divine spin to his essentially secular self-portrait in 1500 (Spalding 2005: 207). But Morrissey's appeal to the devotional tradition is arguably more committed and particular

Figure 8:6: The pose adopted by Morrissey for *Viva Hate*'s portrait picture recalls the devotional image of Christ known as *The Man of Sorrows*. Reproduced by kind permission © Andrew Cope (2011).

than Durer's earthly appropriation, as the singer's head falls forward, and tilts slightly to one side (whilst his languid eyes avoid the viewer's gaze) to revisit an influential composition associated with the most important aspect of the Passion (Figure 8.6).

When, in the period between 1300 and 1500, devotion ceased to be a purely public matter and became a domestic obligation as well, it was in a guise similar to the *Viva Hate* image, known to art historians as "The Man of Sorrows", that Jesus entered the home; with his head tipped to one side, stressing the weight of a very human body, and the eyes just slightly open to demonstrate a divine triumph over death. Richard Harries, the forty-first Bishop of Oxford, described the embodiment (as it occurred in iconography) as "the most precise visual expression of late mediaeval piety", adding that it was designed to "bring image and viewer together with a religious intensity that has rarely been surpassed" (Harries 2004: 85). It is a "piety" that perhaps helps the occidental eye to overcome the staginess of the pose by subsuming any missionary zeal (that might be associated with the picture's dissemination and display) beneath the ideas of "good" and "natural" that in Christian art were supposed to be understood as inevitable givens, rather than discursively produced meanings.

A more universal convention in iconography, associated with the Classical imperatives of the Grand Manner, proscribed distorted facial features from appearing in any representations of nobility. This meant that however grave the circumstance or immanent the threat, suffering in the convention's imagery always had to be shown as an almost nonchalant form of endurance (Hagan and Hagan 2000: 121). A tradition tested on the sleeve art of 'You Have Killed Me' where an impassive and impressively attired Morrissey lies across a set of train tracks, stoically awaiting the arrival of the inevitable (see also the chapter by Melissa Connor). Much then as the pain of Jesus is accepted in iconography without being abject, suffering in Morrissey's *Viva Hate* portrait, and the folio of its subsequent legacy, is never laboured and only ever exists thanks to the extraneous signifiers that bind the artist's features to ideas of torment.

In the visual arts of the early twentieth century, the painter Egon Schiele had anticipated Morrissey's appropriation of Christianity's visual strategy by advancing Albrecht Durer's pious allusions and displacing religious signs (and their reception) into entirely secular contexts. In one promotional image for an exhibition at the Arnot Gallery (Vienna) in 1914, Schiele assumed the pose of Sebastian stoically absorbing his arrows (Figure 8.7), and Morrissey would adopt a similar comport on the cover of his *Kill Uncle* release. And so, whilst both Morrissey and Schiele doubtlessly intended to evoke symbols of painful martyrdom, there is also, in mocking the sacred, an amount of transgression, perhaps fuelled by the knowledge that their torturers all too often purport to be the agents of God (Whitford 1993). A clearly painful tension was previously addressed by Morrissey in the lyrics of his song 'Yes I Am Blind' where the singer struggles to come to terms with the eagerness of the devout to kill, then cook and devour the very symbol of Christ on earth, the lamb.

Ultimately then, the suffering Morrissey communicates is the wretchedness of the vanquished which – in an ironic yet inevitable fate, that has befallen on many of his own outsider heroes – keeps propelling him towards, rather than away from, an institution which he often contests. Nevertheless, the historical "sense" that always matches and complements Morrissey's historical knowledge gives him some scope to register and strategically exploit elements of the tradition's narrative (and emotional appeal) without being entirely subsumed or lost beneath the weight of its meanings.

Typical are the artist's evocations of Michelangelo's *Dying Captive* (Figure 8.8). It is a recurring form in Morrissey's repertoire of poses and one which allows the singer to read his own needs and poetic aspirations into a trusted symbol of both the Renaissance's metaphysical foundations, and its classical quality. History deems that the pose signifies anguish, but Morrissey has used his own contemporary story and context to privilege nuanced subtexts. For instance, on the sleeve of his *Live in Dallas* DVD (previously an *NME* cover image) Morrissey takes full advantage of the opportunity that the pose provides for displaying his hairless physique – and in doing so the singer simultaneously asserts some fidelity to an Antique precedence, whilst complicating the meaning by appealing to its modern relationships with ideas of innocence and prepubescent powerlessness. Sexuality and notions of purity are thus embroiled into the circumstance to usefully collude *with*, rather than simply distract from, the disapproval of his antagonists. And such aesthetic

Figure 8:7: The pose adopted by Egon Schiele for his self-portraits as a Saint Sebastian figure impaled by arrows. Reproduced by kind permission © Andrew Cope (2011).

Figure 8:8: After Michelangelo's *Dying Captive*. Reproduced by kind permission © Andrew Cope (2011).

tactics have arguably helped Morrissey to constitute, and feed, the fiercely protective attitude that shoots right through the scene that has grown up around him.

Morrissey's live appearances have subsequently become characterized by a contagious enthusiasm that often tips into a religious fever, leading Michael Bracewell to describe such fanatical events in terms of "the inexplicable being pursued by the insatiable" (Bracewell in Sterling 1992: 1). So, whilst Morrissey's shows are undoubtedly entertaining, his touring also seems to provide an opportunity for his following to satisfy a palpable thirst for some intimacy with their hero. A need that the singer clearly anticipates and tries to answer from his elevated stage position (which in the live context seems to help the singer transcend his human frame, and affirm his ascendance to some canonized status) by frequently extending an open palm out above the crowd (Figure 8.9), an inviting presentation that is itself met by a flock of yearning hands, each seeming to belong to a suddenly stifled soul, temporarily frozen in gesture and apparently waiting (not unlike Michelangelo's languishing figure of Adam as it is painted on the Sistine Chapel ceiling) to receive some kind of regenerative release through the fingertips of life's authentic source.

It is perhaps this experience above all then – a happening that seems to embody and exemplify both the lone and the gregarious aspects of existence – that takes the Morrissey

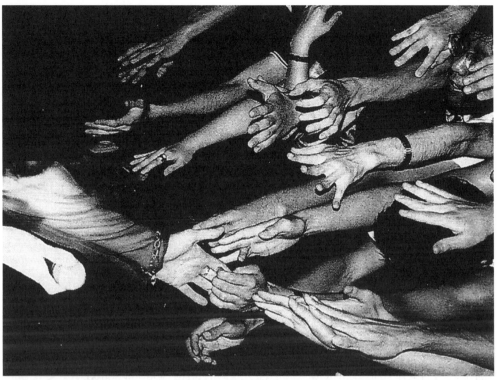

Figure 8.9: A photograph of Morrissey in concert (c.1991) by Linder Sterling. Reproduced by kind permission © Linder Sterling (1991).

phenomenon through, yet beyond, the ambivalent status of irony (appropriate for postmodern purists, such as David Bowie, who knowingly exploit but never exceed pop's plastic quality) and towards some much more cathartic and culturally significant mimetic contract – one which might yet come to make Morrissey's claim for some earthbound martyrdom seem, if anything, a little understated.

> Nature is a language, can't you read?
>
> (Morrissey, 'Ask', 1986)

References

Baudrillard, J. (1983) *Simulations*, 1st edn. US: Semiotext[e].

Bolton, R. (2004) *A Brief History of Painting: 2000 B.C. to A.D. 2000*, 1st edn. London: Constable & Robinson.

Bracewell, M. (1995) 'A walk on the Wilde side', *The Observer*, 26th February, p. 77.

Butler, J. (1999) *Gender Trouble: Feminism and the Subversion of Identity*, 2nd edn. London: Routledge.

Cawthorne, N. (2005) *The Sex Lives of the Roman Emperors*, 1st edn. London: Prion.

Clark, K. (1973) *The Romantic Rebellion: Romantic versus Classical Art*, 1st edn. London: John Murray.

Clark, K. (1969) 'The hero as artist', in K. Clark, *Civilisation*. London: The British Broadcasting Corporation and John Murray, pp. 117–138.

Davey, N. (1999) 'Art, religion and the hermeneutics of authenticity', in S. Kemal and I. Gaskell (eds) *Performance and Authenticity in the Arts*. Cambridge: Cambridge University Press, pp. 66–93.

Gill, M. (1989) 'Something rich and strange', in M. Gill *The Image of the Body*. New York: Doubleday, pp. 382–428.

Gombrich, E. H. (2002) 'Ritualized gesture and expression in art', in E. H. Gombrich *The Image and the Eye: Further Studies in the Psychology of Pictorial Representation*. London: Phaidon Press Ltd., pp. 63–77.

Hagan, R. and Hagan, R. (2000) *What Great Paintings Say: Masterpieces in Detail*, 1st consolidated edition. Koln: Taschen.

Harries, R. (2004) *The Passion in Art*, 1st edn. Aldershot: Ashgate Publishing.

Hobsbawm, E. (2002) 'The world revolution', in E. Hobsbawm *Age of Extremes: The Short Twentieth Century 1914–1991*. London: Abacus, pp. 54–84.

Huxley, D. (1998) '*Viz*: gender, class and taboo', in S. Wagg (ed.) *Because I Tell a Joke or Two: Comedy, Politics and Social Difference*. London: Routledge, pp. 273–290.

Kelly, D. (1985) 'The further thoughts of Chairman Mo', *NME*, 8th June, available: *http: //www.foreverill.com/interviews/1985/chairman.htm*.

Lambert, R. (1997) *Beloved and God: The Story of Hadrian and Antinous*, 2nd edn. Phoenix: London.

McCullough, D. (1983) 'Handsome devils', *Sounds*, 4th June, p. 13.

Morrissey, S. (1983), *James Dean is Not Dead*, 1st edn. Manchester: Babylon Books.

Parsons, T. (1993) 'What now, Mozzer?', *Vox*, April, pp. 20–23.

Pollitt, J. J. (1993) 'Rome: the republic and early empire', in J. Boardman (ed.) *The Oxford History of Classical Art*. Oxford: Oxford University Press, pp. 217–296.

Pywell, G. (1994) *Staging Real Things: The Performance of Ordinary Events*. London and Toronto: Bucknell University Press.

Rogan, J. (1994) *The Smiths: The Visual Documentary*, 1st edn. London: Omnibus Press.

Schechner, R. (2002) *Performance Studies: An Introduction*, 1st edn. London: Routledge.

Schwartz, H. (2002) *The Culture of the Copy: Striking Likenesses, Unreasonable Facsimilies*, 1st paperback edn. New York: Zone Books.

Slee, J. (1994) *Peepholism: Into the Art of Morrissey*, 1st edn. London: Sidgwick & Jackson.

Smiths, The (1986) 'Bigmouth Strikes Again/Vicar in a Tutu (live)', *The Old Grey Whistle Test*, available: *http: //www.youtube.com/watch?v=Igg_2ZqyMzQ*.

Spalding, J. (2002) *The Art of Wonder: A History of Seeing*, 1st edn. Munich: Prestel Verlag.

Spicer, J. (1991) 'The Renaissance elbow', in J. Bremmer and H. Roodenburg (eds) *A Cultural History of Gesture*. Oxford: Polity Press, pp. 84–128.

Sterling, L. (1992) *Morrissey Shot*, 1st edn. London: Secker & Warburg.

Whitford, F. (1993) *Egon Schiele*, 1st edn. London: Thames and Hudson.

Woolf, M. (2008) 'David Cameron: heaven knows I'm triumphant now', *The Sunday Times*, 23rd March, available: *http: //www.timesonline.co.uk/tol/news/politics/article3602643.ece*.

Chapter 9

Moz: art: Adorno Meets Morrissey in the Cultural Divisions

Rachel M. Brett

> There's a cash register ringing and /It weighs so heavy on my back.
>
> ('You Know I Couldn't Last')

Although it is possible to purchase the music of someone such as Mozart alongside Morrissey CDs at supermarkets, this is not a reason to celebrate the cultural egalitarianism of these artists. While there may be distinctions between the histories of these two artists, what is not distinct is the commercial system that mediates both artists in late modernity.[1] Be it the monarchy or a record label, the system of patronage and funding that enables the recordings of Mozart's compositions to be marketed, reproduced and sold analogous to Morrissey's music rests upon economics. To be precise, this system is commercial and is responsible for constructing the distinction that institutionally categorizes one as high art, and the other under the rubric of pop culture.

In the advancements of the western world, boundaries between categorization became variable, while almost any aspect of popular culture can be academically validated through a post-structural approach. As such, what follows will not be a textual analysis of Morrissey's work in order to overdetermine his value. Rather this essay proposes a dialectical project, in order to regard the complexities and conflicts of popular music's status in relation to the function of art's value and the canonizing process.

> [T]he origin and functions of the hit song within capitalism is not questioned at all.
>
> (Adorno 2002: 432)

This hypothesis is premised upon a split between high and low culture that was critically outlined by the philosophers Adorno and Horkheimer in their conceptualization of and book of the same name, *The Culture Industry* (hereafter abbreviated to CI). I will attempt to magnify certain aspects of Adorno's dense philosophical observations of music's role in the CI from his works: 'On the fetish-character in music and the regression of listening' (Adorno 2002: 288–324) and 'On popular music' (Adorno 2002: 437–470).

The social situation of pop that Adorno described will be reconsidered through punk as an historical model. The aims of my approach anticipate that this will provide a contextual framework in which to discuss the composition and themes, such as standardisation, class, self-referentiality and voice within Morrissey's work. These emerging aesthetic qualities can then be contemplated as an art form, which confronts an advanced form of popular music under the prevailing conditions of production in society. In concluding, I will suggest that the residual resistance of punk's genesis at the kernel of Morrissey's art demonstrates pop's submission to the CI is not absolute, while simultaneously proposing that institutionally the insufficient theoretical position on pop music must recognize its potential aesthetic value if it is to reveal itself as art after all in a post-pop world.

> Some men here, they know the full extent of my distress.
>
> ('Why Don't You Find Out For Yourself')

Pop music and the culture industry

In their work on the CI, Adorno and Horkheimer proposed that in modern society, culture had became equivalent to economics as an ideological tool. They argued that through capitalist production methods of industrialization, the CI produced a predetermined division between high and low culture that disguised the transactional values between them (Adorno and Horkheimer 1997: 135). Within the philosophical conception of the CI, Adorno particularly focused on pop music's status. He stated that despite pop music's *historicism*, it was *important* as a socially communicative object and dialectic product, but because pop was valued as a "low" cultural form it lacked philosophical and academic examination. What can be understood from these comments then is that it is necessary to examine pop not just technically or descriptively but also symbolically, to theorize it by demonstrating the dialectic links between the social production of music and its aesthetic qualities (Adorno 1989: 426).

Adorno made his critiques of music at the beginning of an epistemological rupture when pop was in its infancy, before any nuances or modernization *within* the divisions had developed. Therefore, his criticism and theorization of mass produced hits was based upon his appreciation and defence of classical, composed music in opposition to the manufactured pop of the CI. However, Adorno also explained how the CI defused the rebellious power of the social function of low cultural forms, which created a disproportion between music's condition and its potential (Adorno and Horkheimer 1997: 99).

"Our frank and open" ('Our Frank')

The language of pop is a complex and valid candidate for questioning the limits of the cultural split, particularity after the advent of the punk paradigm. Indeed, Morrissey's career cannot be divorced from pop music and the encoded cultural value that it contains based upon the commercial status of its production and distribution. Adorno questioned the social conditions that have constructed the divisions in musical forms, and this is relevant because it demonstrates that pop music's ability to communicate relates to the evolution of productive forces unfolding in the layers of music's development (Adorno 1989: 203). Thus, pop can only critique its social role in negative terms, by refusing to accept its status as a commercial object, while simultaneously participating in it. This is precisely what punk did – the public face of Morrissey and his work persist in challenging these restrictions, because he acknowledges the dilemma of pop within a commercial culture but also its power of communication to reveal the artificial foundation upon which this construction is built and maintained: specifically, economic and class divisions.

> For this reason, the divisions between light and serious music is to be replaced by a different distinction which views both halves of the musical globe equally from the perceptive of alienation; as halves of a totality which to be sure could never reconstruct through the addition of the two halves.
>
> (Adorno 2002: 395)

The fetish character of listening (to popular music)

In his essay 'On the fetish-character in music and the regression of listening', Adorno applied Marx's concept of the fetish character of the commodity to explain how the phenomena of the CI appeared to objectively reduce the distinction between popular culture and art (Adorno 2002: 313). Specifically focusing on music, he claimed the mechanical reproduction of music transformed its essence into a commercial property of pure exchange. By amalgamating aesthetics and economics, the mass-produced form of pop became an anti-artistic device within modern culture.

Additionally, Adorno (2002) claims that the immanent logic of music, its ability to use its aesthetic qualities and the internal problem of its own material to express its commercial production was predetermined by class divisions. As such, the pleasure and value of pop are problematic and cannot be considered in isolation from the relationship of labour. For just as the masses are separated *within* the production process and from *the result of their toils*, so is mass culture removed from the ideal of bourgeois art. Cultural goods appear as an objective part in social relations yet the social labour process that created them is disguised through the ideology of consumption. However, neither the CI nor music are ahistorical concepts, and therefore, it is helpful to reflect on a transition from aspects of Adorno's original thesis in order to maintain the relevance of his theories to an understanding of Morrissey as an artist.

Standardisation

Adorno identified several characteristics of cultural goods that have been mass manufactured. One characteristic he termed "Standardisation", which was the result of universalizing particular critical aesthetic details of art's character (Adorno and Horkheimer 1997: 123). Entertainment, art and everyday life become amalgamated into a seamless repetitive transaction and are used as details to exaggerate comparisons between goods. Hence, genuine innovation is utilized to reinvigorate the market as an omnipresent negation of reality.

> If the concept of decay, which cultural philistines love to cite against modern art, is justified anywhere it is in popular music.
>
> (Adorno 1989: 22)

In music, the CI imposes standardisation by borrowing from existing formats and/or applying technology to reproduce arrangements, composition, structure, pitch, chords or timing. Choruses frequently repeat the title at timed intervals like an advert for the song, while the external format of music is forced to fit the situation in which it will be heard, like the radio or work place (Adorno 2002: 295). The style of singing and voice become the hook, or the use of certain instruments turn sounds into motifs that synchronically function to preoccupy the listener. Adorno explained how instruments and the autonomy of sounds should interact by continually critically opposing each other, then dissolve to confront the whole meaning of a piece of music, rather than dictate the composer's ideas (Adorno 2006: 102). The separate, standardized format of these parts reflects for Adorno the industrial division in the labour process. This is also apparent in the repetitive use of time in the recording of music and playback in both studio and domestic spaces.

Thus, the meaning and use of time become abstract and unpredictable through the internalized duration of time in the music itself. This in turn becomes a permanent lapse in relation to the external movement of time in which the music is heard. In other words, pop music constructs time analogy to the industrial mechanism of work (for instance shift work).

Adorno stated that mass manufactured music used technology to re-create the industrial beat of modern life, producing a "rhythmically obedient listener" (Adorno 2002: 460). This standard productive rhythm has never been more prevalent, and now that technology has advanced to such a level of sophistication, music can be entirely created and distributed by a machine. While this in itself is emancipating, the danger is that sounds can become even more homogenous. Yet, the material of all music retains a residual of tensions between aesthetics and commodification. Adorno cited Beethoven as an artist who expressed this contradiction through his music:

> [H]e is the most outstanding example of the unity of those opposites, market and independence, in bourgeois art. Those who succumb to the ideology are precisely those who cover up the contradiction instead of taking it into the consciousness of their own production as Beethoven did.
>
> (Adorno 1991: 157)

This implies that the use of technology is not always immediate or in consensual relationship with economic and social ideologies (Adorno 1989: 22). Therefore, high and low cultural forms both contain a truth as different "episodes" of the social reality. This sketch of Adorno's ideas is intended to establish an understanding of pop, in order to reflect on Morrissey's position within the CI. To summarize, the CI's irrational and relentless surplus supply of records reduces art's power by reconciling aesthetic details to produce standard recognizable genres preventing alternative forms of music from emerging.

Morrissey: An expert listener

An historical vantage can now permit a reconsideration of Adorno's comments in light of pop developing a critique of its own contradictions: its purposelessness *and* function in society. Punk is important to this argument because it confronted the music industry by subverting the CI's method for combining the relationship between life, art and commodities. By invading the pattern of supply and consumption, it demonstrated that the pleasure of music was conditioned by the context in which it is produced and received. This reconfigured method would historically reinvent pop as an object of protest and communication. Punk made manifest Adorno's point that music's content conceals social divisions in the production and distribution mechanisms. This was revolutionary in influencing pop's development and the instigators were experts: the listeners themselves.[2]

"Turned sickness into [un]popular song" ('On The Streets I Ran')

Morrissey is an expert listener who continues to tackle the music industry while operating within that system. Punk's critique of the record industry and society was a multifaceted and unpredictable revelation in the commercial exchange of signs, upon which it depended. In subverting pop's status, it critically disrupted the identity between producer and receiver, to reveal that pop culture does have the capacity to objectively communicate and transcend its unified relation to the commodity form, by developing internally through the style and sound of the music. The most influential legacy of punk developed through the audience taking control of production, and this DIY approach legitimized the practice of social relations in the creative development of pop music. It could be argued that without this, Morrissey's voice may never have had a chance to be publicly heard.[3]

By Morrissey's standards

Since the demise of The Smiths, Morrissey has worked with different musicians and producers who added variation to his oeuvre.[4] Styles shift from a standard structure to complement the narrative atmosphere, to more unpredictable sounds that can be loud and aggressive, adding tension or appearing to attack the overall themes in the songs. Refrains give way to indicate a change of mood, for instance the children's choir on 'The Youngest Was The Most Loved' and 'The Father Who Must Be Killed'. Different instruments like keyboards are introduced in 'Everyday Is Like Sunday' for instance, the tempo builds up, then gives way to a gentle fade, mirroring the pace of the day as he describes it.[5]

The music on the album *Southpaw Grammar* seems out of control and no longer contained by the songs, as vocals and lyrics are left behind. Each track varies in length, with long intros, lack of definition between the verses and chorus, unexpected endings with no indication from vocals or music that the song is about to fade out. In conventional pop songs, the standard arrangement of these sections are smooth and flow together in a pre-arranged harmony which reconcile any tensions that are produced between them, but the internal parts in Morrissey's music are exemplified and occur unexpectedly, giving space for an interaction between the elements. The autonomy of individual "parts'" relation to the overall "whole" composition is a common theme throughout Adorno's discussions on popular music and the CI.

Sampling/montage

To understand the nature of what Adorno means by a "part", his discussion of Brecht and Weil's appropriation of montage in their theatre work serves as a good example. Adorno contemplated innovative structures in popular music by considering how their montage technique drew attention to the function of the internal structures; it demonstrated how music could internally criticize its own form as a social object. The "part", which is montage, is a method that distorts the possibilities for art forms by exposing the social conditions that construct them. Therefore, popular music could be "legitimatized as a vehicle of dialectic communication" (Adorno 2002: 409). The method of montage that Adorno described could be understood as a formative style of sampling. This is a particular aesthetic characteristic in Morrissey's music, which is derived from varied sources such as dialogue from film, radio and "found" sounds, and even his use of guest backing vocalists and "quoting" from other characters function as samples.

This is an application of technology to create sounds that develop internally, and rather than adopting these parts as a novelty, the samples function to maintain a uniqueness and resistance to trends. These elements are introduced into his songs not merely as a selling point or hook, but maintain individuality because they are innovatively used with precision to function as a vital component within the structure of the music as a whole or to construct an internal dialogue indicating a shift in perspective in the songs storyline.

In the track 'Disappointed', for instance, when he announces "This will be the last song I will ever sing", the sample of a cheering crowd responds. When our unpredictable singer changes his mind again, it sounds like the crowd jeers. These sonic moments are low in the mix and their function is understated, yet these sounds are of equal value to the vocals. Further illustrations where samples function as integral parts include, 'Asian Rut' where vocals are overdubbed adding emphasis, and by the placing of sardonic laughter. It raises the question, with whom does our narrator sympathize the victim or assailant? Shutters snap like fireworks on 'The Harsh Truth Of The Camera Eye', the claps mirroring the greedy grabbing lens of the paparazzi. There's the football crowds rousing battle cry on 'We'll Let You Know', and the strangers' voices suddenly giving guiding directions from Suggs on 'Piccadilly Palare'. The sound of a woman crying, band members chatting, engines firing up, choirs harmonizing, radio interference and dialogue from films are all moments when samples operate as autonomous parts within the songs. 'Margaret On The Guillotine' is framed with a perfect use of sampling that introduces the song and dramatically ends with another sample, defining the track as the final act/scene on the album. 'Dial A Cliché', the album's penultimate track, ends with church bells of a traditional funeral march echoing in the death of a person who is "lost in the fog" following the unnamed subject of the song. This eerie signifier has a subtle ambiguity that points to the final statement in 'Margaret', where the sampled sound waits for the listener to reach the end of the song. The sound of a blade then chillingly drops and cuts the song dead, underlining Morrissey's point in what remains one of his most political songs, but its timing is also imperative. This sample marks the fictitious end of Margaret's life, the song and the album, but it also marks the end of The Smiths. From then on, all records that followed would be Morrissey's solo material, so in this sense the role of the singer in that band was also killed off and reborn. These parts are not irrefutable like a film or photograph portraying a copy of the thing itself, rather like theatre, or paintings, these individual elements within the songs require the listener to make their own connections. This internal and external relationship between performer and the audience is a progression from passive consumption by audience to its active presence becoming part of the performance.

Pseudo individual

Returning to Adorno's characteristics of the CI's goods, he proposed that the standardisations of forms eventually become transparent, so a "pseudo individual" character disguises this (Adorno and Horkheimer 1997: 153). For instance, personal details like regional accents and surnames become promotional signs that create a pseudo sense of identity. Adorno understands aesthetics function in music as the boundary between reality and art. It is through the tensions between the aesthetic presentation of form, namely the record as a commodity, and the content, that the listener's needs are produced. Pop music manipulates these two realms and reconciles the tensions to offer an escape or solution, by turning one aspect into a novelty or presenting an idealized scenario that pacifies listeners through over-identification (Adorno 1989: 27).

Everyday themes functions as parody, while any negative emotion that may accompany these genuine scenarios is expressed as an external obstacle to be overcome (Adorno 2002: 444–446). Civil disobedience and revolt are portrayed as punishable acts, thus the message in these forms is that happiness only comes from conforming and surrendering. Music's role in this capacity functions within the contradictions of "free time" by offering listeners a false sense of identity that promises instant gratification (Adorno and Horkheimer 1997: 120–167). Under the capitalist regime, the CI is an instrument to suppress subjects' desire for freedom, and weakens their ability for self-reasonability. The CI proves the public can survive capitalism's exploitation so long as it continues creating and gratifying the needs of the audience's members are weakened. But this also means that any distrust of its goods or any outsider's opinion is a potential peril to the CI's domination.

Indeed Morrissey, by his own admission, is an 'Ambitious Outsider' who uses the mechanisms of society as material within his music. Morrissey's treatment of themes, however, refuses to unify these realms or to offer pacification for the listener. Instead, he injects his lyrics with an aesthetic sensibility, intelligent, witty and literary quality that he uses like an artist's choice of paint to create rich imagery and experiences. These aspects function as "parts" within the "part" and "whole" relationship of artworks described by Adorno. The songs' contentious points are often subtle, because as complete works they are closer to the medium of theatre, that is to say there is a space between the "parts" for the listener to interpret the songs for themselves.

The "Other"

Unlike visual medium such as films or photographs, the beauty and value of the songs are their lack of closure, they do not reveal the whole story or offer reproducible ready-made emotional reactions. Instead, Morrissey narrates ambiguous Proustian details and imagery nuanced through the unexpected turn of phrasing as poetic devices. Such "parts" add richness to the songs, prompting listeners to follow clues and construct their own connotations. The lyrics communicate reoccurring themes: class, race, religion, suicide, fame, love, isolation, death, history, gender and sexuality. What becomes apparent in his treatment of these themes is the prevailing idea of the *Other*, be it the voiceless, the disabled, the dead, the rejected, the overweight, the poor, the antihero or the mute witness. This *Other* is framed through the social circumstances he describes – the media producing stars, the press exploiting the concept of evil, politics generating greed, the blood hungry crowds at football or boxing matches, the lost male working-class youth at a fascist meeting, the murdering of a parent or child, a vigilante attack, rejecting work and never voting conservative, the bad people on the right with government schemes, refusing to reproduce or marry, but instead choosing to resist the social establishment of the family unit and its ideological function.

His representations of these themes are reflected through the omnipresence perspective of the protagonist, while illustrating how the *other* is ultimately our projection by uncovering our private thoughts, and essentially laying bare and calling into dispute taboos. What his songs emphasize are the human traits such as jealousy, anger, violence and nonconformity. In psychoanalytical language, these could be aspects people might "split off" or deny feeling. In particular, there is always an absence at the centre of the themes, be it loneliness, rejection or the ultimate absence of death.

Class

Morrissey holds the typical tropes of popular culture to ransom: he is cruel to women, celebrates the villain, humiliates himself, demands society accounts for its faults, and is unfailing in his belief in the working-classes. His entire career has contained references to class, and unlike "protest" singers, Morrissey's treatment of class is pluralistic, as the working-classes is not a unified body of people as the media and popular culture portrays it. His songs, interviews and quotes offer an abundance of examples.[7] The use of class as a subject matter by Morrissey is particularly powerful because he is being authentic not only to the class from which he came and understands, but to his convictions for the potential of the working-classes. This highlights an essential point, that Morrissey is aware of the function of cultural commodities' power over the working-classes, and while Morrissey may not be consciously [aware/engaged with] the theoretical conception of CI, I am suggesting that in practice he highlights and uses the concealed aspects of popular music that Adorno perceived. This makes Morrissey partisan, like Punk before him, and he uses the materials of his own form to express the very conditions that established them, but in a nuanced art form.

Self-referentiality

As a cultural product Morrissey never promises the false ideas that the pop industry does, instead he presents an art form, which requires the audience to recognize themselves as subjects and uncover the truth in his work for themselves individually. One of the fundamental themes in Morrissey's work is the self-referential commentary on precisely the social and historical conditions that Adorno argued the CI concealed through the process of aesthetization. Morrissey is fully aware of the commodity status attached to him, and he carefully employs every word he utters, to make manifest the contradiction in the content and form of his art. Morrissey's eloquent self-expression offers his listeners the opportunity to reflect on his work that reveals mechanisms of the CI. However, it is because Morrissey is working in the medium of pop music that his art must bear the weight and constriction of that system, thus criticism is always directed at him *personally*, rather than the system itself.

In a multitude of ways, Morrissey consistently reminds the audience that they are individuals. His music is a vehicle through which we can see the subjects he portrays, but it is the listener's responsibility to connect the various parts and complete his work. Morrissey utilizes the tensions of pop as self-referential themes in themselves in tracks like 'Why Don't You Find Out For Yourself', where the record company men have a special interest in his career, or the fading star in 'Papa Jack', 'Little Man What Now', 'You know I Couldn't Last', 'On the Street I Ran' or 'Get off The Stage'. In 'Sing your Life' for example, his voice is clear and inviting, echoing the punk ethic to instruct the listeners to use the medium themselves, explaining the structure of pop music is standardized pointing out "First chorus, middle eight, break fade". Making no separation between himself and the audience, he tells us how effortless it is to sing our lives before confirming that those who do "stole the notion from you and me".

In 'Speedway' and 'Hated For Loving' he tells us he has taken his responsibly to be true to us seriously, but to hear the truth also carries a responsibility. This sentiment is the nexus of Adorno's argument that understands the relationship between reader and author as a dialectical one. By making manifest the system in which pop operates, Morrissey illustrates how the material form of pop can comment on its conditions of possibility. This would disrupt the predetermined identity of passive consumers indicating the dialectic relationship between the contents of the record, listening habits and the future production of records. Ultimately, Morrissey's entire back catalogue has told the audience that to resist the structure of society deems one "maladjusted". As modern man in a culturally driven market, he exists as the artist cast out of Plato's Republic for provoking excessive emotions. As modern men and women, the audience members are alienated from themselves and each other, discovering any disagreement with society is punishable by isolation.

Listening to music

Adorno highlights a discrepancy between the receptions of art as opposed to the reception of standard popular music. Adopting a psychoanalytical approach, he explained a typology of listening. He claimed that it takes time and concentration for the free association of the imagination's engagement with the variety of elements and connections within music. The CI turns pop into repetitive structures denying listeners the invitation of participation to engage with alternatives so the ability to make judgements is reified, forcing listeners to forget the conditions that constructed the music. Conversely, because capitalism dominates people's time, listening to music becomes a habit that is replayed in their free time when only standardized parts of songs like the chorus or the sounds of instruments are appropriated (Adorno 2002: 452–457). Consequently, the music becomes refigured or distorted in their memory through selective hearing. The audience internalize the effects of pop music in a psychological transference, transforming a song into a receptacle object where personal gratification can be placed. This identification represses any real desires as unrecognizable so that subordination to everyday life is maintained. Listeners, however, are afraid to acknowledge this deception so experience the false narcissistic power of the aesthetic and expressive quality of music as a defence of their tastes (Adorno 2002: 452–462). This regressive psychological effect is reinforced by the CI's industrial method of *distribution*, for as a commodity each new record that is produced invariably destroys the value and effects of the past ones.

If the fetish character of exchange has alienated people to the extent that they are removed from their pleasure, listeners' are then concealing their self-contempt and forcing themselves into submission to the CI. However, the transference of the "external order" to "internal manipulation" is not a passive act if people actually decide to conform. Therefore, if music's function in modernity is failing to reach people's consciousness, what is the nature of pleasure in pop music (Adorno 1989: 39)? Perhaps, there could be a possibility for music to expose this alienation and for the pleasure to be experienced through the expression of surviving *within* these tensions. This would reintroduce the "particular" individual response rather than a general one, which in turn would confront the CI to reveal that sensual pleasure of reception is subjective, and not pre-manufactured.

Hearing: Voice

Modernity has privileged the ocular, arguably replacing the elusive power of the voice with the visual. For instance, a classically trained voice as an indexical sign is embodied by the image of a gendered body. Even pop voices are stylized and focused upon to convey a personality, which infects narratives and characters in songs that the voice rhythmically brings to life. As such, the singing voice is a creative tool that the CI exploits through recording technology to produce a pleasant standardized sound, which becomes reinterpreted upon receivership by the listener. The process of production fetishizes songs, which predetermines the voice as representational, rather than having an individual quality that is unique to the material it is singing. This makes listeners value the reactions to the sensations that have deliberately been provoked, rather than how the voice may function and contain value in itself. Voices do have a distinctiveness though, and it is this aspect that disrupts passive listening, because the voice can transport the listener to the borderline where the imaginary meets symbolic and it is in this gap that the subjective can be discovered. Thus if a song can interpolate listeners, it is a recognition that brings a subject into being, through the combination of repeated performance.

Music then affords a space that allows the subject to take up a multitude of positions. In this way, it can temporally emancipate listeners from the culture that endeavours to pacify the audience. The voice also has a metaphysical life because it can describe political positioning, it can take on a visibility in the ruling orders that makes up society. Morrissey's voice is an instrumental element that can disguise or reinforce the text and his personality as a performer. He often sings from different perspectives within the same song; this is when the phrasing, non-verbal acts like pauses in the breath, whistling, growling, moaning and yodelling can emphasize words or echo like ghosts of the other characters' positions.

The excessive emotional expression in his voice sounds like an evocative struggle to escape the structure of the songs, disrupting the coherence of communication between the lyrics and the feeling associated with them, in the process producing a sense of oppression and proposing alternative meanings.

The distinctive characteristics of Morrissey's voice have matured from the vernacular accent, becoming richer, deeper and wider in range. He masterfully utilizes the performative element of the voice, which as a human "part" retains its autonomy as an "instrument" intrinsic to the aesthetic quality of his music. Mostly his vocal is even in the mix to articulate themes, but when the volume alters or dominates, the theatrical use of his voice creates disunity between the sounds and enhances the nuances within the vocal arrangements. This leaves neither listener nor singer in control, while the style and arrangement of the vocals decentre the power in the music. Technology is not excessively used to manipulate his voice; it is only layered or over dubbed, when it enhances different elements of the song.

Moreover, the uniqueness of his voice embodies the performance, and it is this element that communicates the unspoken aspects of the songs. His voice allows a powerful use of language that exists beyond the visual, which can provide a transcendental experience for the listener.

The confessional character of his voice at times guides the listener to follow it; consequently, when his vocal is a challenge to hear, the voice risks its own eminence as a commodity. The fragmented, unrestrained cries cling to their autonomy in the realization that their existence depends on the necessity of the record. The result echoes the listener's subconsciousness to construct a subjective meaning in reply to the music as a whole, in contrast to a standard pop song that reproduces aspects of real life by literally describing them as a way to manipulate sensual pleasure and produce a uniform response.

In comparison, Morrissey's songs are like subverted modern hymns that twist music's traditional relationship with topics like religion, faith, modernity and love into an anti-celebration by poetically expressing the negative aspects of society and the everyday. The hope that pop songs often convey is reconfigured as a dystopian tragedy set against the shattered dreams of the past, thus negating the CI's entertainment value by withholding reconciliation. The typical notion of romance, love, desire and the conventional identities of gender roles are deconstructed as unrecognizable false ideals, in contrast to the images portrayed by pop that frequently position a woman as the central object. The addressee in Morrissey's songs is often unclear and all these aspects negate the CI's value of entertainment by postponing reconciliation.

The voice and lyrics, as separate parts, can alert the listener to respond as they unfold in relation to the energy of music as a whole. Listening, like singing, has a subjective involvement that can be manipulated to hierarchically order everything else around it. Therefore, although tones, rhythms and ironies change meaning, listeners can insert themselves into this space to make sense of these meanings, or subvert them, but this demands a subjective self. In other words, listeners do project their personal image back into songs, which demonstrates that music is a two-way street.

Conclusions

Symbolic shifts in the circulation of culture

It is impossible to return to a pre-CI world and in late capitalism the shift from traditional industrial production increased the competitive relation between capital and culture, so aesthetic production and marginal originality were integrated much quicker than in earlier stages of the CI. As a result, a symbolic exchange that colonized all aspects of civil life in the ideological merging of the distinctions between a mass production economy and the circulation of culture as signs, acquired limitless meaning and value. As an extension of promotional homogeneity, this pervasive and instrumental appropriation of self-identity delimitated and valorized the commercial exchange principle in the CI's goods.

In postmodern terms, the CI recognized the incorporation of life and culture as an erosion of distinction between high modernism and mass culture (Jameson 1991). This transformed meaning from cultural objects into the image of the object, thus placing emphasis on the visual. Music, however, lacked a visual product, which was counteracted by the invention of MTV, placing an obligation on musicians to make promotional videos to influence the commercial success of their records.

This transformed the experience of music because the narrative of a song was either mediated (or detached) from the accompanying visual of the video. MTV exploited the representational aspect of music and extended it into a pre-made image that gives way to depthless simulacra and nostalgia. This confused the relationship between music, meaning and image but extended the circulation of songs as consumable objects.

The theorization of pop music can be problematic because it slips between the boundaries of cultural and subcultural divisions, which can often be vague in themselves. Since the Frankfurt School and the evolution of media studies, pop music, as a child of popular culture, has been over-invested in through post-structuralist theories to focus on consumption as active moments producing positive subjectivities. Nevertheless, the ambivalence and rationality of pop music's existence is political precisely because its latent content is the repetition of society itself. Music is a space where image, voice, sound and text all interrelate, which manifests a danger that could erupt at any moment through the collective ideals it fosters. If Adorno's arguments are not used dialectically, pop, as an object of study, is vulnerable to being over-determinant and reductive of music's oppositional potential.[8] Alternatively, it can be described as a pacifying commodity, denying the complexity of the relationship between the tensions of pop music and its value as an imminent art form. This is because pop records, as low cultural forms, lack what Adorno termed the disinterestedness and autonomy of high art (Adorno and Horkheimer 1997: 157–158). Although as aesthetic objects, they are dialectic and contain tensions of their conditions just as art does.

Adorno did not invest in analysing the potential of popular music as an historical expression of its situation, but this did not mean he dismissed the *possibility* of it. I have attempted to employ Adorno's method of critical theory to demonstrate his ideas are relevant to Morrissey, because his argument that music and theory should be fluid rather than a formula remain.

Adorno understood that when the relationship between parts or aspects of songs was manufactured to produce a standard connection to the whole, it was to produce typical reactions in listeners. This contrived construction of pop that was discussed earlier in this chapter exposes the social truth of isolated subjectivity. This is a result of the discontinuity between use and exchange values, thus music's material contained "congealed histories" (Adorno 1998: 15–16). In other words, pop records are produced as commodities, but sold as a distraction from the commodification process. Morrissey reflects the truth of these social relations by expressing the *lack* of them as a constant theme in his music. By acknowledging the system that manufactures and distributes pop music, he is creating an art form that contains the potential to reintegrate social relations.

A song cannot be an absolute representation of the intangibility of emotions, to the extent that Adorno or maybe even Morrissey's fans claim that rather it is the particular, and not the general in reception, which reveals that sensual pleasure is subjective and *different* for different classes and genders. It is the production and distribution process of music that transforms the quality and content, so the relevance of emotional responses, regressive or otherwise, is ambiguous and not an accurate or deciding feature to measure pop's value. Adorno conceptualized pop music as a commodity that distracts its audience from this truth by appearing as a consolation for the circumstances of the nature of production. Put another way, the symbolic codes of pop disguise the conditions of leisure time that allow listeners to celebrate their false consciousness in modern culture. Adorno made his critique of pop culture over 70 years ago, and since then the CI has accelerated. The limits and content of pop music have expanded, particularly after punk; nevertheless, it continues to be commercially produced. Therefore, it is necessary to re-negotiate the relationship with the CI, so as to uncover moments when a three-minute pop song actually provokes a listener's attention by confronting them with the nature of the CI.

There has always been an economic and class element to the accessibility of live performances, and the private consumption of records. Classical music was initially made to be heard live, but it is no longer bound to live performances or court patronage, while pop artists no longer depend on record labels to produce and distribute their music. In comparison, consumers now appear to have freedom of choice, but that choice is still mediated by the CI mechanisms, only it is now more disguised than ever.

Therefore if the initial divisions of culture can be understood as economically based constructions, it would be possible to hear *all* music's internal and external conflicts as representations of the society that shaped the music in the first place. Morrissey developed from a tradition that produced and distributed music in opposition to the mainstream, which allowed it to sonically and lyrically express the contradictions in an artful and authentic style. Hence, by transforming the conditions of production and consumption into a creative force, popular music can prove to be an artistic material with the capacity to reflect critically on the relations of its condition. As a social object, this reconfigured the romantics of pop and created tensions that had not previously existed, by re-presenting class, gender and sexual codes. The pleasure in this music came from the ambiguities that showed how music was consumed and used to regulate.

Music does not exist in a vacuum removed from art; as a counterpart it continues to communicate and is a powerful tool for propaganda, profit, passivity and desire. As a material product of social relations, it is an instrument of knowledge and a container of history; the changes it has undergone reflect the manifestations of society. The struggle that remains is to maintain the particulars of these forms within the general and to reflect on the resistance and submissive dialectic of those particulars.

If we were to state there is little distinction between Mozart and Morrissey, it would ignore the cultural divisions. Indeed, the insidious operation of the CI forges an amalgamation of these "torn halves" (Adorno: 2000: 395). Institutionally however, composers such as Mozart are contemplated as a topic of art history, aesthetic, philosophy and musicology, while pop music is relegated to culture studies.[9] It is debatable if other disciplines would consider Morrissey with the same regard as high art. As a sign, pop music is only valued for its economic and symbolic exchangeability. Unlike the plastic arts, music is not judged for its "purposelessness".[10] The epistemology of this subject awaits institutional approval to give it theoretical substance, but in the mean time, its knowledge is experienced in praxis every time someone listens to a song, purely because it does *say something to us about our lives.*

However, to focus on the polemic between the values of high and low culture is to miss the point. The point is this distinction was constructed for economic ends. While Adorno was right, that the standard official music of the charts and radio playlists fails to convince listeners about the truth of the contradictions that exist within society, and the songs themselves, this is not to deny these songs still contain similar contradictions. This is why artists like Morrissey became categorized as "alternative", for presenting an authentic representation of society's contradictions and pointing out that culture was and continues to be ideologically responsible for creating false desires.

In this chapter I have attempted to draw attention to this division through Adorno's understanding of the CI's influence over the categorization between high and low art forms. Mozart may have been "popular" in his time, but the distinction is subtle; "popular" did not equate to low culture or standard forms. Despite the disruption of genres and forms, pop music is still controlled by the CI. While subjective political meaning can also be found in the textual readings of a pop song. What is of relevance are the conditions of possibility. Morrissey is exceptional because he continues to challenge the possibilities of the pop format. By naming the process, he maintains human agency for himself as a commodity form and his audience as consumers alike.

Reader meet author indeed

Morrissey's cult like status could now have a contradictory effect once fans start to place a function upon his music, and expect the songs to give answers. Like art itself Morrissey is in danger of becoming a victim of his own circumstances. The CI takes the genuine experience of the audience, reformulates it and then sells it back to them as unrecognizable. *"Amusement under late capitalism is a prolongation of work"* (Adorno and Horkheimer 1997: 137). Adorno continually asserted that only when individuals could activate their own subjectivity by listening and responding to music would it enable a dialectical progression of the subject and object.

Morrissey is only supplying the text, it is up to the audience to complete it by interpretation. Thus unless we are accountable for the creation of our tastes as subjective acts, the particular will always be subsumed within the whole.

The technological revolution within the domestic production and consumption of music could signal a post-pop world. Had Adorno met Morrissey in such a world, how could he have failed to disagree with the demand: "Hang the deejay – because the music they constantly play, says nothing to me about my life". Class and aesthetics are not separate objects under Adorno's arguments, nor in Morrissey's work. In concluding, I have not intended to reveal that Adorno's arguments about pop music were misguided, whilst I also hope to have avoided presenting a biased adulation towards Morrissey. Rather I have used Adorno's theory to draw out the critical aspects of Morrissey's work, while dialectically relating Adorno's relevance to the current emerging aesthetics of music, and their categorization thereafter. Academia is one such institution of power that can maintain or uncover ideologies and produce frameworks for critically analysing society. Maybe it is time for theorists to take a punk approach and infiltrate the system from within by acknowledging fissures in the system. Just maybe, following Morrissey's cue, this publication is a partisan-like start.

Notes

1. Mozart is not of particular relevance to this essay, he is used merely as an example of the classical tradition in contrast to popular culture.
2. See bibliography for further reading on the development of Punk.
3. What is meant by this comment is that punk influenced the development of independent record labels, and an intervention into the standard charts that existed. See bibliography for further reading.
4. Morrissey has worked with various people like Vini Reilly, an established figure in the punk/post punk Manchester scene; he was also a member of the Nosebleeds, whom Morrissey auditioned for, Stephen Street, who went on to champion Brit Pop, Jerry Finn, who worked with younger American punk bands and the Italian Composer Ennio Morricone.
5. These examples are just an indication of variations and not exhaustive of distinctive musical moments through Morrissey's career.
6. When Adorno discusses "parts", he is mostly referring to classical compassions, therefore those parts are different instruments, and the sections played. Thus in a pop song any other element of a song could be conceived as a "part", for example, voice, lyrics, stature of the music and phrasing.
7. For an excellent analysis, see Power's chapter in this volume.

8. The value of disciplines is a much wider topic that cannot be expanded on here. For Adorno's comments on pop music and academia, see 'On the social situation of music' in Adorno (2002).

9. See Bibliography for texts by Marcus, who equates punk with avant-garde art movements; also the texts by Hebdige and Frith.

10. "Plastic arts" is an art history term referring to any art form that can be 3D.

References

Adorno, T. (2006) *Philosophy of New Music*, trans. Robert Hullot-Kentor. Minneapolis: University of Minnesota Press.

Adorno, T. (2002) *Essays on Music, Selected, with Introduction, Commentary and Notes by Richard Leppert*, trans. Susan H. Gillespie. Berkeley: University of California Press.

Adorno, T. (1989) *Introduction to the Sociology of Music*, trans. E. B. Ashton. New York: Continuum.

Adorno, T. and Bernstein, J. (ed.) (1991) *The Culture Industry*. London: Routledge.

Adorno, T. and Horkheimer, M. (1997) *Dialectic of Enlightenment* trans. John Cumming. New York: Continuum.

Attali, J. (1985) *Noise: The Political Economy of Music*, trans. Brian Massumi. Minneapolis: University of Minnesota Press.

Cook, D. (1996) *The Culture Industry Revisited*. Marylands: Rowman and Littlefield.

Denora, T. (2000) *Music in Everyday*. Cambridge: Cambridge University Press.

Durant, A. (1984) *Conditions of Music*. Albany: SUNY Press.

Frith, S. (ed.) (1988) *Facing the Music: Essays on Pop, Rock and Culture*. London: Madarin.

Frith, S. (1983) *Sound Effects, Youth Leisure and the Politics of Rock*. London: Constable.

Frith, S. and Horne, H. (1987) *Art into Pop*. London: Methuen.

Graham, D. (1994) *Rock My Religion Writings and Projects 1965–1990*. Massachusetts: MIT Press.

Haslam, D. (2000) *Manchester England: The Story of the Pop Culture City*. London: Fourth Estate.

Hebdige, D. (1979) *Subculture: The Meaning of Style*. London: Methuen.

Home, S. (1995) *Cranked Up Really High: Inside Account of Punk Rock*. Hove: Codex.

Heyin, C. (1993) *From the Velvets' to The Voidoids Pre Punk History for a Postpunk World*. London: Penguin.

Jameson, F. (1991) *Postmodernism or the Cultural Logic of Late Capitalism*. London: Verso.

Kellner, D. (1989) *Critical Theory, Marxism and Modernism*. Oxford: Polity Press.

Marcus, G. (1993) *In the Fascist Bathroom, Punk in Pop Music 71–92*. Massachusetts: Harvard University Press.

Marcus, G. (1989) *Lipstick Traces: A Secret History of Twenty Century*. London: Secker and Warbura.

Paddidon, M. (1996) *Adorno, Modernism & Mass Culture*. London: Karn and Averill.

Paddidon, M. (1993) *Adorno's Aesthetics on Music*. Cambridge: Cambridge University Press.

Reynolds, S. (2005) *Rip It Up and Start Again, Post Punk 1978–1984*. London: Faber & Faber.

Saban, R. (ed.) (1999) *Punk Rock: So What?* London: Routledge.

Savage, J. (1991) *England's Dreaming*. London: Faber & Faber.

Thompson, S. (2004) *Punk Productions: Unfinished Business*. Albany: State University Press of New York.

Witkin, W. (2003) *Adorno on Popular Culture*. London: Routledge.

Witkin, W. (1998) *Adorno on Music*. London: Routledge.

Chapter 10

Speedway for Beginners: Morrissey, Martyrdom and Ambiguity

Eoin Devereux and Aileen Dillane

Introduction

Representing a sort of latter day 'De Profundis', it is somewhat surprising that the epic song 'Speedway' written by Morrissey and Boz Boorer has not, in spite of its popularity amongst fans and critics alike, received much by way of scholarly attention. With the exception of Hawkins (2002), there has been scant critical engagement with this important composition which dramatically brings to a close Morrissey's 1994 album *Vauxhall and I*.[1] Fans and music critics alike have speculated – without much real foundation – on its supposed meaning. Morrissey's post-Madstock persecution by the music press (and the *NME* in particular), his relationship with Johnny Marr and even the impending (1996) court case mounted by former Smiths drummer Mike Joyce have all been highlighted as possible motivations behind Morrissey's lyrics.[2] Notwithstanding these interpretations, 'Speedway', for us, represents a rich and multi-layered example *par excellence* of how tropes of martyrdom persist across Morrissey's creative work as both the leader of The Smiths and as a solo-artiste. Our interest in this theme stems from an overarching research interest in the presence of the religious and the occultural within popular culture (see Devereux 2010; Partridge 2005; Flory and Miller 2000; Lynch 2006; Sylvan 2005) and in Morrissey's work in particular. Although defiant in tone and mood, *Vauxhall and I*[3] contains strong themes of martyrdom and victimhood, and it is not entirely coincidental that one receptive review of the album included an illustration of Morrissey recast as Joan of Arc and tied to a stake[4] (see Figure 10.1). Sketched by Graham Humphreys, the Morrissey caricature is foregrounded with the phoenix, who within Christian mythology rises from the ashes and symbolizes Jesus Christ's resurrection. Conforming to previous media constructions of the singer, the review itself is presented as a series of meditations on Morrissey and is replete with religious discourse (Devereux 2010). Emphasizing Morrissey's messianic dimensions, it makes explicit reference to Morrissey as Joan of Arc, to his beatification and to him being Christ-like. 'Speedway', in particular, we are told sees Morrissey "beat up and beatific" while the overall album smells of "human flesh at the stake" (Bailie 1994).[5] Taken together, the review and its accompanying illustration can be read as symbolizing Morrissey's martyrdom (by disloyal friends; by former colleagues; by the music press; by the music industry; and the British establishment)[6] but also his resurrection and renewal.

In this chapter we offer a close critical reading of 'Speedway'. Our approach is as much sociological as it is musicological – that is to say that we are equally interested in the initial "making" of the song, its performance and delivery as well as its possible meaning(s). We

Figure 10.1: And Now I Know How Joan of Arc Felt … Reproduced by kind permission © Graham Humphreys (1994).

examine 'Speedway' in three main ways. Our discussion begins with an account of the writing and recording of 'Speedway'. We then present a critical commentary on the song's lyrics and music and suggest an alternative reading of the text. Taking as our cue a review of *Vauxhall and I*, which perceptively remarked that 'Speedway' "could be Oscar Wilde singing on the witness stand and flirting with the judge" (Sheffield 1994), we offer a reading of the song which suggests that Morrissey adopts Wilde's martyr persona in addressing an array of his/their enemies.[7] Finally, we discuss how Morrissey's persistent use of ambiguity and irony (both lyrically and sonically) serve as a crucial device in his songwriting (see Devereux 2009). In Morrissey's case, martyrdom is a two-way street in that constructions of Morrissey as a martyr stem from both himself and from the music press.

Why speedway?

While the word "speedway" is referred to in the lyrics of a much earlier Morrissey/Marr composition – 'Rushholme Ruffians'[8] – other than in its title, speedway does not appear anywhere in this song. Previous accounts have made reference to a range of reasons as to why Morrissey may have chosen this title.[9] These include Johnny Marr's time as a

Figure 10.2: Themes of martyrdom and persecution have been a consistent feature of Morrissey's career. Reproduced by kind permission © Douglas Cape (1985).

motorcycle speedway assistant in Cheshire; Morrissey's negative adolescent experience of a violent incident at a fair in Stretford Road[10] and the suggestion that it is the title of one of his favourite films starring Elvis Presley and Nancy Sinatra.[11]

We hold that Morrissey's decision to use the word as a title may in fact signify something else entirely. As a term with multiple possible meanings, speedway is polysemic. It refers to two track-based motorsports;[12] it is the title of a 1929 silent film starring William Haines and it is also the name of a place traditionally associated with Gay subculture in Santa Monica.

If its use is in reference to either of the two danger-laden motorsports which bear its name, Morrissey's use of the word may be simply metaphorical. Like the motorcycle rider in speedway racing (where the bikes have no brakes), its use here may serve to signify a world where the song's protagonist (not unlike James Dean) is heading off all sorts of dangers and threats with reckless abandonment. *Speedway* is the title of two films which use stock-car racing as their respective settings. In addition to the movie featuring Elvis and Nancy Sinatra (1968), the original (silent) film *Speedway*[13] (1929) starred William Haines, who, before becoming a very famous interior designer, was victimized by the Hollywood movie industry and who heroically refused to conform to a "straight" sexual identity.[14] Coincidentally (or otherwise) Haines was responsible for the interior design in Morrissey's house in Lincoln Heights (LA) when it was owned by the comic actress Carole Lombard. Speedway the place, is, as Hawkins (2002) observes, located in Santa Monica. This oceanfront thoroughfare has had a long history of association with Gay subculture. Bret (2004) notes that it was a favoured cruising area for actors including James Dean, Rock Hudson and Montgomery Clift. Thus Speedway may also signify a place of pleasure imbued with danger.

So in addition to a possible nostalgia for Speedway the motorcycle sport, for its adolescent emotional resonances, for possible homoerotic longing for speedway operators, for its associations with Johnny Marr and with Elvis Presley, the word Speedway can connote danger, victimization and the liminal world of gay sexual encounters.

Writing and recording 'Speedway'

The original demo upon which 'Speedway' is based was called 'Rock of Ages'.[15] Composed by Boz Boorer, the song was written for Morrissey in the usual way, that is, the guitarist gave him a demo of the soundtrack to which Morrissey added his lyrics. Although the key used in the end version shifted from E to F sharp, the recording of the song does not differ in any substantial way from the original demo. Three particular production devices were used featuring the use of two ebows,[16] a chainsaw sample and drums which were recorded in two separate locations. Although some confusion abounds as to what device was used to create the sample at the start of the song, both Boz Boorer and producer Steve Lillywhite confirm that it was indeed a chainsaw.[17] In attempting to re-create the sound of a speedway motorcycle, a number of implements were used. The producer tried recording a drill and a lawnmower engine without much success and settled in the end on a chainsaw to produce the required sound.[18] Lillywhite wanted the song's percussion to build gradually from a light drumming to a thundering cacophony. The drums which are heard in the song's climax were recorded in the dining room at Hook End Manor (Goddard 2006: 214). In stark contrast to the other ten songs on the album, 'Speedway' stands apart from the overall "lush" sound which Lillywhite brought to their production.

Reading 'Speedway'

Lyrically, Morrissey manages to write a very complex song that combines ambiguity and irony in order to address his/the song's protagonist's detractors. At first glance, it is clear that the song has martyrdom as its primary theme, but it is uncertain as to *who* is being addressed and *who* is being martyred. Is it aimed at an ex-lover or a former collaborator? Is his venom directed at the music press or those who spuriously accused him of being racist in 1992? Is his quarry the music industry or the establishment in general? While any of these readings are indeed possible, we hold that 'Speedway' is a much more elaborate text that successfully manages to conflate the real or imagined martyrdom of Morrissey with that of Oscar Wilde. In doing so we present two readings of 'Speedway', with the first focused on Morrissey's experience prior to the writing and recording of *Vauxhall and I* and the second on Oscar Wilde's spectacular fall from grace.

Elsewhere in this collection Baker describes in detail the so-called Madstock incident. The reporting of and subsequent fallout from "Madstock" is the most common context by which 'Speedway' is read by both commentators and fans alike. If we were to accept this interpretation of the song, then the finalé of *Vauxhall and I* is simply an address by Morrissey to his enemies in the music press who have engaged in a witch-hunt against him. Unnamed journalists and editors have martyred Morrissey, metaphorically crucifying him through the spreading of rumours. They are digging his grave ("Can you delve so low?"), punishing him ("And when you are standing on my fingers") and attempting to break his spirit. These enemies will not be satisfied until the singer is silenced and dead. Stark as all this may seem, the song's subject then turns the tables on his opponents by stating (coyly) that both the rumours and lies written about him may have had some basis in truth. Somewhat strangely, 'Speedway' shifts focus in its last nine lines with Morrissey addressing another unidentified subject whom he admits to being still fond of. Is he merely intimating a love–hate relationship with those who have set out to persecute him? Or is he singing to more than one person?

Morrissey's own few pronouncements on the song are not particularly helpful, but he has admitted to its complexity and the possibility of the song simply being a wind-up. He told one interviewer that 'Speedway' is "even knottier than it appears" (Macioni 1994) and according to Goddard one decade later he admitted "somewhat flippantly, that the lyrics were just his way of winding up his detractors at the time", adding the remark "Life's a game isn't it?" (Goddard 2009: 411). Unsurprisingly, Morrissey's characteristic evasiveness does not bring us very far.

An alternative reading of 'Speedway' in terms of Oscar Wilde's story is perhaps a more fruitful way of uncovering what the song may be about. In this reading of the song, three separate people are being addressed, namely, his trial judge(s), the Marquess of Queensbury and Lord Alfred "Bosie" Douglas. While the opening lines of 'Speedway' ("When you slam down the hammer") might be read as making reference to the crucifixion of Christ (and Morrissey), the hammer[19] may also be that of a judge about to pass sentence. The unspecified rumours[20] (mentioned three times in the song) may refer to those concerning Oscar Wilde's sexuality before his trial(s) and ultimate imprisonment in 1895. Having appealed for mercy from the trial judge, Wilde addresses his nemesis – the Marquess of Queensbury. Queensbury who has succeeded in ruining Wilde is told: "You won't sleep / Until the earth that wants me / Finally has me / Oh you've done it now." The line which follows reminds us that in both Morrissey and Wilde's world-view, tragedy and comedy are close bedfellows. "You won't rest / Until the hearse that becomes me / Finally takes me / Oh you've done it now." So, in a camp fashion (and with a typically Wildean flourish), Morrissey notes that being sartorially sophisticated matters and that even in death he will be a Dandy (see Hawkins 2009). Our contention that this part of the song is directed at Queensbury is copper-fastened by the existence of a coded reference to homosexuality and numerous mentions of lies. Queensbury's intense homophobia about Wilde's sexual relationship with his son Bosie is alluded to when Morrissey sings "And you won't smile / until my loving mouth / Is shut good and proper / FOREVER." The admission that "All those lies / Written lies / Twisted lies / Well, they weren't lies / They weren't lies" may refer to the original (misspelt) calling card left by Queensbury in which he wrote "For Oscar Wilde, Posing Somdomite [sic]" and which spurred Wilde to (unwisely) take the case for criminal libel against Queensbury. The third "You" in 'Speedway' can be read as a reference to Bosie. Even though Wilde was initially strongly critical of Bosie in 'De Profundis',[21] here, his persona is protective of his ex-lover in stating "I could have mentioned your name / I could have dragged you in / Guilt by implication / By association."[22] Added to this in the final lines of the song is Wilde's realization that in spite of all that has happened (imprisonment, disgrace, financial ruin and separation), he still loves Bosie thus "I've always been true to you / In my own strange way / I've always been true to you / In my own sick way / I'll always stay true to you." This echoes the first section of 'De Profundis', where Wilde is heavily critical of Bosie at the outset but his venom gives way to forgiveness as he still loves Bosie in spite of everything that has happened.

Speedway: Structure and performance

Having introduced the social context, biographical details, critical views of the genesis and meaning of the song (lyrically and as social text), we now wish to discuss the song structure specifically in terms of formal structural musical elements and the performative processes which bring them to life. It is interesting to muse on just how many Morrissey fans, or indeed listeners to music in general, are able to speak about song lyrics and their (multiple) meanings but struggle to articulate what it is in the music structure that makes songs so moving and memorable (or not, for that matter) (Juslin and Slobda 2001). This interplay between lyrical content and musical structure is central in our understanding of how the idea of martyrdom and ambiguity is played out and performatively embodied in 'Speedway'.[23] Such formal analyses, combined with social and historical contexts (Brackett 2002; Clayton et al. 2003; Cook 1998; Negus 1996), see readings as interpretations and not givens or reified "products", and like the song 'Speedway' itself remain open to interpretations and reinterpretations.[24] 'Speedway' is, after all, a song, not a poem and the sounds of music, the relationships between gesture and affect, structure and feelings, reference and allusion, are central to its provisional understanding.

Harmonic orientation and the grain of the voice

Our analysis comes in two parts. First, we turn our attention to the macro structure of the song and place particular emphasis on the harmonic orientation, which we argue underpins this notion of ambiguity in its constant deferral of a home key. We also point to certain key structural elements that play with the quasi-religious undertones of the composition. Second, we focus on the grain and texture of Morrissey's voice where we further argue that Morrissey's performance in the recorded version plays very much with the idea of the priest-hero-martyr in terms of tone, timbre and delivery, in its careful and deliberate approach.[25]

As we have pointed out earlier, "martyr" has two meanings, both of which are played on in this song and both of which find expression in the song structure itself. The concepts of martyr and of ambiguity are intrinsically linked. Morrissey as "martyr for the cause" is very evident in this song in terms of his demand for freedom of expression in one's performance life, or indeed even in one's sexual orientation (both of which are played out through the persona of Wilde). This martyr is charismatic, authoritative, a leader and one who inspires devotion with almost saintly devotion. To be a martyr, however, is also to be someone who plays for empathy, who seeks attention. Thus the martyr persona as performative category is equally ambiguous – a genuine hero-sufferer versus an indulgent seeker of sympathy. This doubleness, played out as much in harmonic structure as it is in mode of delivery and subjective/objective positioning is at the core of our discussion where we expand upon the notion of the singer/narrator referencing Oscar Wilde specifically, and move to a broader, more metaphorical interpretation of Wilde's evocation. Here it acts as metaphor, drawing us towards the larger sense of testimony as found in the Christian church. Which martyr persona triumphs ultimately remains unanswered as Morrissey takes us to places of empathy as well as resistance.

Structural ambiguity and tonal deferral

Like so many of Morrissey's songs, 'Speedway' is deceptively simple and, in terms of performing ambiguity, very clever in its harmonic (and by extension, melodic) construction, revealing the interface between simple structures and complex productions of meaning (Brackett 2000: ix–x).

'Speedway' is constructed in an apparently quite typical verse and chorus format but it is not quite so straightforward as it appears. It commences with a verse fragment "And when you slam [...] heart", followed by a chorus "All the rumours [...] unfounded", which reappears a couple of more times. The first full verse, comes in three phrases, the first being a recapitulation of the opening question but now elongated with "can you delve so low"? Two more questions are asked, the chorus returns, then a new verse with not three but rather four questions, the last of which ends abruptly. After that next chorus, the structure again changes in that the verse is no longer made up of questions but of defensive answers. These macro structural elements are underpinned by important harmonic changes, and this emphasis on the number "three" or thirds (and "four" in the third verse) find parallels in the harmonic language deployed, which acts in as much a symbolic capacity as it does in a structural one.

The song uses a relatively limited tonal/chordal palette. It is, we argue, this specific, even somewhat banal palette, that generates the sense of ambiguity central to the theme and text of the song. This is achieved by avoiding the establishment of a clear tonal centre and therefore a commitment to a specific key or mode.[26] This lack of clarity is based on well-worn conventions of resolution in the tonal language of western music, from which much of popular western song forms draw their harmonic language.[27]

The opening gesture to which the lyrics "And when you slam down" are set begins on a C# minor chord, which, between a pause in the lyrics, morphs into an E major, followed by a hanging A major chord at the end of the question, "can you feel it in your heart?" And so the listener is left poised as the chainsaw/motorbike sound jars and shatters the silence.[28] There is another question. Is this song in the key of C# minor or is it more likely in E major? The C# minor is a natural minor key, or the lonesome Aeolian mode (on the C#), in contrast with E major which is a naturally bright and "happy" key.[29] This very uncertainty of which is the "home" key is all the more powerful not because the "other" key is so different, but rather it is so very close and familiar. C# minor is the relative minor of E major, thus intrinsically tied to E major – in fact the two scales share the exact same notes, only differing in the sequence of tone/semitones.[30] But this shared behaviour nonetheless manifests differently according the orientation of the home note or tonic.

Immediately after the rude chainsaw, the band break into a powerful descending riff – C# minor chord to a B major to an A major to an E major. This is the basis for the rest of the song, featuring over and over in all of the verses. The cadence from A major to E major (which for now is the temporary home key) is important as it represents a chord sequence of IV to I, a cadence termed the Plagal Cadence but more popularly known as the "Amen" cadence due to its ubiquity in religious choral music, English choral music in particular.[31] Not only is it apt that this Amen chord should be so prominent in this martyr narrative with its religious overtones and subconscious referencing of religious music, but from a structural level, given the absence of a leading note, which truly defines a key, the progression is unable to confirm a definitive key. This ambiguity is further structurally underscored by the frequency of this progression, one which is unable to articulate and commit to a formal closure and hence a sense of resolution. Against this descending sequence of chords the lead guitar punches out a counter melody, one which has an ascending orientation with the notes E, F#, A and G# coinciding with the change of chords in four beat durations.

Chordal structure:	C# min	B maj	A maj	E maj
Lead guitar notes:	E	F#	A	G#

Figure 10.3: Harmonic and Instrumental Interplay in 'Speedway'

There is nothing surprising here as the lead guitar notes are all picked out of the chordal triads which they accompany. What the guitar line does, however, is push the key more towards the major side of the fence. But on coming back to the verse, where the chord frequency doubles, that is, chords last for eight as opposed to four beats, C# asserts itself again, and is underscored by the appearance of its chord V, G# major, at the end of the phrase. G# is the root of chord V in C# minor but it is also the third of E major, the chord against which it appears. With such shifting tonal perspectives and contradictory usages, the tonal ambiguity continues to be played out. The fact that guitar functions as another voice, another perspective, and is structurally integral to the song adds another dimension to threads of narration happening here.[32]

Third and fourth relationships

This relationship of the third, which features so prominently in the harmonic structure of the song, is also key to the melodic structure of not just this Morrissey song, but also so many others. Taking the opening lines, "If you slam [...] heart", the song starts on the third of E major, on G#, and rises to B, a strong major third gesture internally from G# to the B but also in terms of being the two other notes in an E major chord.

G#	B	B	*B	G#	A	B	G#
And	when	you	slam	down	the	ham-mer	

G#	G#	C#	B	G#	B	B	E
Can	you	feel	it	in	your	hea-rt	

*chord sequence starts here…

Figure 10.4: Melodic Orientation of Vocal Line in 'Speedway'.

But against a C# minor chord, B is the leading note, so is just as important in establishing the key of C# minor, or more tellingly Aeolian mode beginning on C# here.[33] The chord sequence which goes with this section moves from C#min to Emaj to Amaj, chord I–IV, a mirror of the IV–I or Amen cadence referenced earlier.

Interestingly, in the many versions of the chord structure of 'Speedway' to be found on the Internet, very few go on to outline the chord sequences of the closing verse, which in actual fact differs from the previous verses and further underscores this vacillation between the major and minor keys happening here, neither of which really ever triumphs in order to fully secure one single tonal centre.[34] 'Speedway', it seems, is destined to remain Janus-faced to the very end. The by now very familiar sequence C#min, Bmaj, Amaj, Emaj is replaced every second turn, by an ascending sequence that seems to promote E major more thoroughly on one hand, but, on the other, must be seen as more directly related to the relative minor, that of C# minor. This sequence starts on a firm E major chord which seems to signal its dominance, yet it is followed by an F# major (the supertonic of E major and not a likely chord really to help centre the home key, yet is the fifth of C# minor, to which it is more closely related). This sequence goes E maj, F# maj, A maj, E maj, so though there is more E major here, the F# major does enough to destabilize things slightly. By then moving back to the older sequence of C#, B, A, E, the ambiguity is continued. Tellingly, against the line "shut good and proper", there is a cessation of harmonic accompaniment as the chord sequence shuts down, referencing death, surely, but also, ironically, further underscoring the lack of resolution in the absence of sound and structure.[35] This emphasis on the structuring nature of the third and the fourth is further tied back into the presentation of the lyrics, as mentioned earlier, where the verses take the format of three questions per verse and then expanding to four in the final verse. The degree to which this is a conscious undertaking is not what is at stake here but rather the manner in which a close reading can reveal all kinds of interconnectedness.[36]

Grain of the voice[37]

Taking our prompting from Barthes' (1984) essay of the same name, particularly in light of the textual reading we are performing here, we now turn our attention to Morrissey as singer/musician, focusing on his style of delivery and the manner in which it plays a crucial role in articulating and performing the martyr. It may be addressing the historically potent incident of Oscar Wilde and his trial or indeed it may be both, where the singer is using Wilde in a kind of performative ventriloquism. Either way, *how* Morrissey does this – the process involved – is what we focus on, particularly as Morrissey's voice is central to his self-conscious styling and is recursively influenced by this styling.

On hearing the track from the album *Vauxhall and I*, one is immediately struck by the high levels of production and the lushness of the instrumentation and overall sound, complementing and setting the tone for Morrissey's own lush and dulcet approach.[38] Given the directness, even harshness of some of the lyrical content, such a smooth approach seems at odds with the message, creating a sense of ambiguity on one hand, but on the other, underscoring the menace of the attack/defence of the singer/narrator with its highly contrasting tone. This is where ambiguity is at its most powerful and persuasive.[39]

The tone adopted in the vocal style of Morrissey has other rich allusions. The sound of the hammer does not just reference Wilde's court appearance or the kind of scrutiny and populist trial Morrissey is undergoing. It may also be linked to the notion of the Christian martyr who, when speaking, was viewed as giving testimony to his noble, if often misunderstood, cause.[40] Finally, in terms of the sound effect of Morrissey's delivery, there is one more code to be revealed. There is something cajoling and also gently reprimanding in this style of delivery, very akin to the style adopted by sermonizing priests addressing their (oftentimes lowly) flock (of fans/followers). The diction is clear and paced, the tone laced with a certain level of restrained though disappointed acceptance, in line with the lyrical content. Even in the more dramatic parts of the song, particularly the motorbike effect, and the abrupt stopping after the verse towards the end of the song, the former is an allusion to fire and brimstone, the latter perhaps reminiscent of dramatic pauses in the highly stylized rhetoric of religious figures.

Conclusion

Morrissey does not just perform 'Speedway'. 'Speedway' performs martyrdom, ambiguity and Morrissey himself, in all his multiple personae, as Wilde and as martyr/saint/priest. Songs are not merely reflective of society, telling a story of what has happened. To paraphrase Jacques Attali, songs and music may be predictive of society, engaged in a recursive process where they make and are made.[41] 'Speedway' can only be interpreted in relation to its social and historical context, but it draws also upon a rich tapestry of allusions to other traditions, religious ideas and iconic figures (e.g. Wilde, Jesus). In this way, 'Speedway' invites multiple readings, of which this has been, we hope, a compelling one.

As the final track on what many believed at the time to be Morrissey's very last record, 'Speedway' served to perpetuate Morrissey's construction of himself as a martyr. Tropes of martyrdom were in evidence from the early days of The Smiths and continue to be present in Morrissey's more recent work. In presenting himself as a martyr, Morrissey manages to side with the oppressed whilst at the same time be narcissistic. Such explicit connections with the oppressed provides a very interesting set of contexts in which many fans connect with their anti-heroic icon. Morrissey's use of martyrdom, we concede, may also however function at an ironic level. His presentation of himself as one of the persecuted (as Joan of Arc; St Sebastian; Oscar Wilde; Padre Pio; Jesus) may simply be an ironic device that he deliberately uses to send up the music press that has consistently represented him as tortured and condemned.

Notes

1. Recorded in 1993 at Hook End Manor Studios, *Vauxhall and I* – Morrissey's fourth solo album was produced by Steve Lillywhite. Representing a marked departure from Morrissey's rockabilly incarnation, the album was a critical and commercial success – reaching number one in the UK charts. Although Lillywhite describes the album's sound as having a "lushness", the overall sound of *Vauxhall and I* has been characterized as funereal, introspective and sombre – a fact usually attributed to the deaths in 1993 of three of Morrissey's close associates (musician and producer Mick Ronson, video director Tim Broad and manager Nigel Thomas). It was widely believed at the time that this would be Morrissey's final recording. Given Morrissey's tendency to obfuscate, much speculation has surrounded his choice of title for the recording. *Vauxhall and I* may be a pun on the cult film title *Withnail and I* (1987); it may refer to either the seventeenth-century Vauxhall Gardens or the Royal Vauxhall Tavern famed for its drag-queen acts; alternatively, it may be in reference to someone who in Morrissey's words was "born and braised" in Vauxhall.
2. See for example Simpson (2002: 213–214); Rogan (2006: 213–214); Goddard (2009: 409–410); Bailie (1994) and Brown (2008; 192).
3. Bailie (1994). For this and other reviews of *Vauxhall and I*, see www.luckylisp. com and most notably those by Andrew Collins, Shaun Phillips and Simon Renyolds. Given the theme of this chapter, it is of interest that a number of reviewers take up on the theme of martyrdom in their commentary on 'Speedway'. Phillips writes of Morrissey being "tortured and demonised" and Renyolds refers to how the song "dramatizes Morrissey's sense of being a martyr" who in 'Speedway' "turns this persecution complex into a panoramic epic".
4. Personal communication between the authors and Graham Humphreys, 26th August, 2010.
5. Bailie's review is of the opinion that *Vauxhall and I* represents Morrissey's response to his critics in the wake of Madstock. For its part, 'Speedway', he argues, is a "bizarre address to those critics leading the witch-hunt" and specifically this (the *NME*) "cage-rattling journal".
6. For example 'The More You Ignore Me The Closer I Get', 'Why Don't You Find Out For Yourself' and 'I Am Hated For Loving'.
7. As well as referring directly to Oscar Wilde (e.g. Cemetry Gates) and using Wildean quips, Morrissey has subsequently written songs from his hero's viewpoint, for example, 'I'm Throwing My Arms Around Paris'.
8. From The Smiths album *Meat is Murder*, Morrissey's sexually ambiguous lyrics state "And the grease in the hair of a Speedway Operator is all a tremulous heart requires". For a critical account of Morrissey's dexterity in terms of gender roles, see Hubbs (1996).
9. See for example, Bret (2004: 208–209); Simpson (2002: 213–214); Rogan (2006: 213–214) and Goddard (2009: 411–412).
10. In an interview with Robert Chalmers in 1992, Morrissey stated "I remember being at a fair at Stretford Road; it was very early, about 5 pm, and I was just standing by the speedway. And

somebody just came over to me and head-butted me. He was much older than me, and much bigger. I was dazed for at least five minutes. What I find remarkable is the way you just accepted it. That was just the kind of thing that happened. I don't think it was even that I looked different in those days. There never needed to be a reason."

11. *Speedway* (1968) directed by Norman Taurag.

12. Speedway can refer to both motorcycle speedway and to stock or sports car speedway racing.

13. *Speedway* (1929) directed by Harry Beaumont and also starring Anita Page.

14. Haines left home aged 14 with his boyfriend. He refused to bow to pressure to live as a straight man by MGM and instead lived openly with his lifelong partner Jimmie Shields.

15. Interview with Boz Boorer, 12th August, 2010.

16. In live performances of 'Speedway', it has only ever been possible to make use of one ebow.

17. Interview with Boz Boorer, 12th August, 2010 and Steve Lillywhite interviewed on WXPN's *World Cafe*, 17th December, 2008, available: www.npr.org.

18. Steve Lillywhite recalls "I remember distinctly bringing the chainsaw into the studio and firing it up and it stunk the place out 'cos of all of the gas in there […] the petrol […]but it was great." He also notes that it is the "one jagged element of this whole album". See also Bret (2004: 208); Rogan (2006: 213) andGoddard (2009: 214). Boz Boorer remembers that the attempts to use either the drill or the lawnmower to re-create the sound of a motorbike were rejected as they sounded "like a hairdryer". Interview with Boz Boorer, 12th August, 2010.

19. Slamming (down) a hammer may also refer to what happens when you pull the trigger in a gun.

20. Note the parallel between these lyrics and Wilde's 'De Profundis' when he writes "A great friend of mine – a friend of ten years' standing – came to see me some time ago, and told me that he did not believe a single word of what was said against me, and wished me to know that he considered me quite innocent, and the victim of a hideous plot. I burst into tears at what he said, and told him that while there was much amongst the definite charges that was quite untrue and transferred to me by revolting malice, still that my life had been full of perverse pleasures, and that unless he accepted that as a fact about me and realised it to the full I could not possibly be friends with him anymore, or ever be in his company."

21. Originally published in 1905, the 50,000-word letter from Wilde to his lover Bosie takes its title (meaning "from the depths") from Psalm 130. Divided into two distinct parts, 'De Profundis' deals with Wilde's relationship with Bosie and then his suffering and his martyrdom shifts to a focus on how Christ offers redemption.

22. Following the first trial Wilde wrote a letter to the editor of the *Evening News* on 5th April, 1895 in which he stated "It would have been impossible for me to have proved my case without putting Lord Alfred Douglas in the witness box against his father. Lord Alfred Douglas was extremely anxious to go into the box, but I would not let him do so. Rather than put him into so painful a position I determined to retire from the case, and to bear on my own shoulders whatever ignominy and shame might result from my prosecuting Lord Queensbury."

23. For example, taking the line – "I never said, I never said, that they were completely unfounded" – it could be argued that playing with the comma mid-phrase (shifting it after "that") suddenly offers a very different readings of this line – "I never said, *I never said that*, they were completely unfounded". In other words, the narrator denies the charges. However, when hearing this line sung/performed in real time, it is clear the emphasis is not on "that". In fact, in the melody line, "that" glides by as an adjunct to the rest of the sentence, restoring the more ambiguous interpretation that, in spite of the narrator's resistance, he is admitting that he never insisted that such rumours were without foundation. Therefore, the interplay of the music and text is key to a full reading of the song in its entirety in certain instances.

24. Brackett (2002), Clayton et al. (2003).
25. It is worth mentioning at this point that in so many live performances of 'Speedway', Morrissey tends to take on a saintly pose with a single spotlight illuminating him as he sings.
26. For further reading on "tonality", "harmony", "scales" and "modes", see www.grovemusiconline.com.
27. For examples of analyses in this vein, particularly in relation to Morrissey's oeuvre, see Hawkins (2002); chapter 3 is entitled 'Anti-rebel, lonesome boy: Morrissey in crisis?' and specifically references 'Speedway'.
28. Hawkins refers to this as serving an "assailing" function, as part of the experience of "caustic wit" (2002: 96), while we are more inclined to interpret it metaphorically and structurally here.
29. This characterization of major/minor, happy/sad, is somewhat of a generalization but nonetheless it is broadly understood as such in western pop music. See McClary (2001).
30. The major key is structured as follows (where T=tone, and S=semitone) – TTSTTTS; the minor or Aeolian is structured thus – TSTTSTT. The distribution of tones and semitones gives a very different feel to each scale and to the chords and triads which are built upon these notes.
31. For a solid introduction to music theory, see Benward and Saker (2003).
32. See Askerøi in this collection for a more detailed discussion on the role of the guitar.
33. As an aside, the Aeolian mode is one of the most common in Irish traditional music and perhaps the persistence of such modes in Morrissey's music, as well as the orientation of his vocal lines and the intervallic leaps and dips, so reminiscent of Irish song structures and performance practice, points to a distinct influence of traditional/folk idioms in his work, something which we do not have the space to discuss here at this time.
34. Of the many searches we performed on the various chord/tab sites in order to perform a comparative analysis, all seemed to come from one source, *abraha'n garza*. This version, which was promulgated across the web, is the same as discussed here by us except the final verses are not mapped out harmonically. Instead we get a "you get the idea" prompt, which is, in fact misleading, as the chords do change towards the end. One site (ultimateguitar.com) did spell the prominent G# major chord as Ab major, which, under the rules of conventional harmonic progression is a mistake, but sonically sounds the same (therefore providing a practical more ergonomic alternative for some, perhaps?). Interestingly here too the chords in the final verse were omitted. The song was also presented in A minor/C major with the direction to put the capo four frets up in order to sound it in C# minor/E major. It is worth noting that the song itself is recorded up another whole tone (or two fret positions) in F# major/D# minor.
35. It might be argued that to build a thesis around such closely related keys is a stretch because they are so alike sonically and so interrelated structurally, but we would counter that this is precisely the reason why this song construction (and our subsequent reading) works so well. Within the laws of tonality and the contained palette on offer, 'Speedway' is able to be in both keys, without ultimately committing to one. In the final analysis, the harmonic ambiguity represents different sides of the same coin without having the need to succumbing to one definite label. This is a musical structuring and sounding, surely, of Morrissey's own political and ideological stances?
36. The degree to which such structural (and structuring) elements can be connected to the discourse on third and fourth gender is beyond the scope of this study but invites further investigation elsewhere.
37. Barthes (1984).
38. In terms of the voice itself on this track, Hawkins refers to it as "crooning" (2002: 96). While the influence of crooners Faith, Fury and Richard may be heard, we would add the sermonizing style is also present.

39. This interpretation contrasts somewhat with Hawkins', who argues that the indifference of the music gesture negates their [the lyrics] intensity and imaginative profundity (2002: 96–97). Quite the contrary, we believe it underscores them for that very reason.
40. Wunthnow (1998: 494–497).
41. Attali (1985). Also see Attali in Qureshi (2002).

References

Bailie, S. (1994) 'His Astra's voice', *NME*, 12th March.

Barthes, R. (1978) *Image, Music, Text*. New York: Hill and Wang.

Benward, B. and Saker, M. (2003) *Music: In Theory and Practice, Vol. I*. Boston: McGraw Hill.

Brackett, D. (1995) *Interpreting Popular Music*. Berkeley: University of California Press.

Brown, L. (2008) *Meetings with Morrissey*. London: Omnibus.

Bret, D. (2004) *Morrissey: The Scandal and the Passion*. London: Robson Books.

Caplin, W. (1998) *Classical Form: A Theory of Formal Functions for the Instrumental Music of Haydn, Mozart and Beethoven*. New York: Oxford University Press.

Chalmers, R. (1992) 'Morrissey flowers again', *The Observer Magazine*, December.

Clayton, M., Herbert, T. and Middleton, R. (eds) (2003) *The Cultural Study of Music*. New York: Routledge.

Cook, N. (1998) *Music: A Very Short Introduction*. Oxford: Oxford University Press.

Devereux, E. (2010) 'Heaven knows we'll soon be dust: Catholicism and fan devotion in The Smiths', in S. Campbell and C. Coulter (eds) *Why Pamper Life's Complexities? Essays on The Smiths*. Manchester: Manchester University Press.

Devereux, E. (2009) 'I'm not the man you think I am: ambiguity, authenticity and the cult of Morrissey', in V. Rautavuoma, U. Kovala and E. Haverinen (eds) *Cult, Community and Identity*. Jyvaskyla: Research Centre for Contemporary Culture.

Flory, R. E. and Miller, D. E. (2000) *Gen X Religion*. New York: Routledge.

Goddard, S. (2009) *Mozipedia: The Encyclopedia of Morrissey and The Smiths*. London: Ebury Press.

Hawkins, S. (2009) *The British Pop Dandy: Masculinity, Popular Music and Culture*. Farnham: Ashgate.

Hawkins, S. (2002) 'Anti-rebel, lonesome boy: Morrissey in crisis?', in S. Hawkins *Settling the Pop Score*. London: Ashgate.

The Complete Letters of Oscar Wilde.

Hubbs, N. (1996) 'Music of the "Fourth Gender": Morrissey and the sexual politics of melodic contour', in T. Foster, Siegel, C. and Berry, E. (eds) *Bodies of Writing, Bodies in Performance*. New York: New York University Press, pp. 266–296.

Juslin, P. N. and Sloboda, J. A. (2001) *Music and Emotion: Theory and Research*. Oxford: Oxford University Press.

Lynch, G. (2006) 'The role of popular music in the construction of alternative spiritual identities and ideologies', *Journal for the Scientific Study of Religion*, 45: 4, pp. 481–488.

Macioni, S. (1994) 'Hello cruel world', *Q*, April.

McClary, S. (2001) *Conventional Wisdom: The Content of Musical Form*. Los Angeles: University of California Press.

Negus, K. (1996) *Popular Music in Theory: An Introduction*. Cambridge: Polity Press.

Partridge, C. (2005)*The Re-Enchantment of The West: Alternative Spiritualities, Sacralization, Popular Culture and Occulture (2 Vols.)*. New York: T & T Clark International.

Phillips, S. (1994) 'Vox album of the month', *Vox*, April.

Qureshi, R. B. (ed.) (2002) *Music and Marx*. New York: Routledge.

Renyolds, S. (1994) 'An enigmatic Morrissey still battles his demons', *The New York Times*, April.

Rogan, J. (2006) *Morrissey: The Albums*. London: Calidore.

Sheffield, R. (1994) 'Platter du Jour', *SPIN*, April.

Simpson, M. (2003) *Saint Morrissey*. London: SAF Publishing.

Sylvan, R. (2005) *Trance Formation: The Spiritual and Religious Dimensions of Global Rave Culture*. New York: Routledge.

Wunthnow, R. (ed.) (1988) *Encyclopedia of Politics and Religion (2 vols.)*. Washington, DC: Congressional Quarterly.

Chapter 11

No Love in Modern Life: Matters of Performance and Production in a Morrissey Song

Eirik Askerøi

As time speeds up, nothing changes. People become more lonely. And the more they surround themselves by electronic gadgets, they become more isolated and lonely, and I think there'll be a reaction against that.

(Morrissey 2009)

Introduction

Narratives of loneliness, marginalization and vulnerability have been recurring themes in Morrissey's music, both throughout his years as front man for The Smiths and during more than 20 years as a solo artist. Through the musical delivery of these narratives, and also through his off-stage media persona, Morrissey has been raising questions concerning the politics of identity, as well as taking an opposing stand against the commercial record industry. Understandably, music journalists, scholars and fans have devoted most attention to his lyrics and vocal performance. My main argument in this chapter is that the musical backdrop to his persona, with special reference to the electric guitar, plays a vital communicative role. Ever since The Smiths-era, there has been a special connection between the guitar and the voice in Morrissey's music. The relationship between Morrissey and guitarist Johnny Marr was built on collaborative songwriting, and formed one of the most characteristic trademarks of the 1980s. Rogan has described this relationship as "another exercise in doublethink: The Smiths projected a semblance of pop group solidarity and camaraderie, but all the power and influence lay with Morrissey/Marr" (Rogan 1992: 227). Marr's distinctive guitar arrangements, often with subtle melodic lines on top of the harmonic structures, positioned the electric guitar compatibly to the lyrical content and vocal performance. During his solo career, Morrissey has continued to write songs in collaboration with his guitarists Boz Boorer, Alain Whyte and later also Jesse Tobias. He recorded with producers such as Steven Street (*Viva Hate, Bona Drag*), the late Mick Ronson (*Your Arsenal*), Steve Lillywhite (*Vauxhall and I, Southpaw Grammar, Maladjusted*), Tony Visconti (*Ringleader of the Tormentors*) and the late Jerry Finn (*You are the Quarry, Years of Refusal*), all of whom have made their artistic marks on the musical result. In this light, Morrissey's lyrics and vocal performance are conveyed through a specific pop aesthetic.

My focus in this chapter falls on the expressive dimensions of production. I argue that the dialogue between lyrics, vocal performance and the aesthetic qualities of the electric guitars plays a major role in Morrissey's performance strategies. Through an analysis of

'Something Is Squeezing My Skull', the powerful opening track of *Years of Refusal* from 2009, I intend to illustrate how certain aesthetic qualities of the production contribute to the song's narrative. Structured by an excursion into details of pop production, this chapter falls into three sections. In the first section, I will focus on the vocal production, especially in relation to the main melodic hook of the chorus. Not only is this moment charged with a considerable physical exertion, but also the technological processing would appear to play a major role. In the second section I will explore the dialogical relationship between the singing voice and the sonic qualities of the electric guitars[1] employed in this song, with a focus on how Morrissey, through his lyrics and vocal performance, potentially alters the discursive framework of the heavily distorted electric guitar – and vice versa. Finally, in the third section, I will consider Morrissey's performance strategies and how they relate to the socio-political climate around the song's release in 2009. In this section, the focus will fall on how the meaning of this song can be contextually bound by the production aesthetics. The goal of this chapter is thus to develop a model for exploring how certain musical sounds, represented by instruments or studio effects, can appear as *sonic markers*, through the ways in which they affect what is being communicated. This does not mean that the affective qualities of music as technological artefact would be the same in every musical context. On the contrary, as I will emphasize, the impact of the sonic markers relies strongly on the specific musical context in which the markers are applied. More specifically, 'Something Is Squeezing My Skull' provides an example of how elements of vocal processing and aesthetic features of electric guitar sound and style can be read as sonic markers in relation to the lyrical content, the vocal performance and the cultural context in which they appear.

Lyrics and vocal performance

Before turning to the questions of production, I want to spend some time on the communicative power of Morrissey's lyrics and vocal performance. Through his lyrics, Morrissey appears to offer a way into the mind of a self-reflective, critical and strong, yet vulnerable, lonely man. Songs like 'Satan Rejected My Soul', 'Maladjusted', 'Suedehead' and a range of others feature Morrissey in first person, emphasizing his position as a misfit of bourgeois society. In other songs, like 'We Hate It When Our Friends Become Successful' and 'Interesting Drug', he includes the listener through the collective and general "we", either directly or by assuming that the listener has the same political standpoint as him. With few exceptions, it is either "I" or "we" in the main role. In other words, he opens up for an emotional dialogue with the listener. In addition, a characteristic feature of his lyrics deals with what Hopps has labelled oxymoronic mobility: "a light footed tendency to turn on himself, and then turn on this turning, and in doing so inhabit without being identified with a variety of divergent positions" (Hopps 2009: 62). Often the verses start with punchy one-liners, which are followed up by a sudden, unpredicted turn. In 'Something Is Squeezing My Skull' we meet Morrissey apparently teetering on the verge of madness, stating that he is "doing very well". The lyrics alone contain ambiguous elements, hinting that some things are not quite as they should be. An example of his mobility is found in the ironic tone of the lyrics, which becomes manifested through the first verse:

> I'm doing very well
> I can block out the present and the past now
> I know by now you think I should have straightened myself out
> Thank you drop dead

Undoubtedly, Morrissey's lyrics offer an important insight into his music. Still, a key reference for interpreting the meaning of his songs is the way in which his characteristic vocal style adds a strong, emotional dimension to the lyrical content. Herein lies one of the main clues as to why he appeals to the listener's personal feelings. Morrissey's own awareness of his powerful vocality comes through in an interview with Zane Lowe of MTV, where he expressed that

> [s]ometimes the great singers are not singers who have great voices, but they are just people who catch your attention. [...] There is something very sexual in the singing voice, and it draws you in. And it doesn't necessarily mean you want to be physical with the person, but the person is pulling at your very being, and your heart and so forth.
>
> (Morrissey 2009)

By making a distinction between having a great voice and being a great singer, his observation suggests that the listener can become emotionally drawn to a voice. In his seminal text 'The grain of the voice', Barthes makes a similar differentiation between what he labels *pheno-song*: "everything in the performance which is in the service of communication, representation, expression" and *geno-song*: "the volume of the singing and speaking voice, the space where significations germinate 'from within language and in its very materiality'" (Barthes 1977: 182). Being located within the space of the geno-song, the grain, according to Barthes, is the bodily presence in the voice. It could be argued, though, that such a distinction is somewhat idealistic, mostly because Barthes seems to be suggesting that the geno-song is extra-cultural. Emphasizing the problems in locating a voice outside culture, Steinskog has argued that traces of the body are always left in a voice, even when disembodied:

> The voice, as an abstract entity in the singular, is a construct; there is no singular voice, but rather different vocal expressions. And when we hear a voice, we simultaneously hear a body. The voice emanates from the body, and the body – with all its different characteristicscolors the voice.
>
> (Steinskog 2008: 2)

Even though there is an intimate relationship between the voice and the body, the difficulties encountered in pinning down vocal sound in words require terms for any kind of deconstruction to take place. With this in mind, the idea of the geno-song is a useful platform for discussing aspects of the voice, which are *not*, to borrow Barthes' phrase, "customary to talk about" (Barthes 1977: 182). The principal point is that a singer's bodily presence is always interlinked with the vocal expression and that these bodily traces contribute to eliciting an emotional response.

Morrissey, according to Hawkins (2002), has a remarkable ability to evoke empathic response through his vocal style. Central to the evocation of empathy is the ability to communicate. The idea that the body might be represented in vocal style offers a vital clue as to how emotional response can be evoked through sound. For Hawkins, the specific use of expressive parameters, such as inflections of pitch, precise enunciation and vocal timbre, can suggest a detached self-irony (Hawkins 2002: 84). Within the context of the commercial pop scene, this is what defines Morrissey's strong, independent voice. At the same time, as Hawkins argues, Morrissey's persona relies on a display of vulnerability that might well be "faked". Accordingly, his navigation between strength and independency on the one hand and vulnerability on the other emerges as a vital element in the social contract between him and his fans. In his account, Hawkins insists that Morrissey is "motivated by the significance of his words" (Hawkins 2002: 87), and during the process when straining to reach top notes, he intermittently fails. In this way, the personal discrepancies of the vocal performance signify sincerity through the detailed delivery of the words, which may be interpreted as sloppy singing - hence, contributing to his appeal. Thus, empathic response is actualized by certain moments in the music, and in 'Something Is Squeezing My Skull' one of the most discernible vocal moments is perhaps the fanfare-like melodic hook of the chorus (Figure 11.1).

Figure 11.1: Fanfare-Like Melodic Hook of The Chorus.

An interesting aspect of this particular moment is the precise manner in which Morrissey actually reaches the top note (the high G) of the chorus (Figure 11.1). This opens up several possible interpretations. On the one hand, it would be plausible to read this as a sign of conformity, in that he has finally resigned himself to formal and technological demands for "clean" singing. On the other hand, it could also be a way of underlining the ironic tone of the lyrics. For example, he does not reach this high G without tremendous effort.[2] The lyrical motivation for arriving at the word "skull" comes through in the last tonal leap from D to G due to the rhythmically delayed pronunciation and slight, timbral alteration. While I will not speculate as to whether or not his voice has been tuned in the studio, something is definitely squeezing the timbral qualities of his voice at the word "skull".[3] As he reaches this particular word, he holds back the attack on the "s" (though, of course, you can not really "sing" an "s"), mobilizing with a full punch the "kull". As the word rings out on the double "ll", a rapid vocal vibrato further underlines the timbral difference between the calm build-up and this desperate temporary climax of the song.

Whereas the question of technological processing in itself may not be of great importance to most people, there are certain affective qualities in this particular moment that catches our attention. This is largely due to a timbral change in the vocal sound. As in all his songs, Morrissey's voice reveals a range of stylistic markers that make it recognizable on the sonic level of communication. Hawkins argues elsewhere in this volume that the similarities between his singing voice and the way he speaks decreases the potential distance between on- and off-stage personae. In this way, both his singing and speaking voice contain traces of his "real" body, validating his authenticity. When it comes to this particular moment, however, the timbral alteration seems to indicate a tiny moment of disembodiment. Could this suggest conformity? I would rather argue that this tiny detail plays a part in the story. Even if the voice only loses contact with the body for a few seconds through technological manipulation, it is still long enough to mark out a difference. Interlinked with the lyrics, this difference, which potentially comes as a result of technological processing, gains a strong narrative importance for the song. In turn, what could be read as an attempt to control Morrissey's *geno*-song becomes instead a sonic representation of the medical treatment used as a metaphor in the song's mid-section, a section to which I will return to shortly.

So far, I have focused on aspects of vocal performance and production. Yet, the question still remains: how is lyrical content and vocal performance conveyed? After all, the three-and-a-half-minute pop song is Morrissey's main channel for meeting his fans. It is through his music that he touches the listener. In the following section, I will therefore demonstrate how certain aesthetic features of the musical performance play a vital role in conveying these narratives of intimate communication achieved through technological disembodiment. More specifically, I will direct the focus towards one of the most pertinent sonic features of this song, namely the electric guitar.

The electric guitar as sonic marker

Even though Morrissey has been performing as a solo artist since The Smiths split up in 1987, his performances, both live and on record, have always been characterized by a strong and stable "band mentality". Since 1991, guitarists Boz Boorer and Alain Whyte have been credited as regular co-writers, a relational consistency, which according to Brown was a tale of the unexpected: "Against all expectations, these creative relationships would persist well into the 21st century; over three times longer than Morrissey's famous liaison with Johnny Marr" (Brown 2008: 172). Insisting that his solo career was more or less thrust upon him, Morrissey describes his relationship with his band as a personal one: "The musicians are handpicked, really. They are not just anybody who turns up to play. [...] The point is I couldn't simply play with session musicians or people whom I didn't like" (Morrissey 2009). The music for 'Something Is Squeezing My Skull' was written by Whyte, whereas Jesse Tobias, who replaced Whyte as regular band member in 2004, performs the guitar parts alongside Boorer on this recording. As the band members and different producers seem to be given a central creative position, the question is whether we can speak of a certain Morrissey-sound that they all conform to or to what extent their personal sonic marks would affect the narratives?

One way of identifying the narrative importance of a sonic marker like the electric guitar would be to think of Morrissey's songs as "utterances". Shifting focus from the novel to aspects of speech communication in his later writings, Bakhtin argued that any utterance is inseparable from its *thematic content, style and compositional structure* (Bakhtin 1986: 60). The thematic content of the utterance then would always be heavily intertwined with *how* this content is delivered. From this perspective, speech communication has a lot in common with recorded music in a narrative sense. If we leave the thematic content to the lyrics, then how is the meaning of the song affected by the musical style and compositional structure the song represents? Building on Bakhtin's theories of dialogic meaning in speech communication, Middleton has construed musical texture and processes as dialogues of style-elements and their associations, through which a multiplicity of *voices* speak (1995). For Middleton, these voices are defined in a broad sense, which also would include instrumentalists. This perspective paves the way for taking the communicative powers of musical sound into question. Middleton points further to popular music's ability to actualize multiple listener positions. "The dialogic interplay of 'voices'", he says, "offers a range of possible points of identification: not just this style but also that, not just lead vocal […] but also other voices in the texture" (Middleton 1995: 478). Central to Middleton's argument are the discursive axes of difference actualized by the various voices in the music. Hence, the electric guitar can be read as a separate voice, or a sonic marker, that through the cultural manifestation of its sonic qualities reinforces the communicative power of the song. First, the stylistic approach to the instrument reflects the level of subjectivity mobilized in relation to the technology at hand. Second, the electric guitar has come to hold a strong symbolic and ideological position in western popular music.

To start with the last point, the ideological positioning of the electric guitar is traceable back to the cultural and political climate of the 1960s. Wicke (1995) has described how rock music gradually went from representing commercial interests in the 1950s to becoming a symbol of political protest through the 1960s. Individuality and the importance of individual change figured at the centre of these politics, and Wicke observes two main driving forces of this process. On the one hand, the British art school, whose influence on popular music in the 1960s has been profound, celebrated creativity as a main source of individuality. On the other hand, on the opposite side of the Atlantic, Bob Dylan and other musicians were fronting a nationwide protest against American capitalism. At the hub of this political and cultural watershed stood the electric guitar, marking these events sonically. According to Wicke, rock was long held as "merely an unappetising expression of capitalism's ideological powers of temptation" (Wicke 1995: 102). The sensuous pleasures of dancing were especially contentious and seemed to put the seriousness and consciousness of the class struggle at risk. This resistance from the folk movement peaked commercially with Dylan bringing electric guitars on stage at Newport Folk Festival in 1965 – which initially seemed to be a betrayal. However, as Wicke observes, celebrating creativity, communication and sense of community, rock music would eventually become the new soundtrack of the revolution, sonically marked by the most powerful instrument of its time: the electric guitar.

Placed somewhat to the background, the quality of the production in 'Something Is Squeezing My Skull', nevertheless provides a solid platform through which Morrissey's lyrics are conveyed. Bannister has argued that an important role of, what he labels the "guitar heroes" of bands like The Smiths and REM, was "to normalise the aestheticism and tendentiousness of the lead singers by grounding them in 'rock and roll'" (Bannister 2006: 109). I would argue though that, for Morrissey, the electric guitar also acquired a narrative purpose with Johnny Marr's distinct style. Rather than adapting to a given genre, like punk or mainstream heavy metal, Marr's guitar arrangements marked The Smiths songs with musical codes[4] that signalled a difference. For example, one of the aspects that characterizes Marr's guitar style in The Smiths is the way in which he opens up the chords, combined with his choice of guitar sound. Holding Phil Spector as one of his main influences, Marr has expressed that "I wanted my guitar to sound like a whole record" (Carman 2006: 45). By expanding the chords with open strings, often with a "clean" (in terms of not distorted) guitar sound, he could be decisive and demand a lot of space in the recording without overrunning the singer, while at the same time adding a characteristic colour to the music. In turn, this gave Marr much of the same insisting character as Morrissey has with his melodic motifs, while at the same time contrasting in its more "optimistic" character. As Carman points out: "While The Smiths over the years earned an undeserved reputation for glumness, Johnny's guitar lines were resplendent in their optimism, as fresh as a walk at dawn on a cool spring morning" (Carman 2006: 43).

During the 1980s the pop music industry became increasingly focused towards synthesizer-driven constellations, especially due to the invention of MIDI in 1981 (Théberge 1997; Hawkins 2002). At the same time, the growing heavy metal scene celebrated the guitar hero as the symbol of masculine power and authenticity (Walser 1993). Somewhere in between these opposite poles of the commercial music industry, independent rock, or "indie", rose from recurring DIY punk ideals (Bannister 2006), deploying the guitar. In this way, Marr's guitar playing came to represent a specific form of expression, opposing both sides of the commercial record industry, and thus further underlining The Smiths' ideological and autonomous standpoint. The production aesthetics have been, and still are, playing a major part in Morrissey's performance strategies. Since then, the electric guitar has become a prerequisite in any rock recording, and the way the guitarist approaches it stylistically, both through performance and effect processing, to a large extent, plays a major part in forming the production aesthetically.

In 'Something Is Squeezing My Skull', the electric guitars assume a lead role stylistically. The heavy, crunchy wall of guitars tends towards what, in broad terms, could be referred to as punk pop. Producer Jerry Finn, apart from producing the 2004 release *You Are The Quarry*, was also well known for his work with punk pop acts, such as Blink 182, Sum 41 and Green Day. With these bands, heavily distorted guitars and crystal clear and tightly produced drums have become stylistic idioms, adapted from indie rock on the one hand and metal on the other, and polished to fit the more commercial pop market. This sound grew into the commercial market through indie and grunge in the early 1990s. With bands like Nirvana and Pearl Jam, the electric guitar re-entered the commercial pop scene, despite, and perhaps because of, certain pessimistic predictions of "the death of rock". Building further on this into the noughties, a punk pop aesthetic has come to represent an institutionalized yet heavier adaptation of these codes. In this way, the stylistic codes mobilized by the electric guitar seem to be suggesting commercial connotations to a larger degree than on earlier recordings. If we accept that traces of punk pop aesthetics can be identified in 'Something Is Squeezing My Skull', one needs to question the extent to which these codes affect and/or generate the song's meaning.

During the first eight bars, the powerful tone and syncopated rhythmic motion of the guitars set the scene. Due to the amount of overdrive and the rhythmic pattern, an aggressive tone insists on a youthful "in your-face" attitude. The distorted and sustained tones rest on every second beat, mobilized by sixteenth note triad attacks. Morrissey's vocal style, however, disturbs this image, mainly because it does not resemble what have become the stylistic idioms of punk pop. The most significant aspect of this song is therefore the way in which the guitar, despite its stylistic diversification from the voice, still relates to and also underlines the song's narrative structure. In a compositional sense, there is actually a strong correlation between textual variation and melodic, harmonic and rhythmic build-up in the guitar. Indeed, as a culturally coded mediator of nonverbal communication, the electric guitar operates as a powerful sonic marker, providing a stable platform for Morrissey's lyrical critique, with its punk/rebellious referents.

The song's aesthetic content suggests an overall aggressive tone. This, in turn, is central to the compositional structure of the song. Based on lyrical density and musical dynamics, we might consider the song in three sections. The first section consists of intro, verse, chorus, verse and then double chorus, and conforms to the build up of a regular pop song, and contains the lyrical presentation of the narrative. From a musical perspective, this has tonal, timbral and textural implications. At first, the guitars keep a steady pattern, with mute-release pumping throughout four bars, as Morrissey proclaims that he, despite what the listener presumably believes, is in fact doing very well (Figure 11: 2).

Figure 11.2: Guitar Pattern Against First Line of The First Verse.

This illusion is, of course, soon broken, and we witness how the meaning is conveyed. As the tone of the lyrics changes, the left speaker guitar, which is the one processed in heaviest overdrive, takes on a melodic movement for eight bars, almost contrapuntal to the sung melody, although on a micro level, this would be an example of how Morrissey's mobility relates to the music. I would argue that the musical backdrop allows for this mobility by assuring a generic consistency. As Morrissey starts singing about how he is now able to block out the past and present, and describes his sheer excitement when seeing taxis in motion, the electric guitars support this lyrical ambiguity, both tonally and texturally. Here, the timbral qualities of the guitars, and this guitar in particular, guarantees the idiomatic grounding of the song.

Figure 11.3: Contradictory Guitar Patterns Against The Following Lines of The First Verse.

Following this is a short mid-section that also serves as the song's dynamic resting point, where Morrissey offers a brief overview of the various anti-depressive treatments available. Heavy medication as well as Hormone Replacement Therapy (HRT) and Electroconvulsive Therapy (ECT) are reeled off in an almost *bel canto* style, accompanied by a chord progression that closely resembles the famous intro of Led Zeppelin's 'Stairway To Heaven'. "How long must I stay on this stuff?" he sings with gradually increasing intensity, and although it takes up a relatively short time span in the song, this particular section has huge narrative importance. By providing a dynamic contrast to the rest of the song, and through the ironic contrast between lyrical content and vocal style, this section builds up towards the final section thematically, stylistically, and in terms of its part in the compositional structure.

The first section then could be read as a sarcastic comment on the lack of human love in our society, accompanied by an aggressive yet restrained band. In contrast, the last section, which stretches over one whole minute of the song's total run time, consists of Morrissey desperately shouting "Don't gimme anymore!" with direct reference to the medical treatments listed in the mid-section. After 16 bars, as the drums change to a march-like snare beat, the other band members support him by shouting "Hey!" on every second and fourth beat hinting to older British punk bands or perhaps even football supporters. Finally, after another eight bars, a widely panned tom break flares through the soundscape, displacing the drums slightly to the left. "You swore!" he shouts, as the right speaker guitar embarks on upward octave slides. Crash cymbals on every beat, underlined by sixteenth notes on double kick drum further intensify the density of the texture. In addition, a synth-string line, low in the mix, first introduced in the second half of the first verse, now becomes a disturbing element by operating at the same frequency area as the voice. The song culminates with Morrissey drowning in the sound of guitars, strings and drums. It is as if he has resigned to the "treatment" and that the fight is over.

Discourses of irony and terror

So far I have been arguing that the aesthetic features of the performance, with special reference to vocals and the electric guitar, play a major role in the communicative power of a song. Yet, if the electric guitar affects the narrative through its dialogical relationship with Morrissey's voice and words, then this should also have contextual implications. If we return to Hawkins, who has argued that the analyst must carefully seek "sets of characteristics and details that make the logic of statements possible" (Hawkins 2001: 6), the question remains which roles the electric guitar sound and style details play in Morrissey's performance strategies. One of the most prevalent aspects of Morrissey's performances is his use of irony. Either when dealing with friendship or with gender politics, his wry take on serious questions has been a thread running through his entire career. Hawkins has argued that in music, irony functions as a relational strategy between the effects of the musical codes and their relationship with words (Hawkins 2002: 91). He exemplifies this in the guitar solo on 'Billy Budd', which "harks back to the Smiths, soliciting a nostalgic reading of the beginning of Morrissey's fraught love-hate relationship with Johnny Marr" (Hawkins 2002: 93). Certainly, the guitar solo in 'Billy Budd' hints at Marr's guitar style.[5] Yet, the main aspect of this reference is the ironic take the guitar potentially represents. As Hawkins claims: "Not only does this stylistic code echo the Smiths' sound, but it also functions as an ironic marker" (Hawkins 2002: 93).

In contrast, the guitar playing on 'Something Is Squeezing My Skull' seems more distanced from this part of Morrissey's past. I would not speculate as to whether or not this is done deliberately. Arguably, in terms of production, the song is delivered in an up-to-date package adhering to the standards of 2009, omitting any hints or references to Marr's guitar style. At the same time, the ironic tone of the utterance is still present. This is evident in the ways in which Morrissey's lyrics and vocal performance communicate with the musical codes of the guitar. If we accept that the guitar sound may function as an ironic marker, I would argue that in this case it is not pointing to Morrissey's own past. The guitar sound rather underlines the ironic take within the lyrics that deal with recent social and political developments in western society. For example, both the choruses culminate in statements about modern life. In the first chorus, after having expressed that the "something" that is squeezing his skull probably is beyond description, he sums up that "There is no love in modern life". In the second chorus, which is double the length of the first, he states that "There is no hope in modern life" in the first round. The last round of this chorus contains the lines:

> Something is squeezing my skull
> Something I can't fight
> No true friends in modern life

From this perspective, I would argue, the ironic attitude in 'Something Is Squeezing My Skull' can be interpreted in relation to two notions that were dominating the socio-political discourse at the time the record was released. The first notion concerns the "war on terror", and ways in which this might have had a gathering effect through collective fear. According to Baudrillard, our western society is grounded in what he labels a zero-death system: "a system that operates on the exclusion of death" (Baudrillard 2003: 16). Introducing the term as a possible key to explaining the elevated fear of terrorism in the aftermath of 9/11, Baudrillard points out how terror has removed this basic premise of this system. And, although perhaps not present at all times, the socially constituted fear of terror in everyday life has still left an irreversible mark of angst in our society. The second notion rests on the idea that Internet-based media like YouTube, MySpace and Facebook have become mediators of increased freedom (and alienation) for the subject.

If we return to the opening quote of this chapter, Morrissey expresses his concerns about how loneliness and immobilization come as a result of the growing number of electronic gadgets that invade our everyday life. This also comes across as one of the motives for writing this song (Morrissey 2009). Not only are people afraid of the terrorist threat, but they also become increasingly immobilized and lonely through the extended use of electronic gadgets. Together, these socially constructed notions give rise to what Butler refers to as a normative framework (Butler 2009). The consequence of such a framework would provide an applicable context for reading 'Something Is Squeezing My Skull' as an utterance. For, as Butler argues:

> The consequence is that the normative framework mandates a certain ignorance about the 'subjects' at issue, and even rationalizes this ignorance as necessary to the possibility of making strong normative judgements.
>
> (Butler 2009: 143)

Through the mass media's coverage of the war on terror, the binary oppositions of good/evil, right/wrong, East/West and with us/against us have grown stronger. Supported by a wide range of visual, audible and written material, which proves the cruelty of the Other, these binaries become easier to accept, particularly, as Morrissey suggests, if people become passive and lonely due to increased interaction with new media. In this sense, the notion that a "war against terror" is necessary for protecting democracy gets further reinforcement through the deployment of these media. So-called terrorists have been known to utilize these media as channels of posing their threats against the west, and also, perhaps most potently, the feeling of freedom and democracy becomes embodied through these channels.

Though Morrissey has not been engaged with questions of the war against terror in his songs, he has always been a spokesman for subjectivity and difference. 'Something Is Squeezing My Skull' is no exception. If we accept, as I have suggested in this chapter, that the choruses could be read as summaries of how he experiences the human condition in modern life, the verses become reminders of who is speaking. In particular, two assumptions stand out that assure his biographical presence. In the first verse, he sings that "I know by now you think I should have straightened myself out", possibly with reference to any assumptions concerning his age and occupation. After all, Morrissey turned 50 in May 2009, the same year as the record was released, and he is still playing in a rock band, which occasionally sounds more rough than ever before. Building further on this in the second verse, he proclaims that "It's a miracle I even made it this far", as if to ensure that surviving what he has gone through is not to be taken for granted. Morrissey has spoken openly about his own depression, and around the time of *Vauxhall and I*, there were even speculation as to whether he was possibly suicidal. He has also spoken quite frankly about what he thinks of the therapy and the medications. As he expressed in an interview with *Details* in 1992:

> I've tried them [Prozac and Lithium]. A lot of extreme things happen to you on them, which sometimes cannot seem to be worth it, because I don't want something that's going to effect me in any way other than to perhaps cure me. I don't want anything that's going to make me different.
>
> (Morrissey 1992: 2)

Combined, then, with the lack of love in human life, which he suggests results from the increasing amount of communication technology, any form of social ambiguity would be in danger of representing general instability and unpredictability. In addition to his depression, Morrissey has been subject to such accusations by not abiding to established social norms. In turn, a person who celebrates ambiguity, by not conforming to established categories, comes over as different, and perhaps even as mentally unstable. He might even be institutionalized and medicated, a metaphor around which 'Something Is Squeezing My Skull' is continuously pivoting. From this perspective, the "something" that apparently is squeezing Morrissey's skull might well be linked to a social and political framework, which is normatively constructed around binary oppositions. Ultimately, this juxtaposition reinforces the message. This is not to say that he has not expressed similar concerns before, but, considering the socio-political context in which the song appears, perhaps we are more prepared to listen?

Conclusions

The purpose of this chapter has been to present a tentative model for reading a pop song by means of the aesthetics of performance. The importance of the voice and the lyrics will of course vary according to the music in question, and the goal has not been to present this as a universal solution. What I have attempted however is to show how certain details of musical sound can affect the larger musical narrative. The main focus has been to show how the dialogical relationship between lyrics, vocal performance and production aesthetics is crucial to understanding the communicative power of Morrissey's music. How, then, can a concept of sonic markers say anything about what is being communicated and how does this become relevant in a chapter about Steven Patrick Morrissey?

The most significant sonic marker in 'Something Is Squeezing My Skull' is perhaps the massive electric guitar sound. Yet this markedness does not stem from the sound itself as this guitar sound can be identified on a range of recent pop and rock records. Bands like Placebo, Foo Fighters, Blink 182 and Green Day, as different as they may seem, have all taken an aesthetic turn in the same direction when it comes to guitar sound. In this way, the sonic qualities of the guitar would represent the constitution of a musical trend rather than a significant difference in itself. Furthermore, the possibility that Morrissey's voice may have been exposed to technological manipulation in parts of the choruses fulfils a vital narrative function and thus becomes a sonic marker. As most voices in popular music today have gone through some form of tuning in order to fit the commercial market, it is not sufficient to simply label these narrative functions as results of technological processing. How, then, can these musical parameters stand out and communicate so strongly when they are probably some of the most typical technological techniques employed in contemporary popular music? My argument has been that it gains a narrative function due to the musical context of operation.

Even if a heavily distorted electric guitar does not necessarily appear as a sonic marker, it does to some extent still dictate a certain stylistic direction of the music. On a detailed level, the amount of overdrive or distortion (technology), and the guitarist's utilization of this (style), will always have a communicative function. Yet, what is being communicated will always be contextually bound. This means that as a sonic marker in this particular song, the sound and style of the electric guitar is destined to relate to the vocal performance and eventually also to the lyrics. This is why Bakhtin's dialogical concept of speech communication functions as a useful platform for the analytical model presented in this chapter. Any utterance is inextricably linked to a range of non-verbal components of communication, as well as contextual considerations. Similarly, in music, the geno-elements of the vocal performance, the aesthetic qualities of the production and socio-political context of appearance all contribute to the ways in which we perceive the song. As we have seen, one of the main keys to Morrissey's appeal lies in his ability to evoke empathic responses through his vocal style.

Keeping the lyrics and vocal performance in focus, the sound of the electric guitar and conjectures about vocal tuning provide a basis for a discussion of how established musical codes affect the meaning of the song. On the one hand, the aesthetic surface of 'Something Is Squeezing My Skull' fits well with the contemporary time code. On the other hand, Morrissey's biographical presence is assured through his voice and lyrics. Ultimately, 'Something Is Squeezing My Skull' becomes an utterance through the internal dialogue between lyrics, vocal performance and the aesthetics of production, as this is contextualized within a certain normative framework. As we become more isolated and lonely through a mix of technological devices and fear of an unstable and ambiguous Other, Morrissey's sonic double take becomes a reminder of how such mechanisms might lead us away from love and real friendships in human life.

Notes

1. The two electric guitars, which are present on this track, are panned left and right as in a traditional rock recording. Yet, the one in the right channel, played by Jesse Tobias, is processed with heavier overdrive and becomes more dominating in the soundscape. Although Boz Boorer's guitar in the left channel has an important rhythmic function, the Jesse Tobias' guitar will figure as the main focus in this chapter.
2. In music notational programs such as Finale and Sibelius, this G-note is the last "legal" note for male singers, suggesting a norm for the upper limit of the male voice.
3. Indications of technological treatment of Morrissey's voice also come through the fact that this song is always transposed down a tone when performed live, suggesting that Morrissey's vocal range or comfort zone is actually lower than that on the recording.
4. My application of musical codes builds on the work of musicologists such as Richard Middleton (1990), David Brackett (1995) and Stan Hawkins (2002). Stylistic codes build more specifically on Hawkins' divide between stylistic and technical codes (Hawkins 2002: 10).
5. Alain Whyte, songwriter and guitarist, wrote the music for 'Billy Budd'.

References

Bakhtin, M. (1986) 'The problem of speech genres', in C. Emerson and M. Holmquist (eds) *Speech Genres and Other Late Essays*. Austin: University of Texas Press, pp. 60–102.

Bannister, M. (2006) *White Boys, White Noise: Masculinities and 1980s Indie Guitar Rock*. Aldershot: Ashgate.

Barthes, R. (1977) 'The grain of the voice', in R. Barthes *Image, Music, Text*. London: Fontana, pp. 179–189.

Baudrillard, J. (2003) *The Spirit of Terrorism*, 2nd edn. London: Verso.

Brown, L. (2008) *Meetings with Morrissey*. London: Omnibus.

Butler, J. (2009) *Frames of War: When is Life Grievable?* London: Verso.

Carman, R. (2006) *Johnny Marr: The Smiths and the Art of Gun-Slinging*. Shropshire: Independent Music Press.

Hawkins, S. (2009) *The British Pop Dandy: Masculinity, Popular Music and Culture*. Aldershot: Ashgate.

Hawkins, S. (2002) *Settling the Pop Score: Pop Texts and Identity Politics*. Aldershot: Ashgate.

Hawkins, S. (2001) 'Musicological quagmires in popular music: seeds of detailed conflict', *Popular Musicology Online*, 1.

Middleton, R. (1995) 'Authorship, gender and the construction of meaning in the Eurythmics' hit recordings', *Cultural Studies*, 9: 3, pp. 465–485.

Hopps, G. *Morrissey: The Pageant of His Bleeding Heart*. New York: Continuum, 2009.

Morrissey, S. and Lowe, Z. (2009) 'Zane Lowe meets Morrissey', MTV TWO, available: *http: //www. youtube.com/watch?v=026c_Q9tARg*.

Morrissey, S. and Keeps, D. (1992) 'Homme Alone 2', *Details*, December.

Rogan, J. (1992) *Morrissey and Marr: The Severed Alliance*. London: Omnibus Press.

Steinskog, E. (2008) 'Voice of hope: queer pop subjectivities', *Trikster*, 1.

Théberge, P. (1997) *Any Sound You Can Imagine: Making Music/Consuming Technology*. Hanover: Wesleyan University Press.

Waksman, S. (1999) *Instruments of Desire: The Electric Guitar and the Shaping of Musical Experience*. Cambridge: Harvard University Press.

Walser, R. (1993) *Running with the Devil: Power, Gender, and Madness in Heavy Metal Music*. Hanover, NH: University Press of New England.

Wicke, P. (1990) *Rock Music: Culture, Aesthetics and Sociology*. Cambridge: Cambridge University Press.

Chapter 12

'Vicar In A Tutu': Dialogism, Iconicity and the Carnivalesque in Morrissey

Pierpaolo Martino

The carnivalesque

In his cult study *Rabelais and His World* (1984) Mikhail Bakhtin identifies a shift from popular life to literary culture, arguing that Rabelais's taste of parody, linguistic richness and emphasis on the grotesque body are strictly related to the practices of carnival in the Renaissance period. According to Bakhtin, "carnival celebrated temporary liberation from the prevailing truth and from the established order; it marked the suspension of all hierarchical rank, privileges, norms and prohibitions. Carnival was the true feast of time, the feast of becoming, change and renewal" (Bakhtin 1984: 10). With its emphasis on the bodily life, carnival "made a man renounce his official state as monk, cleric, scholar" (Bakhtin 1984: 13) in order to experience a communalism freed from commerce and power relationships.

Interestingly, in 1985 The Smiths wrote a song, entitled 'Vicar In A Tutu', about a clergyman who chooses to preach the gospel dressed as a classic dancer, which is rich in carnivalesque images and complex associations. As Hopps (2009: 235) observes "the song is like a miniature *Carry On* film, with a cast of momentary but memorable characters". The narrative starts with the image of the first person narrator "lifting some lead off the roof of the Holy Name Church" who is positively surprised with the "blistering sight of a vicar in a tutu". Some lines later, the narrator mentions Rose who first collects and then counts "the money in the canister," and a "monkish monsignor with a head full of plaster" addressing the vicar, and indirectly the narrator, with the sentence "my man get your rile soul dry-cleaned". The narrator, in the guise of a sort of criminal, is himself of particular interest, because somehow engaged in a complex dialogue with other narrative voices. As, indeed, Hopps (2009: 235) observes in the song "the ostensible speaking perspective is not consistently or prominently sustained and is subverted by a species of free indirect discourse", as in the case of the line "it is worthwhile living a laughable life". Moreover, as the critic observes, the repeated lines defending the vicar ("he's not strange") "suggest the involvement of a supplementary omniscient perspective" (Hopps 2009: 235). In short, 'Vicar In A Tutu' is a very good instance of Morrissey's capacity of introducing a literary sensibility and complexity into the realm of pop. More importantly, with this grotesque song Morrissey is able to turn the world of the Church, and its official culture, topsy-turvy.

If the notion of the carnivalesque "can be extended to include all those cultural situations in which the authority of a single language of authority is called into question, notably by the simultaneous co-presence of other languages which can challenge it" (Dentith 2000: 23), then 'Vicar In A Tutu', with its mix of the religious, of vaudeville, parody and transvestitism is undoubtedly a carnivalesque song. The "laughable life" of which Morrissey sings is, indeed, a version of Bakhtin's carnival laughter and defines an important aspect of Morrissey's discursive strategy, namely *innuendo*. Making reference to Bakhtin, Hopps (2009: 142) observes that

> Like Carnival laughter, innuendo has a democratic foundation: in pointing towards the drives and processes to which all human beings are subject, it involves a "suspension of all hierarchical precedence" and reveals a realm of "purely human relations" ("Vulgar" in its primary etymological sense means "of the common people"). Such humour would therefore obviously appeal to Morrissey whose work […] – both in its concern for the marginalized, the damaged, the fallen and the "queer", and in the animosity it evinces towards institutions, nations and individuals that appear to deny the claims of common humanity – is centrally bound up with the defence of the human. Its appeal might also lie in the fact that innuendo is the mirror image and hence perhaps the ideal opponent of hypocrisy in that it intimates behind all fine appearances a […] brotherhood in corporeality.

Hence the emphasis is on the body, which characterises all of Morrissey's performances. In this sense, the very enunciation of 'Vicar In A Tutu' is, especially in his live rendition (and in particular in the *Rank* album version), characterized by a carnivalesque use of the singer's voice, implying all those performed noises (groaning, sneezing, etc.) through which Morrissey renders "the apparently absent body visible and assert(s) the importunate claims of the flesh" (Hopps 2009: 24).

The song is significantly included in *The Queen is Dead* (1986) whose title-track offers a similar parody of Queen Elizabeth II and Prince Charles. According to Simon Goddard in 'The Queen Is Dead', Morrissey's "blunt dismissal of the monarchy as outmoded, uncaring and parasitical is also a rejection of England itself" (Goddard 2006: 205). Early in the song Morrissey offers carnivalesque images of "her very lowness with a head in a sling" and of her eldest son, Prince Charles, who is asked if he has ever craved "to appear on the front of the Daily Mail" dressed in his "mother's bridal veil". "The provocative suggestion of closet transvestitism" (Goddard 2006: 205) is followed by the image of Morrissey himself as an intruder breaking into Buckingham Palace "armed with a rusty spanner and sponge, presumably to bludgeon Her Majesty before mopping up the mess" (Goddard 2006: 205), which suggests a sort of carryonesque vignette. The song closes on a bitter note voicing the author's sense of displacement and solitude, with the repetition of the line "life is very long, when you're lonely", namely when you feel you do not *belong* to a nation dominated by the monarchy and the church. The only possible approach to this world is a parodic, carnivalesque one.

In this sense, in the final line of 'Vicar In A Tutu' – which being the eighth track on the album stands, in a sense, as one of the nine answers to the questions asked in the title track – Morrissey declares himself to be "a living sign" of the carnivalesque stance embraced by the vicar, indeed the "I" of the song's final enunciation "dilates to include the singer as well as the song's vicar (and arguably its putative speaker too [...]. The utterance is thus crowded with a multiplicity of distinct speakers, whose divergent voices resonate simultaneously" (Hopps 2009: 236). The line is sung with an extraordinary intensity; in this sense, one can get the impression that one of the speakers, that is, Morrissey himself, is trying to shift from the song's narrative to a larger one in which to refer to his condition as a "living sign", that is, living icon, within the vast and complex frame of contemporary pop culture.

Iconicity

In Charles Sanders Peirce's semiotic theory (1931–58), the icon stands as a specific typology of sign along with the index and the symbol; while the index is a sign that signifies its object by a relation of contiguity, causality or by some physical connection, and the symbol is a sign in consequence of a habit (usually determined by a code), the icon is characterized by a relation of similarity between the sign and its object. The icon is the most independent sign from both convention and causality/contiguity: an icon stands for something or for some particular meaning in an unpredictable, often escaping way. However, in contemporary culture, the notions of icon and iconicity, even preserving their semiotic, Peircean connotation, can cover a vast and complex range of meanings.

According to the *Oxford English Dictionary* (1999: 704), a (cultural) icon "is a person or thing regarded as a representative symbol or as worthy of veneration". In this sense, Morrissey represents the alternative cultural icon, a *pop icon* who – never giving in to commercial pressures – has been faithful to his artistic and personal beliefs, and is still admired by thousands of fans who, *iconically*, try to emulate him, to look like, that is to be *similar* to him (in the Peircean sense), to share his tastes, his sympathies and antipathies. Paradoxically, Morrissey is both an icon and an iconoclast; in a sense, he is the *anti-icon*. Indeed, he used and still uses his art to attack – through parody and subversion – sacred icons, which include not only the already mentioned vicars and queens, but also political leaders such as Margaret Thatcher and George W. Bush.

It is interesting to note how the term icon can also refer to "a devotional painting of Christ or another holy figure" (*Oxford English Dictionary* 1999: 704). Ironically, there is something religious about Morrissey's (anti)iconicity, which brings admirers to worship both his image and the world connected to that image. It is not by chance, perhaps, that one of the best critical studies on the British artist is entitled *Saint Morrissey*. According to Mark Simpson, author of the study: "[Morrissey] has achieved in life the transcendence that other performers have only achieved in death [...] Morrissey is the only "saint" to be canonised before his death" (Simpson 2004: 213).

Morrissey has certainly gained his iconic, saint-like status through the difficult performance of himself in terms of "same-other" (Ponzio 2001), that is, through his extreme faithfulness to a highly recognizable *persona* which, however, he has always been capable of (self) translating and reinventing in different and complex ways. In this sense, the singer's visual aspect is particularly relevant.

In his Smiths' years, Morrissey paid much attention to his *look* and to that of his band. The Smiths' visual aspect was a highly peculiar one; they all were short-haired and they all dressed like ordinary people in a period in which every pop performer wanted to gain the audience's attention through the display of eccentric and colourful dress, hard make-up and elaborated hairstyles. However, The Smiths' concerts and TV appearances saw the band employing some specific *signs* which contributed to the construction of the band's iconic originality. Some of them were of considerable relevance, in particular the flowers used on stage and the hearing aid and the glasses worn by Morrissey in performance.

The Smiths used flowers since their first concert at Manchester's Haçienda Club in 1983. Making reference to that concert, Morrissey explains the meaning of the flowers in these terms:

> "They're symbolic for at least three reasons. We introduced them as an antidote to the Haçienda when we played there; it was so sterile and inhuman. We wanted some harmony with nature. Also, to show some kind of optimism in Manchester which the flowers represent. Manchester is semi-paralyzed still" [...] Looking back the singer later noted "The flowers were a very human gesture [...] It had got to the point in music where people were really afraid to show how they felt. To show their emotions. I thought that was a shame and very boring, the flowers offered hope".
>
> (Rogan 1993: 158)

Besides, as Johnny Rogan observes, "the floral spectacle owed much to Morrissey's mentor Oscar Wilde who was notorious for decorating his Oxford rooms with lilies. As his fame increased, Wilde's love of flowers captured the public imagination and Morrissey clearly wanted to achieve something of the same" (Rogan 1993: 158). For Smiths' fans flowers became a language by which to communicate with their hero, often laying gladioli at his feet during the concerts.

Another important sign within The Smiths' visual repertoire was represented by the hearing aid used first by the singer during a performance at *Top of the Pops*. Morrissey explained that the idea "emanated from a fan letter he had received from a deaf girl, Morrissey empathized with her disability and wore the device as a gesture of support" (Rogan 1993: 185–186). A similar function was played by the NHS spectacles worn by the singer to express his solidarity with boys and girls who were considered unattractive. In youth culture, "bespectacled" is often a synonym for "undesirability" (Williams 2002). In short, these visual signs, in particular the glasses and the flowers, were cleverly used in The Smiths' narrative in order to amplify the effect of their musical and verbal enunciations, which were addressed to outsiders of any kind.

The very peculiar iconicity of the group's visual choices was matched by the complex iconicity of the singer's voice. Morrissey's, indeed, was an extremely peculiar voice, with a *grain* (Barthes 1977a) in between male and female; more precisely, Morrissey's voice was that of the Northern Woman, characterized by "a certain intensity mixed with a certain breeziness, a certain desperation mixed with a lot of self-irony" (Simpson 2004: 49). Hopps identifies a double side of Morrissey's voice, one connected with a kind of dandyism represented by a tendency to sing with a correct, clear diction and the other with the carnivalesque, which, as we have already seen, "is most apparent in his penchant for performed noises: groaning, sneezing, stage belching, spoof vomiting, etc [...]. Hence, in contrast to the 'health and efficiency' of New Pop, where the body is a source of pleasure and pride, in Morrissey's songs it becomes a source of trouble and embarrassment" (Hopps 2009: 24). In this way the singer gives particular prominence to the unpoetic and the low within the realm of pop itself. Besides, these sounds are *iconic* themselves because they exceed the symbolic, that is codified aspect of verbal language, to access a realm of motivated, often onomatopoeic signification. Other aspects of Morrissey's unconventional singing are represented by his use of melisma (the singing of multiple notes to a single syllable of the text), yodelling, which evidences "a daring and comical appropriation of the kitsch" (Hopps 2009: 26) and his trademark falsetto, through which, interestingly, he is able to access female territory through a male body.

It is important to note how the very choice of calling himself just Morrissey expressed the artist's desire to reject the name as sign of gender identification, in order to inhabit a sort of borderline from which to address outsiders of both sexes.

The Smiths' choice of their singles and album covers shows how one of the band's major achievements was the mixing of iconic recognizability and clever intertextual quotation from other medias (cinema, TV). Featured on the cover of the single 'Bigmouth Strikes Again', James Dean was to be the biggest iconic obsession of the young Morrissey who was attracted by the actor's handsomeness, by his sexual ambiguity, by his fascinating restlessness and, to a degree, unhappiness. Dean was also the symbol of transcendence, of the immortality Morrissey wanted to achieve as a pop star. With the *death* of The Smiths, Morrissey appeared for the first time on the front cover of a recording of his own – in a full and definitive enunciation of his iconic status – with the publication of the single 'Suedehead' in February 1988, whose video was shot in Dean's hometown of Fairmount, Indiana (see Hazard's chapter in this volume).

The biggest cinematographic obsession of Morrissey was, however, represented by the British 1960s new realism films, which, within his rich intertextual world, represent a point of conjunction between the visual and the literary. Speaking about these films during a 1985 interview on Australian Radio Morrissey confessed:

I'm afraid that they probably remind me of my childhood because I lived in lots of those circumstances and I also think that [...] I gaze upon them fondly because it was the first time in the entire history of film where regional dialects were allowed to come to the fore and people were allowed to talk about squalor and general depression and it wasn't necessarily a shameful thing. It was quite positive [...] people were allowed to be real instead of being glamorous and Hollywoodian, if that is a word, and I sincerely hope it isn't.

(Simpson 2004: 58)

This form of realism was to affect deeply Morrissey's writing. Morrissey's favourite films include *Saturday Night, Sunday Morning* (1960), *Billy Liar* (1962) and *A Taste of Honey* (1961). This last film was an adaptation of Shelagh Delaney's play by the same name, which represents the most important intertext of Morrissey's poetic work. According to Simpson, *A Taste of Honey* represents:

The landscape, the mother country, the heart of Morrissey's work [...] it is a lyrical play whose affecting but plain-speaking poetry proceeds from ordinary people showing their extraordinary side [...] Likewise, it exists narcissistically in a word of its own, where it is everything to itself: the drama and all the characters seem to proceed from Jo's adolescent imagination; they are merely aspects of her own predicament, conversations between her emotions.

(Simpson 2004: 60)

This is precisely what happens in Morrissey's lyrical production, where, again, different characters and aspects of the artist speak to each other.

Dialogism

Morrissey has been capable of translating his "polyphonic consciousness" – inhabited by what Bakhtin (1981) saw as multiple, dissonant, even contradictory voices – in a literary landscape of rare beauty and complexity whose rich intertextuality perfectly responds to the singer's internal dialogism. According to Roland Barthes:

A text is [...] a multidimensional space in which a variety of writings none of them original, blend and clash. The text is a tissue of quotations [...] the writer can only imitate a gesture that is always anterior, never original. His only power is to mix writings, to counter the ones with the others, in a such a way as never to rest on any one of them.

(Barthes 1977b: 146)

Morrissey is at once a (living) text and a writer in the Barthesian sense; his lyrics are a constant translation, re-articulation (and often direct quotation) of other literary texts. Delaney is just one of the voices inhabiting his work along with William Shakespeare, Christopher Marlowe, John Milton, Charles Dickens, George Eliot, Herman Melville, Elizabeth Smart, John Fowles, D. H. Lawrence, T. S. Eliot, Graham Greene, Richard Allen, Pier Paolo Pasolini and Oscar Wilde. Within this long list the author, who besides Delaney, has exercised the most powerful influence on Morrissey is undoubtedly Oscar Wilde, who according to Michael Bracewell (1997) stands as the first British pop star.

Wilde became a global celebrity during his Tour of the United States; as with any contemporary pop star, in order to become a proper celebrity, he had first to be *big* in America. The chance was given by the success of Gilbert and Sullivan's operetta, *Patience or Bunthorne's Bride* which focused on the look and manner of the aesthete in the character of Bunthorne. Richard D'Oyly Carte, the show's producer, offered Wilde a series of promotional lectures to offer American audiences the chance to see a real life aesthete; a similar practice was to become quite popular in the 1960s with British rock and pop artists, such as The Beatles (and later The Smiths themselves), promoting their albums in long American tours. Interestingly, Wilde did not link his name with opera as a form of high art, but with operetta as a form of low culture entertainment. In America, Wilde gave lectures such as "The English Renaissance of art" and "The decorative arts" and hundreds of photographs were shot of the aesthete in his poses, like the famous Sarony photos, which, according to Simon Waldrep (2004), perfectly capture Wilde's look and capacity for self-promotion. On his arrival in New York a customs official asked him if he had anything to declare, Wilde promptly answered "I have nothing to declare except my genius" (Ellmann 1987: 152). Wilde, among other things, notoriously declared to have put all his genius into his life and only his talent in his work. This maxim can be perfectly applied to Morrissey. Indeed, even though The Smiths' songs are characterized by images and themes which are clearly Wildean (see 'This Charming Man' included in 1984 *The Smiths*) and some of them ('Cemetry Gates' included in 1986 *The Queen Us Dead*) even feature the Anglo-Irish writer as a character besides Keats and Yeats, Wilde's strongest influence must be detected in the "living sign" named Morrissey.

Like Wilde, Morrissey spent a considerable effort in the construction of his *persona*, often using resources provided by Wilde himself. Many of the interviews given by the singer in the early years of his career featured a number of epigrams and paradoxes which were clearly Wildean and that contributed to the construction of Morrissey's intellectual complexity, something which was strongly at odds with the superficiality of many pop stars of the early 1980s. It must be added that Wilde's influence on Morrissey represents a space where, again, the literary and the visual meet. It is worth mentioning again the singer's obsession with flowers, which was clearly a way for Morrissey to pay tribute to his favourite writer.

The flowers on stage, the hearing aid, the NHS spectacles, the pop icons on the album covers, the 1960s films, the works of Shelagh Delaney and Oscar Wilde are some of the main signs and intertexts used by Morrissey in the construction of his persona in The Smiths years. His solo years see the artist embracing other signs and discourses, from the 1970s imagery, which nourishe his debut album *Viva Hate* (1988), to his tribute to Glam Rock with *Your Arsenal* (1992), to his love for gangs, criminals and boxers in the mid-1990s, which can be detected in *Vauxhall and I* (1994) and *Southpaw Grammar* (1995).

The unique appeal of Morrissey's persona is, in short, given by the artist's capacity to present himself in dialogical terms, that is, using – often through direct quotation – multiple discourses at once. As we have seen, Morrissey is not just a "living sign" but also and foremost a "living text", that is, a space in which different signs, different voices and discourses speak to each other. If according to Brummett "a text is a set of signs related to each other insofar as their meanings all contribute to the same set of effects or functions", then Morrissey stands as a "multimodal text" (see G. Kress and T. van Leeuwen 2001), one in which the visual, the musical and the literary meet to articulate a complex critique of the cultural and political establishment. In the mid-1990s, this very establishment aimed decreed the end of Morrissey's solo experience.

While in the Brit-pop years everybody could play with nationalist imagery (in particular with the Union Jack) without creating any scandal, in the early and mid-1990s Morrissey – who during the *Your Arsenal* period had sympathized with skinhead imagery, wrapped himself in the Union Jack, and written a complex and ambiguous song such as 'The National Front Disco' (See Baker's and Foleys' chapters in this volume for discussions of these issues) – became the privileged target of a number of media attacks concerning his unclear political position. Some commentators focused on the low quality of his albums (in particular of 1995 *Southpaw Grammar*), often comparing them with his masterpieces in The Smiths years, while others focused on the court case with Joyce about The Smiths earnings in 1996, in which Judge Weeks described Morrissey as "devious, truculent and unreliable" (Dee 2004: 112). In short the "living sign" became a "living target", main accusation against him was that he had embraced a number of discourses which did not fit within the much loved Smiths' narrative. *Maladjusted* (1997) was to be his last album for a very long time; Morrissey's unfavourable media profile, the scarce success of his last work and the economic collapse of the Mercury label determined the end of (the first part, at least of) his solo career and led the artist to embark on a long exile in America and away from his beloved England.

You are the Quarry (2004) represents the return of Morrissey from the periphery, from the margins of the cultural establishment to its very centre. A return which has seen Morrissey introducing discourses about the margins in the very heart of the system, *attacking* its ideologies through the same channels by which he had been attacked seven years before. Morrissey's discographic return was preceded by a number of interviews given by the singer to the British press. Morrissey used the interview as a discursive mode to introduce some of the issues analysed in the album. On the other hand the *NME* – which ironically 12 years before had labelled him racist – gave extreme relevance to Morrissey's artistic and political return, paving the way to the great success of the album.

The title, *You are the Quarry*, seems to make reference to the idea of dialogue. The deictic dimension is absolutely central to understanding the *dialogic* informing the whole album; indeed, in the different *chapters* of Morrissey's work there is always an "I" referring to a you – as person or personification (for example, America) – or to a third participant in a particular space and time. The title's "you" has at least three different referents. According to Simpson, the title is "a comment on the British media's treatment of him as a national blood sport for much of the previous decade" (Simpson 2004: 193). On the other hand, in an interview Morrissey declared: "*You are the Quarry* is actually a title [...] aimed at my audience in general saying they are a target for me to win their affection now" (cited in Bret 2004: 265).

However, associating the title to the cover's image (Morrissey's embracing a machine-gun), the reader is induced to interpret Morrissey's words as a reference to American (colonial) politics towards the peripheries of the world. This impression is confirmed by the very moment of Morrissey's enunciation, which is May 2004, one year after the attack on Iraq. Moreover the album's opening track is entitled 'America Is Not The World'.

It is important for a proper understanding of the song to make reference to Morrissey's enunciative position. The singer is speaking to America from its very heart, indeed in 1997 – after *the break* with Britain – he moved to Los Angeles; in this sense Morrissey's discourse *sounds* particularly convincing as the speech of someone who asserts at once his otherness ("you have nothing to say to me") and closeness ("I love you") to America. Hence the colloquial tone – America is addressed through personification ("your head", "you is"), and it is immediately defined as "big-head", an expression making reference to America's incapacity for self-questioning. The image of America as a land of freedom and opportunity – something ironically presented in biblical terms ("America / the land of the Free, they said and of opportunity / in a Just and Truthful way") – is soon deconstructed through the reference to the impossibility of a black, female or gay president. After making reference to President Bush ("Steely-blue eyes with no love in them, scan the world") Morrissey voices the other main theme of the whole album, that is love, and in particular the theme of love's place in a world of war, a world dominated by the ideology of power and money ("and I / I have got nothing / to offer you just this heart deep and true which you say you don't need").

We can maintain that 'America Is Not The World' introduces Morrissey's postcolonial voice (Young 2003), a voice speaking for (and preoccupied with) the other, a voice giving voice to Estonian uneasiness with the very idea of America ("don't you wonder why in Estonia they say 'hey you, you big fat pig'"). During the album sessions he also recorded a song entitled 'Mexico', written some years before and included in the late 2004 special edition of the album, where again he attacks America's politics ("in Mexico / I went for a walk to inhale / the tranquil, cool, lover's hair / I could taste a trace of American chemical waste"). Mexico and Mexican-Americans were to be a great passion of Morrissey during his American exile during which he was strongly supported by his Latino fans. Commenting on Morrissey's appeal to many young Mexican-Americans, Simpson observes:

> To a certain American audience, Morrissey is familiar but exotic, American but un-American, alternative but timeless. He is the pop cultural soul in a world made soulless by pop culture; a distinctively Catholic voice in a distinctly Protestant country. A man who lives between borders, an insider-outsider.
>
> (Simpson 2004: 187)

In 'Irish Blood, English Heart' Morrissey focuses on his particular human condition, that of someone inhabiting the borderline between differences, between identities ("Irish Blood, English Heart this I'm made of"). The first chorus lines in the song "no regime can buy or sell me" make reference to Morrissey's otherness in relation to any system and regime, and yet they indirectly and ironically refer to his position of artist sold and bought within the capitalist system. However, since his voice is speaking from the very heart of this system, Morrissey's discourse has a truly deconstructive effect. Morrissey sees his personal condition as a perspective through which to address and analyse the condition of England; Morrissey's partial Irishness is indeed a sort of blackness (see Simpson 2004: 51), a form of hybridity, a postcolonial perspective through which to question Britain's identity. In his treatment of both America and Britain Morrissey presents images connected with power; in particular, he concentrates on some signs, or better symbols, associated with the British colonial empire, like for instance the Union Jack ("I've been dreaming of a time when / to be English is not to be baneful / to be standing by the flag not feeling / shameful, racist or partial"). Here there is also an indirect reference to the Finsbury Park accident; Morrissey is finally clarifying his political position, openly asserting his rejection of racism.

In the second chorus of the song the references to the colonial empire and to English politics become even more precise ("I've been dreaming of a time when / the English are sick to death of Labour / and Tories / and spit upon the name Oliver Cromwell / and denounce this royal line that still / salutes him / and will salute him forever"). Commenting on the song during an interview, Morrissey explained that

> it's a comment on the whole British monarchy. Oliver Cromwell was no more than a general, but he behaved like some of them by slaughtering thousands of Irishmen just to get them out of the way. As for British politics, the only choice you have is between the Tories and Labour, neither of which are spokesmen for the people. It's an age-old, ridiculous circus.
>
> (in Bret 2004: 257)

It is interesting to note that the publication of the single – two weeks before the album – was accompanied by the release of a video-clip consistently played at MTV, which in this way "promoted", in visual terms, Morrissey's counter-discourse on the establishment's favourite discursive channel (television). The video features Morrissey singing the song with his musicians and a few people as audience in a relatively small (underground) *marginal* space. The focus of the video's director is on Morrissey's voice, on his words and hence on the importance of "listening" to those words. Morrissey is portrayed as a middle-aged singer who asserts his otherness in relation to the "young and beautiful" prototype often *reproduced* in music television. Dressed in a white jacket – which besides being a pacifist symbol is perfectly in tune with the singer's choice of wearing extra-elegant (Rat Pack-like) suits during concerts and public appearances from 2002 onwards – Morrissey accompanies his words with a mime, which amplifies the verbal contents, in particular on the words "spit", "denounce", "salute", that is, the expressions more directly related to the ideology of resistance.

In short, in *You are the Quarry*, and in particular in 'Irish Blood, English Heart' Morrissey questions the very idea of polarity as a static dimension, as a space of identification and exclusion. Here he seems to inhabit the borderline, the limit, the "coma" which at once joins and specifies his Irish origins and his English sensibility, translating it into a world-view. This is a belated and yet extremely powerful response for those who saw in Morrissey a nationalist and a racist, obsessed with England's historical and cultural superiority over the rest of the world.

Hopps (2009: 59) defines Morrissey's in-betweeness in terms of "oxymoronic self", something which he explains by making reference to Oscar Wilde. Wilde's most interesting feature is, indeed, as queer theorists have shown, his liminality, his capacity of never taking sides, of rejecting a fixed, predictable, centralizing frame of mind, and so in his resistance to the irreconcilability of contradictory, even opposite realities. Something similar happens with Morrissey. He is, for example, typically described as an "ordinary working-class 'anti-star' who nevertheless loves to hog the spotlight, a nice man who says the nastiest things about other people, a shy man who is also an outrageous narcissist" (Hopps 2009: 6). Hopps analyses Morrissey's elusiveness, his oxymoronic self, in terms of mobility and multiplicity; with the former he implies, among other things, the artist's capacity of moving from one position to another in few lines of a song (as witnessed in 'Cemetry Gates' in which a well-learned person criticizes a plagiarist to be later criticized himself), with the latter his capacity of being many different things at once, and in particular his capacity of mixing levity and gravity.

The image of Morrissey as a "translated man" – which we borrow from Salman Rushdie (1991) – that is as a living text moving freely between different ways of being and different cultures (and spaces) is what connects *You are the Quarry* to *Ringleader of the Tormentors* (2006). In *You are the Quarry* Morrissey's enunciative position coincided with Los Angeles; *Ringleader*, instead, sees the artist addressing his fans from Rome, where he moved in 2005. There is however some stylistic and thematic continuity between the two albums.

The very title of the album makes reference to the gang dimension, with Morrissey declaring in different interviews of being himself the ringleader mentioned in the title. It must be added that one of the more incisive songs of the album 'The Youngest Was The Most Loved', a "saga of a spoilt child turned killer" (Rogan 2006: 299), thematically recalls *You are the Quarry*'s 'First Of The Gang To Die', which focused on Los Angeles street gangs. However, the connections between the two albums are even deeper. The first track of the new album is entitled 'I Will See You In Far-Off Places' and is thematically linked to 'America Is Not The World'. The song is a meditation on life, death and immortality; however, the philosophical tone of the opening sharply contrasts with the reference to America's (and UK's) responsibility for the deaths of thousands of innocent people in Iraq ("Destiny for some is to save life / but destiny for some is to end life"). This very first song investigates the complex dialogic between religion ("If your God bestows protection upon you / and if the USA doesn't bomb you / I believe I will see you somewhere safe") and death which will inform – along with the artist's renewed interest in sex – the whole album.

'Dear God Please Help Me', perhaps the album's most important track in both lyrical and musical terms (thanks to Ennio Morricone's impressive string arrangement), opens with the narrator making reference to his enunciative position ("I am walking through Rome / with my heart on a string") and asking for God's help in facing the temptations of the flesh. The song features the most direct reference to sex ever included in a Morrissey song ("then he motions to me / with his hand on my knee"), something which attracted many critic's attention. However, what matters here is not Morrissey revealing his homosexuality – which is also a risky interpretation given the narrative complexity typical of the author – but the capacity of the narrator of establishing a very fascinating dialogue with God, making Him both saviour and confidant ("dear God did this kind of thing / happen to you?"). The song closes in a circular way with the narrator walking through Rome, but this time with a free heart, most probably the effect of sexual accomplishment.

Rome is the *space* of enunciation for both 'Dear God Please Help Me' and the powerful 'You Have Killed Me'. Here Morrissey mentions two cultural icons strictly associated with the Italian city – Pasolini, with whom the singer identifies ("Pasolini is me / Accattone you'll be), and Anna Magnani, who worked on maybe Morrissey's favourite Pasolini film: *Mamma Roma* (1962). Speaking about the Italian director and poet during an interview Morrissey confessed:

> I've seen all the films [...] There's nothing flash about them. You're seeing real people without any distractions, just the naked person, with everything taking place on the streets [...] He didn't have to be anybody else, he was being himself in his own world and even though he was obsessed with the low-life that was all he wanted.
>
> (Rogan 2006: 298)

Morrissey found Pasolini's realism absolutely fascinating, something at once very close to and yet very different from the British 1960s film realism he had so much loved in his twenties. Pasolini's realism was essentially about the bodily existence, about a low-life which, at least in the early 1960s, had nothing to do with the official culture (see Pasolini 1976) and with mainstream trends; on the contrary, through its emphasis on the naked body, swearwords and dialect, it stood as a space absolutely resistant and subversive in relation to high- and middle-class life. No wonder Morrissey found Pasolini absolutely attractive. Moreover, speaking about Morrissey's love for Rome, Beaumont suggests that what the singer probably enjoys about the city is "the closeness of the bodies" and the particular spontaneity of the people.

'You Have Killed Me' makes reference – like 'Dear God Please Help Me' – to the sex / love theme through some beautiful lines ("I entered nothing / and nothing entered me / till you came / with the key / and you did your best"), which again give the idea of a finally freed bodily life. It is not by chance that the album closes with a track entitled 'At Last I Am Born', which is a sort of confession about the suffered achievement of a state of physical and emotional serenity. Even the album cover – featuring a serene Morrissey playing violin – suggests "a state of mind verging on the harmonious" (Beaumont 2006: 23). Once again Morrissey's great gift is in the capacity of articulating his complex enunciations, using different discourse modes almost simultaneously.

Years of Refusal (2009) signals, on the contrary, a departure from this kind of serenity and a refusal of any kind of conventional dialogue and relationship. The cover of the album turns Morrissey into a living (assertive) sign of human alienation, which the baby he holds can not but emphasize. It is an album about refusing and being refused; the whole collection is, indeed, centred on a poetics of rejection and on a concern for loneliness, for solitude as a kind of strategy to react, to respond to past events, as witnessed in such tracks as: 'I Am OK By Myself', 'One Day Goodbye Will Be Farewell' and 'It's Not Your Birthday Anymore'. Love and its bruising unobtainableness, along with the exploration of mortality, seem to be the other main concerns of the album. What seems particularly interesting is that here Morrissey seems to have forgotten Rome in order to embrace Paris, which here, however, becomes a kind of non-place, a symbol again of solitude, a belated version of the bedroom of his adolescence.

In conclusion we can argue that Morrissey is not just a "living sign" but also a sort of *hyper*text, a text whose internal dialogism asks for further dialogues and contexts of enunciations. Morrissey's carnivalesque utterances – delivered in the specific guise of the "vicar in a tutu", but also in the more general form of albums, concerts and interviews – are always addressed to a "listener", who in turn is compelled to rethink his/her own identity, possibly reshaping it through an intelligent recombination and re-articulation of the artist's most loved signs and texts; it is important, indeed, to underline that Morrissey is a fan himself of Oscar Wilde, David Bowie, The New York Dolls, Patti Smith etc. In one sense, the Morrissey fan is asked *to play* with his/her favourite *icon*, in a dialogical process in which the self becomes more and more *other*, and identity, like music itself, starts to be considered in iconic (that is in escaping) more than in symbolic (encoded) terms.

References

Bakhtin, M. (1986) *Speech Genres and Other Late Essays*, ed. C. Emerson and M. Holquist, trans. Vern W. McGee. Austin, TX: University of Texas Press.

Bakhtin, M. (1984) *Rabelais and His World*, trans. H. Islowsky. Bloomington: Indiana University Press.

Bakhtin, M. (1981) *The Dialogic Imagination: Four Essays*, ed. M. Holquist, trans. C. Emerson and M. Holquist. Austin, TX: University of Texas Press.

Barthes, R. (1977a) 'The grain of the voice', in *Image-Music-Text*, ed. S. Heath. London: Fontana Paperbacks, pp. 179–189.

Barthes, R. (1977b) 'The death of the author', in *Image-Music-Text*, ed. S. Heath. London: Fontana Paperbacks, pp. 142–148.

Beaumont, M. (2006) 'The new Roman emperor', *NME*, 25th February, pp. 20–23.

Bracewell, M. (1997) *Oscar*. BBC documentary.

Bret, D. (2004) *Morrissey. Scandal and Passion*. London: Robson Books.

Brummett, B. (2006) *The Rhetoric of Popular Culture*, 2nd edn. Thousand Oaks, London and New Delhi: Sage Publications.

Davis, J. (2003) 'Paint a clever picture', *NME The Smiths*, 7th June, pp. 20–21.

Dee, J. (2004) 'I'm not sorry', *MOJO Morrissey & The Smiths Special Edition*, pp. 111–113.

Delaney, S. (1959) *A Taste of Honey.* London: Theatre Workshop.

Dentith, S. (2000) *Parody.* London and New York: Routledge.

Ellmann, R. (1987) *Oscar Wilde.* London: Penguin.

Goddard, S. (2006) *The Smiths. Songs that Saved Your Life*, revised and expanded edn. London: Reynolds & Hearn.

Hopps, G. (2009) *Morrissey: The Pageant of His Bleeding Heart.* London and New York: Continuum.

Jakobson, R. (1959) 'On linguistic aspects of translation', in R. A. Brower (ed.) *On Translation.* Cambridge, MA: Harvard University Press, pp. 232–239.

Kress, G. and Van Leeuwen, T. (2001) *Multimodal Discourse: The Modes and Media of Contemporary Communication.* London: Arnold.

Morrissey (2009) *Years of Refusal.* London: Sanctuary Records.

Morrissey (2006) *Ringleader of the Tormentors.* London: Sanctuary Records.

Morrissey (2004) *You are the Quarry.* London: Sanctuary Records.

Morrissey (1997) *Maladjusted.* London: Mercury.

Morrissey (1995) 'Boxers'. London: Parlophone (EMI).

Morrissey (1995) *Southpaw Grammar.* London: RCA Victor.

Morrissey (1994) *Vauxhall and I.* London: Parlophone (EMI).

Morrissey (1992) *Your Arsenal.* London: Parlophone (EMI).

Morrissey (1988) *Viva Hate.* London: Parlophone (EMI).

Mullen, J. (2004) 'Detest and survive', *MOJO Morrissey & The Smiths Special Edition*, pp. 86–87.

Oxford English Dictionary (Concise) (1999), ed. by J. Pearsall. Oxford: Oxford University Press.

Pasolini, P. P. (1976) *Lettere Luterane.* Torino: Milano.

Peirce, C. S. (1931–1958) *Collected Papers of Charles Sanders Peirce*, eds A. Burks, C. Harthstorne and P. Weiss. Cambridge, MA: The Belknap Press of Harvard University Press.

Ponzio, A. (2001) 'Lo Stesso Altro: il Testo e la sua Traduzione', in S. Petrilli (ed.) *Athanor. Lo Stesso Altro*, n. 4, pp. 5–7.

Rogan, J. (2006) *Morrissey. The Albums.* London: Calidore.

Rogan, J. (1993) *Morrissey and Marr. The Severed Alliance.* London, New York and Sidney: Omnibus Press.

Rushdie, S. (1991) *Imaginary Homelands.* London: Granta Books.

Simpson, M. (2004) *Saint Morrissey.* London: SAF.

Smiths (The) (1988) *Rank.* London: Rough Trade.

Smiths (The) (1986) *The Queen is Dead.* London: Rough Trade.

Smiths (The) (1984) *The Smiths.* London: Rough Trade.

Smiths (The) (1984) *Hatful of Hollow.* London: Rough Trade.

Waldrep, S. (2004) *The Aesthetics of Self-Invention. Oscar Wilde to David Bowie.* Minneapolis: University of Minnesota Press.

Williams, Z. (2001) 'The Light That Never Goes Out', *The Guardian*, 23rd February.

Young, R. (2003) *Postcolonialism. A Very Short Introduction.* Oxford: Oxford University Press.

Chapter 13

Smiths Night: A Dream World Created Through Other People's Music

Dan Jacobson and Ian Jeffrey

It was Sunday night, in New York City, at 'The Smiths Dance Party' when all hell broke loose as the DJ played 'Bigmouth Strikes Again' (Morrissey and Marr 1986). A girl would not stop dancing, even though a piece of broken glass was deeply embedded in her foot. She did not care – she just kept dancing – spraying blood all over the crowded floor. The floor was really more of a long corridor, a digestive tract, connecting the bar in the front and the toilets in the back. The young dancers had to fight to keep their footing against the drunken elbows pushing through – either to get a drink or take a piss. Although there is a smoking ban in New York City, past the velvet rope cigarettes were flaunted. On this night, the smoky atmosphere was punctuated by flowers in the air. Not just the petals, but also the remains of a long-stemmed bouquet that was gleefully snapped by the aimless grasping of the dancers. Someone had brought them in their back pocket as a sly reference to Morrissey.

The decor was modelled on a Moroccan Kasbah with ornate iron lanterns, as big as disco balls, which hung down on delicately linked chains that allowed them to be swung back and forth by the crowd. Eventually, one of the fixtures got out of control and crashed against the ceiling, sending shattered pieces of glass into the brightly dyed hair below. A gang of plastered twenty-somethings tried to lift one of their friends into the air to crowd surf, but the bouncer grabbed his purple Nikes and pulled him back down.

The bartenders had left their post to try to clean up the girl's blood. One of them irritably pushed through the crowd, clearing a path with a flashlight, while his partner followed behind with a mop, jostled violently by the dancers' passion. It was futile. The blood had already stained the hems of everyone's designer jeans and sneakers.

Several minutes earlier, I had noticed the girl on the other side of the room. She was attractive with dark flowing hair and a draped sequined blouse. Staring through the jumble of legs, I saw that she was missing one of her braded leather sandals. She stood elegantly on one leg like a flamingo, her bare foot propped against her knee to protect it from the shattered glass. She scanned the dark floor of the club with the dim blue light of her open phone, while the two boys who were with her looked on their hands and knees. The search was on, until she heard the guitar intro of 'Bigmouth Strikes Again'. Suddenly, filled with aggressive abandon, she slapped the phone closed and I saw her lips mouth an exaggerated "fuck it", faintly audible even over the tremendous bass. She grabbed the shoulders of her two friends, pulling them up to dance as she slammed her bare foot down into the hazardous floor. I was swept up into the flow of bodies as she disappeared into the crowd. Everyone sung along with the music: "Now I know how Joan of Arc felt" (Morrissey and Marr 1986).

DAN JACOBSON: We have been discussing what we think about this girl ever since this happened.[1] On the one hand she might have been drunk, or coked up, and sometimes you go out of your mind when you are out partying. But on the other hand, this girl with her overtly romantic gesture personifies something about The Smiths which reveals their essence. She found a means to approach sincerity at Sway,[2] a place where sincerity itself has become insincere. This transformation happens by collapsing the present into a broader historicized past.

IAN: It is not so much that the present and the past collapse into each other, becoming one thing, it is more like there is an alignment that occurs, allowing us to see the difference in context. What has remained the same? What is different? "Has the world changed, or have I changed?" (Morrissey and Marr 1985). The historical point of reference in question here is Joan of Arc. There is a triangulation between Joan of Arc as a symbol, Morrissey's use of this symbol in the song 'Bigmouth' and the girl at Sway whose gesture we are analysing.

DAN: Indeed, it does not take much of a leap of imagination to see her as a veritable patron saint of Smiths Night. The symbol of Joan of Arc has been used for many different purposes, but the themes that it usually calls to mind are: heroism, religious passion, nationalism, gender reversal, teenage fearlessness, dying for your cause and abandonment. Morrissey assumes all of these connotations in his comparison of himself to Joan of Arc in 'Bigmouth'.

IAN: It is pretty clear that this song is an attack directed at the music industry. What makes it the most successful of Morrissey's songs in this vein is that it is not totally up-front about this, like for example, 'Frankly Mr. Shankly' (The Smiths 1985) or 'Paint A Vulgar Picture' (The Smiths 1987). It takes the form of a love song – or at least a song around relationship issues – the typical form of expression in popular music. Morrissey uses this form to vent his frustration. But this is not the sexual frustration that would usually be found in a pop song, it is the frustration of the misunderstood artist.

DAN: Exactly, it takes the cliché and turns it on its head. The narrative of the song is that "Bigmouth" has sarcastically insulted his lover: "Sweetness, I was only joking when I said I'd like to smash every tooth in your head" (Morrissey and Marr 1986). "Sweetness" does not understand the irony underlying this offhanded insult, and continues to hold a grudge against him. This lack of forgiveness prompts Morrissey to take the hyperbole to another level by comparing himself to Joan of Arc burning at the stake for her sins. The subtext is, of course, that Morrissey feels that he is always misunderstood and misquoted by the music press. However, this misunderstanding is flirted with, and occurs precisely because Morrissey's lyrics are always full of this kind of ironic ambiguity.

IAN: You are referring to a certain self-awareness about operating on several contradictory levels at once – a double consciousness if you will. Morrissey exhibits this kind of intention all the time. I remember you showing me a video of him being interviewed on *The Old Grey Whistle Test* (1985) where he attempts to explain this point:

Interviewer: Are you as profoundly miserable as everybody wants to believe?

Morrissey: No, not really, not really, again that just simply becomes somewhat of a pigeonhole, somewhat of a tag, if you like – label.

Interviewer: But the lyrics would suggest that you're permanently on the verge of despair and suicide.

Morrissey: Well, in a way I think they do, but in another more serious and affecting way they don't because I feel that I write with humour, and I never get recognition for this. But, when people say Morrissey is so miserable, to me its just lazy journalism … I don't want to make it sound trivial, but we're not doom laden by any means.

IAN: The two levels that Morrissey mentions in this interview are absolutely essential. He resists easy commercial categorization, which for Morrissey is not the same thing as resisting popularity – after all he named one of his albums *The World Won't Listen* (The Smiths 1986). He does not want an exclusively underground following like Mark E. Smith and The Fall. It seems that Morrissey's lyrics are able to be part of "alternative" music because they have these contradictory levels of meaning. I would also add that Morrissey is a contrarian and if the interviewer had asked, "Are you really always as witty in real life as everybody wants to believe?" He would have responded that really he's miserable. And if the interviewer pressed him, "But the lyrics suggest that you live to take the piss out of everyone." He would have responded, "Well, in a way that's what I'm doing, but in another more serious and affecting way I write out of despair, and I never get recognition for this." I sense that what he is really angry about is that the question never would have been posed in this way. Did anyone decide to pick up a Smiths record because they thought it would be funny? (Ewing 2010).

DAN: When I started listening to The Smiths, it was because I was miserable. The more I have listened to them though, the more I enjoy Morrissey's sense of humour. I think 'Bigmouth' would be too melodramatic if he did not have satirical images like "as the flames rose to her Roman nose and her hearing aid started to melt" (Morrissey and Marr 1985). There are even the little snippets of Morrissey's voice pitch shifted, almost like a caricature of a girl-group backing vocal. Even though this tragic–romantic fervour is being referenced, it is also being made fun of simultaneously. In short, he is making himself ridiculous in order to be serious.

IAN: That is exactly what is happening with the girl at Sway. She made a ridiculous scene, and now we are discussing it as though it is serious. Maybe I am making assumptions, but she seems like one of these girls who moves to the city, and probably has to have an internship so her parents can see that she is in New York for a reason. But her real reason is the parties and the shopping. I am not saying this is a shallow existence, maybe – like most people – she just does not know what she really wants yet. But despite this, she really does know how Joan of Arc felt – she knows it physically. She *feels* how Joan of Arc felt, along with Morrissey, who feels it aesthetically, like when you read, and you can feel what a character in a work of literature feels. Instead of burning at the stake, she bled all over everyone at the club – just look at the relics she made out of your converse high tops! She becomes a "misplaced Joan of Arc".[3] But remember, this is happening all at once; she is dancing because 'Bigmouth' is playing.

DAN: Misplaced in the sense that Sway is not a place where you would find sincere passion. There is always a certain detachment. Sway, in the true tradition of "downtown cool", is a place where irony itself is worn as a badge of sophistication.

IAN: This attitude seems like the fallout from the New York of the 1970s and 1980s: CBGBs, New York Dolls, Warhol and No Wave. But this idea of "cool" has been eaten up and regurgitated over and over again for the last 25 years. At this point there is a certain bored nostalgia. As the composer, Glenn Branca, recently complained:

> Is it that people just don't want to hear anything new? [...] Of course, we could all just listen to all of our old albums [...]. there are a lot of them now. Why bother making any new ones? Why bother doing anything new at all?
>
> (2009)

If we are all just going to listen to our old records, then the difference between an artist and a non-artist becomes nothing more than knowing what record to play next. This does not sound paralyzing to me, it sounds like it could be a party. It is just a different kind of energy now. I think this is what Branca is concerned with – that nothing seems to have the same urgency anymore. That it is a "borrowed nostalgia for the unremembered eighties" (Murphy 2002).

DAN: Yes exactly! It is a DJ culture: a sort of "LCD Soundsystem style" re-presentation of pretty much anything that has been considered cool in the last 40 years.[4] And it is a "borrowed nostalgia", it is not as if the crowd at Sway is necessarily interested in The Smiths. For the most part, they are only interested in going out.

IAN: But they go to this party in particular, out of the hundred others that they could be at. There must be an identification with something about The Smiths that keeps them coming back week after week. The party has been going on since the 1990s and there is always a line down the block.

DAN: I think the appeal goes back to this idea of two contradictory levels that we identified in Morrissey's interview. I have seen a girl arrive wearing a garbage-bag as a dress, and other girls dressed up fabulously as presents wrapped in giant bows. They wear fake prescription glasses, sailor uniforms, ripped leather pants or English lumberjack shirts with kimono sleeves. But of course, they all show up and sing along with Morrissey, proclaiming in one voice: "I would go out tonight but I haven't got a stitch to wear" (Morrissey and Marr 1984). And the party is on a Sunday night, really the most unsuitable night for a party.

IAN: But it is a great opportunity to sing 'Everyday Is Like Sunday' (Morrissey 1988), although if you think about it, the lyrics would be more appropriate to sing on any other night.

DAN: It is the same way that the DJ[5] always plays 'Panic', which invites the crowd to chant "Hang the DJ!" although the songs on rotation say everything to me about their lives (Morrissey and Marr 1986). Maybe it is an appropriate song to play; this is a Smiths *Dance Party*. The Smiths are not exactly the first band you would think to play in a dance club. Morrissey has never written a lyric like "I went to a party and wanted to dance all night, so I swivel my hips and shake 'em on down to the ground. I wanna dance!" (ESG 1982). All of Morrissey's songs are about inaction. He does not want to go out dancing, he would rather be alone, go to sleep and never wake up (Morrissey and Marr 1985).

IAN: And if he does go out to a club, he is just going to stand on his own because he knows he is going to end up going home to cry (Morrissey and Marr 1984). There is a difference between being lonely while you are alone and being lonely in public. When you are alone, you can preserve the fantasy that "you might meet somebody who really loves you" (Morrissey and Marr 1984). But when you are around other people, loneliness has a different, more egoistic, quality. The idea of a Smiths Dance Party in New York, where everyone is constantly alone in a crowd, explores this distinction.

DAN: All in all, we are talking about a place where the crowd will wait 15 minutes to push their way up to the bar and order Manhattan-priced Curaçao cocktails, Negroni martinis, or whatever other brightly coloured drink they can think of. They sit on the divans and roll their eyes at Chloë Sevigny "disco-training" her way through to the VIP room only to work her way back to the bar ten minutes later. They smoke a Nat Sherman or maybe a joint for the sheer "naughtiness" of it all. As the night progresses and they move onto the dance floor, they put their hands daintily over their hearts or perhaps on their hips.

IAN: It is a very stylized pose, but there is a casualness about it too; it is like sloppy voguing. There is a sense of fashion photography, but there is also a consciousness of the poses that Morrissey makes on stage.

DAN: I guess that is why in the middle of all of this, it is shocking that a person would end up bleeding all over everyone. How could anyone in a downtown club be truly serious about suffering in the name of the music? This kind of action is the opposite of the very cool and affected way that most people behave. It breaks all of the rules, and she becomes a "misplaced Joan of Arc" just like Morrissey in 'Bigmouth'.

IAN: Yes, but the relationships between these three connections are actually more rich and complex. It would be inappropriate for her to bleed everywhere at *any* club. The only reason why we are able to bring this girl and her action into this field of references, making this an academic paper instead of just another bar story, is a precedent that Morrissey has set by his use of historical material. He does this through using lyrics borrowed from other texts, samples from BBC sound effects compilations and the photographs he uses as "cover stars" for the records. For example, on the cover of the 'Bigmouth Strikes Again' 12-inch, he uses an image of James Dean on a motorcycle wearing glasses (Morrissey and Marr 1985).

DAN: It is interesting that the image would not be of Joan of Arc, perhaps from Dreyer's *The Passion of Joan of Arc* (1928). It is easy to imagine Morrissey using a still of Maria Falconetti's face in an expression of religious ecstasy and pain. He did something similar to this on 1986's 'Shoplifters Of The World' single when he chose to use a picture of Elvis on the cover in conjunction with a reference to an Elvis lyric.[6] There's no mention of James Dean on 'Bigmouth'.

IAN: But putting James Dean on the cover is just like putting Joan of Arc on the cover. James Dean is another figure that stands for teenage rebellion and died tragically young. Morrissey further emphasizes the connection between himself and James Dean (and by extension Joan of Arc) by placing a cropped version of the cover photo on the verso as well. It seems to emphasize both James Dean's youthful teenage appearance and the fact that he is wearing glasses. Morrissey often wore glasses himself as a statement about his affinity for bookishness and the first rock n' roll stars.

I have noticed that these references also colour the source material. Lately I have been looking at a photography book called *Rock 'N' Roll Times* (Volmer 1983). The book is organized into two parts. The first shows images of The Beatles during their amphetamine-fueled residency in Hamburg in the early 1960s. The second part contains images of the 'Rocker' subculture that was developing in Hamburg and Paris around this new music. I tracked down this book expressly because Morrissey used photos sourced from it for *The World Won't Listen* (The Smiths 1986). While looking through it, I can not separate my own gaze from my awareness of Morrissey engaged in the same activity. I cannot simply view the images alone for what they are because his act of looking at them before me has left an indelible trace over my perception. In the same way, my ideas about Manchester in the 1960s are largely based on The Smiths. It seems to me that there is a connection between this modern literary process that Morrissey uses as a means of artistic expression and the way that the crowd at Sway expresses itself.

DAN: You're right because *Rock 'N' Roll Times* also shows that these strange social rules that exist inside exclusive clubs like Sway have been around since the beginning of rock n' roll. Jorgen Volmer shares an anecdote about the Kaiserkeller, a club that the 'Rocker' sub-culture centred around.

> I remember an incident in the Kaiserkeller. It was The Beatles' last day before going back to Liverpool for a few months. I had the idea to bring them five roses. Astrid [Kirchherr] was supposed to give them to George [Harrison]. It was difficult to get those long-stemmed roses into the Kaiserkeller without detection. We hid them under our table. But while this rose idea was created in the outside world earlier that day, we now once again were slowly absorbed into the dream world we loved, where our adoration had to take the form of submission. Our intended ritual – a gift of roses – had to be re-evaluated, re-thought, and at last discarded. I ended up destroying the roses under the table with my feet.
>
> (Volmer 1983: 27)

DAN: The rules at the Kaiserkeller are different than those at Sway, but they both serve to construct what Volmer terms the "dream world". In the "outside world" an act like giving flowers as a farewell gesture makes perfect sense. But when brought into this other context, just the thought of this action becomes embarrassing, something a leather-clad rocker might beat you up for.

IAN: Instead of destroying flowers with her feet, our "misplaced Joan of Arc" destroyed her feet with broken glass.

DAN: When Volmer and his friends brought the flowers into the club, they immediately exposed the sub-cultural rules of their "dream world", in the same way that dancing in broken glass exposed something about the sub-culture at Sway.

IAN: The question is: Why not express everything in a more direct way? Why all of this ironic detachment and double meaning?

DAN: I think we can answer these questions by analysing The Smiths' music in more depth. Morrissey's play of intertextuality extends to the general artistic methods used by The Smiths as well. Look for example at The Smiths song *par excellence*, 'There Is A Light That Never Goes Out' (Morrissey and Marr 1985). The riff used in this song by Johnny Marr and the lyrics sung by Morrissey have a very complex history whose genealogy traces the path of how we got to a place where sincerity can be insincere. Let me read you a quote from Johnny Marr that will begin to introduce this idea:

> There is this little in-joke in there to illustrate how intellectual I was getting. At the time everyone was so into the Velvet Underground, and they stole the intro to 'There She Goes Again' – da da da-da, da da-da-da, Dah Dah! – from The Rolling Stones version of 'Hitch Hike', the Marvin Gaye song. I just wanted to put that in there to see whether the press would say, "Oh, it's The Velvet Underground!" 'Cos I knew I was smarter than that. I was listening to what The Velvet Underground were listening to.
>
> (Goddard 2002: 187)

IAN: There is something strange about Johnny Marr's quote though. Why would he insist that he is taking the riff from The Rolling Stones' cover, instead of from the original Marvin Gaye version? I mean, if anything, would not that be even harder for the music journalists to identify? I can not quite imagine Johnny Marr sitting around agonizing over whether to use The Stones' version or the original. He is an artist and he worked through this process in his own idiosyncratic manner, and this reveals something about his taste. It could simply be that The Stones' version was what he was actually listening to and thinking about. So what is the attraction? I think it has to do with The Smiths having, in effect, the same ambition as The Rolling Stones: to be the archetypical rock band. Morrissey and Marr's partnership can be read as an historical re-enactment of the partnership between Jagger and Richards. There is certainly an understanding of this parallel at Sway. The DJ has cued 'Jumpin' Jack Flash' right before cutting to 'Bigmouth' (Jagger and Richards 1968).[7] In the same way that we have been discussing a "misplaced Joan of Arc", The Smiths can be seen as a "misplaced Rolling Stones".

DAN: Both of these bands are centred around the collaboration of the lead singer and the guitarist. We have been talking primarily about Morrissey's contribution, but it is important to consider Marr's process as well to understand what is happening in their music.

To further expand upon Marr's explanation, let me share my understanding of the historical progression of 'There Is A Light That Never Goes Out'. In 1962, Marvin Gaye released a single entitled 'Hitch Hike'. Its lyrics, which are very typical of early Motown and R&B records, deal with love and the stupidity and mania that characterize our actions when we are under its influence. In 'Hitch Hike', Gaye sings of his commitment to travel all over the world to find his 'baby', whom he fears he will never see again. Gaye's soulfulness gives the listener a genuine feeling of excitement, and empathy, while the lyrics give us a sense of desperation that is only adequately described as distinctly African American with its description of poverty and outsider discrimination "Got no money in my pocket so I'm gonna have to hitch hike all the way" (Gaye and Stevenson 1962).

In 1965, The Rolling Stones, great fans and admirers of Gaye, covered the song, and translated the soulfulness of the original into a white British-invasion screamer. It is a straight cover, except now, being preformed by a white group, it has become viable for broader white audience in a way that Marvin Gaye never could. The white audience really wanted to hear black people's songs without actually listening to black people sing them.

IAN: Mick Jagger does not quite capture the specificity of what Gaye is singing about.[8] However, is not this what pop music is? It is about entertainment. Pop music aestheticizes thoughts and emotions, allowing you to feel them *only* through a process of commercialization. It is a product manufactured by a company to make money, but this product (i.e. a record) can become a medium for artistic expression. There is a consciousness of this contradiction in both the music of The Rolling Stones and The Smiths. Both groups are engaged with what it means to be a popular band.[9] By interpolating The Rolling Stones, The Smiths were able to become historically "displaced".

DAN: So, if Johnny Marr insists he took the riff from The Rolling Stones, it must be because he felt alienated by the more straightforward meaning in the original Marvin Gaye song. The genuine feeling that Gaye expresses would be naïve to reiterate in this new context. Those sentiments would ignore the contradictions art faces in a society where commercialism is the dominant mode. Everything is now a "product", but who would want to buy into a product, either financially or emotionally, that exhibits no awareness of its own commodification? This sceptical attitude is projected at Sway as well.

Likewise, The Velvet Underground were one of the first bands to make music where artistic integrity was more important than popularity. In 1967, when The Velvet Underground took the riff, they were no longer doing a cover of 'Hitch Hike'; they were doing an ironic critique of it. On 'There She Goes Again' (Reed 1967) the percussive quality of the riff is emphasized and paired with lyrics about misogynism and general downtown depravity. It literally stands in for the sounds of clinched fists beating a vamp. This resulting combination is a further example of the double consciousness that we have been discussing. Pop music is revealed to be an empty fantasy, and this new sarcastic version, complete with Motown-style backing vocals, is the definitive "hip" version.

IAN: The Smiths are more indirect, they are consciously making pop songs, but pop songs inheriting the artistic tradition of The Velvet Underground. Songs that manage to make the conventions of pop music meaningful and personal. They are able to do this because the riff and the lyrics were stolen. It is the same sensibility as when a DJ plays records at a club. Even though the records may not obviously have anything to do with one another, a DJ is able to take them and put them together, recreating a "live" experience within the club for that given moment. I mean, even Morrissey's lyrics are mostly taken from The New York Dolls' 'Lonely Planet Boy': "You're out drivin' in your car [...] But how could you be drivin' down by my home, when you know I ain't got one" (Johansen 1973). He uses other people's words and music to speak about himself. He avoids embarrassment because, on one level, he is not confessing anything about himself, he is not a singer-songwriter with an "acoustic guitar".[10]

While actually, on another level, he is able to be totally sincere and personal. But "personal" is perhaps too relative a term. I get the feeling that Morrissey's aesthetic experiences are more real to him than his lived experiences. It is counter-intuitive, almost perverse, that you would feel something as deeply as you do when you listen to a song – perhaps even more deeply than with an actual experience.

DAN: Morrissey deals with this paradox in his music all of the time. Oscar Wilde is one of his most important influences and he tends to echo the sentiment that "poor, probable, uninteresting human life will only try to reproduce the marvels of art […] Art never expresses anything but itself" (Wilde 1889: 918). If a song can save your life, it can do so in that it is a song, and not your life (Morrissey and Marr 1985). The most accurate way for him to express himself is to use stolen words and motifs. For example both the original 'Hitch Hike' and 'There Is A Light That Never Goes Out' centre around the idea of needing a ride, wanting to be picked up, taken away down the highway in search of love. It is almost as if Morrissey is able to recreate Gaye's original tone through his ironic presentation, and translate the personal hardship from one milieu into another. In this way The Smiths are able to give us a window through which we can view the pop culture of the past. This is how the girl at Sway can be viewed as ironic and sincere simultaneously. She embodies Joan of Arc mirroring Morrissey in his invocation of Joan of Arc. It is ironic and sincere, historical and current. At The Smiths Dance Party, Ben Cho's DJ sets invoke the method through which The Smiths made their music. He facilitates this whole referential process through his style of "DJ'n". He plays The Smiths and other Manchester bands, but also girl groups, and rockabilly. Benji knows what The Smiths were listening to and includes these sources in his sets. He expresses something about his loves and hates and passions through playing other people's music.

IAN: As we said before, the party itself seems like it is not so much about going out to a club: it is about "going out to a club" very much in quotation marks. This party is a self-conscious comment on going-out in general. As Ben Cho told us, he used to sit by himself, play chess and listen to The Smiths on Sunday nights before he started the party at Sway. He said "I decided it would be nice if there were some other people there to hear what I was playing for myself." Instead of going out to a club, it is as if each person there is having their own night in. These psychological spaces are analogous to the bedrooms documented in *Rock 'N' Roll Times*. There are these photographs of the 'Rockers' sitting in their rooms listening to records. You immediately notice that on their walls are all of these posters of their idols like James Dean and Elvis, in the same way as Morrissey would put them on the covers of 'Bigmouth Strikes Again' and 'Shoplifters Of The World'. It is lying in awe on your bedroom floor, listening to the songs that made you cry and the songs that made you laugh. Is not this what is at the heart of rock 'n' roll? It is the vulnerability of listening to music and becoming who you want be, if only for a moment, by becoming someone else. Sway creates a dream world where this can happen in a crowd.

Notes

1. Our methodological approach took the form of a conversation, centring primarily around the records we were listening to. These sources offered us access into Morrissey's thought process as he was constructing the music of The Smiths. His explorations set a precedent for ours. As we were writing our conversations down and revising them, it sometimes became unclear who had originally said what. Thoughts were transposed, exchanged between us and grew offshoots into many directions. We would imagine that this is similar to compositional process of writing music in a band.

2. Sway Lounge LLC is a nightclub located at 305 Spring St, New York, NY 10013. Their website is accessible at www.swaylounge.com.

3. The term is borrowed from the Patti Smith song Kimberly:

> Ah, here I stand again in this old 'lectric whirlwind,
> The sea rushes up my knees like flame
> And I feel like just some misplaced Joan of Arc
> And the cause is you lookin' up at me
>
> (Smith, Lanier and Kral 1975)

4. 2002's *Losing My Edge* is LCD Soundsystem's 7: 53min. opus on this particular breed of New Yorker. James Murphy sarcastically name drops his record collection, gently makes fun of every downtown cliché but at the same time, weaves a sentimental meditation on getting older, no longer in touch with this idea of cool (see Murphy 2002).

5. The DJ is Ben Cho who started the party, the official name being "Ben Cho's Regulars Only Night". He dropped out of fashion school but still became famous by designing handbags and the aforementioned gift-wrapped present dresses.

6. On 'Half A Person', the B-side of the single, Morrissey sings, "I went to London and I booked myself in at the Y – WCA" (Morrissey and Marr 1986). He is paraphrasing Elvis' 'Guitar Man', "I hitch-hiked all the way down to Memphis, got a room at the YMCA" (*ELVIS – Trouble/Guitar Man* (Remastered Audio)). Elvis recorded Jimmy Reed's 'Guitar Man' as part of a medley to open his 1968 comeback special in order to harken back to his early days when he was young and successful. Morrissey seems to be harkening back to his early days when he was unsuccessful, because the girl of his affections liked him more when he was hopelessly poor. This comparison shows yet again the historical alignments that Morrissey is always creating.

7. Johnny Marr has said that he modeled the guitar part on 'Bigmouth Strikes Again' from 'Jumpin' Jack Flash' (Goddard 2002: 184). The Rolling Stones released this single as a return to form after their psychedelic experimentation. Similarly, 'Bigmouth Strikes Again' was a comeback single for The Smiths after a nine-month gap since their previous single 'The Boy With The Thorn In His Side'. This was the longest gap in their short career.

8. A 1964 promotional short film makes this evident. It opens with an image of The Rolling Stones, dressed in their "swinging 60s" British outfits, walking down the side of a speedway. The narrator intones:

> Just another lot of hitch hikers. That's what they look like to motorists speeding towards Hull […] Little do they know, they're having their legs pulled […] because these are five of the most talented boys in show business: The Rolling Stones!

The hitch-hiking in the original Gaye song was an authentic image of despair and hardship, but in The Stones' version becomes a façade and practical joke – a marketing tool for image and fad. Take for another example this excerpt from the back cover of The Rolling Stones American release *Out of Our Heads* (1965) on which 'Hitch Hike' first appears:

> It's a new ROLLING STONES album, strictly OUT OF their HEADS, and out of those five talented heads come twelve great new sides recorded in LONDON, CHICAGO, and HOLLYWOOD!

It is clear that the promoters of this record are not concerned with the heartache of love, nor with a genuine desire to get people "OUT OF their HEADS" as it is so strangely typeset, but rather with selling records. There is a danger that the songs are left empty, bankrupt and devoid of any real feeling.

9. 'I Can't Get No Satisfaction' also appears on the same album as 'Hitch Hike'. On 'Satisfaction' the integration of art and commercialism is much more complex. Mick Jagger sings "When I'm drivin' in my car and that man comes on the radio, He's tellin' me more and more about some useless information, supposed to fire my imagination" (Jagger and Richard 1965). The tension here between commodity and art is that Mick Jagger *became the man* on the radio and it is 'Satisfaction' that did it by breaking them in America.

10. In 'Shakespeare's Sister' "Mamma" makes the assumption: "I thought that if you had an acoustic guitar it meant you were a protest singer" (Morrissey and Marr 1985). Morrissey is concerned with the fact that his music is not a spontaneous and direct form of expression like a hippie at a train station. He feels embarrassed that anyone would even think that this image has anything to with him.

References

Branca, G. (2009) 'The end of music', Opinionator Blog-NYTimes.com, available: http: //opinionator. blogs.nytimes.com/2009/11/24/the-end-of-music.

La Passion de Jeanne d'Arc (1928) Dir. Carl Theodore Dreyer. Criterion Collection, New York.

ESG. (1982) Sound recording, Dance. On: *ESG Says Dance to the Beat of Moody.* US: 99 Records, 99–10 EP.

Jagger, M. and Richards, K. (1968) Sound recording. 'Jumpin' Jack Flash'. US: The Rolling Stones, London Records, L 45.908.

Gaye, M. (1962) 'Hitch Hike', US: Tamla, available: http: //www.youtube.com/watch?v=Gwv HfwDfapI.

Gaye, M. and Stevenson, P. (1965) Sound recording, 'Hitch Hike'. On: *Out Of Our Heads.* The Rolling Stones, US: London Records, LI 3429.

Goddard, S. (2002) *The Smiths: The Songs that Saved Your Life*, 3rd edn. UK: Surrey, Reynolds and Hearn.

Johansen, D. (1973) Sound recording, 'Lonely Planet Boy'. On: *New York Dolls.* Mercury Records, SRM-1-675.

Morrissey, S. (1988) Sound recording, 'Everyday Is Like Sunday'. On: *Viva Hate.* His Masters Voice, 7 90180 1.

Morrissey, S. and Marr, J. (1985) Sound recording, 'Asleep'. On: 'The Boy With The Thorn In His Side'. The Smiths, Rough Trade, RTT 191.

Morrissey, S. and Marr, J. (1986) Sound recording, 'Bigmouth Strikes Again'. The Smiths, Rough Trade, RTT 192.

Morrissey, S. and Marr, J. (1986) Sound recording, 'Half A Person'. On: *Shoplifters Of The World*. The Smiths, Rough Trade, RTT 192.

Morrissey, S. and Marr, J. (1986) Sound recording, 'Panic'. The Smiths, Rough Trade, RT 193.

Morrissey, S. and Marr, J. (1984) Sound recording, 'How Soon Is Now'. On: 'William, It Was Really Nothing'. The Smiths, Rough Trade, RTT 166.

Morrissey, S. and Marr, J. (1984) Sound recording, 'Please, Please, Please Let Me Get What I Want'. On: *'William, It Was Really Nothing'*. The Smiths, Rough Trade, RTT 166.

Morrissey, S. and Marr, J. (1985) Sound recording, 'The Queen Is Dead'. On: *The Queen is Dead.* The Smiths, Rough Trade, Rough 96.

Morrissey, S. and Marr, J. (1985) Sound recording, 'Shakespeare's Sister'. The Smiths, Rough Trade, RTT 181.

Morrissey, S. and Marr, J. (1985) Sound recording, 'There Is A Light That Never Goes Out'. On: *The Queen is Dead.* The Smiths, Rough Trade, Rough 96.

Morrissey, S. and Marr, J. (1983) Sound recording, 'This Charming Man'. The Smiths, Rough Trade, RTT 136.

Murphy, J. (2002) Sound recording, 'Loosing My Edge'. LCD Soundsystem, DFA 2123.

'The Making of "Meat Is Murder"' Interview by Mark Allen (1985) *Old Grey Whistle Test*, 12 February.

Reed, L. (1967) Sound recording, 'There She Goes Again'. On: *The Velvet Underground and Nico.* The Velvet Underground, Verve, V6-5008.

The Rolling Stones (1964) 'The Rolling Stones – Play ABC Cinema Hull 1964 in Colour', available: http: //www.youtube.com/watch?v=GwvHfwDfapI.

Smith, P. , Lanier, A. and Kral, I. (1975), Sound recording, 'Kimberly'. On: *Horses.* Patti Smith, Artista, AL 4066.

The Smiths (1986) Sound recording, *The World Won't Listen*. Rough Trade, Rough 101.

Volmer, J. (1983) *Rock 'N' Roll Times: The Style and Spirit of the Early Beatles and Their First Fans.* Woodstock, NY: Overlook.

Wilde, O. (1889) 'The Decay of Lying', in *The Works of Oscar Wilde.* London: G. F. Maine.

Chapter 14

Talent Borrows, Genius Steals: Morrissey and the Art of Appropriation

Lee Brooks

On 24th November, 2008, David Cohen wrote an article in the *New Zealand National Business Review* under the headline 'Talent borrows, genius steals', discussing charges of plagiarism levelled by the *Sunday Star Times* at writer and broadcaster Noelle McCarthy. Cohen's choice of subject matter is of less interest here than the article's title and its opening passage, which leads off with the humble apology that "we just realised we plagiarised that nifty line you see in the header above from the great Steven Morrissey" (Cohen 2008). Morrissey had, of course, decreed that the line in question be etched into the B side of the 12-inch single of 'Bigmouth Strikes Again', some 22 years earlier. Perhaps the most interesting element of Cohen's self-confessed act of plagiarism is brought to our attention by a poster known only as Chad in the comments section of the publication's online version when he states that the quote "is actually attributed to Pablo Picasso. Morrissey stole it" (Cohen 2008). The fact that the quote is more usually attributed to Morrissey's long time hero Oscar Wilde simply serves to make the irony all the more tangible. What this confusion does reveal, however, is the way in which Morrissey has, throughout his career, appropriated popular cultural imagery in an eclectic fashion and combined it with his uniquely quirky, perhaps studiedly awkward, persona and a sense of whimsical lyricism to conjure up visions of a nation outside of time or space, and a personal identity that is at once a homage to a bygone time and a celebration of a rootless, postmodern condition. This was perhaps nowhere more clearly illustrated than in the song that truly brought The Smiths to the public consciousness, 'This Charming Man', with its famous evocation of a jumped-up pantry boy who never knew his place being almost a direct quote from Sir Laurence Olivier's tirade at Michael Caine's 'blue eyed wop' in Joseph L. Mankiewicz' 1972 film *Sleuth*. In many ways, the combination of artful peculation and broadly drawn, darkly comic characterization in Morrissey's lyrics for this song act almost as a manifesto for a career that has now spanned over 25 years and more than 20 albums.

It is the intention of this chapter to investigate both Morrissey's "genius" for stealing and the seemingly random manner in which he has juxtaposed the fruit of these heists with other cultural references to create a discontinuous narrative that weaves throughout his solo career. In the course of this study I will address three major ways in which these creative loans and juxtapositions have taken place. Firstly I will discuss the way that Morrissey has used both direct quotation, paraphrasing and oblique cultural references within his lyrics. Secondly I will investigate his appropriation of images from within visual mediums such as cover art, promotional video and stage backdrops. Thirdly, and finally, I will turn our attention to examples of the way in which his musical collaborators have complemented his lyrics by occasionally borrowing from the annals of musical history. In taking this circuitous journey through his various solo recordings, I will attempt to identify some of the recurring themes that are woven through this body of work and consider the further ways in which this particular mode of expression has mediated our understanding of Morrissey himself.

In attempting to gain such an understanding of Morrissey's collaging of popular cultural imagery, we must, of course, acknowledge the heritage of just this kind of borrowing at many levels throughout the sphere of popular music. It would not, for instance, take a trained musicologist to listen to Bill Haley and the Comets' 1956 rock and roll classic 'Rock Around The Clock' to notice that the rhythm and metre of its verses were almost identical to Hank Williams' 1947 single 'Move It On Over'. This sort of musical commandeering is anything but rare in the history of popular music, and has indeed always been an acknowledged mode of operation for genres like country and folk music. Such genres have long traditions of lifting parts of, or in many cases entire melodies, from one song and re-using them in another. Socialist anthem 'The Red Flag' for instance originally set Jim Connell's 1889 lyrics to the tune of 'The White Cockade', a melody also often associated with the pro-Jacobite Robert Burns poem 'My Love Was Born in Aberdeen' but has latterly been accompanied by 'Lauriger Horatius', an air more commonly linked with the German Christmas Carol 'O Tannenbaum'. It is also quite clear that this practice has extended to the re-use of lyrics as well as the recycling of melodies. Indeed, in an article for *The New York Times* in 2006 Motoko Rich pointed out just such re-purposing of the words of Confederate Civil War poet Henry Timrod by Bob Dylan throughout his album *Modern Times*, even going as far as to suggest that "Critics and fans of Dylan's have long described his magpie tendencies, looking upon that as a manifestation of his genius, not unlike other great writers and poets like T. S. Eliot or James Joyce who have referenced past works" (Rich 2006). It is not, therefore, the purpose of this chapter to suggest that Morrissey is unique in his borrowing of, and allusions to, existing imagery. Neither is it my intention to raise the spectre of plagiarism in an accusatorial manner that might imply that the impact or originality of his work is in some way compromised, but rather, that he has, just as the title of this chapter suggests, recognized these traits in many of the great artists who have gone before him and embraced them in his own work.

The public image: Constructing Morrissey

If the juxtaposition of borrowed and original imagery of 'This Charming Man' set the tone for his early work, then it could equally be argued that it is his first solo single 'Suedehead', and most notably Tim Broad's promotional video that began the process of constructing the post-Smiths world of Morrissey. As Erin Hazard has discussed in an earlier chapter in this volume, while its early scenes would seem to be a jumble of references to, and perhaps a visual exorcising of, the ghost of The Smiths, it is in its focus on James Dean that Morrissey's artful employment of imagery is at its most interesting. Through the introduction of a young boy resembling James Dean's cousin Marcus (Markie) Winslow delivering a copy of Dean's favourite book, Antoine de Saint-Exupéry's *Le Petit Prince*, Morrissey is transported to Dean's hometown of Fairmont, Indiana, and for the remainder of the video is effectively cast in the role of Dean. Significantly, the Fairmont portion of the video appears to be set in an almost mythical past in which Morrissey uses a vintage camera to take photographs and is dressed in a retro style that could be located in any era from the 1950s to the single's 1988 release date. Indeed, in the scene that shows Morrissey copying a famous pose by the Cal Dean gravestone, there is a hint of a celebration of Dean the legend rather than the man; a sense in which James Dean and Cal Trask are combined into a third entity, in a literal embodiment of the title of Morrissey's 1983 book *James Dean Is Not Dead*. Indeed, in this mythologizing of James Dean and the visual merging of his on-screen persona with Morrissey's own image, there is perhaps a sense in which, for a fleeting moment, Cal represents the intertwining of the Dean and Morrissey facades, two meticulously constructed and equally complex and contradictory signs that at once never were and always will be. In this context, while it is of course important to consider director Broad's role in the film, and despite Morrissey's recent insistence that he has very little creative input into his videos,[1] it is difficult to believe that, given Morrissey's connection to the subject matter, he was not closely involved in the construction of the 'Suedehead' promo's imagery. Indeed, it is in the film's reference to pre-existing relationships between Morrissey and a romantically drawn image of a mythic past that we can begin to identify a recurring theme.

The fascination with James Dean as a construct is perhaps also hinted at earlier in the bathroom scene of the video when the camera briefly pans across the "because I am" letter which bears the signature "James (Brando, Clift) Dean", seemingly in accordance with Elia Kazan's assertion that Dean considered himself to be a synthesis of his two great heroes. That Morrissey should align himself so closely with, and possibly even cast himself as, Dean in this video perhaps offers us an insight into the way that he has similarly constructed a persona from the personalities and characteristics of his own hero worship. Morrissey's celebrated insistence on the use of these heroes in Jo Slee's covers for virtually all of The Smiths' single releases, in place of the band themselves, may be an indication of a retreat into just such a carefully assembled visual style. Similarly his periodic use of physical imagery such as the now famous 1984 *Top of the Pops* appearance in which he performed 'Heaven Knows I'm Miserable Now', whilst wearing a hearing aid, provides us with further evidence of such a facade being constructed. Indeed, a brief investigation into the reasoning behind his adoption of the hearing aid reveals, as so often is the case with Morrissey, two very different stories. On the one hand an empathetic pop star showing solidarity with a young deaf fan who was too embarrassed to wear a hearing aid, while on the other a postmodern artist playfully sporting the stage prop as a gesture of homage towards a personal hero, deaf 1950s American recording star Johnny Ray. While the true nature of his reasoning in the adoption of such a prop might be obscure, perhaps this in itself is the most meaningful measure of its significance. The way in which either explanation, and sometimes both, has been embraced and frequently re-articulated over countless column inches in the music press, and endlessly debated by global fan communities on any number of websites, simply serves to reify the iconography of what the world understands Morrissey to represent. This ongoing construction of the Morrissey myth was perfectly illustrated during his November 2009 appearance on BBC Radio 4's national institution, *Desert Island Discs*. In her introduction to the show, presenter Kirsty Young described Morrissey as "an intensely private person" (Young 2009) before going on to recall an earlier assertion that he did not "really exist anywhere else in life" (Cameron 2004). That Morrissey himself, when challenged on this suggestion, should evade any form of public self-examination in favour of the throwaway remark that he "could be found in the Yellow Pages but nowhere else" adds further weight to the suspicion that he continues to carefully construct a *mélange* of cultural references into the persona of the "outsider's outsider" (Young 2009). The suspicion is only strengthened, throughout the entire interview, by his continued playful evasiveness and steadfast refusal to reveal anything of himself beyond the usual contrary and entertaining sound bites.

When considering this idea of Morrissey as a constructed, almost fictional, character, it is perhaps useful to consider the previously discussed example of Slee's famous cover art for The Smiths. If we accept that this use of Morrissey's own directory of popular cultural icons reflected something of the mythological personality that he was so central to developing for the band, then it is interesting to note that of all his solo albums only two, *Southpaw Grammar* and the *World of Morrissey* compilation album, feature cover stars other than Morrissey himself. Likewise, apart from the sleeves for his 1994 duet with Siouxsie Sioux ('Interlude'), two 1995 singles ('Boxers' and 'Dagenham Dave') and 1997's 'Roy's Keen', every other solo single release has featured a photograph of Morrissey on its cover. One is left to wonder if there is a sense in which this cover art is an admission that Morrissey's need to pay homage to the heroes of his past has been diluted by the fact that the images that these sleeves portray are now such a composite of these references that by displaying them he has himself become the tribute.

It is interesting to note that unlike the cover art of these recordings, Morrissey's live performances during the same period were played out in front of a series of stage backdrops featuring a selection of portraits of famous and occasionally infamous characters. The use of such iconic backdrops seems to be a practice that Morrissey has only really adopted during his solo career,[2] beginning with projected images of Yorkshire born poet, Edith Sitwell, and American movie actor, Harvey Keitel, on the 1991 "Kill Uncle" tour, and continuing throughout all subsequent live engagements up to the appearance of Italian actor, Walter Chiari, on the backdrop for the 2009 "Swords" tour. During this 18-year period and nine major tours the iconography of Morrissey's backdrops has included such varied images as South London gangster, Charlie Richardson, British WBF middleweight boxing champion, Cornelius Carr,[3] and French singer, Sacha Distel, alongside mugshots of various unnamed criminals and a Robert Austin Atherton Jr. picture of a homoerotic, muscle-bound sailor. While there have been a few occasions in which the use of such backdrops have been eschewed altogether,[4] perhaps the most interesting variation was first used during Morrissey's forty-fifth birthday concert at the M.E.N Arena on 22nd May, 2004, in Manchester and then throughout the remainder of the "You are the Quarry" tour. For these shows, rather than performing in front of an outsized photographic projection, Morrissey appeared before a backdrop consisting of nine giant illuminated letters spelling out the word Morrissey. While on the surface this would appear to be a break from the practice of framing a performance with references from his own popular cultural lexicon, a closer inspection reveals more than a passing resemblance to the set of Elvis Presley's famous 1968 NBC TV *Comeback Special*. While he is certainly not the first artist to mimic this iconic image in live performance, this kind of indirect homage to Presley is perhaps another significant milestone in the symbolic construction of Morrissey. Just as we have seen with the use of his own image in cover art, the mobilization of his name in this manner could represent a logical evolution from his gyrations in an Elvis T-shirt on *Top of the Pops* in 1987. By the time of the Manchester performance in 2004 it was no longer necessary for Morrissey to pay tribute by wearing an image of Elvis because, with his name emblazoned behind him in 20-foot letters, Morrissey had become Elvis. Indeed, when we consider the seven-year hiatus between the release of *Maladjusted* in 1997 and *You are the Quarry* in 2004 and the homecoming aspect of a forty-fifth birthday show in Manchester, there is a very real sense in which this was Morrissey's comeback special.

'I Know Very Well How I Got My Name': The artful bricoleur

Lévi-Strauss in *The Savage Mind* identifies the difference between the *bricoleur* and the engineer by the way that, when performing a broad range of tasks the former, unlike the latter

> does not subordinate each of them to the availability of raw materials and tools conceived and procured for the purpose of the project. His universe of instruments is closed and the rules of his game are always to make do with "whatever is at hand", that is to say with a set of tools and materials which is always finite and is also heterogeneous because what it contains bears no relation to the current project, or indeed any particular project.
>
> (Levi-Strauss 1962: 17)

Just as with Levi-Strauss' definition of the *bricoleur*, Morrissey's "set of tools and materials", however eclectic, would appear to be drawn from within a similarly closed universe of cultural reference. The themes that emerge from the lyrics of *Viva Hate*, and develop through the vast majority of his subsequent solo work, tread a path that would seem increasingly to be winding back to the perceived remembrance of a time before the emergence of The Smiths. This is amply illustrated in 'Little Man, What Now?' with its title directly taken from Hans Fallada's 1932 German novel *Kleiner Mann, was nun?* Morrissey paints a picture of a faded teenage idol, believed by many to be *Oliver* star, Jack Wild, who appears forever doomed, to be overshadowed by the image of his own childhood glories. The song also borrows the conception of its protagonist being "too old to be a child star, too young to take leads" from Judy Garland's 1938 hit 'In Between' in which she protests that she is "too old for toys, too young for boys". The overriding feeling of the song, in common with so much of Morrissey's work in The Smiths, is of a baleful, romantic yearning for a lost sense of belonging. Once again, just as Lévi-Strauss remarks of the *bricoleur*, there is a sense that his toolbox of cultural plunder bears little relation to "the current project" and an even stronger sense that he is bound by "the rules" of his own particular game to construct meaning from a set of unrelated images that are constrained by the very importance of being Morrissey. Within this game, oblique reference to relatively obscure German literature and the borrowing of sentiments from a faded icon of the glamour of Hollywood's golden years, who coincidentally died in the same year that the song's central character "murdered every line" on ATV, are entirely consistent with the 'Suedehead' promo's homage to James Dean and visual references to Byron and Saint-Exupéry. While this is clearly a central, supporting structure in the overall construction of *Viva Hate*, a glance back at songs such as 'Cemetry Gates' with its literary league table and Shakespearian misquotes is an indication that it was ever thus. Indeed, it was my own experience as a teenager that, for this very reason, rediscovering British New Wave cinema on VHS felt rather like watching an animated and annotated anthology of Morrissey's early lyrics. On reflection, my own sense of revelation on hearing Jimmy in *A Taste of Honey* declare that "I dreamt of you last night – fell out of bed twice" has, with a growing familiarity with Morrissey's work and influences, become an increasing feeling that what may at first appear to have been the serendipitous juxtaposition of seemingly unrelated imagery may well be a far more considered programme of *bricolage*. Indeed one is left to wonder if the year of Judy Garland's death and the murder of every line in 'Little Man What Now' are such a coincidence after all. This attention to ostensibly trivial detail can be highlighted in many aspects of Morrissey's work from his much-vaunted lyrics to the stage backdrops for his many tours and the choice of images chosen as artwork for singles and album releases during The Smiths and throughout his solo career. The use of a photograph of Pat Phoenix on the cover of the single of 'Shakespeare's Sister' for instance could contain a number of references to Morrissey's declared cultural obsessions. Firstly, and most simply, the photograph is a direct tribute to one of his heroes, the Manchester-born actress whose *Coronation Street* character, Elsie Tanner, Morrissey himself described as "mother, sister and lover to millions" (Morrissey 1985) when he interviewed her in 1985 for *Blitz Magazine*. A further connection to his own cultural lexicon is revealed within this interview with the revelation that early on in her show business career Patricia Pilkington had, at the behest of an unnamed theatre manager, taken the stage name Patricia Dean in tribute to fellow Morrissey idol, James Dean. There is perhaps a further level of symbolism associated with using an image of an actress who took the name Phoenix when we consider the lyrics of 'Shakespeare's Sister' urging its protagonist to "Throw your skinny body down, son" in order to "meet the one I love" in a dramatic tale of death and rebirth. Indeed, there is possibly an even deeper level of significance to the use of such a cover image when we consider that the song's themes of death and ideal love were covered by Shakespeare himself in an untitled metaphysical poem that has since become known as 'The Phoenix and the Turtle'.

The idea that Morrissey reflects the spirit of the *bricoleur* who assembles tools and materials on the basis that they "may always come in handy" (Lévi-Strauss 1962: 17) and uses them, not to signal specific meanings, but as a "set of actual and possible relations" (Levi-Strauss 1962: 17) is well indicated in much of his later work. Perhaps the album that best personifies this trait is 1994's *Vauxhall and I*. The album's opening track 'Now My Heart Is Full' is strewn with a mixture of literary and popular cultural references that are juxtaposed with Smiths-like images of Morrissey's lethargic, youthful dissatisfaction. The refrain recalls names from Graham Greene's *Brighton Rock* alongside little known British actor, Patrick Doonan, in a suggestion that these fictional and lost characters somehow stand in for his own associates when Morrissey implores us to "tell all of my friends" and admits that "I don't have too many". Indeed, one is left to wonder if his choice of an obscure actor in Doonan, who committed suicide in 1958 whilst involved in a mysterious love triangle, represented some association with a tragic notion of doomed romance. The way that Morrissey blurs the edges of his borrowing and juxtaposition is possibly best brought into focus by the assurance later in the song that "Bunnie I loved you". The initial temptation is to assume that Bunnie, alongside Dallow, Spicer, Pinkie and Cubitt has leaked from his subconscious via the pages of the novel, or, given his self professed love of the film (Movieline 1993), perhaps the celluloid of *Brighton Rock*. An examination of Greene's original story or John Boulting's 1947 film adaptation reveals no such character. While there has been some speculation that Bunnie may in fact come from George Rose's character in Lewis Gilbert's 1957 boxing film *The Good Die Young*, there are similar rumours suggesting any number of other candidates from Morrissey's past. The point here is not that Morrissey was intentionally being obscure by interweaving the mysterious Bunnie with borrowed characters and his own heroes, but rather that these references, for all their randomness, conform to the description that Lévi-Strauss offers us of the *bricoleur* considering the project at hand. "His first practical step is retrospective. He has to turn back to an already existent set made of tools and materials, to consider or reconsider what it contains and, finally and above all, to engage in a sort of dialogue with it" (Lévi-Strauss 1962: 18). Indeed, when interviewed by *The Face* in July 1984 Morrissey himself confessed: "There's so much buried in the past to steal from, one's resources are limitless. I'm not saying everything I write has been written before but most of the way I feel comes from the cinema" (Van Poznack 1984).

While on the one hand we can see how this declaration fits comfortably with the *bricoleur's* search through an existing inventory of tools and materials to produce, or perhaps reproduce a solution to a particular problem, there is clearly a contradiction in Morrissey's assertion that "one's resources are limitless". It is in this contradiction and his later confession that "most of the way I feel comes from the cinema" that we can begin to trace a turn towards the postmodern, particularly a trait that Featherstone has described as "the aestheticization of everyday life" (Featherstone 1991: 65). Featherstone identifies "an emphasis upon the effacement of the boundary between art and everyday life […] a general stylistic promiscuity and playful mixing of codes" (Featherstone 1991: 65) as one of the defining characteristics of the postmodern condition. In these terms we can look at Morrissey's introduction of the obscure Bunnie alongside the likes of Dallow and Spicer, not simply as a quotation from the novel but as a manifestation of a genuine personal engagement with and embracing of the reality of Graham Greene's characters. This is not to suggest that Morrissey in any way believes *Brighton Rock* to be factual but rather that his relationship with these personalities in print and on screen transcends the boundaries of their respective media and consequently obliterates the line between art and life. It is surely no coincidence in this context that his call to them in the song should follow the admission of a lack of friends and the intermediate description of "some raincoated lover's puny brothers". Examples of this "effacement of the boundary between the real and the image" (Featherstone 1991: 65) are littered throughout both the lyrics and the use of sampled audio in much of his solo work. A cursory glance at the track listing of *Vauxhall and I* reveals one song title, 'Billy Budd', taken directly from the name of a Herman Melville novel, or, given Morrissey's affinity with films in general and the 1962 adaptation's star Terence Stamp in particular, the Peter Ustinov motion picture of the same name. The song, whose title character would appear to be a thinly veiled reference to Johnny Marr[5] also, concludes with an audio sample of Anthony Newley, as the Artful Dodger from David Lean's 1948 version of *Oliver Twist*. Another track, 'The Lazy Sunbathers' gets its title from a remark made by Marlene Dietrich about those among her Hollywood peers who spent the Second World War lounging by Californian swimming pools, and then mobilizes it as a savage critique of society in the wake of contemporary atrocities.

'Noise Is The Best Revenge': Sculpting the sound of Morrissey

While in no way as prolific as Morrissey's lyrical and visual borrowings, there have also been a number of occasions throughout his solo career in which his collaborators have plundered the annals of musical history to complement his vocal performances. Perhaps the most obvious example of this can be heard in the song 'Certain People I Know' from the 1992 album *Your Arsenal*. There is little doubt that the guitar line, written by Alain Whyte, is directly lifted from the 1970 single 'Ride A White Swan' by T. Rex. The fact that this guitar part was actually played by legendary glam-rock producer, Mick Ronson, who also produced the album, adds a further layer of meaning to this unconcealed homage to one of Morrissey's oft-declared heroes. That Linder Sterling should produce such an obvious pastiche of T. Rex covers in her MOZ sleeve for the single simply serves to underline this. Indeed, even in the song's lyrics, that have no noticeable connection to Bolan's esoteric tale of fantasy and wizardry, there is perhaps another oblique example of Morrissey's playfully self-referential style. Goddard's *Mozipedia* contains a reference to Morrissey's claim that "people literally were breaking their necks against the stage" (Godard 2009: 38) during the T. Rex gig that he attended at the Belle Vue arena in 1972. This recollection leads one to wonder whether the "incredible" impact of this concert on the young Morrissey may have been recalled in his assertion that certain people he knows "break their necks and can't afford to get them fixed". A slightly more obscure, but possibly even more blatant, example of this gift for eulogy through appropriation can be heard in the B side to the 12-inch version of the 1990 single 'November Spawned A Monster'. 'The Girl Least Likely To', written by Morrissey and former Smiths' bassist, Andy Rourke, owes its structure almost entirely to a 1963 B Side by American R&B girl group, The Cookies, entitled 'Only To Other People'. Of course, Morrissey's input to the authorship of this track would have been lyrical. However, given his affinity for the genre and the fact that The Smiths famously performed another Cookies track, 'I Want A Boy For My Birthday' during their first official gig at The Ritz in Manchester in 1982, it is virtually inconceivable that he would have been unaware of its lineage. Indeed, perhaps this is exactly the point for an artist who has, more than once, emphasized his faith in a knowledgeable and intelligent audience and dismay at the fact that, as he suggested during his *Desert Island Discs* interview, "it is very difficult to find anybody in pop music who has anything to say". With this position in mind it would seem entirely possible that unlike the plagiarist who fails to reference the work of others, in the hopes that it may be assumed to be his own, Morrissey does so expressly because he believes that those who are drawn to his music will or, perhaps more pertinently, should know it is not.

In conclusion we can clearly see that Morrissey's adoption of the line "talent borrows, genius steals" is not simply the glib projection of a clever slogan but rather, it would seem, a credo around which he has developed his particular mode of expression. From the very earliest Smiths' recordings and throughout his entire solo career Morrissey has, like a *bricoleur*, delved into a toolbox of cultural references that is at once limitless yet apparently limited by an overwhelming connection to a particularly individual remembrance of the past. A cursory scan through some of Morrissey's more celebrated and occasionally vilified reminiscences of the past reveals connections to some of the groups and subcultures that have been most closely associated with the construction of style through the practice of *bricolage*. Hebdige, in his hugely influential text *Subculture: The Meaning of Style*, points particularly to Punks, Skinheads and Glam Rockers, all groups who have by turns influenced and obsessed Morrissey, as iconic examples of this process in action. Indeed, it is easy to see obvious parallels with Morrissey's own use of imagery in Hebdige's comparison between the subcultural *bricoleur* and Max Ernst's assertion that the creator of a surrealist collage "juxtaposes two apparently incompatible realities on an apparently unsuitable scale [...] and [...] it is there that the explosive junction occurs" (Ernst 1948 in Hebdige 1979: 106). In the case of Morrissey's rich, career-long collage, the explosive junction would seem to direct his fans through a discontinuous narrative of "precious recollections" (Goddard 2009: vii), some experienced first-hand, some consumed through music, literature or cinema and many simply absorbed through an all-consuming obsession with popular culture. That this narrative is often tangled with contradictions should hardly come as a surprise from a man who at once states that "I really do want to be remembered" (Goddard 2009: vii) and also 'I Don't Mind If You Forget Me'. Goddard attests to just such inconsistency in his assertion that "the more his surface is scratched, the more puzzlingly contrary he becomes" (Goddard

2009: vii). Indeed, could there be a more telling comment on the complex tapestry of images and preoccupations that construct the fan's-eye view of Morrissey than the existence of a 500-page encyclopaedia dedicated exclusively to him with entries as disparate as Myra Hindley, Marcel Proust and Hattie Jacques?

While so much of his work is underscored with themes of nostalgic longing, there is a further sense in which this manifests itself in a desire for a past, and often a Britain, that is created by the blurring of the lines between memory and fiction. Indeed, when a February 2009 article in *City Magazine* entitled 'Little Englanders' suggested that "it's not really Wilde who's on Morrissey's side – it's Philip Larkin" (Weiss 2009), it was largely due to their shared disdain for the modern world and longing for a forgotten England that probably never existed. In Morrissey's impassioned and controversial cries to "David" in 'The National Front Disco' about a mythical, idealized country that one day he would like to live in, we can trace an echo of Larkin's fatalism for an England that "will be gone" (Larkin 1974) but for a trace that will "linger on in galleries" (Larkin 1974: 21–22) in his 1972 poem 'Going Going'. This process would appear to extend beyond the scope of the lyrical content of his music into virtually every facet of the production, whether it be the imagery of promotional videos, the choice of stage backdrops for live performance or sometimes even the music itself. This *bricolage* would seem, initially, to be the work of an artist intent on drawing together the varied threads of cultural reference to project his work as a richly textured, colourful collage of social critique and homage to his heroes. While this reading of Morrissey's genius for cultural plunder would seem true, it is perhaps only a partial understanding of his reason for it. We can, throughout his career, trace an almost pathological need to pay tribute to the popular cultural icons that have shaped, not just his music, but our very understanding of Morrissey himself. Perhaps more than any other performer of his generation Morrissey has used this personal *bricolage* to carefully construct a persona that allows a fanatically devoted fan-base to at once know everything and nothing of their hero. Slee suggests in the preface to her 1994 collection of Morrissey's visual imagery, *Peepholism*, that his lyrics while "apparently frank, disarming and explicit [...] in fact give nothing away" (Slee 1994: 1) and at the same time she confirms his almost compulsive control of every facet of the presentation of both The Smiths and his early solo work. Meanwhile his own hero worship of shadows from the remembered past has moved beyond the directness of The Smiths era into an increasing projection of a self that has become so saturated with popular cultural idolatry that its very existence acts in place of the earlier imagery of cover stars and verbatim quotations. In this context we can trace a very real sense in which his own admission that "unfortunately, I don't really exist anywhere else in life" (Cameron 1994) is thrown into sharp relief. In short, the ethos of "talent borrows, genius steals" has not just shaped Morrissey's music but also constructed the very nature of Morrissey himself.

Notes

1. During his appearance on BBC's *One Show* on 16th February, 2009, Morrissey told presenters Adrian Chiles and Christine Bleakly that he has 'very very little' creative input into his promo videos, claiming that he says to the director "here's the song, how do you see it, off you go" and while he was insistent that he did not do as he was told he did suggest that he lets 'someone else hammer the story board together.'
2. Though The Smiths did use a projected backdrop of *The Queen is Dead* album cover on the tour of the same name this was not common practice during previous live performances.
3. Morrissey told Jules Holland in a 1995 interview that Cornelius Carr was his favourite boxer, a claim that would seem to be borne out by his appearance on the covers of the *World of Morrissey* album, the Smiths single release of 'Sweet and Tender Hooligan' and the promotional video for the 'Boxers' single in the same year.
4. The 2002 tour and dates in certain locations during the 1999–2000 "Oyé Esteban" tour did not use stage backdrops.
5. The song 'Billy Budd' contains the line "Things have been bad / Yeah, but now it's 12 years on" which would seem to be a reference to Marr as the albums release date was 12 years after the formation of The Smiths. The choice of a Herman Melville novela as the song's title may also be an oblique reference to Marr as Melville published a collection of poetry titled *John Marr and Other Sailors* in 1888.

References

Bret, D. (2001) *George Formby: A Troubled Genius*. London: Robson.
Bret, D. (2007) *Morrissey: Scandal and Passion*. London: Anova.
Cameron, K. (2004) *Mojo*, June, available: *http: //tiptopwebsite.com/websites/index2.php?username= luckylisp&page=23*.
Cohen, D. (2008) *The New Zealand National Business Review*, 24th November, available: *http: //www. nbr.co.nz/opinion/david-cohen/talent-borrows-genius-steals*.
Featherstone, M. (1997) *Undoing Culture*. London: Sage.
Featherstone, M. (1991) *Consumer Culture and Postmodernism*. London: Sage.
Goddard, S. (2009) *Mozipedia: The Encyclopedia of Morrissey and The Smiths*. London: Ebury Press.
Goddard, S. (2002) *Songs That Saved Your Life*. London: Reynolds and Hearn.
Hebdige, D. (1979) *Subculture: The Meaning of Style*. London: Methuen.
Kroker, A. and Cook, D. (1986) *The Postmodern Scene*. London: St Martin's Press.
Larkin, P. (1974) *High Windows*. London: Faber and Faber.
Levi-Strauss, C. (1962) *The Savage Mind*. Paris: Weidenfeld and Nicholoson.
Morrissey, S. (1985) 'Never turn you back on mother earth: Morrissey interviews Pat Pheonix', *Blitz Magazine*, May, available: *http: //www.foreverill.com/interviews/1985/phoenix.htm*.
'Sound & Vision: An Interview with Morrissey', *Movieline Magazine*, March 1993.
Passions Just Like Mine Urban Cowgirl Productions. Dir. Kerri Koch. http://www.passionsjustlikemine.com.
Rich, M. (2006) 'Who's this guy Dylan who's borrowing lines From Henry Timrod?', *The New York Times*, 14th September, available: *http: //www.nytimes.com/2006/09/14/arts/music/14dyla.html*.
Slee, J. (1994) *Peepholism* London. Sidgwick and Jackson.

Van Poznack, E. (1984) 'The Face interview', July, available: *http: //foreverill.com/interviews/1984/ mozface.htm*.

Weiss, M. (2009) 'Little Englanders: Morrissey and Philip Larkin morose brothers', *City Journal*, 27th February, available: *http: //www.city-journal.org/2009/bc0227mw.html*.

Young, K. (2009) *Desert Island Discs*, BBC Radio 4, 29th November.

Chapter 15

'I'm Not The Man You Think I Am': Morrissey's Negotiation of Dominant Gender and Sexuality Codes

Elisabeth Woronzoff

Introduction

In the popular cultural text that is the 1980s, Morrissey and the Smiths created their own cultural texts for adolescents that openly embraced non-normative sexuality and questioned, negotiated and deconstructed hegemonic ideologies regarding sexuality and gender. However, Morrissey does not deconstruct popular culture to such an extent that it is unrecognizable from its original entity. What Morrissey does that is so unique is that he acknowledges the dominant codes but parlays an alternative means of decoding them. Using the encoding and decoding language of Hall, I read Morrissey as one who does not actively oppose dominant discourse. I hold that what he does do is settle in the middle, and presents us, in the words of Hall, with a negotiated discourse. This negotiation of both dominant and oppositional codes allows fans to decide and interpret Morrissey's language, lyrics and appearance as reflections of their own identity. Consequently, they are able to relate to Morrissey in ways that are not reachable by Boy George, David Bowie's Ziggy Stardust and other transgressive types, whom theorists Hubbs and Butler understand as parodies of gender.

Basing my work on the theories of Bersani, Hawkins, Reynolds and Press, Hopps and Hubbs, I use Morrissey's musical repertoire to demonstrate how he embraces gender fluidity and never settles at either end of the gender binary long enough to provide the normative constructions credibility. As Hopps (2009) demonstrates, Morrissey does not destroy gender construction but strips the binary of any stable meaning.

By not establishing himself as a marker of normative gender roles, Morrissey is capable of breaking the confines of strict masculine codes. More so, Morrissey demonstrates a change in the understanding of masculinity. Using the work of Hawkins, I read Morrissey as the signifier of a type of masculinity that is more than macho and emotionless but capable of demonstrating vulnerability and sensitivity without being homosexual. The type of masculinity Morrissey embodies is far more expansive and fluid than the simplistic rhetoric espousing men as active and women as passive. Morrissey demonstrates an ability to be both. Hawkins sees Morrissey as a queerer of gender identity and I further that notion by using Morrissey as the exemplar of the availability of a polymorphous identity, that is, a life not set within the concrete systems of male or female.

Sexuality, sex roles and sexual fluidity are frequently synonymous with gender roles. Yet Morrissey is one of the few pop artists capable of separating sexuality and gender. Morrissey's own sexuality underwent public change thus he demonstrates the complexities of sexualities extend further than gender roles, sexual paradigms and power structures. I understand Morrissey's song 'Pretty Girls Make Graves' (1983) as a demonstrator of the complexities derived from non-normative sexuality. And from the lyrics to 'You Have Killed Me' (2006), Morrissey represents the ability to deconstruct the regulating of the behaviour of male and female bodies according to preconceptions of masculinity and femininity. Both songs share one trope: sexual activity is strictly representational of the culture that creates it and therefore sexuality is capable of change.

Typically, adolescents, or any person struggling with identity consciousness, are forced to reconcile their behaviour within a binary: normalized or abject, male or female, homosexual or heterosexual. This behaviour is often dictated by sexualized power structures, dominant understandings of gender and sexuality or popular media institutions. With celebrities and individuals such as Morrissey living out loud the availability of a negotiated understanding of codes, it provides a new narrative to all. This narrative fearlessly and confidently represents a solace with oneself while shepherding others to do the same. As Morrissey sings in 'At Last I Am Born' (2006), "Leaving the one true free life born /I once thought I had numerous reasons to cry / And I did, but I don't anymore / Because I am born, born, born." For the free life that is constructed from dominant discourses is not free at all. But the moment one realizes that a life cannot neatly fit into a binary, then this is the moment of rebirth. This type of narrative, one which questions, plays with, throws away and recycles dominant structures, creates a powerful influence on those who accept it as a new alternative to what is commonly considered the truth.

Cultural codes and individual agency

As with any type of system, popular culture presents codes to society that carry ideologies and social constructs. Hall's classic understanding of codes from the essay 'Encoding/decoding' in the text *Culture, Media, Language* can be applied to Morrissey's performance, lyrics and image. A reading of Morrissey confirms his acknowledgement of dominant gender codes but his performance and lyrics parlay the existence of gender codes not previously widely considered. In that these actions signify meaning that is then read by Morrissey's fans as a negotiated discourse. For Hall:

> Codes of this order clearly contract relations for the sign with the wider universe of ideologies in a society. These codes are the means by which power and ideology are made to signify in particular discourses. They refer signs to the "maps of meaning" into which any culture is classified; and those "maps of social reality" have the whole range of social meanings, practices, and usages, power and interest "written in" to them.
>
> (Hall 2005: 129)

These codes, as dictated by popular culture, masquerade its ability to control and position the body amongst the mainstream. By inserting a specific language and ideology into discourses, these codes emphasize control of the individual. When reinforcing codes, institutions like the *Top of the Pops*, MTV, magazines, television and even the presence of a celebrity performing on and off the stage, expose viewers to dominant codes. Therefore these institutions act like machines for transforming and controlling people, rendering individuals obedient to dominant discourses.

Radio and television are cultural machines which establish and perpetuate normative and dominant structures or codes which adolescents are predisposed to embrace. The media provides the dominant codes that the majority of audiences can easily understand and can define, align and relate to. As Hall argues:

> [T]he dominant definitions, however, are hegemonic precisely because they represent definitions of situations and events which are "in dominance" (global) [...] they relate events to the "national interest" or to the level of geo-politics, even if they make these connections in truncated, inverted or mystified ways.
>
> (Hall 2005: 132)

Popular culture in the 1980s dictated a space of affluence, heterosexuality and homogeneity, yet the presence of Morrissey renegotiated these understandings. Knowingly, Morrissey was not the pioneer of dominant discourse deconstruction. However, the world popularity of The Smiths and Morrissey's prolific solo career positioned Morrissey in a unique situation to present a subversive discourse to his fans and critics. Morrissey used his stardom to present a subtle yet readable negotiation of dominant social constructs. This runs in contrast with other individuals who firmly situated themselves within dominant or oppositional discourses. Decoding within the negotiated version contains a mixture of adaptive and oppositional elements. According to Hall "it acknowledges the legitimacy of the hegemonic definitions to make the grand significations (abstract), while, at a more restricted, situational (situated) level, it makes its own ground rules – it operates with exceptions to the rule" (Hall 2005: 133). The lyrics and the image of Morrissey present a negotiated code resisting the hegemonic power paradigm by consciously adopting behaviour that appears threatening.

Conceptions of masculine, feminine, and in-between

A close reading of Morrissey deconstructs the understanding of the deep-rooted pressure to conform to normative and hegemonic gender roles. Morrissey's acknowledgement of gender norms foremost dictates to fans a problem: the conventions of hyper-masculinity and the very specific examples of masculine characteristics are issues in popular discourse. These characteristics are still embodied in the gender roles and norms expected and conceived in today's society. Such a notion echoes Laquer's historical understanding of the "one-sex model" from *Making Sex: Body and Gender from the Greeks to Freud*. Here Laquer understands the historical roots of gender conceptions: women, based on acknowledged differences between men and women, are as a result inferior or are incomplete men (Laquer 1992: 14). Further, such a model yielded exact characteristics of femininity and masculinity: men are reasonable, women are emotional; men are active and women are passive. Within the music industry a similar gender paradigm is reinforced but when it is obviously transgressed, it is done so in a comical or outrageous way (which I discuss in reference to Bowie's dressing as the alien Ziggy Stardust.) As Hubbs writes in "Music of the fourth gender: Morrissey and the sexual politics of melodic contour":

> A female vocalist may, occasionally, cover a boy's song: she is understood to take on the purportedly neutral and universal masculine perspective of the song's first person subject, and thus, as a stand-in of sorts, she may sing love songs to another "she". This is "allowable" partly because the singer's subjective identity, being feminine (and hence passive, nonpenetrating), is not so overpowering as to pose a threat to the understood heterosexual arrangement. But clearly a male singer is less free to sing girls' songs; pronouns are assiduously altered, or more often this threatening situation is avoided altogether. For it places a man in position to assume the gender-marked, nonuniversal identity of the feminine Other – or even to sing love song to another "he". The taboo energy accrued at such boundaries is evident in those instances when they are transgressed, as when artists tap this power for parody or other humorous purposes, or expressly to shock, provoke, or titillate.
>
> (Hubbs 1996: 275)

Hubbs describes the gender binary in popular music as a manifestation of either normative power or reductive humour. On one hand, Hubbs understands the power given to the pronoun to determine and demonstrate the sexuality of the musician, yet on the other hand, views/sees the tendency to dismiss gender nonconformity as humorous or an extension of entertainment rather than as expressions of self-identity. For Morrissey, he neither believes nor positions himself within this gender binary but rather uses his celebratory status to convey a negotiated understanding of gender norms. In an interview with David MacCullough, Morrissey discusses the notion and conception of gender:

> I'm very interested in gender. I just want something different. I want to make it easier for people. I'm bored with men and I'm bored with women. All this sexual segregation that goes on, even in rock 'n' roll. I just so happen to be completely influenced by feminist writers. It will never be realized beyond that because this society detests strong women.
>
> (Woods 2007: 17)

Here Morrissey demonstrates the ability for both men and women to step outside of normative gender norms. Importantly, by saying "I want to make it easier for people" Morrissey brings credence to people who already live outside of gender norms but are lost amongst the attention and influence of hegemonic gender discourses.

Looking at Morrissey's lyrics, it is also apparent that he understands gender as a more fluid concept than a simple and concrete binary. Typically, Morrissey resists using gender determining pronouns in lyrics and will provide characters with proper names. By resisting the use of gender specific pronouns, Morrissey avoids locking his characters in a fixed gender identity. When characters are identified by pronouns, their gender fluidity is emphasized. For example in the song 'Sheila Take A Bow', Morrissey sings "take my hand and off we stride / Oh, la / You're a girl and I'm a boy / La / Take my hand and off we stride / Oh, la / I'm a girl and you're a boy / La." Here Morrissey taking the position of first person narrator understands the character's gender as fluid between both dominant understandings of male and female. By doing so, Morrissey actively transgresses dominant ideologies and lyrically deconstructs gender. But Morrissey's lyrics do not deny that the gender categories of male and female exist but rather they are unstable, capable of flexibility and changing. As a result, fans are given a text through which they also can move in between the gender binary.

Hopps (2009) understands Morrissey's language as a means to bring visibility to gender and sexual nonconformity without destroying cultural definitions.

> Deconstruction, we should note, is not destruction – which is why things "live on", in spite of the unhinging of their foundational logic – but a seismic disturbance which reveals an instability or "anarchy" that was always already in play […] it reveals that the values and concepts that structure the discourse of popular music are differentially constituted and have no stable foundation or essential meaning.
>
> (Hopps 2009: 56)

The idea of a gender binary, as in the concrete understanding of distinct male and female bodies, demonstrates the dominant understanding of gender. Yet in 'Sheila Take A Bow', the image of the character moving between two gendered bodies brings visibility to the concrete and defined social binaries, at the same time drawing attention to the existence of a space where gender is mutable rather than a seminal identified characteristic.

Hopps furthers his analysis of Morrissey by understanding the language in 'Sheila Take A Bow' as light and playful therefore further deconstructing the gendered language from its dominant meanings.

> There is likewise a sort of capricious "etc." in Morrissey's "la la la", which with a wonderfully playful defiance underlies the subversive teasing away of words, even as apparently fixed in their reference as "girl" and "boy", from any stable meaning.
>
> (Hopps 2009: 57)

The minimalist understanding of dominant gender consciousness found in 'Sheila Take A Bow' reflects a negotiated treatment of how gender is perceived, as if it were not a concrete system positioned within a binary. Morrissey, as a pop star, brought forward the existence of lives that are too complicated to be defined by simplistic language. Morrissey diminished the creation of otherness perpetuated by the dominant and inflexible gender ideologies.

Gender roles and the confines of masculinity

For many fans, Morrissey's identity serves as a tool by which they negotiate and deconstruct heteronormative conceptions of masculinity. As specified by Lacquer and Hubbs, emotions become the key to dichotomizing genders. As Hubbs argues "there are boys' songs and there are girls' songs, and specific (though tacit) laws governing each" (Hubbs 1996: 275). Morrissey echoes this statement when he reflects on the popular music gender divide: "female singers were allowed to be very expressive and dramatic whereas male singers couldn't sing in a sexually open way about their heart and how they felt" (Brown 2008: 94–95). In a society where the volume of manhood is measured by machismo and virility, Morrissey is renowned for adorning a sort of masculine sensitivity. He embodies what are commonly understood to be female characteristics such as delicacy, vulnerability and sensitivity. For instance, in the song 'He Cried' (1997), Morrissey sings: "I need you / simple words / But words which had never been heard from people where I come from / They survive without feelings or blood / I never could / So he froze where he stood / And he looked to the ground / And he cried / He cried." Here Morrissey expresses the desire to be needed, and he juxtaposes this desire with a socially enforced tendency for men to repress emotions. Typically, these are not the characteristics which frame the dominant definitions of manliness and machismo. Fiske, in his essay titled 'British cultural studies', tackles the construction of masculine and feminine ideals when he builds on Shere Hite's list of the qualities which creates the idea of a man:

> The list of characteristics she generated began with such qualities as self-assurance, lack of fear, the ability to take control, autonomy, and self-sufficiency, leadership, dependability, and achievement [...] self-sufficiency which stresses the absence of a need to depend on others.

> (Fiske 1987: 293)

When Morrissey sings "I need you", he reveals himself as man who does depend on others, lacks self-assurance and autonomy. Morrissey embodies a man who is emotional, capable of feeling and even crying yet is able to survive a society that opposes him. Despite cultural and social constructs which define masculinity as callous and emotionless, and presents men as providers of safety and protection, Morrissey shows that men are capable of feeling emotion and have a deep desire to be loved, needed and protected.

Furthermore, Morrissey uses the stage to create a new safe cultural space where gender is fluid and where he can resist gender normativity. The stage acts as a space for fans to tenderly hug him, give Morrissey flowers or offer gifts. These are the same gifts that Morrissey will gently accept and display moments before ripping open his shirt presenting his male body to the audience. Here, Morrissey swiftly moves between culturally constructed understandings of female and male behaviour, without pausing to give one more emphasis than the other. Morrissey's singular body encompasses both. Thus, Morrissey can be seen as an agent attempting to break apart from the hegemony of normative culture. The stage becomes a space that is not controlled or regulated by dimorphic understandings of gender, and serves as a way for the powerless body to negotiate normativity.

Sexuality, sex roles and sexual fluidity

Morrissey's performance and representation offered a means through which it became possible for young heterosexual, homosexual, bisexual and questioning fans alike to address the complexity of their own sexualities and desires. For example in the song 'Pretty Girls Make Graves' Morrissey's lyrics expand the focus of the song to encompass both homosexual and heterosexual fans. Assuming the narrator is male, he can be interpreted as gay because he rebukes the advances of a woman and exclaims:

> I'm not the man you think I am / I'm not the man you think I am / End of the pier, end of the bay / You tug my arm, and say: Give in to lust, / Give up to lust, oh heaven knows we'll / Soon be dust [...] Oh, I'm not the man you think I am / I'm not the man you think I am / I could have been wild and I could have Been free / But Nature played this trick on me.
>
> ('Pretty Girls Make Graves')

Here the narrator tries to understand his lack of interest in the female character, therefore reflecting an adolescent's own questioning of self-identity. As Bersani suggests in 'Is the rectum a grave?'

> An authentic gay male political identity therefore implies a struggle not only against definitions of maleness and of homosexuality as they are reiterated and imposed in a heterosexist social discourse, but also against those very same definitions so seductively and so faithfully reflected by those (in large part culturally invented and elaborated) male bodies.
>
> (Bersani 1987: 209)

Through the narrator, Morrissey establishes a change in the representation of masculinity. Here Morrissey demonstrates the availability of homosexuality as a lifestyle even though it counters the dominant prevalence of heterosexuality. In fact with this piece, Morrissey verifies how men can circumvent normative understandings of heterosexuality as the foundation for masculinity and as a result recontextualize and define their sexual identity without committing to a fixed sexual identity. But this is reading the song's characters as homosexual, what if they are indeed something else?

In *The Sex Revolts*, Reynolds and Press read the character as an "admission of male feebleness in the face of voraciousness [...] but in the song, it's less about a dread of settling down and more about a terror of being devoured. In a witty inversion of rock's rebellion's studly stance, it's Morrissey who's the wilting wallflower, and the woman who's the impatient, sexually precocious ruffian" (Reynolds and Press 1995: 90). As previously discussed with 'He Cried', Morrissey presents, as Reynolds and Press read, an image of gender that is not defined by concrete definitions – in this particular case the role of passive female and active male is reversed and it is the woman who is the active sexual participant. From 'Pretty Girls Make Graves', the line "I am not the man you think I am" becomes a haunting reminder to the listener to be careful of applying gender norms to individuals. Doing so might prove them wrong, for individuals' identities are too complicated and mercurial to categorize as just either male or female. By denying categorization, Morrissey showed how one could jump on the bandwagon of queering identity by stretching sexuality as a cultural construction (Hawkins 2002: 73). Morrissey did not align himself with the popular binary; rather he created his own category that included the possibility of a polymorphous identity.

The acceptance of and ability to understand sexual identity as polymorphic is captured in the song 'You Have Killed Me'. As Hawkins demonstrates elsewhere in this volume, in this song Morrissey identifies himself as Pasolini and Visconti, two Italian directors whose sexuality also underwent public scrutiny. The lyrics of the piece suggest both directors develop an attraction towards their leading female stars Accattone and Magnani. For an unknown reason, both women do their "best but fail" to sexualize both directors. As Morrissey sings "I entered nothing and nothing entered me". But what both women did successfully accomplish is the creation of a question surrounding the men's sexual identity. By doing so, they have killed the understanding of absolute homosexuality. As Morrissey sings: "As I live and breathe / You have killed me / You have killed me / Yes I walk around somehow / But you have killed me / You have killed me / Who am I that I come to be here?" The killing is not the bodily killing of the individual, rather the killing of a concrete and fixed understanding of sexuality. The lyrics of 'You Have Killed Me' demonstrate individuals that are not subject to a singular sexuality. Rather, sexuality is capable of changing and fluctuating and individuals are capable of experiencing and embracing a polymorphic existence. Morrissey himself underwent and publicized his sexual fluidity: his initial bisexuality and later adoption of asexuality and then celibacy bent the strict normative confines of sexuality. And if the lyrics to 'You Have Killed Me' are autobiographical, then it is obvious that Morrissey's sexuality has shifted again.

One more example of sexual fluidity can be derived from Morrissey's 2009 tour, "Years of Refusal". For this tour, Morrissey captured an image from the 1982 film *Querelle*. The backdrop for Morrissey's performance depicted a black and white image of the lead male-role, Querelle, nude from the waste up and raising his arms to flex his arm muscles for the viewer. In this image, Querelle's only accessories are a small sailor hat cocked to the left and a cigar suggestively hanging semi-erect from Querelle's mouth. The synopsis of the film finds the character Georges Querelle arriving in Brest. He first visits a brothel run by the madam Lysiane and shortly thereafter announces his desire to sleep with her. But first, Querelle learns, he will have to throw dice with Nono, Lysiane's husband. If Nono loses, Querelle is allowed to sleep with Lysiane, however if Querelle loses, he must submit to sex with Nono. Querelle deliberately loses the game, allowing himself to be sodomized by Nono. In this instance, Querelle is the celluloid embodiment of sexual fluidity. The symbolism of the seamen landing in Brest and cavorting with men named Nono is obvious. But what is not so obvious is that each character in this film follows their own sexual desires even if it opposes dominant sexual discourses, Querelle being just one example. By the use of Querelle's image, Morrissey largely publicizes the existence of sexual fluidity that is beyond his bodily entity.

The notion of passivity as a female trait becomes important when applied to the act of sex. Passivity for women involves submission to the male, especially the male body in allowing the penis to penetrate the female body. Penetration becomes a physical manifestation of passivity. Morrissey in the song, 'You Have Killed Me' expresses his ability to penetrate and also his potential for penetration: "I entered nothing and nothing entered me." However, as the song progresses, it is fathomable that Morrissey succumbs to penetration when he sings, "until you came with the key". Understanding this metaphor visually, the key acts as the penis (active) and Morrissey's body as the keyhole (passive). Yet, by establishing himself as both the penetrator and penetratee, Morrissey aligns himself with both the dominant understanding of the male and female roles during sexual intercourse. However, this is assuming Morrissey is participating in heterosexual sex. What can one suspect if Morrissey is participating in homosexual sex?

The role of passive and active participants in homosexual sex has undergone transformation regarding the identity attributed to either the passive or active participant. Mastering and subordination become the polarized figures describing sexual participants, a similar dualistic language as applied to heterosexual sex. Revisiting Bersani's 'Is the rectum a grave', he uses a historical understanding of anal sex to address the dualities attributed to homosexual sex:

And while for the Ancient Romans, "the distinction between roles approved for male citizens and others appears to center on the giving of seed (as opposed to receiving of it) rather than on the more familiar active-passive division", to be anally penetrated was no less judged to be "indecorous role for citizen males".

(Bersani 1987: 212)

Bersani sees the relationship created during sexual intercourse as not one of power and social role fulfillment leading to the abdication of power but rather derivations of sexual pleasure. As Bersani continues, the pleasure derived from sex is sometimes in second place to the social and cultural constructs, which ultimately are more influential.

[Sex] can perhaps most easily be exacerbated, and polarized into relations of mastery and subordination, in sex, and that this potential may be grounded in the shifting experience that every human being has of his or her body's capacity, or failure, to control and to manipulate the world beyond the self.

(Bersani 1987: 216)

The need to polarize sex and to group humans within binaries – be it male and female, master and subordinate, top and bottom – controls the language involving sex and sexuality. Bersani argues the pleasure attained from sexual activity is strictly representational of the cultural constructs that create it. Furthermore, sexuality that falls outside the realms of cultural normativity runs the dangers of marginalizing and categorizing participants as "Other". Yet lyrically, agents such as Morrissey demonstrate non-normative sex is just as pleasurable as normative sex, and individuals do participate in it. In the lyrics to 'You Have Killed Me', Morrissey represents the ability to deconstruct the regulating of the behaviour of male and female bodies according to preconceptions of femininity and masculinity. For Morrissey, taking on both the socially constructed roles of passive and active, demonstrates to listeners the ability to live in between or even outside normative conceptions of self and sexuality.

Morrissey actively created a paradigm shift; he spotlighted the existence of individuals not accounted for in dominant ideologies. In 'Music in the global order', Stokes discusses the paradigm shift and space created by dominant and peripheral discourses. As he argues "the inscription in new media and its discursive apparatus of colonial conceptions of otherness (Erlmann 1999; Feld 1994, 2000); processes of musical appropriation that both maintain and disguise Western high-modernist aesthetic hierarchies (Born & Hesmondhalgh 2000a); and the reproduction of the hegemonic relationships between centers and peripheries" (Taylor 1997) (Stokes 2004: 48) However, what Stokes does not emphasize in this quote is the ability to deconstruct the "discursive apparatus" from within the hegemonic structures. When members of the dominant popular industry, such as Morrissey, actively espouse and live narratives that counter dominant ideologies, they prove themselves to be more than cultural allegories. Rather, their negotiated and even oppositional codes create a new discursive rhetoric, one which demonstrates to individuals the possibility to live outside the narrow confines outlined by dominant political and cultural codes.

Queering popular culture

Morrissey's negotiated viewpoint on gender and sexuality is uncommon amongst dominant popular discourses. Therefore the need to understand Morrissey and thus labelling or applying language to him becomes problematic. Unfortunately, there are only two ways to do so: are Morrissey's characteristics male or female? And how are we to understand Morrissey if his identity is neither male nor female? The expression of "feminine" characteristics typically constructs men as homosexual, and the overlap between emotional capability and identity consciousness are drafted against sexuality. When presented with the question "Are you gay?", Paul Woods captures Morrissey's response:

> I feel that I am quite vulnerable and that's quite good [...] I'd rather be thought of as someone who is sensitive who could understand women in a way that wasn't really sexual. I hate men who can see women in a sexual way – to me that's criminal and I want to change that. I don't recognize such terms as heterosexual, homosexual, bisexual, and I think it's important that there's someone in pop music who's like that. These words do great damage, they confuse people and they make people feel unhappy so I want to do away with them.
>
> (Woods 2007: 132)

Not only does Morrissey separate himself from the dominant understandings of sexuality but he also takes an active stance in presenting himself as an agent who negotiates and seeks to change dominant codes. Morrissey represents the ability to deconstruct the dominant and controlling cultural regulations of the behaviour of male and female bodies according to preconceptions of femininity and masculinity. Furthermore, he deconstructs the connection of emotions to gender and sexuality. He believes emotions are not characteristics attributed to one type of person; they are characteristic of all humans. As documented in the song 'How Soon Is Now?', Morrissey sings, "I am human and I need to be loved."

The labelling of Morrissey as gay can be understood in a Foucaultian context surrounding language and discourse. For Foucault, language and discourse define and produce the object of our knowledge; discourse and language create socially acceptable truth. When writing of journalists' responses to Morrissey's sexuality, Simpson notes in *Saint Morrissey: Portrait of This Charming Man*, "the fact that he wasn't 'Straight', he must therefore be 'gay'. What these very helpful, very kind people forgot, however, is that the law 'what isn't one thing must be the other', absolutely correct and inviolable as it is, is a law that only applied to stupid people" (Simpson 2003: 131). Intelligence levels aside, what Simpson does accurately depict is the resolute need to define individuals as straight or gay. However, Morrissey's sexual identity, appearance and interviews cultivate the emergence of a new discourse, one that actively resists normative gender narratives and serves to create a discursive formation. By doing so, Morrissey speaks to fans who are toying with their own sexual identity and understanding of gender. Therefore, Morrissey transgresses dominant understandings of gender by personifying the discourse that decentralizes the powerful heterosexual, white, male image (Hawkins 2009: 77).

Hawkins' recent work *The British Pop Dandy* examines a vital question within musical and cultural studies: how is masculinity conceptualized in pop and performance and how are these notions embodied by pop-dandies? Hawkins develops the image of the dandy as the manifestation of sexuality, music and politics rather than being strictly homosexual. For Hawkins, Morrissey is considered a dandy and therefore the embodiment of political and social conventions that he intentionally manipulates to transgress dominant discourses. Building on Richard Middleton, Hawkins specifically addresses Morrissey:

> Another artist whose biographical material mobilizes signifiers of desire, appeal, control and ironic intent is Morrissey. Known for his ambivalence [...] Middleton points out that a strategy of ambiguity "leaves sexual identification blurred" (Middleton 2006: 27). Invariably, this disrupts norms.
>
> (Hawkins 2009: 70)

Subjectivity and musical performance become the expressions of hyperbolic display. Hawkins uses Morrissey to demonstrate dandyism as the continual acknowledgement of the connection between gender display and musical expressivity where no conventional code is left unexamined. The emergence of an intentional pop image, one centred on style, originality and individualism, is the crux of the dandy, and here Hawkins counters the misconception that dandyism and by extension pop music and its impact on fans are fixed and unmovable. Homosexuality is more than a list of preset characteristics, and Hawkins' understanding of Morrissey as a dandy serves to deconstruct the normative language surrounding gender display while emphasizing the mutability of gender codes.

Morrissey signifies a negotiated cultural and political space similar to that which the dandy occupies. Hawkins states "queering is an agent for social and cultural orders, prescribing difference at the same time as upholding dominant values" (Hawkins 2009: 105). This space further conveys the trends and behaviour patterns that are linked to performance. It also serves to attract the audience, and allows fans to address the complexities of their own identities, sexualities and desires. Hawkins considers the representation of dandies less as effeminate or homosexual and more as a type of masculine sensitivity and vulnerability.

> Dandified display encountered in British pop informs an ongoing narrative of individual agency. What stands for British male dandy is not only a construction that distinguishes from being female, but also a fabricated figuration that marks out the terrain of dissident masculinity. Pop dandyism is about recognizing something intrinsic in the articulation of gender that is adumbrated by nonverbal aural and visual signifiers.
>
> (Hawkins 2009: 35)

By circumventing the limitations of heteronormative and masculine representation, pop-dandies such as Morrissey demonstrate the availability of a negotiated and polymorphous identity. The dandy's queer performance accents gender and works as both compliance and opposition. This fluctuating and mutable identity creates an invaluable connection between performer and audience.

In addition to challenging gender normativity, Morrissey's public acknowledgement of his bisexuality serves to position him as a counter-example to the popular image of the rock star. The images of Bruce Springsteen and John Cougar Mellencamp expressed virility, male physical dominance and hyper masculinity. Morrissey rejected all examples of rock 'n' roll machismo and instead elected to cultivate an entirely unique image. In referencing Morrissey's image, Paul A. Woods writes of: "[Morrissey's] gently haunting vocals whooping suddenly upward into a falsetto, clothed in outsize women's shirts" (Woods 2007: 5). Part of Morrissey's dress was purchased from women's clothing stores, which he donned along with his pompadour and pants. He maintained a fine line between normative male dress and possibly drag performance. As Hawkins writes in his text *Settling the Pop Score: Pop Texts and Identity Politics*:

> How the pop star looks, how he displays his body in performance, how he dresses, how he defines his own social space, and most importantly how he sings, affect the way in which we experience the artist in relation to ourselves.
>
> (Hawkins 2002: 76)

Morrissey's image acted as a representation for those who questioned or resisted gender norms. When thinking about popular music, it is important to remember the glamorized heterosexual fantasyland presented by popular artists. In the context of the 1980s, Morrissey's image and the space he created offered a negotiated discourse to young heterosexual and gay fans, thus providing a counter-cultural narrative to the dominant discourses surrounding sexuality and gender.

It is important to note that Morrissey is not the first musician to bring a type of ambiguity to popular culture. The presence of the band KISS and David Bowie performing as Ziggy Stardust harkens images of hyper-theatrical gender representation. Both the band and musician wore excessive amounts of makeup, decadent wigs, tight clothing and high heels. The 1980s also saw the presence of Boy George, a caricature of stereotypical masculinity, while the early 1990s saw an explosion in popularity of drag queens specifically Ru Paul. As previously discussed by Hubbs, these representations of gender could easily be classified as humorous if not the apex of entertainment. The common themes amongst these examples are an extreme performance of gender and therefore were not accessible to individuals who were simply negotiating gender fluidity or questioning androgyny.

The hyper-theatrics of other notable pop musicians echoes Butler's analysis of gender performativity in *Bodies That Matter: On the Discursive Limits of "Sex"*. Butler specifically constructs performativity around drag, which offers the possibility for a reconsideration of gender categories in its emphasis on the discursive contingency of gender performance. Butler believes that drag cannot be regarded as a deconstruction of gender and drag cannot be understood as "the part of gender that is performed [and …] performance consists in a reiteration of norms which precede, constrain, and exceed the performer" (Butler 1993: 234). In other words, Butler sees gender and sexuality in many ways as signifiers and over-emphasized reiterations of pre-established gender norms. Butler suggests: "drag is subversive to the extent that it reflects on the imitative structure by which hegemonic gender is itself" (Butler 1993: 125). These norms are revisited in the theatrical performance of Ziggy Stardust and KISS and even furthered by heterosexual male popular icons. Morrissey presented a more obtainable yet ambiguous representation of gender through his dress and style. By negotiating the narrow confines of gender, he strategically positions himself in contrast with the heteronormative models of masculinity and the hyper-theatrical performances of other male musicians. The dichotomized man – either hyper masculine or effeminate, if not completely masquerading as female – represents a cultural alteration to masculinity. However, Morrissey's resistance of gender normativity, his ability to perform and present himself in the middle of two extremes presented individuals with a narrative of the availability and possibility to live outside heteronormative characters.

Conclusion

Rather than a fictionalized and idealized lifestyle, Morrissey identifies the mercurial nature of sexual identity, gender, masculinity and femininity. The realism of sexual experimentation and gender fluidity do not fit into the fictional realism depicted in the majority of popular culture. The truth to falling in love, be it with someone of the same or opposite gender, or even with someone who does not define themselves, or does so on occasion, is the reality of many individuals. The compulsory heterosexuality prevalent in popular music is only accessible to a small portion of listeners. Morrissey deconstructed the dominant code, presenting his own negotiated discourse. But what is true is this discourse was the dominant code for many of his fans.

Morrissey stood as an example of a person living among specific gender norms, but questioned and actively resisted gender and sexual constructs. He created a new culture based on outsider dogmas and therefore provided a voice for those on the margins of normative society. Pop figures such as Morrissey demonstrate the need to deconstruct the dominant codes read by audiences and decipher their influence and meaning. It is by way of this construction that adults are able to control and mould youth into acceptable models and participants in current society. Essentially, adolescents are positioned in a society that is created for them and then expected to participate in said society under certain predetermined social constructs. The characters in Morrissey's lyrics are much like himself, as an extension of adolescents living amongst popular culture. They are individuals trapped in a world that is created for them rather than developing their own narratives.

Alternative means of identity structures are available in the mainstream. Morrissey stands as one example of an individual who acknowledges the existence of dominant gender and sexual codes, yet lives and performs outside of their power structures. By doing so, fans are able to read and identify with Morrissey, using his negotiations of gender and sexuality norms to formulate their own self-awareness. Morrissey breaks down the pressure for men to be callous, protective and heterosexual and rather demonstrates the possibility to be emotional, loving and in need of dependence. But most importantly, Morrissey demonstrates how complicated life can be and how a simple binary will never be expansive enough to include all individuals. Identity is an expression of the self, and even though cultural and social factors ultimately influence identity, it is self-awareness that acts as the root of being. The mercurial nature of identity and human nature is constantly mutating and shaping as a direct response to the culture that surrounds it. Morrissey demonstrates to fans that both gender and sexual identity are not concrete constructions but rather are open to polymorphism, to change and fluidity.

References

Bersani, L. (1987) 'Is the rectum a grave?', *AIDS: Cultural Analysis/Cultural Activism*, 43, pp. 197–222.

Butler, J. (1993) *Bodies That Matter; On the Discursive Limits of "Sex"*. New York: Routledge.

Brown, L. (2008) *Meetings with Morrissey*. New York: Omnibus Press.

Fassbinder, R. (1982) *Querelle*. France : Planet Films.

Fiske, J. (1987) 'British cultural studies', in R. Allen (ed.) *Channels of Discourse, Reassembled*. Chapel Hill, NC: The University of North Carolina Press.

Foucault, M. (1977) *Discipline and Punish: The Birth of a Prison*, trans. Alan Sheridan. New York: Vintage Books.

Frith, S. (1990) 'Music and sexuality', in S. Frith and A. Goodwin (eds) *On Record: Pop, Rock, and the Written Word*. New York: Routledge.

Giroux, H. (2000) *Stealing Innocence; Youth, Corporate Power, and the Politics of Culture*. New York: St. Martin's Press.

Hall, S., Hobson, D., Lowe, A. and Willis, P. (1996) 'Encoding/decoding', *Culture, Media, Language*. New York: Routledge.

Hawkins, S. (2002) *Settling the Pop Score: Pop Texts and Identity Politics*. Aldershot: Ashgate.

Hawkins, S. (2009) *The British Pop Dandy: Masculinity, Popular Music and Culture*. Farnham: Ashgate.

Hermes, W. and Michael, S. (2005) *Spin, 20 Years of Alternative Music: Original Writing on Rock, Hip-Hop, Techno and Beyond*. New York: Three Rivers Press.

Hopps, G. (2009) *Morrissey: The Pageant of His Bleeding Heart*. London: Continuum.

Hubbs, N. (1996) 'Music of the fourth gender: Morrissey and the sexual politics of melodic contour', *Genders*, 23, pp. 269–299.

Laquer, T. (1992) *Making Sex: Body and Gender from the Greeks to Freud*. Cambridge, MA: Harvard University Press.

Morrissey (2006) *Ringleaders of the Tormentors*, EMI.

Morrissey (2008) *Maladjusted*, EMI.

Reynolds, S. and Press. J. (1995) *The Sex Revolts*. Cambridge, MA: Harvard University Press.

Simpson, M. (2003) *Saint Morrissey: A Portrait of This Charming Man*. New York: Touchstone.

Stokes, M. (2004) 'Music and the global order', *Annual Review of Anthropology*, 33, pp. 47–72.

The Smiths (1984) *The Smiths*, Rough Trade Records.

The Smiths (1985) *Meat is Murder*, Rough Trade Records.

The Smiths (1987) *Louder Than Bombs*, Rough Trade Records.

Woods, P. (ed.) (2007) *Morrissey in Conversation; The Essential Interviews*. London: Plexus Publishing Limited.

Chapter 16

Melodramatic Morrissey: *Kill Uncle*, Cavell and the Question of the
Human Voice

Johanna Sjöstedt

Introduction

In this chapter, I will offer a reading of Morrissey's second solo album *Kill Uncle* from 1991 as written in the melodramatic mode, although as a piece of melodrama in its oft unrecognized form. While *Kill Uncle* could be described as Morrissey's most atypical album, I firmly believe that to consider it in the light of the melodramatic would show in what respect it differs from his previous releases, and what it reveals about the continuity of his writing. Hopefully, this will prevent *Kill Uncle* being put to the side, viewed as a failure in an otherwise seamless progression of great pop music. Tracing the mode of melodrama in Morrissey from his earlier writing up to *Kill Uncle*, I will also discuss what I take to be the existential concerns underlying this aesthetic category: the question of the human voice as a means for establishing connection between human beings and as a site for the expression of the human condition, thereby also touching upon the human voice as a symbol in Morrissey's lyrics. My theoretical source of inspiration comes from ordinary language philosopher Cavell, whose philosophical concerns share great affinities with those that emerge in the writing of Morrissey. After a critical engagement with Hopps' characterization of *Kill Uncle* as an instance of the aesthetics of camp, I move on to introducing ordinary language philosophy and the reasons I think it deserves a consideration in relation to the ordinary in Morrissey. Against this backdrop, the main analysis of the chapter can finally begin, and I discuss the concept of melodrama in relation to its philosophical underpinnings in order to track down the melodrama of the human voice in Morrissey's writing in general and in relation to *Kill Uncle* in particular.

Camp Kill Uncle?

In general terms, *Kill Uncle* is lowly esteemed in the extant literature on Morrissey. In *The Pageant of His Bleeding Heart*, Hopps argues that *Kill Uncle* has been badly received because critics fail to distinguish between a "deficient version of something one likes, and a successful version of something one doesn't like" (Hopps 2009: 101). While this is surely true, it is also an inadvertent testification to the poor status of the album. Among journalists who have written about it, *Kill Uncle* is considered short, light, atypical in comparison to Morrissey's other work and lacking the emotion that usually marks his music.[1] Given that we accept the view that *Kill Uncle* is different, we should ask why we automatically would take this to be a source of negative critique. To paraphrase Cavell, a change of *style* in the lyrics of pop music is a profound change and should be a subject of critical investigation (Cavell 2007: 102). What I take this to mean is that if we consider *Kill Uncle* as unique, it ought to be the subject of serious critical investigation as to what this difference consists in, not as a ground for rejecting it. In a similar vein it seems highly problematic to dismiss the album on account of the fact that it lacks emotion, since it is not clear what concept of emotion such an evaluation is grounded in. As my analysis will hopefully show, *Kill Uncle* is an album that is ripe with emotion and existential conflict, however in a mode that requires close reading to reveal what I take to be a beautiful attempt to come to grips with human life.

Hopps provides a useful discussion of the issue of lightness in Morrissey, trying to rescue the reputation of *Kill Uncle* by showing that lightness should be judged according to its own criteria, not as lacking with respect to a naïve conception of the serious. Tracing the genealogy of camp and tying it to Derrida's philosophy of deconstruction, Hopps sees the album as the epitome of camp in Morrissey, identifying its lightness and "celebration of surfaces" as positive qualities (Hopps 2009: 102). Camp, according to Hopps, is a "radical overturning of conventional values, discreetly effected by a chiasmus of incongruities, which is typically identified as a matter of treating the serious trivially and taking the trivial seriously" (Hopps 2009: 105). In other words, Hopps accepts the characterization of *Kill Uncle* as "light", but argues that this is a separate aesthetic category and directs his analysis at revealing the implications of this perspective to the reader. His claim relies not on *Kill Uncle* taken as a whole, but is rather supported through an analysis of only three songs, 'Our Frank', 'Sing Your Life' and 'King Leer'.[2] In Hopps' view, 'Our Frank' should be construed as a "tartly lethargic rejection of thinking, depth, sincerity and seriousness, whose gratuitously punning title advertises its frivolity and preference for surfaces – an effect that is dependent upon its very weakness" (Hopps 2009: 106). According to Hopps, then, Morrissey's lyrics reveal what might be described as a *meditated* rejection of deep conversation, where his preference for lightness in this instance is presented simply as a choice of taste between the light and the serious. While it clearly would be a mistake to deny the importance of lightness – whatever we take that word to mean – in Morrissey's writing, I find Hopps' analysis unsatisfying, because it fails to account for the existential predicament that is expressed throughout *Kill Uncle*. Reading for surface as opposed to depth, for style as opposed to content, Hopps ends up claiming that *Kill Uncle*, and 'Our Frank' in particular, is the expression of, if you will, the *ideology* of camp or deconstruction, thereby paradoxically ignoring what is actually said in the lyrics. Thus, if 'Our Frank' contains the lines "Our frank and open, deep conversations / They get me nowhere / They just bring me down", these words, according to Hopps, should not be taken to express a lack of faith in the possibility of human connection through the means of language, but rather as a philosophical rejection of the possibility of fixed meaning, instead exhorting us to delight in the performance and the play of signifiers. I find that to be highly implausible.

Morrissey and the ordinary

In this chapter, taking the philosophy of ordinary language as my source of inspiration, I will try to show what I take to be at least an equally productive way to analyse the lyrics and aesthetics of Morrissey. This also implies exploring and introducing some parallels between the concerns about human life and human connection in the lyrics of Morrissey and the thinking of American ordinary language philosopher Cavell and his predecessors Wittgenstein and Austin. What is distinctly original about the approach of ordinary language philosophy is that it is grounded in the analysis of the use of words in their everyday context, rejecting metaphysical language. In opposition to philosophies that view language in its "messy" everyday use as a problem to be overcome in order to achieve complete clarity, Wittgenstein argues that words separated from their ordinary use are neither better, nor worse than in their original occurrence, but rather *empty*. When we remove words from the situations in which we normally use them, they simply lose all meaning and, to use Wittgenstein's delightful phrase, go "on holiday" (Wittgenstein 1968: 38). Austin suggests that if we want to know the meaning of words, we should proceed by imagining a situation and what words we would use in that very situation, thereby eliciting knowledge about the meaning of words through discovering how we already use them, although in an unreflected mode (Austin 1961: 129).[3] In the philosophy of Cavell, the insights of Wittgenstein and Austin receive a more existential interpretation. According to Cavell, the main problem for the philosopher proceeding by ordinary language is to "discover the specific plight of mind and circumstance within which a human being gives voice to his condition" (Cavell 2007: 240). Ordinary language philosophy takes as its source language used in its everyday context, thus also focusing the situations in which words are expressed. Thereby it also reveals an interest in the problem of the human condition that is at once a question of what constitutes that condition, and the condition in turn for expressing it as such. In my view, the lyrics of Morrissey could be said to share these concerns, revealing a constant reflection and meta-reflection of what it means to desire expression in writing and singing, the problem of knowing oneself through language and the lingering conundrum of the human voice.

As Hawkins has demonstrated elsewhere in this volume, Morrissey has on several occasions expressed a desire to sing about life "as it is lived" as opposed to the glamour of the Hollywood films or the standard pop song – or simply as opposed to "life as it is not lived" (Slee 1994: 45; Haupfuhrer 1985: 106).[4] Indeed, when commenting upon the release of *Kill Uncle*, he simply stated that it was his "views of life as I live it" (Goddard 2009: 209). While the ordinary is an oft mentioned aspect of Morrissey's persona, less interest has been directed at investigating its implications for Morrissey as a writer.[5] However, Morrissey's desire to depict life as it is lived is also reflected in the very choice of language that is used in his songs. During the years in The Smiths, he once explicitly described his writing in terms of the ordinary, opposing it to the esoteric and otherworldly, thus revealing a hidden and as of yet unexplored affinity with the thought of ordinary language philosophy.

I use very fundamental language in my lyrics. I use very simplistic words, but hopefully in quite a powerful way. And by that I mean saying things that people in daily life find so very hard to say, like "I don't want a job", "I don't want to be loved", or, "I'm ugly". I mean things that are really quite simple words but things that people can never really say [...] I don't think it's ever been said in popular music.

(McCormick 1984: 30)

In my mind, this conveys a desire on Morrissey's part to put into words those things and experiences which human beings find almost impossible to express, not because they are extraordinary or unusual, nor because we lack the words to describe them, but because we realize that they would be very difficult to *hear*. They touch upon the very core of the frailty of human connection in everyday life, where my giving voice to my human condition also puts my relationship to the other into question. In other words, expressing in speech my feelings towards the world and the other in itself not only reveals, but furthers the very crisis I was trying to mitigate by speaking out. Thus, it points to an area of human existence which we all – in various degrees, admittedly – seem to experience universally but which nonetheless remains difficult to share in language. If the ordinary language philosophy of Austin takes as its starting point a fictitious situation where we imagine "what we should say when", Morrissey would appear to take his departure from the things we would *never* say in a situation that involves other human beings at all, but still remain integral to what it means to be human and which we therefore have a desire to express. As we saw earlier, Cavell claimed that the issue for an ordinary language philosopher is to investigate the conditions under which human beings give voice to their condition. Here Morrissey would seem to have tracked down a truly tricky domain that is problematic for human beings, artists and ordinary language philosophers alike. To Morrissey, pop music offers a solution to this dilemma and if we take his words seriously, we could conclude that at least one aspect of Morrissey's aesthetic project is to create a space where expressing that which, due to its precariousness and the fragility of the human voice, runs the risk of remaining unsaid is not only put into words, but turned into art.

The melodramatic mode, scepticism and the loss of voice

The aesthetics of melodrama can loosely be described as the "mode of insistent, exaggerated theatricality, an effort to push human expression to its most intense limits" (Moi 2006: 270).[6] Thus, Brooks has defined it as the "desire to express all" (Brooks 1976: 4). In Cavell's view, what underlies this desire is the paradox of a simultaneous fear of revealing too much, and at the same time having nothing to say. "[T]he condition that I find to precede, to ground the possibility and the necessity of, 'the desire to express all', [... is] the terror of absolute inexpressiveness, suffocation, which at the same time reveals itself as a terror of absolute expressiveness, unconditioned exposure; they are the extreme states of voicelessness"

(Cavell 1996: 43). In other words, melodrama could be said to be a reaction to – or perhaps rather an instance of – a feeling or situation where what I express is radically out of my control, whether it be that I reveal myself beyond my intentions, or that I am unable to convey my intentions in any meaningful way whatsoever. These are the polar states of the melodramatic mode. Either way, they express the loss of faith in the human voice as a possible means of communication.

In the writing of Cavell, the terror of voicelessness is closely connected to the philosophical problem of scepticism with respect to "other minds". In other words, whether I can be certain of the existence of other people, whether I can know others and they me. What distinguishes Cavell's thought on scepticism from, for example, the thinking of Descartes and Hume – who in different ways separated the sphere where radical doubt takes place from our ordinary lives – is that Cavell understands scepticism to be a *lived*, rather than *thought* reality (Cavell 1979: 440; Cavell 1996: 157). The question of whether the other is knowable is experienced on a daily basis in human interaction, because "my knowledge of others depend upon their expressing themselves in word or conduct", and yet, "we have cause to be disappointed in these expressions" (Cavell 2007: 254, 1979: 341). Thus, radical scepticism with respect to others is not grounded in metaphysical speculation separated from the human realm, it is a question raised in response to experiences of failure in everyday communication. The spectre of scepticism will thereby persist in all interaction between humans.

Moi traces a specific instance of scepticism in what she labels "linguistic skepticism", which expresses itself through the loss of faith in language and words as a means to get through to the other (Moi 2006: 269). Similarly, for the radical sceptic, the human body may appear not as a source of expression, but rather as an obstacle in my interaction with others. My interest in this chapter lies precisely in the relationship between the melodramatic mode, the question of the human voice and the problem of scepticism. In my view, it is possible to characterize the art of Morrissey in these terms and I find that to be revealed in his writing as subjects of his lyrics, but also constituting a key to the understanding of Morrissey's aesthetic project taken as a whole. Thus, I take the main concern of *Kill Uncle* to be an expression of the *loss of voice*, the feeling of terror that arises when I feel that my words no longer make a difference in the world, whether in the sense that I can not bring myself to enunciation, or, the reverse, that there is no one to whom my words make sense at all. Yet *Kill Uncle* is also a reflection on this most human condition, and offers itself, Morrissey and his voice, to the listener as a solution to this predicament. Before turning to *Kill Uncle*, I will now trace the genealogy of the human voice, melodrama and scepticism in the writing of Morrissey from two perspectives. First I will discuss the theme of the human voice as it is expressed on the album preceding *Kill Uncle*, *Viva Hate* from 1988. Then I will analyse the image of an enclosed inner self as it recurs in Morrissey's lyrics from 1986 to 1991, tying it to the concerns of melodrama and scepticism.

Acknowledgement and voice on *Viva Hate*

While the theme of loss of voice is most explicitly addressed on *Kill Uncle*, the subject appears also on *Viva Hate*. 'Alsatian Cousin', the first track on *Viva Hate* is organized around a very simple, yet poignant question directed to an unknown and ungendered other: "Were you and he lovers?" This phrase recurs thrice; it is both the opening and closing line of the song and it also appears in the beginning of the second verse. In its initial occurrence, the question is followed by yet another query that is more ambiguous in tone: "Were you and he lovers? / And *would you say so if you were*?" Judging by the first line, the song would appear to concern the issue of knowledge – what did actually take place? However, the next line shifts the focus into a question of whether the "you" – should such an event have occurred – would *acknowledge that act in words to the "I"*, thereby putting the first issue into the shade.

The second time the question appears, it is in a slightly altered context: "Were you and he lovers? / And if you were then *say that you were*!" Initially the desire for the speech of the other is phrased by means of a question, now it is expressed as a desperate and exasperated appeal to the other to speak out. Yet the other remains silent, and before the song ends, with the very same phrase with which it was opened, it is revealed to the listener that the "I" has witnessed the sexual act which the song encircles, and the song is brought to a close by the singer conceding that his begging for answers occurs although he already knows what he wants the other to confess: "I ask *even though I know* / Were you and he lovers?" What first seemed to give voice to a desire to know the "facts" thus turns out to be a desire for truth in the voice of the other, a desire that the other acknowledge what the "I" already knows to be true. Knowing the truth and the desire to hear that truth in the words of another person are not the same thing, and it is precisely this problem that constitutes the theme of the song. In the philosophy of Cavell, the lyrics could be interpreted as addressing the problem of the other in terms of *acknowledgement*. While the question of scepticism at first appears to concern whether I can have certain knowledge of the existence of others – here, the initial question of what had taken place – Cavell argues that the problem in fact is one of acknowledgement. "Acknowledgement goes beyond knowledge. (Goes beyond, not, so to speak, in the order of knowledge, but in its requirement that I *do* something or reveal something on the basis of that knowledge)" (Cavell 2007: 257). In other words, knowledge requires confirmation in the voice of the other. In this song, the conflict between truth and the acknowledgement of that truth takes place through the symbolism of human senses, where the knowledge of the eye comes up short against the acknowledgement to be found in the human voice. In the end the listener, as well as the singer, is left where the song began – in the heartbreaking, palpable presence of the other's silence.

If 'Alsatian Cousin' reads as the desperate desire for acknowledgement through truth in the voice of the other, *Viva Hate* also includes a song which poses the problem of the human voice and acknowledgement in completely opposite terms. 'Dial-A-Cliché' is the retelling of a conversation, presumably over the phone, where it is the very exchange of words that yields disappointment. Indeed, what takes place can hardly be called a conversation at all, granted that the word implies at least some dimension of mutuality. Rather, it should be characterized as two parallel monologues, where the first one occurs when the singer listens to the clichéd, stereotype phrases of the anonymous interlocutor: "Do as I do and scrap your fey ways / Grow up, be a man, and close your mealy mouth." Thus, if the other is now present through his words, these words not only fail to bring acknowledgement, they are outspokenly injurious, even instructing the singer to silence his voice. Thereby the possibility of mutual recognition through the means of language is eliminated altogether. The presence of the other consequently comes at the price of the singer's own voice. While the singer keeps quiet in relation to his interlocutor, the song itself is constituted by the portrayal of an inner monologue that is the result of this refusal of acknowledgement, depicting the singer's thoughts and feelings: "But the person underneath, where does he go? / Does he slide by the wayside, or does he just die? / And you find that you've organized your feelings / For people / Who didn't like you then, and do not like you now." Towards the end of the song, it is implied that the singer has previously tried to follow the advice given, resulting only in suffering: "I've changed / But I'm in pain." While 'Dial-A-Cliché' stages a situation, which at first glance by definition should involve communication between human beings by means of the spoken word, the song reveals that this need not be the case. Thus, if 'Alsatian Cousin' is a successful expression of the desire for acknowledgement, and failure to grant satisfaction could be attributed to the absence of reply from the other, 'Dial-A-Cliché' shows the suffocated voice of the singer in the presence of the other's clichéd words, leaving the singer to his private inner monologue, forced to choose between acknowledgement achieved through hiding his inner self and rejecting contact with the other altogether. Either way, he remains alone. Both of these songs, although in different modes, thus offer a picture of the human voice, where it is either my voice or that of the other. No co-existence is possible.

"Zooming into the inner you": Exposure of the private self

Accompanying the idea of scepticism in relation to other minds – that there is a private self that is beyond reach for others – is a concomitant conception that this inner space is completely known by me, or, in other words, that I have full access to myself. In Cavell's view, the existential benefit of having this outlook on the world is that it "relieve[s] me of the responsibility for making myself known to others" (Cavell 1979: 351). That is, I no longer have to go through the painful process of trying to express myself in the face of a possibly indifferent other, only to experience the disappointment of failure. Importantly, this also draws a firm line, impossible to cross, between the world and me as well as between other human beings and me. Clearly, if this were to be realized, it would make any human connection impossible – and unnecessary. Although pointing to an imagined radical separation, what is truly desired is a bond *beyond* the fallacies of human communication, where I am known in an unmediated mode. Cavell thus claims that this fantasy is driven by the very terror that I described above, where "I am powerless to make myself known [… or where] what I express is beyond my control" (Cavell 1979: 351). In that sense, it is related to the same extreme poles of radical seclusion or complete exposure that belong to the register of melodrama. In Morrissey's lyrics, the image of an enclosed, inner space recurs frequently, particularly during the last years of The Smiths and his early solo years.[7] In 'Asleep' the listener encounters what is presumably the last words of a desperate person yearning to get himself elsewhere, here figured as a place beyond this life: "Deep in the cell of my heart, I really want to go." In 'Shoplifters Of The World Unite', we get the vision of a very peculiar revolution, formulated in opposition to the power and energy expressed in the Communist Manifesto, through Morrissey's claim that he "[t]ried living in the real world / Instead of a shell / But I was bored before I even began". Both of these songs thus frame an understanding of the world with a completely separated "I", where the opposite realm is figured either as death or the boredom of the everyday. In 'Angel Angel, Down We Go Together', the image returns once again, this time by virtue of having been broken through, exposing the frail contents of the soul: "When they've used you / And they've broken you / And wasted all your money / And cast your shell aside / I will be here / Believe me, I will be here." Significantly, the song avoids adopting the point of view of the person exposed, as if the violence of the act of intruding on another person's most private domain has robbed that person of his very voice. Instead the narrative is presented from the perspective of a still constant "I" who promises to remain steadfast no matter what. Against the backdrop of my above characterization of the relationship between the aesthetics of melodrama and the fear of exposure and voicelessness, it should come as no surprise that this song reads as one of Morrissey's most melodramatic pieces of writing.

By the time of *Kill Uncle*, the line between the self and the outside is slightly displaced. While the album in its entirety, in my view, should be taken as an attempt to renegotiate the divisions between self and other, between self and world, the image of the enclosed inner self emerges most explicitly in 'The Harsh Truth Of The Camera Eye'. If 'Asleep' and 'Shoplifters Of The World Unite' are told from the point of view of the secluded self, upholding a radical division between the "I" and the world, and if 'Angel, Angel Down We Go Together' shows the breakdown of that separation, speaking from the perspective of a constant bystander, these categories are undermined in several ways in 'The Harsh Truth Of The Camera Eye'. Notably, the song includes two different perspectives, where the major part of the song is told from without, using the word "you", yet receding to the point of view of the "I" in the closing lines. Still, the song has only one person in its purview, the one having his private self exposed by a photographer by means of a camera: "This so friendly lens/It zooms into the inner you/And it tells the harsh truth / And nothing but." The violence of 'Angel, Angel Down We Go Together' is now replaced with an experience of a more ambiguous kind, where the photographer has "had it in for" the protagonist, yet the – perhaps not so – friendly camera still inflicts painful exposure, revealing more than "you ever wanted to know / showing what you didn't want shown". This song thus furthers the symbolic connection between knowledge and the eye and their lacking abilities when it comes to yielding acknowledgement and intimacy. Indeed, the final line of the song consists of a subtle plea: "I don't want to be judged any more / I would sooner be loved, just blindly loved", explicitly indicating that in order for the "I" to be recognized, the judging eyes of the other would have to be closed and the question of truth thereby suspended. The existential predicament behind 'Angel Angel Down We Go Together' and 'The Harsh Truth Of The Camera Eye' is the same and the pain of exposure is imminent in both cases, yet the last song is less melodramatic in tone. To me it reads more as a somewhat resigned though heartfelt wish for things to be different, yet implicating the notion that they never will. 'The Harsh Truth Of The Camera Eye' is perhaps best described as written in a post-melodramatic mode, or in the unrecognized, negative shadow of what we ordinarily take to be the original expression of melodrama.

It is instructive to compare these four songs with 'Found Found Found', the sixth track on *Kill Uncle*. While this piece lacks the image of a secluded self, the song nonetheless gives voice to the philosophy of scepticism that underpins the image of an insular soul. What was earlier merely implied as an underlying existential structure, present only through means of imagery, now becomes an object of reflection. The lyrics are constructed as a pondering inner monologue of the desire to find genuine, unmediated communication with another human being – "Someone who's worth it in this murkiness / Someone who's never seeming scheming" – and yet it reveals a simultaneous fear of being exposed, should your love to the other be expressed: "I do believe that more you give your love / The more you're bound to lose". At the heart of the song is the apprehension that the imagined closeness with another person may very well be a fantasy, that this imagined person "Who wants to be / With me / All the time" may indeed not exist, thereby hinting at the conclusion that the self is metaphysically alone, radically separated from others without any means to establish a connection. As such, it is the gloomiest of pictures.

The ethics of witnessing

At last we are now in a position to discuss *Kill Uncle* at greater length.[8] On *Viva Hate* I analysed the polarity of voice, where the voice of the "I" was either fully expressed in the absence of the other, or suffocated in his presence. I also described the evolution of imagery in relation to an initially secluded self, radically separated from the world, but later on in Morrissey's solo work, subjected to painful exposure through the violent intrusion of others. These genealogies merge on *Kill Uncle* in 'Mute Witness', a portrayal of simultaneous voicelessness and vulnerability beyond comprehension. And if 'Found Found Found' was an expression of the fear that the self be metaphysically alone, this song brings us right back to the melodrama of everyday loneliness in the midst of men.

The lyrics of 'Mute Witness' portray a traumatized woman trying to bear witness to earlier experiences, which remain unknown to the listener throughout the song due to the fact that she is unable to utter a single word: "her silent words describing the fright of last night". Abundant with references to attempted and failed acts of communication, the lyrics further depict the bodily expressions of the woman as "standing on the table with

all arms flailing", describing her "mime in time so nicely". The song also reveals her
less emotional expression as she is "crying so loudly on the floor" to the point of
ing upon alternative means of communication: "will she sketch the answer later? /
will ask her". The song ends with her being sent away in a taxi, literally leaving a scene
d. While the song is told from the perspective of someone who passively registers this
e picture, this person remains very anonymous, which strikes me as an aspect of the
on itself. This extreme state of victimhood and voicelessness is marked by the absence
singular, concrete other, blurring the division between self and other in a manner
robs the other of his very face. The title 'Mute Witness' clearly refers to the woman
question, yet it is also an apposite description of those who watch her break down. The
ere sight of the victimized witness yields new witnesses in turn; people become mute in
esponse to her trying-yet-failing to find a voice for herself. Disclosing more than those
around her can bear, the situation quickly becomes a spectacle, turning the surrounding
crowd into a voiceless audience. Although the song implicates a prior trauma, it primarily
touches upon this double scandal of the human condition, where failure to communicate a
shocking experience produces only silence in return and where the loss of voice generates
voicelessness. In consonance with the imagery of 'Alsatian Cousin', this song thus portrays
the human voice as the site for recognition. Although it is clear that the woman has seen
something – *knows* something by means of the eye – the others depend upon her words in
order to acknowledge her knowledge. Bearing witness can happen only by means of the
spoken word and when that voice is lost, so is acknowledgement. Instead we are left with
the distance of sight and the horrifying picture of the woman imitating the expressions of
genuine connection.

While the narrator in 'Mute Witness' is effaced in the confrontation with acute suffering,
the ethics of witnessing failure in human expression is highlighted also in 'Asian Rut' and
'Driving Your Girlfriend Home'. In spite of the fact that these songs are dramatically different
when it comes to the *effects* of the loss of voice – the first song ending in cruel murder, the
second with a polite handshake – the implications for the onlooker are the same: the terror
of not finding a way to respond to the demands of a human being in pain, as if witnessing
distress itself meant being implicated in the suffering. 'Driving Your Girlfriend Home' – the
title succinctly describing the scene – depicts an everyday situation, much in the same way
that 'Dial-A-Cliché' retold a conversation over the phone. Although the lyrics reproduce
verbatim what the girlfriend says, there is no dialogue, and the words of the song are in fact
directed at the girlfriend's male partner. It is the stark contrast between the heartbreaking,
melodramatic outbursts from the woman and the silence she receives in return from the
driver that forms the centre of this song. Thus, when the girlfriend laments "Why did I
end up / So deeply involved in / The very existance / I planned on avoiding" her words are
met with indifferent silence. The singer laconically concedes: "I can't answer". This section
recurs twice and the second time it is revealed that the driver rather "can't tell her", thereby
introducing a certain amount of ambivalence as to why the singer keeps quiet. While the
first phrase seems to suggest that finding an answer to the girlfriend's emotional demands is

impossible because he does not *know* the answer to her question, the second one indicates that it is the very speech act itself that is too fragile. Indeed, it is the very ambiguity, as to whether the singer knows a truth too painful be told or withholds speech because of the absence of truth itself, that emerges as the strongest theme of this song. Both underline the act of speaking as such, emphasizing once again the inadequacy of knowledge and the frailty of the human voice when it comes to acknowledging others by means of the spoken word.

'Asian Rut', on the other hand, sets the scene of a situation where words no longer seem to be an option. Portrayed as a case of revenge between clashing English and Asian "boys", what we get is only a snapshot in a series of killings which may go on forever. In keeping with the imagery of Morrissey's lyrics, the quiet of the situation and the striking absence of words is marked out as a bad omen. "Peace through the school / It's so quiet in the hall / It's a strange sign for one / Of what's to come". This ill-boding silence is accompanied by metaphors of light, suggesting that the brightness of the day is beyond the ordinary. "Day oh so late / Strangely the sun still shone" – as if the fact that this kind of severe violence may occur in broad daylight in a most regular school adds to the shock itself. After an emotional description of the Asian boy having been "dealt a blow", the song ends in the painful yearning to be elsewhere. "I'm just passing through here / On my way to somewhere civilized / And maybe I'll even arrive?" In this surprisingly light afternoon, the singer, for no reason at all apart from the light that enables his eyes to see, becomes a (mute) witness to an act of violence that produces only a desire to leave. Responding seems to be impossible.

According to Cavell, the concept of acknowledgement does not depend on whether we actually succeed in acknowledging each other. Rather, it is the "category in terms of which a given response is evaluated" (Cavell 2007: 264). Thus there is no way to escape the aspect of acknowledgement in everyday life, since "avoidance of the presence of others is not blindness or deafness to their claim upon us; it is as conclusive an acknowledgement that they are present as murdering them would be" (Cavell 2007: 332). In other words, failure to connect may result in murder or silence, but the helplessness that they inflict upon those standing by the side is similar when it comes to the question of responding. This helplessness is by no means innocent, in the sense that it would absolve us from action or acknowledgement. Rather, it is an instance of the terrifying experience of lived scepticism with respect to others, and the fact that Morrissey's lyrics manage to reveal also the pain of the onlooker, in the very face of the suffering of the Asian boy, the mute witness or the girlfriend, without diminishing the importance of either of them, bears great testimony to his skills as a writer.

The double voice of *Kill Uncle*

By now we have seen multiple components merging on *Kill Uncle*, all sustained by the philosophy of scepticism with respect to others – whether it comes in the reflected mode of 'Found Found Found' or in the description of settings of everyday situations where humans find it impossible to produce a single word or action in response to the urgent need expressed by others. This theme is phrased through the imagery of the human body, where the eye is portrayed as a means for knowledge yielding only distance, disappointment and exposure, whereas the human voice is presented as the site for acknowledgement. However, thus far in our analysis, the voice becomes a symbol of the centripetal force of recognition only by virtue of its *failure* to grant acknowledgement. Before discussing the problem of the human voice at greater length, I should now like to return to the issue of lightness in Morrissey. In the beginning of the chapter I rehearsed Hopps' reading of *Kill Uncle* as an instance of camp, and I criticized it on account of the fact that it failed to take into consideration the existential aspects of the album, presenting the lightness of the lyrics as a mere rejection of the serious. As my analysis shows, this is a rash and misleading description. *Kill Uncle* is nothing but a testification to the tragedy of the failure of the everyday human voice. At the heart of *Kill Uncle* is thus not a "celebration of surfaces" but rather sentiments of desperation at the impossibility of deriving any truly genuine acknowledgement from the words or expressions of the human body at all.

'Our Frank' is the opening track of *Kill Uncle*, and also the first single to be released from the album. It should therefore be taken as a key in the interpretation of it. In a somewhat declamatory mode, the song begins by the almost too straightforward lines: "Our frank and open / Deep conversations / They get me nowhere / They bring me down […] God give me patience / Just no more conversation". The song ends with the desperate melodramatic plea that somebody help the singer stop thinking "so deeply / so bleakly". Against the backdrop of my analysis of the human voice in Morrissey's writing, this seems to come very close to a literal description of what I have taken to be the main theme of this album. My suggestion is that they in fact should be taken at face value. They express what they want to say, no more, no less, and this is the very kernel of their aesthetic value. Clearly, the trickiness in critiquing such lines is not that they are difficult. The problem is rather that the words are too direct, flaunting themselves in the face of the listener, almost inviting a search for a more profound meaning behind the simplicity of the formulations. While Hopps is thus correct to identify this as an aesthetics of lightness in the sense that the words are very straightforward, I think he, too, steps into the trap of being overly theoretical, precisely because he presents it as a matter of a *choice* of philosophy. In my view, the task of the critic is not to explicate these simple words in theoretical terms, *but rather to show the conditions and the significance of the emergence of such a direct mode of expression.*

Similarly, directness is the most prominent feature of 'Sing Your Life'. Here the pain of finding the right words in everyday situations of human interaction stands in stark contrast to the simplicity of artistic expression.

"Sing your life / Any fool can think of words that rhyme / Many others do / Why don't you? / Do you want to? / Sing your life / Just walk right up to microphone and name / All the things you love / All the things that you loathe […] And have the pleasure of / Saying what you mean / Have the pleasure of meaning what you sing."

If my analysis of the melodramatic aspect in the human voice as it emerges in the writing of Morrissey is in any way successful, these words should now be able to stand on their own, requiring no further analysis. Indeed, it is the *sheer contrast* between the melodramatic trouble of finding the right words in everyday situations and the ease with which it is possible to put words to music – most notably so in 'Sing Your Life' and 'Our Frank' – that is the most perspicuous aesthetic achievement of *Kill Uncle*. According to Hopps, 'Sing Your Life' is an instance of camp. This argument – "the sign that its lightness is a refusal of the seriousness and the 'depth' of realist aboutness" – is based on an interpretation of Morrissey's reply to a question posed towards the end of the song.[9] "Make no mistake my friend / Your pointless life will end / But before you go / Can you look at the truth? / You have a lovely singing voice." In Hopps' analysis this answer verges on the bathetic. "[H]aving taken us to the edge of what appears to be an imminent Morrisseyesque disclosure, the singer swerves away with the bathos of a 'knock, knock' punch line." In my view, however, it is *precisely the very beauty of the singing voice that emerges as the sole measurement of authentic truth* in Morrissey's writing. The singing voice suspends judgement and knowledge, and, to put it in Cavellian terms, introduces a sphere where acknowledgement can happen. While *Kill Uncle* thus offers a depressing picture of the human voice as a means of acknowledgement in the daily undertakings of human life, it rejoices in the possibilities of recognition in the aesthetic realm. Finally, then, we are in a position to see the problem of Hopps' attempt to describe *Kill Uncle* as camp. Pitting lightness and seriousness against each other in a deconstructionist mode, Hopps fails to see that the lightness and transparency of the language in *Kill Uncle* receives its value precisely against the backdrop of the difficulty in finding the right words to the demands of other human beings in everyday life, all vividly described on many occasions in Morrissey's lyrics. Rather than camp, I would like to characterize the album as a prime example of what Cavell calls "the discovery that the everyday is an exceptional achievement" (Cavell 1979: 463). While the question of the human voice resonates strongly throughout all of Morrissey's writing, *Kill Uncle* is the album where this theme receives its most thorough exposition. As such, it is a masterpiece.

Notes

1. For a discussion of the reception of *Kill Uncle*, see Hopps (2009: 101). Jounalist perspectives on *Kill Uncle* can be found in these sources: (Bret 1994: 113; Brown 2008: 171; Goddard 2009: 208; Rogan 1993: 301; Rogan 2006: 163; Simpson 2004: 29, 144). Like Hopps, I have found the writing on Morrissey as a lyricist disappointing, and in view of the fact that this chapter is dedicated entirely to the writing of Morrissey, I decided not to discuss earlier Morrissey criticism in greater detail (cf. Hopps 2009: xi).
2. Hopps does acknowledge that *Kill Uncle* varies greatly in tone, thus not taking it as a thoroughly camp album, but still maintains that it is camp in its keynote (Hopps 2009: 108).
3. Literary scholars will surely be familiar with Fish's reading of Austin in 'How ordinary is ordinary language', where he takes ordinary language to be opposed to literary language, claiming that ordinary

language "designates a kind of language that 'merely' presents or mirrors facts independently of any consideration of value, interest, perspective, purpose and so on" (Fish 1980: 97). As Moi shows in her *What is a Woman?* this is very far from the views expressed by Austin and Cavell, where ordinary language is opposed only to metaphysical language (Moi 1999: 209–210). I take it that language that is used in literature, from the perspective of ordinary language philosophy, instead should be seen as a specific modification of ordinary language, without drawing any clear line between literary and non-literary use a priori. Obviously this touches upon the question of what distinguishes literary texts from other texts, a concern I will not address in this footnote. In *Uses of Literature* Felski provides a useful discussion of the distinction made between the literary and non-literary, where she shows that those theories that argue in favour of the literary as an other-worldly category also end up being negative about the ordinary, everyday, merely seeing it as a chaotic ensemble of the non-literary (2008: 6). In my view, Morrissey is an artist that benefits from a perspective that does not draw a radical distinction between the artistic and the non-artistic.

4. Discussing Morrissey in terms of the ordinary is quite common. However, those analyses focus almost exclusively on the image of The Smiths and Morrissey, pointing out the ordinariness of the band name, Morrissey's appearance and his refusal to join in with regular pop culture (Hopps 2009: 14). Sometimes this takes highly dubious turns. For example, when Michael Bracewell claims that Morrissey is ordinary, it is closely connected to his concept of Englishness, where ordinariness is taken to be English in contrast to the international glamour of pop that Morrissey revolts against (Bracewell 1998: 219). Thus, Bracewell establishes what should by now be a well-known dichotomous hierarchy between the authentic and the artificial, the ordinary and the perversion of glamour, between the English and the international. This is a deeply problematic and essentialist understanding of culture, which there are strong reasons to oppose, although I will have to return to that question another time.

5. Hopps briefly compares the ordinary in Morrissey with that of romanticism, which involves similar concerns to mine, and which constitutes a connection I believe is worth further analysis (Hopps 2009: 80). For the time being, my focus lies elsewhere in the sense that I highlight the existential aspects of ordinary language philosophy, tying that to a very close analysis of Morrissey's lyrics.

6. I should make clear that I am not claiming that melodrama is the *sole* possible aesthetic expression of this existential predicament, only that this is the focus of my investigation in this chapter.

7. I do not by any means want to suggest that this analysis is exhaustive when it comes to the question of privacy, separation and seclusion in the writing of Morrissey. The avid listener will surely find more examples of her own.

8. I will not consider 'Tony The Pony' in this reading. It was included only on the American release of the album, allegedly without Morrissey's consent (Goddard 2009: 448). Nor will I discuss 'King Leer', '(I'm) The End Of The Family Line' or "There's A Place In Hell For Me And My Friends", due to limited space.

9. All references to Hopps in this paragraph are to Hopps (2009: 108).

Bibliography

Austin, J. L. (1961) *Philosophical Papers*. Oxford: Oxford University Press.
Bracewell, M. (1998) *England is Mine: Pop Life in Albion from Wilde to Goldie*. London: Flamingo.
Bret, D. (1994) *Morrissey: Landscapes of the Mind*. London: Robson Books.
Brown, L. (2008) *Meetings with Morrissey*. London: Omnibus Press.

Cavell, S. (1979) *The Claim of Reason: Wittgenstein, Skepticism, Morality and Tragedy.* Oxford: Oxford University Press.

Cavell, S. (1996) *Contesting Tears: The Hollywood Melodrama of the Unknown Woman.* Chicago: University of Chicago Press.

Cavell, S. (2007) *Must We Mean What We Say? A Book of Essays*, 2nd edn. Cambridge: Cambridge University Press.

Felski, R. (2008) *Uses of Literature.* Malden, MA: Blackwell Publishers.

Fish, S. (1980) 'How ordinary is ordinary language?', in *Is There a Text in this Class ? The Authority of Interpretive Communities.* Cambridge, MA: Harvard University Press.

Goddard, S. (2009) *Mozipedia: The Encyclopedia of Morrissey and The Smiths.* London: Ebury Press.

Haupfuhrer, F. (1985) 'Roll over Beethoven, and tell Madonna the news: The Smiths' Morrissey is pop's latest Messiah', *People Weekly*, 24th June.

Hopps, G. (2009) *Morrissey: The Pageant of His Bleeding Heart.* New York & London: Continuum.

McCormick, N. ([1984] 2007) 'All men have secrets …', in Paul A. Woods (ed.) *Morrissey in Conversation: The Essential Interviews.* London: Plexus, pp. 27–33.

Moi, T. (1999) *What is a Woman? And Other Essays.* Oxford: Oxford University Press.

Moi, T. (2006) *Henrik Ibsen and the Birth of Modernism: Art, Theater, Philosophy.* Oxford: Oxford University Press.

Rogan, J. (1993) *Morrissey and Marr: The Severed Alliance*, 2nd edn. London: Omnibus Press.

Rogan, J. (2004) *Morrissey: The Albums.* London: Calidore.

Simpson, M. (2004) *Saint Morrissey.* London: SAF.

Slee, J. (1968) *Peepholism: Into the Art of Morrissey.* London: Sidgewick & Jackson.

Wittgenstein, L. (1968) *Philosophical Investigations*, trans. G. E. M. Anscombe, 3rd edn. New York: Macmillan.

Woods, P. (ed.) (2007) *Morrissey in Conversation: The Essential Interviews.* London: Plexus.

Chapter 17

'You Have Killed Me' – Tropes of Hyperbole and Sentimentality in Morrissey's Musical Expression

Stan Hawkins

Morrissey's power as a performer lies in his unorthodox manipulation of sound and movement: the abandon in dance, the unpredictability of gesture, the wayward microphone technique and the unbridled love of eccentric phrasing.

(Rogan 1992: 16)

The description by Johnny Rogan, biographer of the best-seller, *Morrissey and Marr*, almost two decades ago, sheds light on one of the most influential late-twentieth-century figures in British popular culture. For sure, Morrissey has always grasped where he comes from, who his major influences are, and what it means to be a performer as much as a fan.[1]

In actual fact, his performances alone tell us much about the impact of music and reception in a historical context. By attempting to unravel the intricacies of his subjectivity, my main objective in this chapter is to assess the meaning behind a very special recorded performance.

Pop songs, I have argued in earlier studies, are based upon sets of musical rules that shape aesthetic experiences (Hawkins 2001, 2002, 2009), granting us access to the orders within and outside our daily lives. For the song always tells a story, and if anyone knows this, it is Morrissey. One could say his flamboyancy, rooted in a "wayward" and original approach to performance, has fostered an image that highlights the Baudelairean anti-hero, whose temperament is predicated upon realism, fantasy and creativity at the same time.[2] Down the ages numerous renowned British gentlemen have been assigned roles in society, traceable in the different performance traditions of the likes of Beau Brummel, Byron, Wilde, Coward, Crisp, Bowie and others. Historically, Morrissey stems from this strong line of British dandies, his musical style rooted in indie rock, music hall, pantomime, operetta, French *chanson*, as much as British pop. Exhibiting the contradictory features of masculinity, he has always played on the ambivalence of gender roles, and by toying with "otherness", he continuously subverts the safe haven of the white heteronormative male. Proof of this lies in many of the narratives surrounding his songs. Hardly surprising, then, his on- and off-stage personae are a site for much intrigue, where the controversial stories surrounding his personal life – rumours of his gay, bisexual or even asexual identity abound – form part of the spectacle of his act.[3]

In this chapter I want to mainly consider the intricate details of his performance style, mapping them against the musical expression in a song from his 2006 album, *Ringleader of the Tormentors*, which reached number one in the UK album charts. The song I have selected, 'You Have Killed Me', the album's first single, was played for the first time on radio station BBC 6 on 4th February, 2006. Used for the marketing of this song and album, a range of powerful images and photo shots would document Morrissey's life at this point in time. As Melissa Connor's analysis of Morrissey's use of visual imagery elsewhere in this volume demonstrates, iconography in pop accounts for a good deal of the pleasure experienced by fans, as much as the music. For sure, details of visual packaging complement the sound of the artist, and, in no uncertain terms, album covers mediate much to an artist's fans. The image on *Ringleader of the Tormentors* bears this out. Poised in the heat of the moment, Morrissey is depicted as the maestro in full flight, dressed in black tie and looking ever so earnest. Instantly, this comes across as an impudent allusion to the world-renowned classical label Deutsche Grammophon, with the cover appropriating a near identical logo and design. More than a touch of parody is invested in the monochrome photo, conceitedly positioning Morrissey as virtuoso instrumentalist within a genre he could not be less part of – the trained orchestral musician *par excellence*.

Publicity shots of this ilk are clearly cunning marketing ploys, characterizing him as someone we know full well he is not – *je ne suis pas se que je suis*. Broadly speaking, the subject matter of *Ringleader of the Tormentors* is about the theatricality of the pop performance, relayed through both the musical and visual codes of attire, attitude, masking, pose and so on. Essentially, the superficiality of this image – its self-denigrating send-up – reveals Morrissey's construction in relation to his "real self", or better, his ordinariness. Also, it reminds us that through music the body obeys the generative rules of movement: hand gestures, shoulder shrugs, arm sweeps, awkward facial contortions, eyebrow winks, head nods and pouting. For all intents and purposes, the expressivity captured in the unlikely pose of Morrissey clutching a violin is an outright admission of self-irony, for it signifies insiderism and is fully dependent on his fans grasping his parody.[4]

Many musical features can impact our understanding of an artist, not least the characteristics of the singing voice. This begs the question: how is music mediated through the voice, and how does it affect the artist's status? Notably, Morrissey's sung voice closely resembles his spoken voice – something that is not as common as one would think. Of this he is well aware, as revealed in numerous interviews. Intentionally, his voice comes over "natural" and "untrained" – by untrained I am referring to that particular type of voice that defies the *bel canto* tradition. This type of voice succumbs to the ordinariness of speech through a range of technicalities, such as pitch slippage, straining and controlled exertion (see Moore 2001; Hawkins 2002, 2009; Hopps 2009).[5] Certainly, Morrissey's voice helps stage his credibility (read: authenticity) as he accesses his fans on an intimate level. Pop artists, as Nicola Dibben has argued, tend to operate through complex channels of authentic emotional expression where the voice occupies a central position: "The normative staging of pop voices provides aural intimacy with the star and therefore contributes to the notion of access to a 'real' person behind the star-image" (Dibben 2009: 331). Thus, in mediating his "real self" through the framework of his star-image, Morrissey draws on, if not caricatures, a lineage of alternative musicians, indie artists and groups. Recycling his cultural heritage through a range of strategies, then, he turns to a singing style that challenges fixed forms of categorization. In this light, his persona needs to be contextualized in a broader narrative of male identity, ethnicity, Irish roots, social class, a Mancunian background, a British pop sensibility and so forth.

Hyperbole and sentimentality

Morrissey's songs protest on many levels. And this has to do with tactics of control and disengagement. For instance, the carefully regulated narrative he pursues in the track 'You Have Killed Me' reveals storytelling antics that are brought to life vividly. To explore this, I want to activate the terms "hyperbole" and "sentimentality", my intention being to consider how style and rhetoric is fashioned *musically*. Hyperbole, in my analysis, is a communicative device intended to evoke strong feelings, which, in musical performance, becomes a discursive code for representing an artist's sensibility. Musical hyperbole functions in unique ways and is integral to Morrissey's strategy, affecting both interpretation and reception; it is a powerful device that has a connotative role. Moreover, it underlies the artist's spirit of engagement, his idealism, his earnestness and ironic distancing on all matters. If hyperbole is an ingredient of Morrissey's musical style, it is also a signifier of attitude and mannerism, making things seem "natural" when they are not. Indeed, we might even be swayed to believe that hyperbolic delivery is a reflection of reality as we identify directly with the ideological representations of the performer in question.

When it comes to sentimentality – a literary device for inducing heightened emotional responses through a sympathetic contract with the listener – a musical performance can be shrewd, evoking feelings such as anger, indignation, mourning, sorrow, pathos and so on. In effect, how we become engaged with sentiments can be mirrored in our responses to any musical performance. Put differently, if the intention is to deliver a song in a manner appropriate to its social, historic and cultural context, the performer's strategy is in part a self-dramatization. With this in mind, I want to identify sentimentality as a hallmark of Morrissey's appeal and skills in negotiation. My contention then, is that Morrissey's style lends itself to hyperbole and sentimentality in a way that is double-coded: on the one hand, the strategy is to parody, exaggerate and subvert, while, on the other hand, it is to ascribe to a range of emotions that are calculatedly excessive and permissive.

Written by Morrissey and the Texas guitarist, Jesse Tobias, who toured with him and played lead guitar on the *Years of Refusal* album, 'You Have Killed Me' signals something unique musically. In contrast to the album cover, the single's cover is emphatically macabre. Morrissey lays strewn over a rail track, looking as much ravished as dead. Gazing ahead demurely, an ever so slight smirk accompanies his stare – a hint of pleasure and pain?

'You Have Killed Me' would become Morrissey's joint highest UK chart entry (with his hit, 'Irish Blood, English Heart', from the 2004 album, *You are the Quarry*), entering the UK singles chart in 2006 at number three. Instantly one is struck by the abundance of Italian references and cryptic insinuations of carnal love. Why Rome, why love and murder, we might ask? In the comfort of a room on the fourth floor of the Dorchester, journalist Paul Morley failed to get Morrissey to kiss and tell:

MORLEY: Listening to the new record, it's one of the first things the listener will think
            – he's in love, and it's not nosiness to want to ask about that [...] well, it is
            [...] But it's also wanting to give the songs some kind of wider framework.
            So, in a situation like this, you being there, and me being here, together in
            this lovely room overlooking Hyde Park on the notable occasion of your
            new record, it seems right and fitting to ask: are you in love?
MORRISSEY: I'm in love with something. I often am.
MORLEY: Not someone?
MORRISSEY: Not a human being, no. And on these songs, I'm in love with something. So,
            keep stabbing away.
MORLEY: You've moved to Rome?
MORRISSEY: I travel so much that I actually live nowhere. I live in the middle of the
            Atlantic Ocean. I left Los Angeles last year after seven years. I became an
            Italianophile, yes.
MORLEY: You moved to Rome with someone?
MORRISSEY: Something.
MORLEY: Because of someone?
MORRISSEY: Something.
MORLEY: Someone?
MORRISSEY: Something.
MORLEY: One.
MORRISSEY: Thing.

(Morrissey in interview with Paul Morley, 2007)

A short while later Morrissey feigns his exasperation: "Does it really matter in the end one way or another, whether I have, haven't, have never, have soon?"[6] Evasive retorts of this kind highlight Morrissey's fugitive identity. He knows that obstinacy is a well-worn strategy of concealment that can be as entertaining as misleading. Thus, by rejecting point blank any clarification of "someone" or "something" (which would inevitably lead to sexual categorization), he verifies his fiercely private nature at the same time he discloses a double strategy of elusiveness that he is aware his fans expect and revel in.[7]

Themes of self-torment, pride, love and death in 'You Have Killed Me' are graphic. "As I live and breathe you have killed me", a delicious oxymoron in itself, elicits all those contradictory responses for which Morrissey is famous. Obviously, the strategy is to keep us guessing: who are his addressees – a lover, a member of the public, the murderer of Pasolini or even us, the fans? And, if he has been killed, what type of death might he be referring to? Could it be *la petite mort* – the little death, the refractory period directly following orgasm – that euphoric moment of almost passing out after the "act"? Or, is it simply a euphemism for all that is detestable, as in Thomas Hardy's *Tess of the D'Urbervilles*, where the "small death" symbolizes a thoroughly unpleasant experience. Death, the main theme in this song, also hints at something Barthesian, with *la petite mort* purporting to the very objective behind reading literature (Barthes used the concept metaphorically in describing what feeling should be experienced from any great literature – *The Pleasure of the Text* (1973)). But, whatever the case, "being killed" or indeed "dying for love" is sentimentalized, with Morrissey egging us on. Thus, what we experience in his music is an element of *pretence* that renders the theme of death farcical yet sinister.

Interpreting a song is no mean task, and can be approached from different angles. Pasolini's untimely horrible death in 1975, and the outrage surrounding this event, takes centre stage in 'You Have Killed Me'. A narrative of betrayal underscores Morrissey's own psychodrama via the fate of Pasolini, as, with great indignation, he openly declares his awkward relationship to the outside world. Seen in the context of *Ringleader of the Tormentors*, the track is one of the more serious songs. In my reading it suggests a bold statement of conflicting emotional states and torment; it is about the putting on and off of masks that allegorize our everyday life. As with many of his other songs, this one is an impassioned response to social politics, with a set of actions that communicate a form of ritual at work. After all, the musical performance often ritualizes play.[8] Let us say that the process of role-playing tests the boundaries of reality in a make-believe world of fantasy, where playfulness is inextricably caught up in serious political work. Identifying Morrissey's "love affair with his public", David Bret views Morrissey as a fascinating artist whose articulacy discloses "a complex individual" through a voice that is "haunting and melancholy" and that of a man "who has experienced every emotion". Bret points out that his songs from the 1980s and 1990s would lend "comfort to bedsit solitude through their leanings towards celibacy, vegetarianism, abstinence from alcohol, cigarettes and drugs, and an aversion to most if not all things modern" (Bret 1994: 1). Interestingly, 'You Have Killed Me' provides a snapshot of an older and more mature Morrissey. Released in the first decade of the new millennium, it is more multi-layered and slick in its production, signifying a development in Morrissey's penchant for storytelling, as we now will see.

Vocal embellishment, nuances and the aesthetics of contemplation

Surely it stands to reason that if the sung voice is a transmitter of empathy, then it conveys what the singer represents. This helps explain the range of different roles one can encounter in any one song or album, although, as I am keen to argue, certain Morrisseyian features inevitably remain constant. At any rate, his now familiar vocal sound is a matter of self-identification and negotiation. As I have argued earlier, 'positions of identification cannot be construed as deterministic in any sense' (Hawkins 2002: 90), which raises questions linked to empathy and pleasure in the musical performance.

The phenomenon of singing can be as baffling as scintillating. This is because the voice transcends lyrical content to retrieve feelings deep from within. Morrissey unleashes his emotional intensity through a high density of melodic embellishment in 'You Have Killed Me'. The technique of elasticizing vowels and over-emphasizing key words is achieved by downward, sliding intervallic motion, which means the lyrics are treated in a nuanced manner that conjure up feelings of ambivalence. Morrissey's ingenuity as vocalist (as much as lyricist) is also borne out by a spate of other details. Take the idiosyncrasies of expressiveness attached to his singing style, the result of a physical exertion that delicately balances sung and half-spoken phrases. An example of this is found in his use of accent, such as that placed on "killed", which is anticipated by the last offbeat of the preceding bar and rendered raw and vulnerable (Figure 17.1).[9]

As I live and breathe You have killed___ me   You have killed___ me

Figure 17.1: As I Live and Breathe.

Slides down to cadence points offer short moments of respite, with Morrissey's characteristic crooned, warble-vibrato coming into full force on the major second interval (D# to C#), where the weight falls on "me" (Figure 17.1). This also occurs on "Magnani you'll never be", but this time with a perfect fifth descent sliding down on "never be" (D#-C#-B-G#) (Figure 17.2). Cadential devices of this kind draw the listener right into the singer's world, evoking empathic response. The intensity of melodic embellishment invariably helps connote sentiments of pathos, as well as underlying Morrissey's ironic retort; a retort that is decidedly cryptic. In the end, we are left wondering who are Visconti and Magnani, what is their relationship to the song's protagonist, and why all the fuss over such infernal cross-references.

Vis - con - ti___ is___ me___   Mag - na - ni___ you'll___ ne-ver be___

Figure 17.2: Visconti Is Me.

In another phrase, musical hyperbole seems more blatant, again shaped through the nuances of tonality and phrasing (Figure 17.3). Through exaggerated inflections he sings, 'Who am I that I come to be here', virtually overdosing on the ornamentation that drives us to the final point of the phrase. The control of syllabic rhythmic and melodic phrasing on the word 'here', stretched over four bars, is so ornate that it literally diverts our attention to the "here and now" of his performance. In musical terms this is an elaborate affair, with Morrissey scatting at length around a D# before resolving unexpectedly to D natural. Taking D# down a semitone serves as a mechanism for transporting the listener on a convoluted journey of intervallic intrigue, in full preparation for the crux of the narrative.

Figure 17.3: 'Who Am I?'

Morrissey's use of vocal inflections and ornamentation through musical hyperbole are also found in the phrase, "I forgive you" (Figure 17.4), which draws the song to its conclusion. The repetition of these words, executed through descending intervals and closed units of rhythmic syncopation with off beats, extracts the message of forgiveness. Exaggeratedly, the message is delivered through an obsequious tone that is jeering. For the most part, the timbre and dynamic variations in such vocal tessitura highlight the ornamentation of the phrase, "I forgive you". Excessive devices like these contribute to the shading of the melody while inducing rhythmic play, with closure achieved by a forlorn sounding minor third resolution to the final long G# (B-G#).

Figure 17.4: 'But I Forgive You'.

One last phrase worth considering is perhaps the most bizarre and perplexing in the entire song, "I entered nothing, and nothing entered me" (Figure 17.5). Contemplatively, the phrase commences with a strong downward movement and culminates with an upward climb to a D#. In this moment the listener might well be left wondering what the intended message might be, and, moreover, who the subject of Morrissey's desire is. Rhythmically simple, the first part, "I entered nothing", consists of straight crotchet beats, while the second half, "and nothing entered me", is syncopated. From this it is evident that the second phrase sets off the first to complicate the message – if we really believe he did not enter someone then are we mistaken?

Resolving to the word "nothing", this, the strongest part of the complementary phrase, signals a sense of *jouissance*, in the form of a strong arrival point, as Morrissey relishes in the intrigue he induces. In particular, his gentle vibrato on the second syllable of "noth-ing" and "me" is erotic, enticing the listener into the intimate world of the protagonist's existence.

Figure 17.5: 'I Entered Nothing'

From start to finish, the song's narrative is delivered with great zest, executed with characteristic grammatical rectitude and precise verbal enunciation. Morrissey's singing style is teasing and weighed down by meticulously selected words and sentences, and, as we have seen, hooks, phrases and single words are reinforced in a variety of ways. Notably, Morrissey avoids full rhyme in his songs as he turns to other techniques, such as alliteration, to drive his words home and, most significantly, to align his lyrics to features in the music (rhythm, melodic and harmonic content, and instrumentation).[10] In sum, I want to again emphasize that his melodic expression comes from his natural speech, and in this way gains its power to signify both bonds and boundaries between listeners. Lawrence Kramer considers melody as "both an act of sympathetic imitation by the music maker and a stimulus to sympathetic identification by the listener" (Kramer, 1998: 50). A melody's imitative character depicts not only the artist's own subjectivity, but, moreover, the relationship between him and the other subject, the listener. One way to define melody is as an entity of symbolic reality, its force of meaning relying on that intermediate space between words and music. Singing, for sure, involves a form of musicalized speaking, which highlights the charismatic state of the melody itself.

One final element worth considering is crooning (ala Frank Sinatra, Serge Gainsbourg, or Robert Goulet), a style of singing that resulted from the advent of the electrical microphone (See Frith 1986: 107). Discernible in the rounded vowels, the clear consonants of Morrissey's Northern accent, and the stretched diphthongs, is a croon (that is extracted from chest and throat). Importantly, crooning is a key aesthetic marker in Morrissey's style, which extracts themes of suffering, misery and despair. I would add that his croon has an immediacy that is empathic; something implicitly melancholic in his timbre heightens the emotive pull in the narrative. From all this, we can deduce that the details of melodic delivery work as a central device for reconstructing his experiences. That is to say, Morrissey's singing per se brings alive the sentiments of his self-expression, and this is accomplished through the vocal idiosyncrasies of his style. The remarkable thing is how natural his singing style comes across.

Self-identification: References of darkness and put-on vulnerability

The gloried hype surrounding 'You Have Killed Me' (and the supposed life-changing experiences in Rome) carries with it a stark reference to the film *Accattone* from 1961, directed by the legendary Italian film director, philosopher and writer Pier Paolo Pasolini. The first two lines of the songs pay homage to him: "Pasolini is me, Accattone you'll be". This is a chilling reminder of Pasolini's brutal murder on the beach of Ostia, near Rome, an incident that has never been cleared up. Furthermore, death, a recurring theme in Morrissey's songs, indicates a leaning towards violence, murder and the macabre. Take earlier songs, such as 'You Know I Couldn't Last', 'Suffer Little Children' (with The Smiths), 'Ambitious Outsiders', 'Death At One's Elbow', and many others, that are dark in their subject matter. Gavin Hopps has noted that Morrissey's use of darkness illustrates "his tendency to represent it from within" (Hopps 2009: 215). Hopps compares Morrissey's first-person perspectives to similar characterizations found in Quentin Tarantino's films, concluding that, like the film director, he "demystifies the 'otherness' of evil". He shows that darkness exists "much closer to home, embodied by people with whom we share something and [is] entangled with mundane or more positive qualities". The handling of darkness in this way, as Hopps asserts, is "to 'invade the mind' and speak with the voice of the criminal, the hooligan and murderer". Not surprisingly, Morrissey's darkness is at its most disturbing when glamorized, suggesting a degree of "carefully reasoned" violence (Hopps 2009: 211).

Although the darkness of 'You Have Killed Me' might not necessarily signify reasoning with violence per se, it certainly critiques it through references to criminals, hooligans, and murderers (as also discussed in Martin J. Power's chapter in this book). Subject matter of this nature is integral to Morrissey's performance style. Indeed, the incongruities of violence form part of a hard social reality, and by plundering the depths of his soul he sets out to confront those who have killed Pasolini. But, as I read it, there is a lot more to this. The darkness surrounding Pasolini's murder expounds upon an incident that involved the killing of an earlier messiah, one who was equally politically outspoken and engaged; ostensibly, Morrissey's mission is to seek justice by pointing to those who murdered the Pasolini and Christ-figure in him.

The build-up in musical momentum during the song is closely aligned to the protagonist's plight, offering Morrissey all the more recourse to sentimentality.[11] With an air of indifference and put-on vulnerability, everything in the performance is affected by the use of much lyrical dexterity and musical hyperbole. Working up a lather of rhythmic and melodic inflections, he skilfully extracts specific phrases and words through his musical expression. For instance, when he nonchalantly sings, 'Who am I', a heavier inflection is placed on these three words than the surrounding lyrics (See Figure 17.3).

The backdrop to Morrissey's recordings is of course the studio where everything is mixed, engineered and produced. The relevance of production cannot be overstated, and Morrissey's recorded voice, as I have already stated, becomes a potent marker of his persona. Much of this is down to his producer Tony Visconti, whose detail for (re)producing Morrissey's voice is intriguing. Staging the voice convincingly is ultimately what we buy into, and indeed the recorded voice functions as an imaginative canvas for aestheticizing the combined effect of a song's delivery. Not without a touch of irony, a pointed reference is made to Visconti, whom Morrissey cryptically claims he has become, "Visconti is me" (See Figure 17.2). Yet, ambiguity reigns once again, this time in the form of another Visconti, Luchino Visconti (1906–69), Italian theatre and cinema director and writer, best known for his films, *The Leopard* (1963) and *Death in Venice* (1973). With this play on names, we are reminded that Morrissey is always involved in processes of "double enactment", where his role is to keep several acts buoyant at once.[12]

Further clues to understanding his tactics are located in the promotional video of the song, directed by Bucky Fukumoto, where Morrissey plays an entrant in the 1970 Eurovision contest. Full of parody, the video opens with an Italian compere introducing the foppish Morrissey to a bemused audience who are decidedly bourgeois. There is something nostalgic about Morrissey's address. Performing to a crowd from the 1970s, discernible by their hairstyles, clothes and spectacles, much attention is drawn to their disenchantment with him. Given that Morrissey was 47 when recording this song and video, there is a sense that he milks the nostalgia of his own legacy. Notably, the video blatantly references earlier videos from the Smiths' period, 'This Charming Man' and 'Panic', and is filmed with analogue video cameras from the 1970s. Immaculately turned out in a light suit, over an open black shirt, he is positioned on stage with his band in the background, silhouetted against a garish pink backlit wall. A repertoire of flamboyant gestures impassions his delivery. Swaying to the music, Morrissey is rendered positively comical as he jerks his head back defiantly on high notes, eyes rolling, upper lip curled in an Elvis snarl, with an expression that trivializes his earnestness.[13] The band, cool and nonchalant in their pose, frames all this perfectly. Strikingly, this video spectacularizes the disciplining of the Eurovision *chanseur*. Brimming with sentimentality, Morrissey's performance is clearly self-referential. One is struck by his showmanship, which functions as an extension of his own biography, an admission, arguably, of his own dramatized subjectivity.[14] In fact, his camped-up, dandified performance is knowingly frivolous. Frivolity is not only a matter of what is being said but *how* it is being said, and "being killed" does not necessarily imply violence and death. Rather it might suggest a broken heart – a veritable cliché in countless Eurovision songs – and a very poetic way of saying you have been let down, ever so badly. In effect, the artist's claim to having been killed (by love, by his fans, by a prejudicial audience?) has a critical function, namely releasing any number of ambiguities.

Aside from its sheer entertainment quality, flippancy of the sort Morrissey exhibits can also relay mixed signals of hope and despair in an overtly nonchalant way. The vocal hook, "you have killed me", becomes all the more expansive as the artist drives home his message. All the way through, a seductive tone belies this catchy hook, which is not only excessive, but also weirdly affectionate. Consequently, the hook's incessant repetition is a fitting example of how figurative language is shrewdly exploited to connote powerful feelings. There can hardly be any mistaking that devices of this kind form a major constituent of his musical rhetoric, with his vocal exhortations contingent on a subtle degree of variation and inventiveness. As he howls out the last lines of the song, "I forgive you", resolution in the video is also attained, with him throwing his arms out to the audience who burst into rapturous applause. In this moment everything seems over the top. Why? Well, not only is Morrissey's gesture overplayed in the confines of a tacky Eurovision setting, but it also cleverly references another dramatic moment in pop video history, the performance of Sid Vicious's 'My Way' from 30 years earlier, where he opens fire on the audience at the end of the song, killing some of them.[15] But Morrissey's onlookers are spared this indignity. Well, at least so far.

Conclusion

There can be little doubt that Morrissey performs with an extraordinary level of self-reflection. Rife with whimsical conjectures of sentimentality, 'You Have Killed Me' is indicative of a stylized, narcissistic performance, and Morrissey meticulously stylizes the character his fans will relate to. One might say his strategy of role-playing is a self-empowering motive, a distinguishing marker of his musical rhetoric. This idea alone sheds light on the points of identification that signify both the enigmatic and the familiar. From this it would seem that Morrissey's personal struggles, on- and off-stage, are part of a deeply personal critique that is entrenched in ambivalence and self-obsession. Yet, this comes with a price. Over the years Morrissey has maintained a problematic "masochistic relation" to his fans, frequently eroticizing men in terms of their "powerful working-class masculinity" (Bannister 2006: 152). Matthew Bannister has proposed that in flirting with his fans he intimates that he is "saving himself " for "that impossible moment" (Bannister 2006: 154) when he might meet them person-to-person. Could this indeed be the fantasy that keeps the flame alive? If Morrissey's masculinity and homoerotic sensibility, as Bannister insists, is linked to feminism and the emergence of new roles amongst males, his success hinges on him uncovering the anxieties associated with the normality of social class, race, ethnicity and sexuality.

This is why Morrissey is a fitting example of how pop subjectivities work. As we have seen, his subjectivity is based upon him playing the male hysteric: 'Who am I that I come to be here? [...] Yes I walk around somehow [...] But you have killed me'. Indisputably, his Englishness, a distinctly Northern variant, represents something special – a universal sensibility – that gains its appeal as much abroad as locally. Instinctively, Morrissey has grasped that pop music shapes myths around ideas of individuation on a large scale. Surely it is this that turns him into an international symbol of wide-reaching appeal geographically and politically.

Popularity on such a scale also owes much to the vulnerable display of the troubled self. We know that many British pop acts are steeped in a tradition that is preoccupied with satirizing norms and assumptions linked to the politics of gender and sexuality. Indeed, Morrissey assumes a level of non-conformity in relationship to the dynamics of idealized masculinity, which underlie both his complexity and appeal; I am referring here to a subjectivity that works as a resilient buffer against the constraints of dominant roles in society. Personifying the cynic, the anti-hero, the underdog, Morrissey exhibits class and sexual hostility in songs that deal with the tedium of everyday life. Moreover, his gendered-ness, as I interpret it, is symbolic, for its meaningfulness has to do with a dissident masculinity. In this sense, possibly his most beguiling characteristic is a profound vanity that is mischievously deceptive. Thus, in the setting up of a trusting relationship with his fans, it is this quality that becomes located in a cult of the self, where the pleasure in entertaining others, and gaining their support, becomes the prime goal of self-gratification.

Inevitably, Morrissey's performance strategies are linked to the social and cultural circumstances of people's lives in Britain during the 1980s and 1990s. This would explain why his songs are useful for evaluating the changes in society two decades later (at the time of writing this chapter). Yet, we need to ask to what extent Morrissey relishes in the construction of his own passive, "feminine" emotional disposition, and what indeed is the psychopathology behind his vulnerable display?

'You Have Killed Me' is all about someone who "came with the key". And if we are to believe that redemption comes through Morrissey's sense of self-sacrifice, then this is surely an indictment of his very narcissism. Playing around with codes of ambiguity, Morrissey reinforces a narrative of self put-downs that run through a lifetime of songs. Uncannily, his songs substantiate endurance and resistance, as well as permitting a degree of self-mockery. In turn, his strategy underscores something subversive. While things are expressed simply, he knows they are poetically dark and ambivalent, and musically he makes this compelling. This happens through intricately sculpted tunes, crafted studio productions and poignantly expressed lyrics. Sensitively conveyed through a distinctive singing style his songs make us listen closely: in fact, so closely that we have to ponder long and hard. This is because his performances ghost his very presence, the effect of which spells out that special quality in pop music that creates empathy. 'You Have Killed Me' employs the past tense in the choruses, and the present tense in the verses; and all this unfolds in a way that engages our desire in *his* bid for sentimental retrospection. From this it would seem that the pop song allows listeners to experience things without necessarily being forced to intervene or get involved in the actuality of the drama. As with opera arias, pop songs are staged events whereby social dramas arise from conflict situations; they can theatricalize the most horrendous incidents into an aesthetic experience. And, with the aid of the music video, it is not unusual to involve audiences within the storyline through the actualization of the musical process. After all, the pop artist's prime goal is to make a text take on a life of its own, creating a host of possibilities.

From this we might say 'You Have Killed Me' dispels the trivia around us by drawing on the merriment of satirical performance through memorable tunes, simple rhythmic accompaniment and quirky chords. Tenderly, Morrissey croons in a way he knows his fans wish to experience him time and again, and this is executed with immense panache and melodrama. One effect of 'You Have Killed Me' is that it gives us a glimpse into his moments of human struggle and pain, as, almost religiously, he cries out, "I forgive you". This line, if not parodic, is at least spiritually tied up with the song's meaning in a myriad of ways. So, whether we choose to love him or hate him, or, indeed, accede to him forgiving us, the message seems uncompromising; for it is one of solidarity and sincerity, directed to the marginalized and afflicted. It is precisely this that makes Morrissey's performances such powerful commentaries, which, in the end, can save us more than once.

Notes

1. Rogan (1992) has provided a fascinating insight into Morrissey's childhood, detailing his obsession with popular music right from the outset. Significantly, it was the events going on in Manchester from the 1960s onwards, in the metropolis in which Morrissey grew up, that would have a profound effect on the artist's growth and development.

2. I have theorized this point in detail through a discourse on pop dandyism, which I connect to Baudelaire and numerous other authors (see Hawkins 2009).

3. My employment of the term "performativity" is primarily Butlerian in that it refers to the nuanced ways of performing out one's gender. In this sense, gender is an act that is learnt and rehearsed, and, most significantly, only becomes a reality when performed. Judith Butler insists that a person plays out their gender according to prescribed performatives, and when falling outside the conventions of a given social context, these are considered as a rebellious act against "nature" (see Butler 1988, 1990). Unorthodox gender displays in certain pop acts confront reality because they are perceived as an affront to the stability of a "settled existence". My use of the concept of performativity, then, is derived from the wider field of performance studies and points to the construction of a sense of social reality through the construction of both Morrissey's gender and ethnicity.

4. In an earlier study of Morrissey, I have attempted to theorize his ironic markers as a means to understanding his affective charge. Morrissey's regulation of intimacy with his fans is largely based upon an exclusivity that requires a shared awareness. Turning to songs, such as 'Billy Budd', 'Hold On To Your Friends', 'I am Hated for Loving', 'Speedway' and 'Used to be a Sweet Boy', I argued that irony resides in the degree of intentionality. One of the interesting conclusions of this study was a realization of Morrissey's reflexive approach to irony and the fascinating point that intended responses to humour are never guaranteed. Irony permeates Morrissey's song as a form of ritual which is cunningly performed out through the brilliance of his lyrics as much as his musicality. See Hawkins (2002: 91–97).

5. Gavin Hopps makes a similar point about the "untrained" voice in a section in his book on Morrissey, subtitled, "The Homeless Voice". Hopps asserts that his voice marks him as "other" through his use of melisma and falsetto. Turning to the term "ineptitude" to describe Morrissey's "untrained" or "imperfect" vocality, Hopps points out how this very quality enhances the expressive effect of the voice (Hopps 2009: 26–31).

6. From the interview with Paul Morley (2007) 'The last temptation of Morrissey', in *Morrissey in Conversation – The Essential Interviews*, ed. Paul. A. Woods (London: Plexus), pp. 203–218.

7. This is central to the way empathy works, and, as I have argued previously, it is through the process of mediating his emotional state that Morrissey charms his fans. His poetic delivery of every phrase through the nuances of lyrical and musical reinforcement, often to the point of exaggeration, strikes up a special rapport between artist and fan. See Hawkins (2002: 83–91).

8. Play is an integral part of Morrissey's performance strategy – it is about temperament and mood, and can involve a spur-of-the-moment flare-up. Through satire, irony and parody, play commonly subverts power structures and systems. Intrinsically, play is part of the rhetoric of Morrissey's performance because it embraces the make-believe at the same time it places the performance under the aegis of rational thought. In Morrissey's performances, there is a tension between the organized and the unpredictable, the latter suggesting a Nietzschean approach to play, where the gods can alter the rules of the game without any warning. On the social strategies of play and the power rhetoric that defines the self and the imaginary, see Sutton-Smith (1997).

9. At this point in the chapter my thanks go to Eirik Askerøi, who not only helped with all the transcriptions, but also, as a Morrissey fan/scholar, provided a useful buffer for discussing the numerous assertions I make throughout.

10. Johnny Rogan, in his discussion of Morrissey's singing style, has made an interesting connection with Chaplin's simplicity. Rogan describes the sounds that flow forth as "pure Morrisseyspeak", and goes on to clarify what he means: "Single syllables are stretched to breaking point and merge with otherworldly gargles, close microphone kisses and indecipherable phrases which, in their own way, probably say more than can be gleaned from any lyric sheet" (Rogan 1992: 16). These are the features that make his relationship to his audience wonderful.

11. I am suggesting here that the outpouring of excessive emotions in melodramatic songs is affectedly mediated through singing. There is a sense that Morrissey's sentimentality is marked by feelings of idealism rather than reason or logic. My argument is that his brand of excessive sentimentality traverses masculinity as a discursive formation, and this throws light on the politics of affect in late twentieth century popular song. To exemplify this point, Morrissey's brand of sentimentality is an antithesis to that of Ernest Hemingway's quite paranoid anti-sentimentality only some decades earlier, and can be read both as a site for idealism and nostalgia.

12. Pop performers, as Frith insists, move "in and out of character", which opens the possibilities for looking forward while reminiscing (1996: 212).

13. In moments like this we are reminded that the bodily movements in performance function as powerful aids for communicating the internal emotional state of an artist. In turning her attention to Robbie Williams, Jane Davidson (2006) has related his gestural types to his on and off stage personae. Davidson makes the argument that gestures and movement depend on the interpretation of "adaptor movements", which cater to physical and emotional needs.

14. For a truncated reading of the video, 'You Have Killed Me', see my earlier study in Hawkins (2009: 70–72).

15. See my analysis of Vicious's version of 'My Way' and discussion of his rejection of mainstream values in Hawkins (2009: 176–179).

References

Bret, D. (1994) *Morrissey: Landscapes of the Mind*. London: Robsons Books.

Butler, J. (1998) 'Performative acts and gender constitution: an essay in phenomenology and feminist criticism', *Theatre Journal*, 40: 4, pp. 519–31.

Butler, J. (1990) *Gender Trouble*. New York: Routledge.

Davidson, J. (2006) '"She's the One": multiple functions of body movement in a stage performance by Robbie Williams', in A. Gritten and E. King (eds) *Music and Gesture*. Aldershot: Ashgate, pp. 208–225.

Dibben, N. (2009) 'Vocal performance and the projection of emotional authenticity', in Derek B. Scott (ed.) *The Ashgate Research Companion to Popular Musicology*. Farnham: Ashgate, pp. 317–333.

Frith, S. (1996) *Performing Rites: On the Value of Popular Music*. Oxford: Oxford University Press

Frith, S. (1986) 'Art *vs* technology: the strange case of popular music', *Media, Culture and Society*, 8, pp. 107–122.

Hawkins, S. (2009) *The British Pop Dandy: Masculinity, Popular Music and Culture*. Farnham: Ashgate.

Hawkins, S. (2002) *Settling the Pop Score: Pop Texts and Identity Politics*. Aldershot: Ashgate.

Hawkins, S. (2001) 'Musicological quagmires in popular music: seeds of detailed conflict', *Popular Musicology Online*, 1.

Hopps, G. (2009) *Morrissey: The Pageant of His Bleeding Heart*. London: Continuum.

Kramer, L. (1998) 'Primitive encounters: Beethoven's "Tempest" sonata, musical meaning, and enlightenment anthropology', *Beethoven Forum*, 6, ed. Glenn Stanley. Lincoln: University of Nebraska Press, pp. 31–65.

Moore, A. (2001) *Rock the Primary Text: Developing a Musicology of Rock*, 2nd edn. Aldershot: Ashgate.

Morrissey, S. (2006) *Ringleader of the Tormentors*. Sanctuary.

Morrissey, S. (2006) 'You Have Killed Me', *Ringleader of the Tormentors*. Sanctuary.

Rogan, J. (1992) *Morrissey and Marr: The Severed Alliance*. London: Omnibus Press.

Sutton-Smith, B. (1997) *The Ambiguity of Play*. Cambridge, MA: Harvard University Press.

Notes on Contributors

Eirik Askerøi is a Ph.D. scholar at the University of Agder, Norway, where he is writing a thesis entitled 'Reading pop production: markers of musical subjectivity'. Besides his academic activities, he works as a professional musician and co-manages a recording studio in the centre of Oslo. His favourite Morrissey song is 'Interesting Drug'.

John H. Baker teaches English Literature at the University of Westminster in London. His research interests include Howard Barker, David Peace, Philip Pullman and, more generally, English literature and the Bible. He is currently editing *The Art of Nick Cave*, a collection of essays on the Australian singer-songwriter, for publication by Intellect. His favourite Morrissey song is 'Life Is A Pigsty'.

Rachel M. Brett was pronounced "fed up" upon arrival. Refusing to accept the life sentence of being born and buried in the Midlands, she avoided Home Economics lessons, and the obligation to learn a trade. Having escaped to London she took a degree in Art History at Middlesex University and a Master's in Aesthetics and Art Theory at the Centre for Research in Modern European Philosophy. She has since written a collection of short stories based on the first Smiths album. Rachel is currently writing her first novel. Her favourite Morrissey song is 'Everyday Is Like Sunday'.

Lee Brooks is a Lecturer in Media Arts at St Mary's University College, Twickenham. His research interests include the articulation of Englishness in popular music and the cultural and social impact of Disney theme parks. Alongside these theoretical pursuits, he has developed his previous training in graphic design and typography into a practical specialism in motion graphics. His favourite Morrissey song is 'A Swallow On My Neck'.

Len Brown was born in the Scottish borders, and started writing for *NME* in 1983 and first set eyes on The Smiths that September at London's Venue; it was the night they first played 'This Charming Man' live. He wrote the band's *NME* obituary in 1987 and began to get to know Morrissey in early 1988 before the release of 'Suedehead'. His biography, *Meetings with Morrissey* (published in 2008), is a memoir of his many encounters, conversations, communications and interviews with "Semisorry" for over 20 years. (The book has been translated into Swedish, German and French.) Having moved into television production in 1989, Len's many music documentary credits (as producer, director or executive producer) include the *My Generation* series for Channel Four (The Animals, The Kinks, The Troggs, The Yardbirds, The Small Faces and Herman's Hermits), *The Brit Girls* for Channel Four (Cilla, Sandie, Marianne and Lulu), *A Fine Romance: The New Romantics, Rod Stewart and The Faces: Wine, Women and Song* (for BBC1) plus the definitive television documentary about Marc Bolan – *T.Rex: Dandy in the Underworld*. He has also worked as a storyliner on *Coronation Street* and his play *Ghosts at Cockcrow* is currently being performed by Three Wee Crows Theatre Company in Argyll. His favourite Morrissey song is 'Now My Heart Is Full'.

Melissa Connor holds a Master's in Visual Arts from the School of Art, Architecture and Design, University of South Australia in Adelaide. She completed an Honours thesis on Morrissey fans in 2008 and her Master's research looks at the resurgence in craft practices as facilitated by online blogs. Her favourite Morrissey song is 'Alsatian Cousin'.

Andrew Cope is a Ph.D. student at the University of Plymouth. His interdisciplinary project is exploring the contribution that art and performance might make to material culture studies' growing repertoire of research methodologies. His favourite Morrissey song is 'Alma Matters'.

Eoin Devereux is Senior Lecturer and Head of Department in the Department of Sociology, University of Limerick, Ireland. He co-organized two symposia on Morrissey at the University of Limerick in 2008 and 2009. He has published a number of articles/book chapters on Morrissey and The Smiths including '"Heaven Knows We'll Soon Be Dust": Catholicism and devotion in The Smiths' in S. Campbell and C. Coulter (eds) *Why Pamper Life's Complexities: Essays on The Smiths* (2010) (Manchester: Manchester University Press); and 'I'm Not The Man You Think I Am: Authenticity, Ambiguity and The Cult of Morrissey' in E. Haverinen, U. Kovala and V. Rautavuoma (eds) *Cult, Community, Identity* (2009) (Finland: Research Centre for Contemporary Culture of the University of Jyväskylä). He saw The Smiths play in Galway in 1984 and never really recovered. His favourite Morrissey song is 'Speedway'.

Aileen Dillane is a Lecturer in Music at the Irish World Academy of Music and Dance University of Limerick. A traditional Irish music performer and ethnomusicologist, Aileen's interests include critical and cultural theory, in particular issues of ethnicity and identity, in relation to the popular and traditional musics of Ireland, the United Kingdom, the United States and Australia. She received her Ph.D. from the University of Chicago where she was a Fulbright Scholar and Century Fellow. Her favourite Morrissey song is 'Asleep'.

Lawrence Foley is completing a Ph.D. at Queen Mary, University of London. His research examines the role of bullfighting as a prominent motif in the art and literature of Modernism.

Lawrence obtained his Bachelor's degree in English from Queen Mary in 2007, and in 2009 was awarded a Master's degree in Modern literature by University College London. Having been an admirer of Morrissey and The Smiths for many years, Lawrence is particularly interested in the influence of literature on Morrissey's lyrical output. His favourite Morrissey song is 'The Lazy Sunbathers'.

Stan Hawkins is Professor of musicology at the University of Oslo, Norway. He is author of *Settling the Pop Score* (2002) and *The British Pop Dandy* (2009), and co-editor of *Music, Space and Place* (2004) and *Essays on Sound and Vision* (2007). His many publications appear in edited books and journals, with research specialities within music analysis, masculinity, sexuality, subjectivity and music sociology. He is editor-in-chief of *Popular Musicology Online,* as well as serving on the editorial teams of *Popular Music, Journal of the Royal Musical Association, Swedish Journal for Music Research* and *Journal of the Musical Arts in Africa.* From 2010–14 Hawkins is leading a project funded by the Norwegian Research Council, entitled *Popular Music and Gender in a Transcultural Context.* His favourite Morrissey song is 'You Have Killed Me'.

Erin Hazard was the editor of the Morrissey zine *Maudlin Street* in the early 1990s. She received her Ph.D. in Art History from the University of Chicago in 2007 and was Assistant Professor of Art History at Western Washington University from 2008 to 2010. Her work has appeared in the journal *Nineteenth Century Studies* and the essay collection *Literary Tourism and Nineteenth-Century Culture.* She currently lives in Chicago. Her favourite Morrissey song is 'Late Night, Maudlin Street'.

Dan Jacobson is an artist currently residing in New York City. He graduated with a BA in Theatre/Philosophy in 2007 from the New School For Social Research and is now pursuing his masters degree in Liberal Studies. His first feature length documentary film entitled 'Looking For Roots, Finding Flowers.' premiered in 2009. He is currently working on a new film, 'Everyone But You,' and producing rock and roll music with his band *The Bedroom Feel* which will see the release of its first EP in 2011. His favourite Morrissey song is 'Late Night, Maudlin Street'.

Ian Jeffrey is an artist currently based in Boston, Massachusetts where he graduated in 2008 from the School of the Museum of Fine Arts, Boston. Ian's drawings frequently use images from popular music to reflect on artistic production and the culture of fame. His artwork has been exhibited in New York, Boston, and most recently with the Anthony Greaney Gallery at Cottage Home, Los Angeles. His favourite Morrissey song is 'I Don't Mind If You Forget Me'.

Daniel Manco received a Master's degree in Popular Culture from Ohio's Bowling Green State University, where he wrote his thesis on disability representation in the music and persona of Morrissey. He also holds a Bachelor's degree in English and Psychology from

Indiana University at Bloomington. He currently is employed at Bowling Green State University. His favourite Morrissey song is 'The World Is Full of Crashing Bores.'

Pierpaolo Martino is *ricercatore* (research fellow) of English Literature at the University of Bari, Italy. His areas of enquiry include postcolonial, translation and cultural studies. He has published on Oscar Wilde, Virginia Woolf, Kamau Brathwaite, Colin MacInnes, Linton Kwesi Johnson, Salman Rushdie, Hanif Kureishi, Hari Kunzru, Radiohead, Morrissey and The Smiths. (*Exodus. Studi sulla letteratura anglo-caraibica*, 2009; *Down in Albion. Studi sulla cultura pop inglese*, 2007; *Virginia Woolf. La musica del faro. Pagina e improvvisazione*, 2003). His favourite Morrissey song is 'Everyday Is Like Sunday'.

Martin J. Power is a Lecturer in Sociology at the University of Limerick, where he teaches courses on "The Welfare State" and "Inequality and Social Exclusion". He co-organized "The Songs That Saved Your Life (Again)", a two-day symposium on Morrissey, held at the University of Limerick in April 2009. He has previously published on the persistence of class inequality in the Irish education and social welfare systems, and on media constructions and representations of stigmatized public housing estates in Ireland. His favourite Morrissey song is 'Jack The Ripper'.

Johanna Sjöstedt is a postgraduate student at University of Gothenburg, Sweden. Her main intellectual interests are contemporary feminist theory and philosophy and their history, along with the gender debate in eighteenth century France involving authors such as Rousseau, Laclos, Marquis de Sade and Wollstonecraft. Her five favourite songs by Morrissey/The Smiths are, for the time being (and not ranking them): 'Alma Matters', 'Let Me Kiss You', 'November Spawned A Monster', 'Jeane' and 'The More You Ignore Me, The Closer I Get'.

Colin Snowsell is a Professor in the Department of Communications at Okanagan College in British Columbia, Canada. His essays and short stories have been published in *Rhetor, Journal of the Canadian Society for the Study of Rhetoric, Maisonneuve Magazine, This Magazine, Ryga Journal, Prairie Fire Journal* and *PopMatters*. He is the author of the novella *The Frollett Homestead*, and has been nominated for the National Magazine Award of Canada. His favourite Morrissey song is 'Now My Heart Is Full'.

Elisabeth Woronzoff is currently a graduate student in the American Culture Studies Ph.D. programme at Bowling Green State University, Bowling Green Ohio. She is interested in visual and musical popular culture, and wishes to research the ways in which once subversive musical genres, such as punk rock, evolved into a commodity while expanding the gender, political and cultural boundaries of the independent and mainstream music industry. Elizabeth began studying Morrissey for her Master's capstone project because she was not a fan, and wanted to understand the connection between fans and The Smiths. After 'Years Of Refusal', she became a fan of 'This Charming Man', and now 'Ask(s)' herself why 'These Things Take Time'? In terms of her Smiths' appreciation, 'There Is A Light That Never Goes Out'.

Index